D1882838

# THE JOURNEY
OF
# WILLIAM OF RUBRUCK
TO THE
# EASTERN PARTS OF THE WORLD
1253-55

# THE JOURNEY
## OF
# WILLIAM OF RUBRUCK
## TO THE
# EASTERN PARTS OF THE WORLD
## 1253-55

**AS NARRATED BY HIMSELF**

***WITH TWO ACCOUNTS OF THE EARLIER JOURNEY OF***
**JOHN OF PIAN DE CARPINE**

***TRANSLATED FROM THE LATIN, AND EDITED, WITH AN INTRODUCTORY NOTICE BY***
**WILLIAM WOODVILLE ROCKHILL**

GYAN

*Published by*

GYAN

Gyan Publishing House
5, Ansari Road
Daryaganj, New Delhi-110002
Phone: 011-47034999, 9811692060
E-mail: books@gyanbooks.com

*Distribution Network*
gyanbooks.com
India, USA, Canada, UK, Australia, France

**© Publisher**

All rights reserved. No part of this work may be reproduced, stored, adapted, or transmitted in any form or by any means, electronic, mechanical, photocopying, micro-filming, recording or otherwise, or translated in any language, without the prior written permission of the copyright owner and the publisher.

ISBN : 978-81-212-3651-5 (P.B)
First Published, London, 1900

2nd Impression 2020

*Printed at:* Gyan Press, Delhi.

The book is sold subject to the condition that it shall not, by way of trade or otherwise, be lent, resold, hired out, or otherwise circulated without the prior publisher's written consent.

**The Journey of William of Rubruck to The Eastern Parts of the World 1253-55**
Author: William Woodville Rockhill

# THE JOURNEY

OF

# WILLIAM OF RUBRUCK

TO

# THE EASTERN PARTS

OF

# THE WORLD,

1253-55,

AS NARRATED BY HIMSELF,

*WITH TWO ACCOUNTS OF THE EARLIER JOURNEY OF*

JOHN OF PIAN DE CARPINE.

Translated from the Latin, and Edited, with an Introductory Notice,

BY

WILLIAM WOODVILLE ROCKHILL,

HONORARY CORRESPONDING MEMBER OF THE
ROYAL GEOGRAPHICAL SOCIETY.

LONDON:
PRINTED FOR THE HAKLUYT SOCIETY.

M.DCCCC.

# COUNCIL

OF

# THE HAKLUYT SOCIETY.

---

SIR CLEMENTS MARKHAM, K.C.B., F.R.S., *Pres. R.G.S.*, PRESIDENT.
THE RIGHT HON. THE LORD STANLEY OF ALDERLEY, VICE-PRESIDENT.
REAR-ADMIRAL SIR WILLIAM WHARTON, K.C.B., VICE-PRESIDENT.
C. RAYMOND BEAZLEY, M.A.
COLONEL G. EARL CHURCH.
SIR MARTIN CONWAY.
ALBERT GRAY.
F. H. H. GUILLEMARD, M.A., M.D.
EDWARD HEAWOOD, M.A.
DUDLEY F. A. HERVEY, C.M.G.
ADMIRAL SIR ANTHONY H. HOSKINS, G.C.B.
J. SCOTT KELTIE, LL.D.
F. W. LUCAS.
A. P. MAUDSLAY.
MAJOR M. NATHAN, C.M.G., R.E.
E. J. PAYNE, M.A.
E. G. RAVENSTEIN.
HOWARD SAUNDERS.
H. W. TRINDER.
CHARLES WELCH, F.S.A.

WILLIAM FOSTER, B.A., *Honorary Secretary.*

# CONTENTS.

# PREFACE.

IN publishing the narrative of Friar William of Rubruck, a work which should rank as high in the literature of travel as that of Marco Polo, his better-known successor in the field of Asiatic exploration, the Hakluyt Society, I think, not only renders a service to students, but performs an act of justice long due to a great, though much neglected, traveller, who for six hundred and fifty years has remained imperfectly known and appreciated.

It must be a source of lasting regret to all members of the Society that our great geographer and lamented President, Sir Henry Yule, was not able to undertake the preparation of an edition of William of Rubruck's *Itinerarium*, as he had long contemplated doing; but his high opinion of the narrative, expressed in several of his works, has already greatly contributed towards establishing the traveller's unquestionable right to pre-eminence among the earliest European explorers of Asia. It is sincerely hoped that the present volume will further aid in showing the equity of Friar William's claim to the highest recognition.

It is an interesting fact that to England, and England alone, the great French traveller owes the chief contributions to the establishment of his fame. From England came the first notice of his work in the *Opus Majus* of Roger Bacon; by Richard Hakluyt the relation of his journey was first made known to the world; to Samuel Purchas he owes the first publication of the complete text of his narrative. I trust that it will now be found that from an English Society he receives full recognition of his great and lasting worth.

In the Introductory Notice no attempt has been made to give in detail the history of the early relations between Western Europe and the Mongol Empire; this subject has been elaborately and lucidly treated by such high authorities as Abel Rémusat, Baron d'Ohsson, Sir Henry Howorth, Cahun, and others. The object of the editor has simply been to give an idea of the knowledge possessed by Western Europe concerning the Mongols down to the time of Friar William's journey; and to show the sources of information of which that traveller could, and very probably did, avail himself as a preparation for his journey.

Among the most valuable sources of information to which Friar William had access, was the narrative by Benedict of Poland of his journey to the Court of Kuyuk Khan, in 1246, in company with John of Pian de Carpine. It is highly probable that Friar William met Friar John before leaving France in 1248, and received advice from him, and possibly communication of his report to the Pope, if it was written at that time. At all events, as the route followed by the latter was for much of the way through the same countries traversed by Friar William and as the two narratives complete and corroborate each other, it has been deemed advisable to give in full the relations of Friars John and Benedict.

As to the first part of the *Historia Mongalorum* of Friar John, relating to the customs and history of the Mongols, I have introduced in foot-notes to the text all such portions of it as bear directly on the narrative of Friar William; and similar use has been made of the account of the mission of Friar Ascelin in 1247, which has reached us in the extracts preserved by Vincent of Beauvais of the report made by Simon of St. Quentin, a member of the mission.

I have largely availed myself of mediæval Chinese works for elucidating or corroborating Friar William's statements, and have had frequent recourse to Oriental writers, Mohammedan or Armenian, for the same purpose. Greek and Latin authors and European travellers, ancient and modern, have been consulted with profit; though, unfortunately, I have not had access to a number of works of the latter class which may contain valuable corroborative evidence of the thorough reliability of our traveller.

It would seem that the MS. of Lord Lumley, published by Hakluyt, divided Rubruck's narrative into a number of chapters, to each of which a title was given, presumably by the copyist: for the other MSS., from which the text of Michel and Wright, the one translated here, was prepared, do not give these head-lines. I have deemed it more convenient to divide the text arbitrarily into sections where the narrative permitted it, and have not given titles to any.

Concerning the spelling of proper names, I have chosen in each case what appeared to me the best reading to be found in any of the MSS., and have retained it uniformly throughout the work. The punctuation in the MSS. is very faulty; I have occasionally altered it, but only where to do so seemed absolutely necessary for a proper comprehension of the narrative.

The above are the only liberties that I have taken with the text of Rubruck: I trust they will be deemed justifiable.

It affords me much pleasure to express here my sincere

appreciation of the services rendered me by Mr. William Foster, Honorary Secretary of the Hakluyt Society, who has, by his kind suggestions, corrections, and general revision of my work while going through the Press, greatly added to its value. I have also to acknowledge with gratitude the assistance given me by many friends in elucidating the text of the *Itinerarium*. To Thomas Watters, formerly of H. B. M. Consular Service in China; to H. Leon Feer, my first guide in Oriental studies, of the National Library in Paris; to Father Alishan, of the Armenian Convent of St. Lazarus at Venice; to F. Grenard, the Central Asian traveller and companion of the unfortunate Dutreuil de Rhins; to Father F. Ehrlé, the learned Prefect of the Vatican Library; and last, but not least, to Panagiotes Calogeropoulos, the genial and scholarly librarian of the Greek Boulé at Athens; I tender my heartfelt thanks.

W. WOODVILLE ROCKHILL.

*Washington*, *D. C.*
*March* 12*th*, 1900.

# INTRODUCTORY NOTICE.

IN 1222 the Mongols, already masters of all northern Asia from the Chinese Sea to Lake Balkash, having destroyed the Khorazmian empire and ravaged Transcaucasia, broke through the Caucasus and spread ruin and terror over southern Russia, then known as the Kipchak, and the valley of the Volga as far north as the modern city of Kazan. But barely a rumour of this invasion reached western Europe, and contemporary writers have left us but a few brief references to it and "the Tartars," as the Mongols and their allies were to be called for ages to come.[1] It was really not till

[1] Albericus Trium Fontium, in his *Chronicon*, and under date of 1222 (p. 150), records that the people called Tartars by the Hungarians and the Comans, and their leader, King David, or Prester John, on learning of the fall of Damietta (in 1219), retreated as best they could to their own country, and the little that was known of them was soon forgotten. Under date of 1239 (p. 571), the same annalist describes the Tartars from information given him "by one who had seen them" in the following terms: "They have a big head, short neck, very big chest, big arms, little legs, and their strength is wonderfully great. They have no religion, fear nothing, believe nothing, worship nothing but their king, who calls himself King of Kings and Lord of Lords." For further information he refers his readers to the narrative of John of Palatio (*sic*) Carpini. On the confusion existing between Chingis Khan and a Christian king, called David, see Yule (*Cathay*, 175), who refers to a *Relatio de Davide Rege Tartarorum Christiano* in Eccard's *Corpus Historic.*, ii.

1238, when a second and greater Mongol expedition against Christendom had carried devastation over nearly half of eastern Europe, that the princes and rulers of western and southern Europe began to awaken to some slight comprehension of the immensity of the danger which threatened them; and that a few of them realised that unless they could unite Christendom against the Mongols they, their crusades, petty wars, and interminable wrangling and fighting between Popes and Emperors would be for ever put an end to, swept away in the rapidly rising flood of Mongol conquest.[1]

Though a mission sent by the Ismaelians to the Kings of France and of England in 1238, asking for aid against the Tartars, may have imparted the first reliable information to western Europe about the Mongols,[2] the following extract from Matthew Paris, under date of 1240, gives such a full description of this new people, embodying practically all the earliest information possessed in western Europe, not excepting that brought by the Ismaelians, of them and their country down to the time of the journey of Friar John of Pian de Carpine to the Mongol court in 1246, that I will translate it in full.

"That the joys of mortal men be not enduring, nor worldly happiness long lasting without lamentations, in

---

[1] Matthew Paris (*Chronica Majora*, iii, 488) says that in 1238 the fear of the Mongols was so great in western Europe that people of Gothland and Friesland did not dare come to Yarmouth for the herring fishery, and that herrings were therefore so cheap that forty or fifty sold for a piece of silver, even at places far away from the coast (see also Cahun, *Introduction*, 356).

[2] From France the Ismaelian envoy despatched one of his suite to plead for assistance with Henry III of England. When he had delivered his message, the Bishop of Winchester, who had taken the cross at that time and was present at the audience, exclaimed: "Let those dogs devour each other and be utterly wiped out, and then we shall see, founded on their ruins, the universal Catholic Church, and there shall truly be one shepherd and one flock" (Matth. Paris, iii, 487).

this same year (*i.e.*, 1240) a detestable nation of Satan, to wit, the countless army of the Tartars, broke loose from its mountain-environed home, and piercing the solid rocks (of the Caucasus), poured forth like devils from the Tartarus, so that they are rightly called Tartari or Tartarians. Swarming like locusts over the face of the earth, they have brought terrible devastation to the eastern parts (of Europe), laying it waste with fire and carnage. After having passed through the land of the Saracens, they have razed cities, cut down forests, overthrown fortresses, pulled up vines, destroyed gardens, killed townspeople and peasants. If perchance they have spared any suppliants, they have forced them, reduced to the lowest condition of slavery, to fight in the foremost ranks against their own neighbours. Those who have feigned to fight, or have hidden in the hope of escaping, have been followed up by the Tartars and butchered. If any have fought bravely (for them) and conquered, they have got no thanks for reward; and so they have misused their captives as they have their mares. For they are inhuman and beastly, rather monsters than men, thirsting for and drinking blood, tearing and devouring the flesh of dogs and men, dressed in ox-hides, armed with plates of iron, short and stout, thickset, strong, invincible, indefatigable, their backs unprotected,[1] their breasts covered with armour; drinking with delight the pure blood of their flocks, with big, strong horses, which eat branches and even trees, and which they have to mount by the help of three steps on account of the shortness of their thighs. They are without human laws, know no comforts, are more ferocious than lions or bears, have boats made of ox-hides, which ten or twelve of them own in common; they are able to swim or to manage a boat, so that they can cross the largest and swiftest rivers

[1] The Ismaelian envoy said they did this so that they could not flee (Matth. Paris, iii, 488).

without let or hindrance,[1] drinking turbid or muddy water when blood fails them (as beverage). They have one-edged swords and daggers, are wonderful archers, spare neither age, nor sex, nor condition. They know no other language than their own, which no else knows; for until now there has been no access to them, nor did they go forth (from their own country); so there could be no knowledge of their customs or persons through the common intercourse of men. They wander about with their flocks and their wives, who are taught to fight like men. And so they came with the swiftness of lightning to the confines of Christendom, ravaging and slaughtering, striking every one with terror and incomparable horror. It was for this that the Saracens sought to ally themselves with the Christians,[2] hoping to be able to resist these monsters with their combined forces. It is believed that these Tartars, of cursed memory, are of the ten tribes[3] who,

---

[1] Pian de Carpine (690) says: "When they come to a river, they cross it in the following way, even if it is a large one: the chiefs have a round, light skin, around the top of which they have loopholes very close together through which they pass a cord, and they stretch it so that it bellies out, and this they fill with clothes and other things, and then they bind it down very tightly. After that they put their saddles and other hard things on it, and the men likewise sit on it. Then they tie the boat thus made to the tail of a horse, and a man swims along ahead leading it; or they sometimes have two oars, and with them they row across the water, thus crossing the river. . . . . Some of the poorer people have a leather pouch, well sewn, each man having one; and in this pouch or sack they put their clothing and all their things, and they tie the mouth of the bag tightly, and tie it to the tail of a horse, then they cross as stated above (*i.e.*, swimming, holding on to the horse's head ?).

*Pei shih* (bk. 94, 16) says the Kitan crossed rivers in the same way; and the Chinese traveller, Wang Yen-tē, who went to Karakhodjo in A.D. 981, says the Ta-ta (or Tartars) used to cross the Yellow River on inflated sheepskins or rafts dragged by camels (Ma Tuan-lin, bk. 336, 12). In 1474 the Venetian Contarini was taken across the Don on a raft tied to a horse led by a Tartar (*Travels*, 153).

[2] Referring to the Ismaelian mission of 1238, previously mentioned. The Assassins had every reason to fear the Mongols; a few years later, they were exterminated by Hulagu and his troops.

[3] Roger Bacon (*Opus Majus*, i, 268) thought it probable that the Mongols who had broken through the Caspian gates were the soldiers

having forsaken the Mosaic law, followed after the golden calves, and whom Alexander the Macedonian endeavoured at first to shut up in the rugged mountains of the Caspians with bitumen-covered rocks.[1] When he saw that the undertaking exceeded the power of man, he invoked the might of the God of Israel, and the tops of the mountains came together, and an inaccessible and impassable place was made. Josephus says of this place : " will God do as much for the believer as he has done for the unbeliever?" So it seemed that God did not wish them to come out ; nevertheless, it is written in sacred history that they shall come out toward the end of the world, and shall make a great slaughter of men. There arises, however, a doubt whether the Tartars now coming from there be really they, for they do not use the Hebrew tongue, neither do they know the laws of Moses, nor have they laws, nor are they governed by them. To which it may be answered that, notwithstanding this, it is credible that they may belong to those who were shut up, and to whom reference has been made. . . . It is stated, however, that the Tartars take their name from a certain river which flows from the mountains which they had at an earlier date penetrated, and which is called Tartar ;[2] in like manner the river of Damascus is called Farfar."[3]

---

of Antichrist. The Armenian historians of the period were of the same opinion (Dulaurier, 198, 248). The Ismaelian envoy of 1238 thought they had started either from the Arctic shores, or from the Caspian mountains, or their vicinity (Matthew Paris, iii, 488).

[1] Conf. Roger Bacon, i, 364, and *infra*, p. xxxi.

[2] The Ismaelian envoy said they took their name from the river *Tar*. Pian de Carpine (645) says a branch of the Mongols called Su-Mongal took their name from the river *Tartar*, which flowed through their country (conf. Vincent of Beauvais, bk. xxix, ch. lxxxix, 422*b*, and *infra*, p. 114, note. Maundevile (127) speaks of " the river of Fassar (or Farfar), which flows by the cyties of Marryoche and Arteyse ;" and he adds, " bessyde the Cytie of Damas ys a Ryvere that cometh from the Mounteyne of Lybane, that men hyt callen

[3] Matthew Paris, *op. cit.*, iv, 76-78.

On April 9th, 1241, the battle of Lignitz was fought and lost by Henry, Duke of Silesia, and the Mongols swept over his dukedom and Moravia, at the same time as another of their armies under the great Batu entered Hungary. The last barrier against an invasion of central and western Europe was swept away, and the Pope, the Church, and the Princes of Europe attempted but feebly and too late to organise resistance. On March 10th, 1241, Henry, Count of Lorraine, wrote to Henry, Duke of Brabant, imploring his immediate assistance.[1] The latter sent a copy of this letter to the Bishop of Paris.[2] The clergy of Germany ordered solemn fasts, and preached a crusade.

But the most important letter written at this critical period was that of Frederic II to Henry III of England.[3] The Emperor, from his long and intimate relations with the Arabs, possessed more correct and wider knowledge concerning the Mongols and their wars than probably any man of his period. In this letter he refers with some detail to the first Mongol invasion in

---

Albane." Vincent of Beauvais (bk. xxix, ch. lxxi, 429*a*) says: "Tartari modo interrogativo clamoroso loquuntur, gutture rabido et horribile. Cantantes mugiunt ut Thauri, vel ululant ut Lupi, voces inarticulates in cantando proferunt, et hanc cantilenam *Ala alali* (*La Allah il Allah!* I suppose) communiter ac frequentissime canunt." The Armenian chronicles speak of the sharp, piercing voices of the Tartars (Dulaurier, 248). Long before this the *Wei shu*, bk. 103, 15, had, in speaking of the origin of the Oguz Turks (*Kao-ch'ê*) who descended from a wolf, noted that to this first father they owed their whining, drawling speech, and that their songs resembled the howling of wolves.

[1] See Matthew Paris, *op. cit.*, iv, 109-111.

[2] See Raynaldus, *Annales*, ii, 258.

[3] It is really an appeal to Christendom: "to Germany, ardent in battle; to France, who nurses in her bosom an intrepid soldiery; to warlike Spain; to England, powerful by its warriors and its ships; to Crete, to Sicily, to savage Hibernia, to frozen Norway." In this letter the Emperor frankly admits that all suppositions as to the origin of the *Tartari*, or *Tartarei*, are baseless, and that no one knows whence they had come.

Europe, the subjugation of the Comans and of southern Russia. Then he passes to the second invasion, to the conquest of Hungary, the defeat of King Bela IV at Pesth, and to the still more overwhelming one of Lignitz. He tells King Henry of the devastation of Poland, of Bohemia, of the marches of Austria ; and dwells pathetically on the urgent need for unity of action of all Christian Princes for the common defence, made so difficult by the cruel attacks on him by the Pope. He finishes his letter by saying that he puts his trust in God, and hopes that by the combined efforts of Christendom the Tartars will be driven finally down into their Tartarus.[1]

So intense, however, was the feeling of a large part of Europe against the Emperor, that we are assured that this letter was not generally accepted as a disinterested call for the defence of Christian Europe, and that to serve his own ends against the Pope he had invented this "plague of Tartars."[2] And so this letter was used by the Church only as further evidence of its great enemy's wickedness, and no effort was made by any of the powers of western Europe to assist Frederic with men or money. The Pope's quarrels, Jerusalem and Constantinople, were their only cares.

On the receipt of the news of the Mongol invasion of Hungary, Pope Gregory IX wrote to King Bela,[3] as he had written the year before to sympathize with the Queen of Georgia, condoling with him, encouraging him to further resistance, and promising all those who should take the

---

[1] *Ad sua Tartara Tartari detrudentur.* In a letter of Innocent IV to the Archbishop of Aquilæa, in 1243, we find this pun again. Joinville credits St. Louis with having also got it off somewhere about this time, and we have it practically in the quotation from Matthew Paris given above. I cannot decide to whom the credit of the discovery belongs, though I am inclined to think that it was Frederic; but then, would Pope Innocent have plagiarized his arch-enemy? (conf. Rémusat, *Mém.*, 15).

[2] Matthew Paris, *op. cit.*, iv, 119.

[3] Raynaldus, *Annales*, ii, 246-248, 259.

cross against the Mongols the same indulgences as if they had gone to the Holy Land. He wrote in the same strain to Coloman, brother of Bela, and issued an encyclical ordering a crusade to be preached.

The defeat of Bela at Pesth, and the loss of his kingdom to the Mongols swiftly followed, and filled the old Pope with alarm and distress. He wrote to Bela on July 1st, condoling again with him, and promising him, if Frederic would but show his contrition by returning to the Church, and thus restore peace to Christendom, to bring all the forces of the Church to the help of Hungary.[1] And so, while the Emperor and the Pope worked to destroy each other, the Pope fulminating against Frederic, and Frederic continuing to wage war against the Pope in Italy, the Mongol invasion was left to run its course. On August 21st, 1241, Pope Gregory IX died, and in December of the same year the Mongol Emperor, Ogodai, followed him to the grave.

Among the Mongols, the emperor was elected by the various members of Chingis Khan's family, and by the great generals and officers of state sitting as a parliament; so the news of the death of Ogodai put an end to the invasion of Europe; the presence of Batu, the Generalissimo, and of all the military chiefs was needed at the great meeting (*kuriltai*), which would soon have to be held near Karakorum, in Mongolia, to choose his successor. Thus it was that, though the Mongols remained in Hungary till 1243, and even detached divisions of their army into Austria and Dalmatia, their great westward movement was stopped, and weak and divided Europe was saved, though it knew it not, but stood helplessly expecting the fatal blow; for the Mongols' claim to universal dominion was now well known over Europe, and no one could entertain any doubt of their ability to enforce it.

---

[1] Raynaldus, *Annales*, ii, 261.

In 1243 Innocent IV was elected Pope; and with his characteristic energy he lost no time in putting to use such spiritual means as he could command to encourage the organization of armed resistance against the supposed impending Mongol invasion. On July 22nd he wrote to the Archbishop of Aquilæa to proclaim a crusade, exhort the Germans to take the cross to go to the help of the Hungarians "against the envoys of Satan, the ministers of the Tartarus," and promising the same indulgences as for a crusade to the Holy Land.[1]

But besides these measures the Pope promptly adopted others more in conformity with his holy calling, his well-known proselytizing zeal, and the deep interest he took in the extension of the labours of the powerful Mendicant Orders of St. Dominic and St. Francis. He organized missions, not only among the various heretical sects of Europe and Asia, and the pagan tribes of north-east Europe, but also to the Mongols; in the hope, as he says in a letter to "the King and the Tartar people," of "averting their onslaughts on Christendom through fear of Divine wrath," and to preach to them Christianity; as well as with the ulterior purpose of finding out through the missionaries exactly the plans of the Mongols as regarded Europe. The Pope must have been encouraged to believe that his representations might have some effect on the Mongol Sovereign by the prevailing belief in the existence, somewhere in the far East, of the Nestorian Christian realm of Prester John; and probably by the more recent information given him by a Russian bishop named Peter, who had fled before the invaders to Lyons, that "the Mongols worshipped one God, and were not without some religious beliefs."[2]

---

[1] Raynaldus, *Annales*, ii, 295.

[2] Matth. Paris, *op. cit.*, iv, 388; see also Rémusat, *op. cit.*, 25, and *infra*, p. 236, note 1. The Bishop, by the way, adds still a little more

The Pope organized two missions to the Mongols, and to the leaders of each of them he gave letters to be delivered, it is presumable, to the first important Chief they should meet, the one in Russia, the other in Armenia or the adjacent countries. He confided both these missions to Franciscans. The ambassador sent to the Mongols in Russia was Friar John of Pian de Carpine[1] near Perugia, who was at that time provincial of his order at Cologne; the other was Friar Lawrence of Portugal, of whose previous life we know nothing. These missions appear to have been organized by the personal initiative of the Pope, and the envoys were ready to leave Lyons before the first sitting of the General Council, for the letters to the Mongol Emperor given to them bear date the 9th March, 1245, and the Council, which was opened on the 26th June, only approved the Pope's action.

The Council of Lyons had been convened more especially for the purpose of "finding a remedy for the Tartars and other spurners of the faith and persecutors of the people of Christ;"[2] but so far as the Tartars were concerned, its action was characteristic of the times, and affords further

---

confusion to the story of Prester John, by apparently confounding him with John the Baptist. He says that the Mongols "say they have saint John the Baptist for chief" (*dicunt se habere sanctum Johannem Baptistam pro duce*). The earliest knowledge gained by Europe of Prester John dates from 1145 (Albericus, *Chronicon*, 307). It is also recorded under the same date by Otto, Bishop of Freisingen (D'Avezac, *op. cit.*, 547. Conf. *supra*, p. xiii, note 1).

[1] The editors of the *Analecta Franciscana* (iii, 266) remark that it would be more correct to write his Latin names *Plano Carpinis* or *de Carpine*, Planum Carpinis or Planum Carpi being the Latin form of the Italian Pian di Carpina, the modern Pian la Magione or Magione, about fourteen miles from Perugia (see also Liverani, 12). We have become so accustomed to speak of Friar John as Pian de Carpine, and of Friar William of Rubruck as Rubruck, that I have retained these names; though we might just as well speak of Thomas of Canterbury as Canterbury, or Robert of Lincoln as Lincoln. Strangely enough Rémusat (*Relations Politiques*, 27, 34) makes out that Lawrence and John were sent together to Batu on the Volga; and Vivien de St. Martin (*Hist. de la Géog.*, 269) repeats this blunder.

[2] Matth. Paris, *op. cit.*, iv, 411.

proof, if such were necessary, of the utter demoralization of Europe. It decided that, "whereas the Tartars are the most bitter enemies of the Christian name, and the Christians are still exposed to their attacks—for not having conquered them all yet, as they in their desire to extinguish the religion of Christ wish to do, they will surely come back, and the horrors seen in Poland, Russia, Hungary, and other countries will be renewed;" therefore it advised, besought, and entreated all Christian people to block every road or passage by which the enemy could pass, either by means of ditches, walls, buildings, or such other contrivances as they might deem best, and to give immediate notice to the Pope of the appearance of the enemy, to the end that he might take additional measures for their protection. The Council further promised that the Church would itself contribute, and cause all Christian localities directly interested in the matter to contribute, towards the expense these defences would occasion.[1]

Friar John of Pian de Carpine set out from Lyons on the 16th of April, 1245; and after various incidents which will be found related in his narrative of his journey given on subsequent pages, delivered the letter of the Pope, not to any Mongol Prince in Russia, but to Kuyuk Khan himself in northern Mongolia, not far from the city of Karakorum. On the 9th of June, 1247, Friar John and his companion, Friar Benedict of Poland, were back in Kiew in Russia; and in the autumn of the same year they again reached Lyons, where they presented to the Pope the reply of Kuyuk to his letter, and related the incidents of their adventurous journey.[2]

---

[1] Raynaldus, *op. cit.*, ii, 332.

[2] The text of Friar John's *Historia Mongalorum*, and of his account of his journey, together with the short narrative of his companion Friar Benedict, have been admirably edited and annotated by D'Avezac in 1839; this work has been of inestimable service to me.

As to the mission of Friar Lawrence of Portugal, we know practically nothing concerning it; no mention is made of it in any work which has come down to us. From a statement in the *Ecclesiastical Annals*,[1] that in 1247 the Pope sent this same Friar as his Legate to Asia Minor, we may infer that he may actually have started on the mission assigned him in 1245, and may have visited parts of western Asia, thus acquiring such knowledge of that region as justified the Pope's selection of him for this new office; but the new mission which the Pope sent in the same year, 1247, to the Mongol Commander-in-Chief, Baidju, in Armenia, tends to prove that Lawrence had not been able to deliver the letter entrusted to him in 1245.[2]

However this may be, in 1427 the Pope determined on sending another mission to the Mongols of Asia Minor, with a letter of similar tenour to those given in 1245 to Friar John and Friar Lawrence; and he chose this time as leader a Dominican friar, Ascelin or Anselm, this Order having already at the time established itself in western Asia. A short narrative of the journey has been preserved to us in Vincent of Beauvais's great encyclopædia, entitled *Speculum Majorum*: he deriving his information from a report which was written by Friar Simon of St. Quentin, a member of the mission, but which has not reached us. It is not without interest, though it adds hardly anything to our general knowledge of the Mongols; nor does it give any details whatever about the route followed by the mission. Friar Simon's narrative, like that of Friar John of Pian de

---

[1] Raynaldus, *op. cit.*, ii, 378.

[2] Additional proof of this is found in the statement made in 1247 by Friar Ascelin, the head of the mission of that year to Baidju, that the Pope did not know who the Great Khan was, nor had he ever heard of Baidju, nor Batu, nor anyone else among them. Rémusat, *op. cit.*, 27, states wrongly that Ascelin's mission was sent by the Pope in 1245, at the same time as that of Pian de Carpine. · Vivien de St. Martin, *op. sup. cit.*, 270, follows Rémusat, and says that Friar John wrote the relation of Lawrence of Portugal's mission.

Carpine, consisted presumably of two parts—the journey proper, and notices on the ethnology and history of the Mongols and the nations contiguous to them ; for we find scattered about in Bks. XXIX and XXX of the *Speculum Historiale*, among much information on the Mongols taken *verbatim* from John of Pian de Carpine's work, other additional details, which can only have been derived from Friar Simon.[1]

Friar Ascelin and his companions were made to suffer all the humiliations and discomforts his predecessors and successors on similar missions were subjected to by Mongol arrogance and natural boorishness. Lodgings far remote from the Court, poor and scanty food, insults, delays innumerable ; nothing was omitted to make the ambassador feel how insignificant he was, and in what low estimation the Pope was held. The envoy's conduct did not improve matters, though we must admit that he was sorely provoked ; he showed himself unbending, and sadly lacking in suavity of manner, or in any desire to ingratiate himself with the Mongols. The result was what was to be expected—a rude reply to the Pope's missive and the utter failure of the mission. It was 1250 before Ascelin ventured back to the Pope and made his report.

When John of Pian de Carpine reached Lyons in the latter part of 1247, a crusade against the Saracens was about to be undertaken, and King Louis IX of France, who had taken the cross on its first preaching in 1245, was on the point of leaving for Aigues-Mortes, there to take ship for Cyprus. But the Pope feared that the departure of the King would leave him exposed to the attacks of that arch-fiend, the Emperor Frederic ; and so, in the hope

[1] I have embodied or referred to nearly all these additional details in subsequent notes to Rubruck's narrative. Vincent of Beauvais had no knowledge of Rubruck or his work. See *Speculum Historiale*, bk. xxxi, chs. XL to LII, 453[a]-454[b].

of inducing the King to defer his departure till his personal safety was amply provided for, he sent, in the early part of 1248, three months after his arrival, Friar John of Pian de Carpine and his companion Benedict the Pole, to Paris, to represent his urgent needs to the King and seek to delay his setting out for the Holy Land.[1]

There was then at the Court of King Louis, among the numerous members of the mendicant Orders of which he was so fond, a Franciscan called William, a native of the village of Rubruck in French Flanders. He was about to accompany the King on the crusade, and St. Louis was to entrust to him some four years later a secret mission to the Court of the Mongol Emperor, the report of which forms the subject of this volume. There is every reason for supposing that Friar William met at Paris the two returning travellers, and heard from their lips the story of their adventurous journey; and he may possibly have conceived at that time the desire to visit those remote regions, preach the true faith, and bring back to the Church of Rome the Christians scattered throughout the Mongol empire, whose existence Friar John had revealed to him. During the next four years Friar William was destined to hear and see much, while with St. Louis, tending to strengthen in him the desire to visit the Mongols, and to supply him with valuable information for his guidance.[2]

---

[1] Wadding, *Annales*, iii, 125. Louis, when on his way in 1248 to Aigues-Mortes, went to Lyons to see the Pope, and presumably to give him an answer to the message brought him by Friar John (William of Nangis, *Gesta*, 357).

[2] The only source of information concerning Friar William known to exist is his own narrative of his journey; my statements are based entirely on it. He speaks several times of the Seine, of Paris, and of St. Denis. His prolonged residence in Paris may be inferred from his reference to the intimate friends (*amicos speciales*) he had there, though he may have become intimate with them while in the Holy Land. If Friar William did not meet John of Pian de Carpine and Benedict the Pole in Paris, he saw, probably as soon as it was

On September 21st, 1248, St. Louis landed on the island of Cyprus, and three months later there arrived at Nicosia an embassy from Ilchikadai, a Mongol General commanding the forces in Persia, bearing letters complimenting the King, "whose renown had already spread throughout western Asia," and who, it was believed by all, was to deliver it out of the hands of the Saracens, and offering Mongol assistance against Islam for the recovery of the Holy Places. The envoy was Sabeddin Morrifat David, or simply David,[1] as he is called by Rubruck. He told the King much pleasing news: he said the name of the Pope was already famous among the Tartars; that the mother of the Great Khan was a Christian; and that on the day of the Epiphany, three years before, the Great Khan himself and the greatest princes of the Tartars had also become Christians, converted by a Saracen bishop called Mallachias; that Ilchikadai even before that had been baptized; that the Great Khan of the Mongols was most favourable to the Christians; and much more to the same effect. This was translated to the King by a Dominican monk, Friar Andrew of Longumeau (or Longumel), who, besides possessing a good knowledge of Arabic, had been among the Mongols with Friar Ascelin's

---

written, the short narrative of Benedict. In the only passage in which he refers to Friar John, he mentions a detail only found in Benedict's account of the journey (see *infra*, p. 38). Antonio de Macro, in Wadding (*Annales*, iii, 207), states that on June 20th, 1248, Friar Benedict the Pole suffered martyrdom for the faith, with another member of his Order, called John of Plano (not to be confounded with John of Pian de Carpine), at Armaloch in Persia. If this be correct, Benedict may not even have had time to go to Paris, but, after making his report at Lyons, have left at once for Armenia. In this case, it is conceivable that a copy of this report was given William of Rubruck by John of Pian de Carpine. Shortly after, William of Rubruck went to the Holy Land, not to return for eight or ten years; but at the time of writing his narrative, in 1255, he apparently did not know of the existence of the work of John of Pian de Carpine, which must have been written not later than 1248, for the author does not appear to have long survived the hardships of his journey (D'Avezac, 599-601).

[1] William of Nangis, 360; D'Ohsson, ii, 237.

mission in 1247, and had there met this same David at the camp of Baidju, the Commander-in-Chief of the Mongol forces in western Asia.[1] King Louis was destined to find out, a few years later, that Ilchikadai's mission had been undertaken without authority from the Mongol Emperor; and that the information vouchsafed him by David was of that unsubstantial kind Orientals are but too apt to give when knowing it will afford pleasure to their hearers.[2] At the time, however, the King was so pleased with it and with the corroborative evidence in a letter from the Constable of Armenia to the King of Cyprus received at about the same time, speaking of the vast numbers of Christians he had found in the Mongol country, through which he was travelling on his mission to the Great Khan,[3] that he at once determined to send, not only a return mission to Ilchikadai, but also one to the Emperor of the Mongols,

[1] William of Nangis (359), Jean Pierre Sarrasin (254), and all contemporary writers who refer to the subject, state that Andrew had been on Friar Ascelin's mission. The chronicler of the mission, Simon of St. Quentin, only mentions Brothers Alexander, Alberic, Guischard of Cremona (who joined the party at Tiflis, to act as interpreter probably), and himself. Sarrasin calls Andrew, Friar Andrieu de St. Jacques, and William of Nangis styles him Andreas, Andrus and Andrien. Joinville refers to him, but not by name. Some writers think that the Friar Ascelin of the mission of 1245 is the same as the Andrew of that of 1249. Rémusat (*op. cit.*, 27) thinks Andrew joined Ascelin's mission during its journey to Mongol headquarters.

[2] Mangu Khan wrote to St. Louis (see *infra*, p. 249) that David was an impostor, but I imagine that we are not to understand this too literally. Ilchikadai had attempted to establish direct relations with the French King without obtaining the sanction of the Emperor; he was consequently, and quite properly, disavowed. D'Ohsson (ii, 238) is of opinion that the envoys were impostors in every sense, and their letters pure forgeries. If this be so, I cannot see why David should have been willing to return with the French mission to the Mongol headquarters in Persia, and how it happened that his companion and accomplice, Marcus, was at Sartach's *ordu* in 1253, when William of Rubruck passed through there, enjoying apparently some influence on account of his knowledge of languages (see *infra*, pp. 102, 105). Copies of the letters brought by David were sent to the Pope and to King Louis' mother, Queen Blanche (see Rémusat, *op. cit.*, 45, who has views identical with mine as to David's mission).

[3] William of Nangis, 360, 361.

who the envoy told him was called Kuyuk Khan,[1] for the purpose of exhorting him and his princes to the performance of Christian duties, and expressing his pleasure at the happy disposition of the Mongols as regarded the faith of Christ. Friar Andrew was naturally chosen as ambassador, and accompanied by his brother, another monk whose name has not reached us, four laymen, one of whom would seem to have been an Englishman, and David, he set out for the Emperor's camp about the middle of February, 1249,[2] bearing letters from the King and Legate, and rich presents, among others a tent made like a chapel, the walls adorned with scenes representing the Annunciation and other events of sacred history, "pour eulz montrer et enseigner comment ils devoient croire." Kuyuk was dead when the mission arrived at the Mongol court on the Imil, and it was the regent, the Empress Ogul Gaimish, who received it, and who promptly put this most unexpected advance of the great Frank sovereign to a very practical use. "When the great King (Queen) of the Tartarins," says Joinville, "had received the messengers and the presents, he sent for several kings, whose security he insured, and who had not yet come to do him homage, and he had the chapel set up, and spoke to them as follows: 'My lords, the King of France has come under my subjection, and here is the tribute he sends us; and if you come not to our mercy, we will send for him to confound

---

[1] Sarrasin (*loc. cit.*) writes the name *Quio Quan*.

[2] Sarrasin (255) says he was accompanied by "un siens frère et maistre Jehans Goderiche et uns autres clers de Poissy, et Herbers li sommeliers, et Gerbers de Sens." William of Nangis (367) says he had two other friars of his Order, two clerks, and two sergèants-at-arms (*serjans d'armes*). He adds that the envoy "envoia assez (tost) lettres au roys Loys de ce que il avoit trouvé; lesquelles lettres li roys envoya en France à sa trés-chiere mere la royne Blanche." Perhaps these letters may some day be found. Rémusat (*op. cit.*, 52) mentions the names of three other persons who, according to various contemporary writers, accompanied this mission: they are John of Carcassonne, Guillaume, and Robert, a clerk.

you.' And many there were among them who, for fear of the King of France, placed themselves in subjection to that King."[1]

In the spring of 1249, St. Louis, Queen Margaret, Friar William of Rubruck,[2] and all the army of Crusaders set sail for Egypt. The fatal battle of Mansurah, the captivity of the King, and the capitulation of Damietta followed shortly after; and in the spring or summer of 1250, the King, with the remnants of his army, was landed at Ptolemais, on the coast of Palestine, a much sadder though hardly a wiser man, as his further conduct showed. Near there, in 1251, while occupied in fortifying the town of Cæsarea, he received Friar Andrew on his return from the Mongol court with the envoys of the Empress-Regent, Ogul Gaimish—that "most abominable sorceress, viler than a dog," as the Emperor Mangu described her a few years later in a letter to King Louis—bearing a letter from her to the French King. It was in the following terms (I will not spoil Joinville's quaint language by attempting to translate it): "Bone chose est de pez; quar en terre de pez manjuent cil qui vont à quatre piez, l'erbe pesiblement. Cil qui vont a deus labourent la terre dont les biens viennent passiblement.[3] Et cete chose te mandons, nous pour toy aviser; car tu ne peus avoir pez se tu ne l'as à nous, et tel roy et tel (et moult en nommoient) et touz les avons mis à l'espée. Si te mandons qui tu non envoies tant de ton or et de ton argent chascun an, que tu nous retieignes à amis; et se tu ne le fais, nous destruirons toy et ta gent aussi comme nous avons fait ceulz que nous avons devant nommez." "And be well assured," adds Joinville,

---

[1] Joinville, *op. cit.*, 48.

[2] I take it that Friar William accompanied the crusade to Egypt, for he speaks of the width of the Nile at Damietta as one who had seen it, and of the annual rise of the river.

[3] *Passiblement*: "laboriously."

"that he (the King) repented greatly for ever having sent thither."[1]

If this mission was a diplomatic failure, it supplied King Louis, nevertheless, with much valuable and original information on the Mongols, their country, origin, customs and history. He learnt that the Tartarins had come from a great sandy desert, which began at the eastern end of the world at some marvellous rocky mountains, which no one had ever passed, and behind which were confined the people of Got and Margoth,[2] who are to come with Antichrist at the end of the world. He then heard of their first great chief and his laws (though Friar Andrew did not mention Chingis Chan by name), of his miraculous conversion to Christianity after a vision in which God had promised him dominion over Prester John, and of his warring with him ; of Christianity among the Mongols ; of the eight hundred chapels on carts seen in one camp; of the German prisoners at Talas;[3] of the many ruined cities passed on the long journey of a year, travelling ten leagues a day ; of the huge piles of bleached human bones marking the devastating march of the Mongols ;[4] of the fires through which they had sought to force his envoy to pass, with the presents he bore, before his audience with the Regent. He must have heard with special delight of the presence in south-eastern Russia of a great Mongol Christian chief, Sartach, son of the mighty Batu—a story believed alike by Christians and

---

[1] Joinville, *op. cit.*, 148.

[2] Clearly a reference to the Great Wall of China. The people of Gog and Magog had been heretofore placed south of the Caucasus (*supra*, p. xvii). Friar Andrew now locates them to the east of the Tartars (conf. *Marco Polo*, i, 276, 283).

[3] See Rubruck's narrative, *infra*, p. 136.

[4] Sempad, brother of King Heythum of Little Armenia, wrote to the King of Cyprus, that along his route to the Mongol court he had passed a hundred thousand (!) piles of bones of those killed by the Tartars (William of Nangis, 360. Conf. Friar John's account, *infra*, p. 13).

Mohammedans; and of many other things equally new and strange, but all encouraging to the Christian King's and to Friar William of Rubruck's hopes of conversion and consequent peace.[1] We are able with the scanty notices at our disposal to gain but slight knowledge of the route followed by Friar Andrew. We know only that he started from Antioch. It seems likely that he went by way of the great northern route through Little Armenia, Cæsarea in Cappadocia, Sivas and Erzerum : the same road followed by Friar William of Rubruck, but in the opposite direction, in 1255. After passing through Tiflis, he went either to Taurinum (Tabriz) or to the camp in the plain of Mugan, where were usually the Mongol headquarters for western Persia ; and where, I suppose, he found Ilchikadai, and delivered the letters he bore ; and where also the prudent David probably left him. Friar Andrew and his companions, having accomplished this part of their mission, skirted the southern shores of the Caspian, and thence, probably by way of the Syr daria valley, they reached Chimkent and Talas.[2] Here they turned eastward, crossed the Chu and Ili rivers south of the Balkash, and reached the camp of Ogul Gaimish on the river Imil, a little to the north-east of the lake. As to the route followed on the return journey, we have but one indication concerning it—

[1] See for the above details, Joinville, 147, *et seq.*, and Rubruck's narrative, *passim.*

[2] William of Nangis (365, 366) says that the King sent "missions" to Ilchikadai and the Great Khan ; but they were both entrusted to Brother Andrew, who is styled *capitaneus et magister.* Rubruck tells us (*infra*, p. 119) that Friar Andrew had skirted the southern and eastern shores of the Caspian ; he also refers (*infra*, p. 136) to this envoy having mentioned (presumably to him in conversation) the presence of German captives at Talas. I take it that he had actually seen them there, for otherwise the extremely careful Rubruck would certainly have noted that Andrew had only heard of their presence. Mangu told Rubruck that Ogul Gaimish received Friar Andrew's mission ; and as this Regent resided in the *ordu* of Kuyuk on the Imil, the envoy evidently did not go further east than this point.

that furnished by Rubruck — that they went along the eastern shore of the Caspian.[1] This suffices, however, to establish the fact that the route followed coming westward from the Balkash must have been, as far as the Caspian, a nearly due east and west one, parallel to that followed later on by Rubruck himself, though perhaps to the south of it.

Friar Andrew had hardly finished relating his adventures, and the King was still at Cæsarea, when there arrived from Constantinople a mission under Philip of Toucy, the son of the former Regent of the Empire.[2] From him the King heard of the wonderful adventures of this knight and other noblemen sent by the Emperor Baldwin II to the Comans of southern Russia. Philip told him of this people's way of swearing friendship by the killing of a dog; of the burial he had seen of one of their chiefs, with whom were interred a squire and a horse; and many other strange tales. It seems likely that among this party of knights (there were ten in all) was one called Baldwin of Hainaut, who had not only been to the Comans' country on this mission, but had actually married while there the daughter of the Coman Prince.[3] More than that, he had

---

[1] It is highly improbable that the mission in going skirted both the southern and the eastern shores of the Caspian, for there was absolutely no reason for the Mongols to make an envoy travelling eastward go up north along the eastern shore of the Caspian, neither Batu nor any of the other great chiefs living between the Caspian and the Aral. King Heythum, in 1253, going from Cilicia to the Mongol court, travelled by way of Derbend and the mouth of the Volga, but then he was anxious to see Sartach.

[2] Joinville says Narjoe (Narjot) de Toucy, but Du Cange and subsequent editors have shown that the envoy to St. Louis must have been Philip, son of Narjot.

[3] There can be little doubt that this Baldwin was on the mission, for Rubruck in his narrative speaks of him as a person well known to King Louis, which he could not have been otherwise, for he had been for many years past in the service of the emperors of Constantinople. On this personage, see *infra*, p. 102.

travelled also through Asia, sent probably on a mission by the Emperor and had gone as far as the camp of the Mongol emperor near Karakorum. From him Friar William of Rubruck got much valuable information, which finally decided him in favour of the road through Russia rather than that by way of Armenia in journeying to the Mongols. The former route he was already familiar with from Friar John of Pian de Carpine's mission, and it had the great advantage of taking him to the camp of Sartach, the Christian Mongol, from whom he might expect help on his journey, and assistance in establishing a mission among the Mongols.

So pleased was King Louis with De Toucy and the knights who accompanied him, that he retained them near him for a year before he would let them go back to Constantinople. This gave William of Rubruck, who had long since made up his mind to try the venture, all the necessary time to complete his preparations. The King readily gave him the small sum of money he needed to defray his expenses, with letters to Sartach and to the Emperor of the Mongols, commending him and his companions to their kindness, but carefully avoiding giving them any official character. After the insolent letter sent him by Ogul Gaimish, self-respect forbade his attempting to open formal friendly relations with this people—at least for the time being. Queen Margaret gave the Friar a beautifully-illuminated psalter, and probably some of the many rich church vestments he carried with him. These, together with a Bible, a present of the King, his breviary, one or two cherished devotional books, and, strangely enough, a valuable Arabic manuscript, composed his simple outfit. And so equipped he embarked, probably at Acre, and with the returning De Toucy mission, some time in the early spring of 1252, reached Constantinople safely, and there remained till May 7th of the following year, when he started for Mongolia.[1]

In the preceding pages I have endeavoured to indicate briefly the extent of the knowledge possessed by Europe of the Mongols and their empire down to the middle of the thirteenth century, and to show the probable sources of information Friar William of Rubruck had available as a preparation for his great journey of over ten thousand miles through Asia. I should have liked to be able to say something of the traveller himself, but we know absolutely nothing about him save his own statement, that at the time of his journey he was "a very heavy man." France can claim him as her child, for there is little doubt that he was a native of the village of Rubruck in old French Flanders, and not of Ruysbrock in Brabant, a few miles south of Brussels, as has been commonly supposed; but the date of his birth is unknown, as is that of his death.[2] His narrative affords us, fortu-

---

[1] There is evidence in Rubruck's narrative that his travelling companion, Bartholomew of Cremona, had been residing in Nicea (*infra*, p. 170). As to his interpreter, nicknamed Homo Dei, it is more likely that he took him along with him from Palestine. That Rubruck left Palestine in 1252 seems to me probable from the strange error he has made concerning the reigning emperor of Trebizonde: an error which he could not possibly have committed had he been with St. Louis throughout 1252, when the mission from Trebizonde arrived at Sidon (see *infra*, p. 46, note 3) Yule (*Ency. Brit.*, xxi, 46) thinks he must have received his commission at Acre, where the King was residing from May 1252 to June 1253.

[2] See Yule's admirable article in *Ency. Brit.* (Ninth Edition), xxi, 46-47; and his *Marco Polo*, ii, 536; Oscar Peschel, *Erkunde*, 165 *et seq.*; F. M. Schmidt, *Ueber Rubruk's Reise*, 163; Michel and Wright, *op. cit.*, 205; de Backer, *Rubrouck*, iii *et seq.*; da Civezza, *Saggio di Bibliografia, San Franciscana*, 503; *Nouvelle Biographie Générale*, xxxii, 938-940; *Hist. littèraire de la France*, xix, 114 *et seq.*

The name of our author's birthplace is variously written. Of the five MSS. used in the preparation of Michel and Wright's edition of the text, four have Rubruc, and one Rubruk. In other works where he is mentioned we find his name spelled *Rubruk*, *Rubruck*, *Rubruc*, *Rubrouck*, *Rubroc*, *Risbrouc*, *Risbrouke*, *Risbrooke*, *Ruysbrok*, *Ruysbrock*, *Ruysbrocke*, *Rubruquis*, *Rubricis* and *Rubriquis*. If, as seems highly probable, the place of his birth was the village of Rubrouck, as written in Flemish, we should write his name in English Rubruck

nately, abundant indications of his character. "These paint for us," says Yule, "an honest, pious, stouthearted, acute and most intelligent observer, keen in the acquisition of knowledge; the author, in fact, of one of the best narratives of travel in existence. His language, indeed, is Latin of the most un-Ciceronian quality—dog-Latin we fear it must be called; but, call it what we may, it is in his hands a pithy and transparent medium of expression. In spite of all the difficulties of communication, and of the badness of his turgemanus or dragoman, he gathered a mass of particulars, wonderfully true or near the truth, not only as to Asiatic nature, geography, ethnography and manners, but as to religion and language . . ."[1]

I would only venture to add to this well-deserved praise of Friar William, bestowed on him by the greatest authority on mediæval geography of our century, that not only was he keen and intelligent, but conscientious and thorough in a high degree. Study of his narrative shows his careful preparation for his work as an explorer. Solinus and Isidorus of Seville are, it is true, his only geographical authorities; still he makes careful use of them, not quoting them blindly, but comparing every statement of theirs with the facts as he observed them. The only quotations he makes are taken from the Bible, and are not always accurate, and from Virgil's *Aeneid*; but we gather from a few passing references in his narrative that he had read historical works and the classical poets, and had specially noted the movements Europewards of the tribes

---

The editors of the *Biographie Générale* say he was born about 1215. Aug. St. John (as quoted by the editors of the text of the *Soc. de Géographie*, 205) puts it at about 1220—Daunou (*Hist. litt. de la France*, 126) thinks he died about 1270, but this is purely conjectural—Da Civezza (*Storia Universalle*, i, 429) says 1230, and Schmidt (163) between 1220 and 1230. There is, so far as I am aware, absolutely no authority for any of these dates.

[1] Yule, *Ency. Brit.*, xxi, 47; conf. F. M. Schmidt, 166.

of western Asia since the time of the great Hunnic invasions: which latter presented to his mind many striking analogies with the Mongol ones just over. While preparing for his journey at Constantinople in the winter and spring of 1253, he saw the Armenian traders who then as now swarmed there, and most of whom had had experience among the Mongols; and from them, and possibly from the resident Armenian monks, he also secured information on the Tartars and the countries he was to visit. During his residence in Asia Minor and in Egypt he had probably acquired a tolerable knowledge of Arabic, as he appears to have been able to converse freely with any of the "Saracens" he met during his journey; and he tells us himself that he picked up enough Mongol to be able to control, or perhaps even dispense with, his very poor interpreter. In short, I think, we may safely say that he left no stone unturned to fit himself thoroughly for the work he had undertaken.

Let us now note what Friar William was able to add by his journey and careful observations to Europe's sum of general and geographical knowledge. His principal contributions to geographical science were the indication of the true sources and course of the Don and Volga, the lake nature of the Caspian,[1] the identity of Cathay with the classical country of the Seres, a description of the Balkash and of the inland basin of which it occupies the eastern extremity, the first description of the city of Karakorum, the first mention of Kaoli or Korea, and of the Tungusic tribes of Orengai, the *Orienguts* of mediæval Mohammedan writers. Natural history owes to him the earliest mention

[1] Albert of Bollstaedt had at about the same date stated that the Caspian was a lake, not a gulf, but he had simply accepted the views of Ptolemy. The fact had already been established by the Arab geographers of the tenth century—by Ibn Haukal for example—but Europe was in ignorance of this.

in western writers of the wild ass or *kulan*, and of the *argali* or *ovis Poli*. Ethnology is indebted to him for interesting facts too numerous to mention. To him linguistics and anthropology owe the first accurate information on the Goths of the Crimean coast, on the identity of the Comans with the Kipchak, Turks and Cangle, on the difference between the Tartars and the Mongols, on the connexity of the languages of the Bashkirds (*Pascatir*) and the Hungarians, on the origin of the Danubian Bulgarians, on the affinity between the languages of the Russians, Poles, Bohemians and Slavs and that of the Wandals, and on that of the Turkish language with that of the Uigurs and Comans. He was the first to give a nearly accurate explanation of the Chinese script, to note the true peculiarities of the Tibetan, Tangutan (Turkish), and Uigur modes of writing. These discoveries in this special line of research are not all we owe to this most perspicacious traveller; but I will not prolong the list, as we have a number of other important ones in the field of the history of religions to credit him with. He was the first to describe the Christian communities in the Mongol empire, and to give details of their rituals and the tenets of their faith; we owe to him the earliest description of the Lamas or northern Buddhist monks, of their temples, their ritual, their Living Buddhas, of their use of prayer beads, and of their favourite formula, *Om mani padme, hum*. He shows the peculiarities of the Uigurs' form of worship, and likewise of their dress. Peculiarities and superstitions of the Greek and Armenian churches did not escape him; in short, no one traveller since his day has done half so much to give a correct knowledge of this part of Asia.

It was Friar William's desire to present his report to King Louis in person; but on arriving in Cyprus in 1255 he found that the King, whom he hoped to see in Palestine, had returned to France; and the Provincial of his Order refused to allow him to follow him there. He took him with him to Acre, to the house of his Order, directing him to transmit his report to the King from that place. This the traveller reluctantly did, requesting at the same time the King to use his influence with the Provincial of the Franciscans in Syria, who appears to have belonged to the Province of France, to have him given permission to make a visit to France, to see the King and the personal friends he had there.

King Louis must have complied with Friar William's request, for we learn from Roger Bacon that he met the traveller in France a few years later, and conversed with him about his discoveries and adventures. We know that he made a careful examination of his report, nearly every geographical detail of which we find embodied in his famous *Opus Majus*.[1]

It was fortunate for Friar William that he met, during his probably short stay in France, this brilliant and appreciative writer, for he alone saved him and the results of his arduous journey from utter oblivion for three centuries and a half: as it was only in 1600 that Richard Hakluyt published a portion of his report from a manuscript belonging to Lord Lumley,[2] which Purchas in 1625 republished and completed, in his *Pilgrimes*, from another

[1] See *Opus Majus*, i, 354 *et seq*. Bacon says he had made special use, in writing his geographical description of the northern parts of the world, of the work of William of Rubruck, "*quem librum diligenter vidi, et cum ejus auctore contuli, et similiter cum multis aliis, qui loca orientis et meridana rimata sunt*" (*Opus Majus*, i, 305). The other travellers were probably returning crusaders. Bacon was familiar, however, with the work of John of Pian de Carpine (*op. cit.*, i, 371).

[2] So little known was Rubruck at the time when Hakluyt published his work, that Gerard Mercator wrote to Hakluyt in 1580, in reply to a letter telling him of the *Itinerarium*: "I have not yet seen the complete treatises of William of Tripoli (*sic*) and John du Plan Carpin; I have only seen some extracts of them in other works" (Bérgeron, *Traité des Tartares*, ii, 116, 121). The extracts were probably solely taken from

MS. in Bennet (now Corpus Christi) College, Cambridge, the text having been supplied him, he says (vol. iii, p. 23), "by Master Hacluits industrie."

Between the date of the writing of Bacon's *Opus Majus* (1264) and the middle of the present century, there are found but the briefest mentions of Friar William in the numerous works written by members of the Franciscan and other Orders. Vincent of Beauvais did not know of the existence of Friar William's *Itinerarium*; at all events, not a single detail concerning the Mongols given by him is traceable to this work. Wadding, the great historian of the Franciscans, makes no mention of him at all in his *Annales*, though he devotes many pages to the missions of Pian de Carpine, Lawrence of Portugal, Ascelin, etc.; while in his *Scriptores Ordinis Minorum* he misquotes an earlier reference to him by John Pitts, though he makes him out to have been a native of Brabant instead of an Englishman, as Pitts had imagined him to be. He credits him with having written an *Itinerarium Orientis, De Gestis Tartarorum*, which many subsequent writers have supposed to be two distinct works, whereas it evidently designates the two parts into which Friar William's report, like that of his predecessor, Friar John of Pian de Carpine, is divided. Lasor a Varea (ii, 297) mentions Risbrooke among the writers who refer to Palestine, and (ii, 555) as having written a work *de Tartarorum gestis.* De Soto (ii, 46) has a short reference to our traveller, gives the title of his work as *Itinerarium ad partes Orientales, una cum relatione Tartarorum*,[1] and refers to the existence of several MSS. of it in the British libraries, to Bérgeron's translation, and to its

Friar John's *Historia Mongalorum*, which had been frequently quoted in works of the thirteenth and subsequent centuries.

[1] Bacon (*op. cit.*, ii, 368), speaking of the Tartars' claim to universal dominion, says that it is referred to "*in libro fratris Gulielmi de moribus Tartarorum*," but this, I take it, is only a sub-title, as it were, of the first part of his work.

having also appeared in Dutch in a collection of travels published in Leyden in 1706.

We must come down to Father da Civezza's *Storia Universalle Delle Missione Francescana* (1857-1861), to find a full account of Rubruck's journey, and appreciation of its great worth, by a member of his Order; and even in this valuable work the author has, it would appear, been content to quote from the faulty translation of Bergeron (1634); and throughout his notice of our traveller he writes his name *Rubriquis*.[1]

The only explanation which suggests itself of this neglect of Friar William's work by writers of his Order, is that his mission, like that of Friar Andrew of Longumeau, equally ignored in their works, was undertaken by order of and for the King of France, and not for the sole advancement of the interests of the Church and the Franciscans. Though this explanation is hardly satisfactory, for the glory gained by the traveller redounded necessarily on the Order to which he belonged, and the Franciscan, Roger Bacon, had promptly made known to the Pope its great value, I cannot but think the neglect in which Friar William was left for so many centuries was, to a great extent, intentional. Even at the present day, the great history of the Franciscan Order which is being published by the Fathers of the College of San Bonaventura, does not contain a single reference to Friar William or Friar Andrew of Longumeau.

---

[1] I have not been able to consult a number of works which have appeared since 1800, containing biographical notices of Rubruck, but those I have seen consider him "untrustworthy," "credulous," "superstitious" (see, *e.g.*, *Nouvelle Biographie Univ.*, xxxii, 938; *Hist. litt. de la France*, xix, 126; and also see Da Civezza, *op. cit.*, i, 429-457). The same writer, in his *Saggio di Bibliografia*, 503, reproduces de Backer's biographical notice of our author, the only good part of the book. Cahun, 392, speaks of "l'inintelligence du moine Rubruquis . . . son étroitesse de jugement et d'informations qui éclate à chaque ligne dans une relation pleine de mots spirituels, mais vide de serieux."

In 1839, the Société de Géographie of Paris published, in the Fourth Volume of its *Recueil de Voyages et de Mémoires*, what may be considered the *editio princeps* of the *Itinerarium*; in which the editors, no less distinguished scholars than Francisque Michel and Thomas Wright, availed themselves not only of the texts published by Hakluyt and Purchas, but of five other MSS. since discovered, three from Corpus Christi College, Cambridge, one from the British Museum, and one from the Library of the University at Leyden. None of the manuscripts present any variations of importance, the different readings in them being clearly attributable in nearly every case to negligent copying; all have been derived from a single original. It is therefore hardly probable that the discovery of any new manuscripts can alter in any important detail the text as given by the two learned editors.[1]

Of the translations which have appeared of Friar William's work little may be said; all of them have been

---

[1] See *Recueil de Voyages et de Mémoires*, iv, 199-212. The MSS. of Cambridge bear the numbers LXVI, CCCCVII, and CLXXXI in Nasmith's *Catalogue of the Parker Collection*. The Brit. Mus. MS. is numbered 14. C. XIII of the King's Library, and the MS. of Leyden is No. 77 of the Vossius Collection. The editors mention (p. 210) another MS., said to exist in the Collection of Sir Thomas Phillips, but they were unable to consult it. Researches recently made by Mr. W. Foster, at the request of the editor of the present volume, have also failed to discover it. As to the MS. referred to by the same editors (p. 202) as existing in the Vatican Library, Father Francesco Ehrlé, the learned Prefect of that library, has very kindly made a careful search for it, but without result. It is true that this MS. is catalogued by Montfaucon (*Bibl. bibl.*, i, 86) as in the Petau Collection under the two numbers 292, 933; but Father Ehrlé is of opinion that the entry is erroneous, or, at all events, that the MS. was not sent to the Vatican when this collection was presented to it by Queen Christina of Sweden. Mr. de Vries, the librarian of the University of Leyden, to whom Father Ehrlé wrote on the subject, is also of opinion that the supposed Vatican MS. is in all likelihood the No. 77 of the Vossius Collection, referred to previously. Henri Cordier (*Odoric*, lxxxiii) mentions a MS. of Rubruck in the No. 686 of the Dupuy Collection of the National Library of Paris. Mr. H. Leon Feer has kindly collated this MS. with Michel and Wright's text, and shown that it is an exact reproduction of the text as published by Hakluyt. It bears date 1646, and was probably copied from Hakluyt's published text.

made on Hakluyt's or Purchas' renderings. Astley, Robert Kerr, Pinkerton in English; Bérgeron, Fleury, l'Abbé Prévost, La Harpe, and more recently (1888) Eugène Müller in French; the *Allgemeine Historie der Reisen* (1747) in German, and many others, are but so many editions of the old English translations. The translations of Hakluyt and Purchas, however valuable, were inevitably inaccurate in many places, for a more thorough knowledge of Asia and the Mongols than was possessed by Europe at the time was necessary for a correct rendering of Friar William's text. Purchas truly remarks: "the Friers Latin, for some barbarous words and phrases, hath beene troublesome to translate." It is, however, to say the least, strange that most writers of the eighteenth and the nineteenth centuries have preferred to avail themselves of these translations, instead of making use of the text as published by Hakluyt, Purchas, or the Société de Géographie. Desguignes, Karamsin, Rémusat, d'Ohsson, and even Henri Cordier in his splendid edition of Friar Odoric, quote from Bérgeron's translation.

Though often quoting him, none of those who have used the rich mine of information opened to them by the old monk seem to have fully realised its value; or, at all events, they have not given adequate expression to their appreciation of his great merit, Purchas alone excepted, who says he holds the Friar's work "a Jewell of Antiquitie." It was reserved for Oscar Peschel,[1] and especially for Sir

[1] Oscar Peschel, *Erdkunde* (165), says: "der Bericht des Ruysbroek, fast unbefleckt durch störende Fabeln, durch seine Naturwahrheit als ein grosses geographisches Meisterstück des Mittelalters bezeichnet werden darf." In 1877 Louis de Backer published a so-called original translation from the Latin of the *Itinerarium*. To the errors of previous translators he has added so many extraordinary blunders of his own that one is astonished that it was ever accepted by the learned editors of the valuable collection in which it appeared. Exclusive of Yule's invaluable notes on Rubruck, the only important work on the subject—and its value is inestimable—is the study of

Henry Yule, to whom geography owes so much, to put Friar William in the high place he so richly deserves among the great travellers of the world. "The generation immediately preceding his (Marco Polo's) own has bequeathed to us," the latter says, "in the Report of the Franciscan Friar William de Rubruquis on the mission with which St. Lewis charged him to the Tartar Courts, the narrative of one great journey which, in its rich detail, its vivid pictures, its acuteness of observation and strong good sense, seems to me to form a Book of Travels of much higher claim than *any one series* of Polo's chapters; a book, indeed, which has never had justice done to it, for it has few superiors in the whole Library of Travel."[1]

---

Franz Max Schmidt, *Ueber Rubruk's Reise von* 1253-1255, published in 1885.

[1] Yule, *Marco Polo*, i, 102.

## ITINERARY

## OF FRIAR WILLIAM OF RUBRUCK.

1253.

| | | |
|---|---|---|
| May | 7. | Left Constantinople. |
| " | 21. | Reached Soldaia (Sudak). |
| June | 1. | Left Soldaia. |
| " | 3. | Met Tartars for first time. |
| " | 5. | Reached Scatay's camp (Remained till 8th). |
| " | 12. | Camp at Isthmus of Perekop. |
| " | 22. | Reached first camp beyond Isthmus. |
| July | 20. | Reached bank of Tanais (Don.—Remained till 23rd). |
| " | 31. | Reached Sartach's camp. |
| August | 3. | Left Sartach's camp. |
| " | 5. | Reached bank of Etilia (Volga). |
| September | 16. | Left Batu's camp. |
| " | 27. | Reached bank of Jaic (Ural). |
| October | 31. | Took southerly course. |
| November | 8. | Reached Kinchat. |
| " | 9. | Took easterly course. |
| " | 18 (?) | Reached Cailac. |
| " | 30. | Left Cailac. |
| December | 3. | Reached head of Ala kul. |
| " | 6. | Accelerated speed. |
| " | 13. | Passed through gorge infested with devils. |
| " | 27. | Reached Mangu's camp. |

1254.

| | | |
|---|---|---|
| January | 4. | Received in audience by Mangu. |
| March | 29. | Left for Karakorum. |
| April | 5. | Reached Karakorum. |
| May | 24. | Audience of Mangu. |
| " | 30. | Public discussion with Tuin. |
| August | 8. | Received permission to leave. |
| " | 18. | Left Karakorum. |
| September | 16. | Reached Batu's camp. |
| October | 16. | Left Batu's camp. |
| November | 1. | Left Sarai. |
| " | 15. | Reached mountains of Alans. |

1254.

| | | |
|---|---|---|
| November | 17. | Reached Iron Gate (Derbend). |
| " | 19. | Reached Samaron. |
| " | 21. | Reached Samag. |
| " | 22. | Entered plain of Mogan. |
| December | 23. | Reached Naxua (Najivan). |

1255.

| | | |
|---|---|---|
| January | 13. | Left Naxua. |
| February | 2. | At Ani. |
| " | 15. | Reached head of Araxes. |
| " | 17 (?). | Reached Marsengen. |
| " | 22 (?). | Reached Camath on the Euphrates (Kara su). |
| March | 23 (?). | Reached Sebaste (Sivas). |
| April | 4. | Reached Caesarea in Cappadocia. |
| " | 19. | Reached Iconium (Konieh). |
| May | 5. | Reached Curta on coast. |
| " | 17. | Left Curta. |
| June | 16. | Reached Cyprus. |
| " | 29. | At Antioch. |
| August | 15. | At Tripoli. |

# TITLES OF BOOKS CITED BY ABBREVIATED REFERENCES.

Abulgasi Bayadur Chan. *Histoire Généalogique des Tartars.* Traduite du Manuscript Tartare par D***. Leyden, 1726. 1 vol., 12mo.

*Acta Sanctorum. Ex Latinis et Graecis aliarumque gentium Monumentis, etc.* Paris. In 4to.

Al Bekri. See Ibn Alathir.

Albericus Trium Fontium. *Chronicon.* Edited by Leibnitz. *Accessiones Historicae.* Hanover, 1698. Vol. ii.

Ammianus Marcellinus. *Rerum gestarum.* Nisard edit., Paris, 1869. In 4to.

*Analecta Franciscana, sive Chronica aliaque varia documenta ad historiam Fratrum Minorum spectantia.* Edita a Patribus Collegii S. Bonaventurae. Ad Cláras Aquas (Quaracchi). 1887-1897. 22 vols., 4to (all published).

Antoninos (?). *Zametki xii-xv veka, otnossiastchiasia k Krymskomu gorodu Sugdee (Sudaku), pripissanniya na Grecheskom Sinaksare.* In Zapiski Odesskago obstchestva istorii i drevnostei, v, 1863, pp. 595-837.

Arrian. *Expeditio Alexandri.* Müller's edit. In Didot's collection.

Assemanus, Joseph Simonius. *Bibliotheca Orientalis Clementino-Vaticana.* Rome, 1721. 4 vols., fol. Tome ii, *De Scriptoribus Syris Monophyritis.*

Atkinson, Thomas Witlam. *Oriental and Western Siberia:* a Narrative of Seven Years' Explorations and Adventures in Siberia, Mongolia, the Kirghis Steppes, Chinese Tartary and Part of Central Asia. London, 1858. 1 vol., 8vo.

Atkinson, Thomas Witlam. *Travels in the Regions of the Upper and Lower Amoor and the Russian Acquisitions on the Confines of India and China.* London, 1860. 1 vol., 8vo.

Baber. *Mémoires de.* Traduits par Pavet de Courteille. Paris, 1871. 2 vols., 8vo.

Bacon, Roger. *Opus Majus.* Edited by John Henry Bridges. Oxford, 1897. 2 vols., 8vo.

Badger, George Percy. *The Nestorians and their Rituals:* with a Narrative of a Mission to Mesopotamia and Coordistan in 1842-1844. London, 1852. 2 vols., 8vo.

Barbaro, Josafa. *Travels to Tana and Persia.* Thomas' translation, edited by Lord Stanley of Alderley. London, 1873. 1 vol., 8vo. (Hakluyt Soc.)

Bartels, Max. *Die Medicin der Naturvölker.* Ethnologische Beitrage zur Urgeschichte der Medicin. Leipzig, 1893. 1 vol., 8vo.

Beal, Samuel. *Buddhist Records of the Western World.* Translated from the Chinese of Hiuen-tsiang (A.D. 629). London, 1884. 2 vols , 8vo.

Benjamin of Tudela. *Voyage au tour du monde*, commencé l'an MCCXXIII. In Bérgeron's *Voyages*, i.

Bérgeron, Pierre. *Voyages faits principalement en Asie dans les xii, xiii, xiv, et xv siècles*, etc. La Haye, 1735. 2 vols., 4to. (Though usually quoted as Bérgeron's, this work is a recast of that writer's work of 1634, by Van der Aa of Leyden. See d'Avezac, *op. cit.* 439-442.)

Bergman, Benjamin. *Nomadische Streiferien unter den Kalmuken*, in den Jahren 1802 und 1803. Riga, 1805. 4 vols., 12mo.

Bitchurin, Father Hyacinthe. *Du Chamanisme en Chine.* In *Nouvelles Annales des Voyage*, Nouv. séric, xxvi, pp. 287-316.

Bouché-Leclerc, A. *Histoire de la Divination dans l'Antiquité.* Paris, 1882. 4 vols., 8vo.

Bretschneider, E. *Notices of the Mediæval Geography and History of Central and Western Asia.* Drawn from Chinese and Mongol writings, and compared with the observations of Western Authors in the Middle Ages. In *Journal of the North China branch of the Royal Asiatic Society*, New Series, vol. x, pp. 75-307.

Bretschneider, E. *On the Knowledge Possessed by the Ancient Chinese on the Arabs and Arabian Colonies and other Western Countries mentioned in Chinese Records.* London, 1871. In 8vo.

Bretschneider, E. *Archæological and Historical Researches on Peking and its Environs.* Shanghai, 1876. In 8vo.

Bretschneider, E. *Notes on Chinese Mediæval Travellers to the West.* Shanghai, 1875. In 8vo.

Bunbury, E. H. *A History of Ancient Geography among the Greeks and Romans, from the Earliest Ages till the Fall of the Roman Empire.* 2nd edit. London, 1883. 2 vols., 8vo.

Busbeck. *Epistolae deque rebus Turcicis.* Leipzig, 1689. 2 vols., 8vo.

Cahun, Leon. *Introduction à l'histoire de l'Asie.* Turcs et Mongols. Des origines à 1405. Paris, 1896. 1 vol., 8vo.

Castren, Matthias Alexander. *Ethnologische Vorlesungen über die Altaische Volker*, nebst Samojedischen Märchen und Tartarische Heldensagen. St. Petersburg, 1857. 1 vol., 8vo.

Castren, Matthias Alexander. *Reisen im Norden.* Leipzig, 1853. 1 vol., 12mo.

Chabot, J. B. *Histoire de Mar Jabalaha III, Patriarche des Nestoriens* 1281-1317), *et du moine Rabban Cauma, Ambassadeur du Roi Argoun en Occident* (1287). Paris, 1895. 1 vol., 8vo.

Chandra Das, Sarat. *Indian Pandits in the Land of Snow.* Calcutta, 1893. 1 vol., 8vo.

Chardin, Le Chevalier. *Voyages en Perse et autres lieux de l'Orient.* Nouvelle édit. Par L. Langlès. Paris, 1811. 10 vols., 8vo.

Chavannes, Edouard. *Le Nestorianisme et l'inscription de Kara Balgasoun.* Paris, 1897. In 8vo. Extract from *Journal Asiatique*, 1897.

Chavannes, Edouard. *Voyageurs Chinois chez les Khitan et les Joutchen.* Paris, 1898. 1 vol., 8vo. (Extracts from *Journal Asiatique*, No. 6, 1897 ; No. 8, 1898.)

*Chien Han shu.* The Book of the Anterior Han, or the Annals of the Early Han Dynasty, covering the period from B.C. 206 to A.D. 24.

*Chin shu.* The Book of the Chin Dynasty, covering the period from A.D. 265 to 419.

*Chou shu.* The Book of Chou, or the Annals of the Chou Dynasty, covering the period from A.D. 557 to 581.

Clarke, Edward D. *Travels in Russia, Tartary, and Turkey.* Edinburgh, 1852. 1 vol., 8vo.

Clavijo, Ruy Gonzalez de. *Narrative of the Embassy to the Court of Timour at Samarcand*, A.D. 1403-6. Translated by Clements R. Markham. London, 1859. 1 vol., 8vo. (Hakluyt Soc.)

Codinus. See *Corpus Scriptorum Historiae Byzantinae.*

Constantine Porphyrogenitus. *De Thematibus et de Administrando Imperio.* See *Corpus Scriptorum Historiae Byzantinae.*

Constantine Porphyrogenitus. *De Ceremoniis Aulae Byzantinae.* See *Corpus Scriptorum Historiae Byzantinae.*

Contarini, Ambrosio. *The Travels of*, to the Great Lord Ussuncassan, King of Persia, in 1473. Edited by Lord Stanley of Alderley. London, 1873. 1 vol., 8vo. (Hakluyt Soc.)

Cordier, Henri. *Les Voyages en Asie au XIVe siècle du bienheureux frère Odoric de Pordenone, Religieux de Saint François.* Paris, 1891. 1 vol., small 4to.

*Corpus Scriptorum Historicae Byzantinae.* Editio emendatior et copiosior, Consilio B. G. Niebuhrii instituta. Bonn, 1831-184 (?) 8vo.

Cosmas Indicopleustes. *The Christian Topography.* Translated from the Greek by J. W. McCrindle. London, 1897. 1 vol., 8vo. (Hakluyt Soc.).

Da Civezza, Marcellino. *Storia universale delle Missione Francescane.* Rome, 1857-1861. 5 vols., 8vo.

Da Civezza, Marcellino. *Saggio di Bibliografia geographica, ethnographica San Franciscana.* In Prato, 1879. 1 vol., 8vo.

D'Avezac. *Relation des Mongols ou Tartares par le frère Jean du Plan de Carpin*, de l' ordre des Frères Mineurs, Légat du Saint-Siège Apostolique, Nonce en Tartarie, pendant les années 1245, 1246 et 1247, et Archevêque d'Antivari, etc. Paris, 1839. 4to. (In 2nd part of vol. iv of the *Recueil de Voyages et de Mémoires publié par la Societé de Géographie.*)

De Backer, Louis. *Guillaume de Rubrouck*, Ambassadeur de Saint Louis en Orient. Récit de son voyage traduit de l' original Latin et annoté par. Paris, 1877. 1 vol., 18mo.

Deguignes. *Histoire Générale des Huns, des Turcs, des Mongols, et des autres Tartares Occidentaux*, etc. Paris, 1756-1758. 5 vols., 4to.

De Morgan, J. *Mission scientifique au Caucase.* Études archeologiques et historiques. Paris, 1889. 2 vols., 4to. Tome ii, Recherches sur les origines des peuples du Caucase.

D'Ohsson, le Baron C. *Histoire des Mongols*, depuis Tchinguiz Khan jusqu'à Timour Bey ou Tamerlan. La Haye, 1834. 4 vols. 8vo.

De Soto, Fr. Joannis. *Bibliotheca universa Franciscana.* Matriti, 1732. 3 vols., 4to.

Devéria, G. *Musulmans et Manichéens Chinois.* In *Journal Asiatique*, IXe série, vol. x.

Devéria, G. *Notes d'épigraphie Mongole-Chinoise.* Paris, 1897, in 8vo. (Extract from *Journal Asiatique*, 1896.)

Du Cange. *Glossarium mediae et infimae Latinitatis*, conditu a Carolo Dufresne Domino Du Cange cum supplementis integris D. P. Carpenterii at additamentis Adelungi et aliorum digessit G. A. L. Herschel. Paris, 1840. 7 vols., 4to.

Dulaurier, Ed. *Les Mongols d'après les historiens Armeniens.* Fragments traduits sur les texts originaux. In *Journal Asiatique*, V[e] série, vol. xi (1858).

Elias, Ney. See Mirza Haidar.

Finlay, George. *History of Greece.* Tozer's edit., London, 1877. 7 vols., 8vo.

Gibbon, Edward. *Decline and Fall of the Roman Empire.* W. Smith's edit., London, 1881. 8 vols., 8vo.

Gombojew, Galsang. *Randbemerkungen zu Plano Carpini.* In *Mélanges Asiatiques de l'Académie des Sciences de St. Petersbourg*, 1856, ii, pp. 650-666.

Grenard, F. *Mission scientifique dans la Haute Asie*, 1890-1895. Paris, 1898. 3 vols., 4to.

Haiton. *Histoire Orientale ou des Tartares.* Traduit suivant l'édition Latine de André Müller, Greiffenhag. In Bérgeron's *Voyages*, vol. ii.

Hakluyt, Richard. *Collection of the Early Voyages, Travels and Discoveries of the English Nation.* London, 1809. 5 vols., 4to. (Vol. i, pp. 80-101, text of Rubruck ; pp. 101-129, translation.)

Hammer, J. de. *Histoire de l'Empire Ottoman*, depuis son origine jusqu'a nos jours. Traduit de l'allemand par J. J. Hellert. Paris, 1835. 5 vols., 8vo.

Hammer-Purgstall. *Geschichte der Goldenen Horde in Kiptchak*, das ist der Mongolen in Russland. Pesth, 1840. 1 vol., 8vo.

Haroldus, Franciscus. *Epitome Annalium Ordinis Minorum.* Rome, 1662. 2 vols., fol.

Haxthausen, A. von. *Transcaucasia.* Sketches of the Nations and Races between the Black Sea and the Caspian. London, 1854. 1 vol., 8vo.

Heyd, W. *Histoire du Commerce du Levant au Moyen-Age.* Edition française par Furcy Raynaud. Paris, 1885. 2 vols., 8vo.

*Hou Han shu.* The Book of the Posterior Han Dynasty, covering the period from A.D. 25 to 220.

Howorth, H. H. *History of the Mongols*, from the ninth to the nineteenth century. London, 1876. 4 vols., 8vo.

Ibn Alathir. *Fragments de geographes et d'historiens Arabes et Persans inedits*, relatifs aux anciens peuples du Caucase et de la Russie meridionale. Traduits et accompagnés de notes critiques, par M. Defrémery. In *Journ. Asiat.*, 4e serie, xiii, 457-522 ; xiv, 447-513.

Ibn Batuta. *Voyages d'Ibn Batoutah.* Texte Arabe, accompagné d'une traduction par C. Defrémery et le Dr. B. R. Sanguinetti. Paris, 1874-79. 4 vols., 8vo.

Ibn Foszlan. *Ibn Foszlan und anderer Araber Berichte über die Russen alterer Zeit.* Text und Ubersetzung mit kritisch-philologischen Anmerkungen, etc., von C. M. Frahn. St. Petersburg, 1823. 1 vol., 8vo.

Ibn Haukal. *The Oriental Geography of Ibn Haukal*, an Arabian traveller of the tenth century. Translated by Sir William Ouseley. London, 1800. 1 vol., 4to.

Ibn Khaldun. *Notice sur les Prolégomènes Historiques de*, par E. Quatremère. In *Notices et Extraits des Manuscrits*, vol. xix, Pt. 1.

Ibn Khordadbeh. *Le livre des routes et des provinces.* Publié, traduit et annoté par C. Barbier de Meynard. *Journal Asiatique*, VIe série, v, pp. 5-127, 446-532.

Ishtakri. *Das Buch der Länder*, von Schech Ebn Ishak el Farsi el Isztachri. Aus dem Arabischen übersetzt von A. D. Mordtmann. Hamburg, 1845. 1 vol., 8vo.

Isidorus. *Sancti Isidori Hispalensis Episcopi Etymologiarum.* Libri XX. In J. P. Migne's *Patrologiae Cursus Completus*, omnium SS. Patrum, Doctorum Scriptorumque ecclesiasticorum qui ab aevo Apostolico ad Innocentii III tempora floruerunt. Vol. lxxxii. Paris, 1850. In 4to.

Jenkinson, Anthony. *Early Voyages and Travels to Russia and Persia.* London, 1886. 2 vols., 8vo. (Hakluyt Soc.)

Joinville, Le Sieur de. *Histoire de Saint Louis.* Francisque Michel edit. Paris, 1867. 1 vol., 8vo.

Jordanus. *The Wonders of the East.* Translated by Henry Yule. London, 1863. 1 vol., 8vo. (Hakluyt Soc.)

Jornandes. *De Getarum sive Gothorum Origine et rebus gestis.* Nisard edit., 1869. In 4to.

Karamsin. *Histoire de l'Empire de Russie.* Traduite par St. Thomas et Jauffret. Paris, 1819-1826. 11 vols., 8vo. Vols. x and xi translated by De Divoff.

Lasor a Varea, Alph. *Universus Terrarum Orbis scriptorum calamo dileneatus.* Patavii, 1717. 2 vols., fol.

Lebeau. *Histoire du Bas Empire.* Brosset edit. Paris, 1824. 21 vols., 8vo.

Le Bruyn, Corneille. *Voyages de*, par la Moscovie en Perse, et aux Indes Orientales. La Haye, 1732. 5 vols., small 4to.

Lejean, G. *Ethnographie de la Turquie d'Europe.* In *Petermann's Geograph. Mittheilungen.* Erganzungsband, 1860 und 1861.

*Liang shu.* Book of Liang, or the Annals of the Liang Dynasty, covering the period from A.D. 502 to 556.

Liverani, Francesco. *Fra Giovanni da Pian di Carpine, nel contado di Magione. Viaggiatore e descrittore.* Perugia, 1876. 8vo.

Ma Tuan-lin. *Wen hsien t'ung k'ao.* In 348 books. (The best-known Encyclopædia in Chinese. It covers the period from the commencement of Chinese history to the early part of the thirteenth century. Books 324-348 relate to foreign tribes and nations, and are composed entirely of extracts from the Annals and other authoritative works. See Wylie, *Notes on Chinese Literature*, 55.)

Mamachio, Th. Maria. *Annalium Ordinis Praedicatorum.* Rome, 1756. 1 vol., fol. (all published).

Marco Polo. *The Book of Ser Marco Polo*, the Venetian, concerning the Kingdoms and Marvels of the East. Translated and edited by Henry Yule. 2nd edit. London, 1875. 2 vols., 8vo.

Masudi. *Les Prairies d'or.* Texte et traduction par C. Barbier de Maynard et Pavet de Courteille. Paris, 1861-1877. 9 vols., 8vo.

Matthaeis Parisiensis. *Chronica Majora.* Edited by Henry R. Luard. London. 5 vols., 8vo.

Maundevile, Sir John. *The Voiage and Travaile of.* Edited by J. O. Halliwell. London, 1883. 1 vol., 8vo.

Menander Protector. In *Fragmenta Historicorum Graecorum*, of C. Müller, vol. iv. Paris, 1868. 4to, Didot edit.

*Mesalek al-absar.* Notice de l'ouvrage qui a pour titre Mesalek al-absar, par M. Quatremère. In *Notices et Extraits des Manuscrits*, vol. xiii, pp. 151-384. Paris, 1838. 4to.

Michaud. *Histoire des Croisades.* Edit. Huillard Bréholles. Paris, 1867. 4 vols., 8vo.

Migne, l'Abbé. *Nouvelle Encyclopédie théologique.* Vol. ix. *Dictionaire de statistique religieuse.* Paris, 1851. 4to.

Mirza Haidar. *Tarikh-i-Rashidi.* N. Elias and E. Denison Ross's translation. London, 1898. 1 vol., 8vo.

Müller, Carolus. *Geographi Graeci minores.* Paris, 1882. 2 vols., 4to. Didot edit.

Müller, Eugène. *Deux Voyages en Asie au XIIIe siècle*, par Guillaume Rubruquis et Marco Polo. Paris, 1888. 1 vol., 18mo.

Muratori. *Scriptores rerum italicarum.* Milan, 1723-1751. 25 vols., 4to.

Nestor. *Chronique dite de Nestor.* Traduite sur le texte slavon-russe, avec introduction et commentaire critique par Louis Léger. Paris, 1884. 1 vol., 4to.

Pachymeres. See *Corpus Scriptorum Historiae Byzantinae.*

Palladius, Archimandrite. *Elucidations of Marco Polo's Travels in North China*, drawn from Chinese sources. In *Journal of China branch of Royal Asiatic Society*, New series, vol. x, pp. 1-54.

Pallas, Professor. *Voyages dans plusieurs Provinces de l'Empire de Russie*, etc. Paris, 1788-1793. 5 vols., 4to.

Pears, Edwin. *The Fall of Constantinople.* London, 1885. 1 vol., 8vo.

*Pei shih.* The Northern History, the history of the Northern Wei, Tse, Chou, and Sui Dynasties, covering the period from A.D. 386 to 581.

Peschel, Oscar. *Geschichte der Erdkunde bis auf Alexander von Humboldt und Carl Ritter.* 2nd edit. München, 1877. 1 vol., 8vo.

Plinius. *Naturalis Historiae.* Traduction de Littré. Nisard edit., 1865. 2 vols., 4to.

Ploss, H. *Das Kind in Brauch und Sitte der Völker.* Anthropologische Studien. Leipzig, 1884. 2 vols., 8vo.

Ploss, H., and Bartels, Max. *Das Weib in der Natur- und Völkerkunde.* Anthropologische Studien. Leipzig, 1895. 2 vols., 8vo.

Pomponius Mela. *De Situ Orbis.* Nisard edit. Paris, 1895. 1 vol., 4to.

Ptolemaeus, Claudius. *Geographia.* Edidit C. F. A. Nobbi. Editio stereotypa. Leipzig, 1843. 2 vols., 18mo.

Purchas, Samuel. *His Pilgrimes.* London, 1625. 4to. Vol. iii Part ii. (Booke i, pp. 1-52, translation of Rubruck.)

Quatremère, Etienne. *Histoire des Mongols de la Perse.* Ecrite en persan par Raschid-Eldin. Tome i (all published). Paris, 1836. 1 vol., fol.

Radloff, Wilhelm. *Ethnographische Uebersicht der Türkstämme, Siberiens und der Mongolei.* Leipzig, 1883. 8vo.

Radloff, Wilhelm. *Aus Siberien.* Löse Blätter aus meinem Tagebuche. 2nd edit. Leipzig, 1893. 2 vols., 8vo.

Rawlinson, George. *History of Herodotus.* A new English version, with copious notes and appendices. London, 1862. 4 vols., 8vo.

Rawlinson, George. *Five Great Monarchies of the Ancient Eastern World.* 4th edit. London, 1879. 3 vols., 8vo.

Raynaldus, Odoricus. *Annales Ecclesiastici*, ab anno MCXCVIII. Lucae, 1747. 21 vols., 4to.

Reclus, Elisée. *Nouvelle Géographie Universelle*, la terre et les hommes. Paris. In 4to.

Reinaud. *Relation des Voyages faits par les Arabes et les Persans dans l'Inde et à la Chine dans le IXe siècle de l'ère chrétienne.* Paris, 1845. 2 vols., 16mo.

Rémusat, Abel. *Mémoires sur les Relations politiques des Princes Chrétiens et particulièrement des Rois de France avec les Empereurs Mongols.* Paris, 1822-1824. 4to.

Rockhill, William W. *The Land of the Lamas.* Notes of a Journey through China, Mongolia, and Tibet. New York, 1891. 1 vol., 8vo.

Rockhill, William W. *Notes on the Ethnology of Tibet.* Washington, 1895. 1 vol., 8vo.

Rockhill, William W. *Diary of a Journey through Mongolia and Tibet in* 1891 *and* 1892. Washington, 1894. 1 vol., 8vo.

Sarrazin, Jean Pierre. See Joinville.

Schiltberger, Johann. *The Bondage and Travels of, in Europe, Asia and Africa*, 1396-1427. Translated by J. Buchan Telfer. London, 1879. 1 vol., 8vo. (Hakluyt Soc.)

Schmidt, Franz Max. *Ueber Rubruk's Reise von* 1253-1255. In *Zeitschrift der Gesellschaft für Erdkunde zu Berlin*, vol. xx, pp. 161-253. Berlin, 1885. In 8vo.

Smirnow, Jean N. *Les Populations Finnoises des bassins de la Volga et de la Kama.* Études d'éthnographie historique. Traduites par Paul Boyer. Paris, 1898. 1 vol., 4to (all published).

Solini, C. Julii. *Collectanae Rerum Memorabilium*, recognovit Th. Mommsen. Berlin, 1864. 1 vol., 8vo.

Spörer. *Die Seenzone des Balchash nach Russischen Quellen.* In *Petermann's Geographische Mittheilungen*, vol. xiv.

Strabo. *Strabonis Geographica.* Graece cum versione reficta C. Mullero et F. Dubnero. Paris, 1853. 2 vols., 4to.

*Sui shu.* Book of Sui, or the Annals of the Sui Dynasty, covering the period from A.D. 581 to 617.

*T'ang shu.* Book of the T'ang Dynasty, covering the period from A.D. 618 to 906. (The "New" (*Hsin*) History is the work here referred to.)

Taylor, Isaac. *The Alphabet;* an Account of the Origin and Development of Letters. London, 1883. 2 vols., 8vo.

Theophanes, Byzantius. See *Fragmenta Historicorum Graecorum*, vol. iv.

Theophylactus. See *Corpus Scriptorum Historiae Byzantinae.*

Thomsen, Vilhelm. *Inscriptions de l'Orkhon dechiffrées.* Helsingfors. 1896. 1 vol., 8vo.

Tott, Baron, de. *Memoirs of, on the Turks and the Tartars.* London, 1785 (?). 2 vols., 12mo.

Tournefort, Pitton de. *Relation d'un Voyage du Levant.* Amsterdam, 1718. 2 vols., 4to.

Tylor, Edward B. *Primitive Culture:* Researches into the Development of Mythology, Philosophy, Religion, Language, Art and Custom. 2nd edit., London, 1873. 2 vols., 8vo.

Tylor, Edward B. *Researches into the Early History of Mankind and the Development of Civilization.* 3rd edit., London, 1878. 1 vol., 8vo.

Vincent of Beauvais. *Speculi Majoris, Vincentii Burgundi Praesulis Belvacensis Ordinis Praedicatorum.* Tomus quartus. Qui *Speculum Historiale* inscribitur. Venice, 1591. 1 vol., fol.

Waddingus, Lucas. *Annales Minorum*, seu Trium Ordinum a St. Francisco Institutorum. Rome, 1731-1745. 19 vols., fol.

Waddingus, Lucas. *Scriptores Ordinis Minorum.* Quibus accessit syllabus illorum, qui ex eodem Ordine pro fide Christi fortiter occubuerunt. Priores atramento, posteriores sanguine Christianam religionem asserverunt. Recessuit Fr. Lucas Waddington. Rome, 1750. 1 vol., 4to.

*Wei shu.* Book of the Wei, or Annals of the Wei Dynasty, covering the period from A.D. 386 to 556.

William of Nangis. In *Recueil des Historiens des Gaules et de la France*, vol. xx. Paris, 1840. In 4to.

William of Tyr. *Historia rerum in partibus transmarinis gestarum.* In *Recueil des Historiens des croisades.* Historiens occidentaux. Tome i. 2 Pts., 1844, fol.

*Wu tai shih.* The History of the Five Dynasties of Liang, T'ang, Chin, Han and Chou; covering the period from A.D. 907 to 959, (The "New" (*Hsin*) History is the work here referred to.)

Yüan-chuang. *Mémoires sur les Contrées Occidentales.* Traduit du Sanscrit en Chinois, en l'an 648, par Hiouen Thsang, et du Chinois en Français par Stanislas Julien. Paris, 1858. 2 vols., large 8vo.

Yule, Henry. *Cathay and the Way Thither;* being a collection of mediæval notices of China. London, 1866. 2 vols., 8vo. (Hakluyt Soc.)

Yule, Henry, and Arthur C. Burnell. *A Glossary of Anglo-Indian Colloquial Words and Phrases,* etc. London, 1866. 1 vol., 8vo.

---

## ERRATA.

P. 102, *line* 5 *from bottom*, *omit* it that.
P. 122, „ 2 „ *read* Batho.
P. 139, „ 15 *read* Lepsinsk.
P. 139, „ 17 „ Balkash.
P. 158, „ 9 *from bottom*, *read* classical.
P. 160, „ 5 „ „ Hai t'ieh shan
P. 162, „ 7 „ „ Kuyuk.
P. 190, „ 19, *transpose reference* (2) *to line* 20, *after wora* daughter.
P. 198, „ 1, *read* Orengai.
P. 253, „ 11, „ his children.

THE

# JOURNEY OF FRIAR JOHN OF PIAN DE CARPINE TO THE COURT OF KUYUK KHAN, 1245-1247, AS NARRATED BY HIMSELF.

## I.

Of the route we went, and of the countries through which we passed.

(733)[1]

WHEN therefore we had arranged, as has been already stated elsewhere, to set out for the (land of the) Tartars we (left Lyons on the 16th April, 1245, and after travelling through Germany)[2] came to the King of Bohemia.[3] And having asked his advice (734), for we were personally acquainted with this lord from of old, which was the best road for us to go by, he answered that

[1] The numbers in brackets are those of the pages of the text in d'Avezac's edition. References to Rubruck's narrative are to the pages of the Latin text.

[2] These details are supplied from Benedict's narrative. See also d'Avezac, 480.

[3] Wenceslaw I, born in 1205, reigned from 1240 to 1253. After having been a friend of the Emperor Frederic, he had gone over to the Pope's party, and become the leader of the German league against him.

B

it were best, it seemed to him, to go by Poland and Ruscia; for he had relatives in Poland, with whose aid we could enter Ruscia; so having given us his letters and a good escort to take us through Poland, he caused also money to be given us to defray our travelling expenses through his lands and cities as far as (the court of) Boleslas, Duke of Selesia, his nephew, with whom also we were personally acquainted.[1]

II. The latter also gave us his letters and an escort and money for our expenses in his towns and cities, as far as Conrad, Duke of Lenczy.[2] At that time, through God's special grace, the Lord Vassilko, Duke of Ruscia,[3] had come there, from whom we learnt more accurately of the Tartars; for he had sent his ambassadors to them, who had come back to him and to his brother Daniel, bearing to the lord Daniel a safe conduct to go to Bati.[4] And he told us that if we wanted to go to them we must have rich presents to give them, for they were in the habit of asking for them most importunately, and if they were not given them (and this is quite true), an ambassador could not conduct his business satisfactorily with them; and that furthermore he was looked upon as a mere nothing[5] (735). Not wishing that the affairs of the Lord Pope and of the Church should be obstructed on this account, with some of that which had

---

[1] He resided at Lignitz (d'Avezac, 481). Karamsin, iv, 21, says he was Conrad's son.

[2] Who was in Cracow (d'Avezac, 482).

[3] Vassilko, Duke of Volhynia and Vladimir, son of Roman and grandson of Rurik (Karamsin, iii, 134, iv, 100, 142; d'Avezac, 482).

[4] Daniel, Duke of Galitch. He had fought against the Mongols in the great battle of the Kalka, 31 May, 1223. Karamsin says Daniel only undertook this journey to Batu's camp in order to deceive him, and inspire the Mongols with confidence in him, the better to be able to prepare means for delivering his country from their yoke. It was for this purpose also that he sought the aid of the Church of Rome, and expressed the wish to march against the Mongols under the Papal flag. Pope Innocent IV gave him the title of King of Gallicia; but Daniel informed him that he wanted troops, not a title. Negotiations were finally broken off between Rome and Daniel in 1249 (Karamsin, iii, 288, 323, iv, 21, *et seq.*).

[5] Conf. Rubruck's remarks, 218, 396.

been given us in charity, so that we should not be in want and for use on our journey, we bought some skins of beavers and of some other animals. Duke Conrad, the Duchess of Cracow,[1] some knights and the bishop of Cracow, hearing of this, gave us some more of these skins. Furthermore Duke Conrad, his son, and the Bishop of Cracow besought most earnestly Duke Vassilko to help us as much as he could in reaching the Tartars; and he replied that he would do so willingly.

III. So he took us with him to his country; and as he kept us for some days as his guests that we might rest a little, and had called thither his bishops at our request, we read them the letters of the Lord Pope, in which he admonished them to return to the unity of holy mother Church; we also advised and (736) urged them as much as we could, as well the Duke as the Bishops, and all those who had met there, to that same end. But as at the very time when this duke had come to Poland, his brother, Duke Daniel, had gone to Bati and was not present, they could not give a final answer, but must wait his return before being able to give a full reply.

IV. After that the Duke sent one of his servants with us as far as Kiew.[2] Nevertheless we travelled ever in danger of our lives on account of the Lithuanians, who often committed undiscovered outrages as much as possible in the country of Ruscia, and particularly in these places through which we had to pass; and as the greater part of the men of Ruscia had been killed by the Tartars or taken off into captivity, they were unable to offer them

---

[1] The duchess was called Grimislawa, the duke's son, Lesko (d'Avezac, 482). Furs were used as currency in Russia at the time; see Rubruck, 329.

[2] On the Dnieper. It had been captured by Batu in 1238, when nearly the whole population was massacred and the city totally destroyed (Karamsin, iv, 10, *et seq.*).

the least resistance;[1] we were safe, however, from the Ruthenians on account of this servant. Thence then, by the grace of God having been saved from the enemies of the Cross of Christ, we came to Kiew, which is the metropolis of Ruscia. And when we came there we took counsel with the Millenarius,[2] and the other nobles who were there, as to our route. They told us that if we took into Tartary the horses which we had, they would all die, for the snows were deep, and they did not know how to dig out the grass from under the snow like Tartar horses, nor could (737) anything else be found (on the way) for them to eat, for the Tartars had neither straw nor hay nor fodder. So, on their advice, we decided to leave our horses there with two servants to keep them; and we had to give the Millenarius presents, that he might be pleased to give us pack-horses and an escort. Before we reached Kiew, when in Danilov[3] I was ill to the point of death; but I had myself carried along in a cart in the intense cold through the deep snow, so as not to interfere with the affairs of Christendom.

V. Having settled then all these matters at Kiew, on the second day after the feast of the Purification of Our Lady (February 4, 1246), we started out from Kiew for other barbarous peoples, with the horses of the Millenarius and an escort. We came to a certain town which was under the direct rule of the Tartars and is called Canov;[4] the prefect of the town gave us horses and an escort as far as another town in which was a certain Alan prefect who was

---

1 Conf. Rubruck's remarks, 247.

2 In Mongol *mingatan*.

3 There are several places called Danilow and Danilowka in Russia, but I do not find any at the present time on the route between Vladimir and Kiew.

4 The present town of Kaniew on the Dneiper, about 75 miles below Kiew.

called Micheas,[1] a man full of all malice and iniquity, (738) for he had sent to us to Kiew some of his body-guard, who lyingly said to us, as from the part of Corenza,[2] that we being ambassadors were to come to him; and this he did, though it was not true, in order that he might extort presents from us. When, however, we reached him, he made himself most disagreeable, and unless we promised him presents, would in no wise agree to help us. Seeing that we would not otherwise be able to go farther, we promised to give him some presents, but when we gave him what appeared to us suitable, he refused to receive them unless we gave more; and so we had to add to them according to his will, and something besides he subtracted from us deceitfully and maliciously.

VI. After that we left with him on the second day of Quinquagesima (19th February), and he led us as far as the first camp[3] of the Tartars, and on the first Friday after Ash Wednesday (23rd February), while we were stopping for the night as the sun went down, the Tartars broke in on us in arms in horrible fashion asking who we were. We answered them that we were envoys of the Lord Pope, and then, having accepted some food from us, they left at once. Starting again at morn, we had only gone a little way when their chiefs who were in the camp came to us, and inquired of us why we came to them, and what was our business. We answered them that we were the envoys of the Lord Pope, who was the lord and father of Christians; that he had (739) sent us to the King as well as to the princes and all the Tartars, because he desired that

---

[1] Conf. what Benedict says of him, *infra*, 34. Micheas' Mongol title was probably *Daruga*.

[2] The name of this Mongol general is variously written Choranza, Curoniza, and Karancha.

[3] *Custodia*. Rubruck uses the word *herbergia* in the same sense. This "first camp" is the same that Benedict (*infra*, 34) states they reached three days after leaving Brother Stephen of Bohemia.

all Christians should be friends of the Tartars and at peace with them. Moreover, as he wished that they should be mighty with God in heaven, he, the Lord Pope, advised them as well through us as by his letters, that they should become Christians and receive the faith of Our Lord Jesus Christ, for otherwise they could not be saved. He told them furthermore that he was astonished at the slaying of human beings done by the Tartars, and especially of Christians and above all of Hungarians, Moravians and Poles, who were his subjects, when they had injured them in nothing nor attempted to injure them ; and as the Lord God was gravely offended at this, he cautioned them to abstain henceforth from such acts, and to repent them of those they had done. Furthermore we said that the Lord Pope requested that they should write to him what they would do and what was their intention ; and that they would give answer to him to all the above points in their letters. Having heard our motives, and understood and noted them down, they said that, in view of what we had said, they would give us pack-horses as far as Corenza, and supply a guide; and at once they asked for presents (740), which we gave them, for we must needs do their will.

VII. Having given them the presents, and taken as pack-horses some from which they got off, we started under their guidance for Corenza ; but they sent ahead a swift messenger to this chief with what we had told them. This chief is lord of all those (Tartars) who are encamped facing the peoples of the West, lest they suddenly and unexpectedly attack them. This chief has under him, we were told, sixty thousand armed men. When we reached him, he made us put our tents far from him,[1] and sent us

[1] This again happened at Batu's camp, see *infra*, 9. Friar Ascelin was treated in like manner at the camp of Ilchikadai in 1249.

his slave stewards[1] who asked us with what (741) we wanted to bow to him, that is to say whether we would make him presents. We replied that the Lord Pope had not sent any presents, for he was not sure we could reach them; and that furthermore we had had to pass through very dangerous places, exposed to the Lithuanians, who make raids along the roads from Poland to near the Tartars, over which we had had to travel; but nevertheless with what we were carrying with us, by the grace of God and of our Lord the Pope, and for our personal use, we would show him our respect as well as we could. But when we had given him a number of things, they were not enough for him, and he asked for more through intermediaries, promising to have us conducted most honourably if we complied with his request, which we had to do since we wished to live and carry out satisfactorily the order of the Lord Pope.

VIII. Having received the presents they led us to his *orda* or tent, and we were instructed to bend three times the left knee before the door of his dwelling, and to be very careful not to put our feet on the threshold of the door; and this we were attentive to observe, for sentence of death is on those who knowingly tread upon the threshold of a chief's dwelling.[2] After we had entered we were obliged to repeat on bended knee before the chief and all the other nobles (742), who had specially been convened there for that purpose, what has been previously said. We presented to him also the letters of the Lord Pope; but as our interpreter, whom we had brought with us from Kiew, was not able to translate them for him, nor was there any one else competent to do so, they could not be interpreted. After this, horses were given us, and three Tartars, two of

---

[1] *Servos suos procuratores.* I presume they were Christian, probably Russian, slaves.

[2] See Rubruck's narrative, 319.

whom were chiefs over ten, and the other a man (*homo*) of Bati, guided us with all speed to that latter chief. This Bati is more powerful than all the other Tartar princes save the Emperor, whom he is held to obey.

IX. We started (for Bati's camp) on the Monday after the first Sunday of Quadragesima (26th February), and riding as fast as horses could go trotting, for we had fresh horses three or four times nearly every day, we rode from morning to night, and very often even at night, and it was not before Wednesday in Holy Week (4th April) that we could get to him.[1] We crossed the whole country of the Comans, which is all a plain, (743) and has four great rivers. The first is called the Neper, along which, on the side of Ruscia, roams Corenza, and on the other side through those plains, Mauci, who is mightier than Corenza. Secondly, the Don, along which roams a certain prince called Catan, who has as wife Bati's sister. The third is the Volga, a very big river, along which goes Bati.[2] The fourth is called Jaec, along which go two Millenarii, one along one side of the river, the other along the other. All these (chiefs) descend in winter time to the sea, and in summer go up the courses of these rivers to the mountains. Now this sea is the Mare-Magnum from which goes out the arm of Saint George which goes to Constantinople. We went along for many days on the ice on the Neper. These rivers

---

[1] The mission left Kiew on February 4th, 1246, reached Corenza's camp on or near the west bank of the Dnieper somewhere about the 22nd, and probably crossed the river between Yekaterinoslaw or Alexandrwsk, where it makes a south-westerly bend.

[2] Friar John is the first western writer to call the Dnieper, Don, and Volga by these names; even Rubruck does not use them. This is explained by the fact that the former had a Russian interpreter, accustomed, like all his countrymen, to use these terms; the latter got his information from the Mongols, and where that failed used the classical terms. Mauci appears to be the Mauchy of Abulghazi; he was the second son of Chagatai. Catan is, I think, the same as Rubruck's Scatai. He must not be confounded with Katan, mentioned in a subsequent passage. Conf. also Benedict's narrative, *infra*, p. 34.

are big, very full of fish, especially the Volga, and they fall into the sea of Greece which is called Mare-Magnum. We went for many days along the shore of this sea, which on account of the ice was very dangerous in several places; for it freezes along the coast quite three leagues out.[1] But (744) before we came to Bati, two of our Tartars went ahead to tell him all we had said at Corenza's.

X. When then we came to Bati on the borders of the Comans' country, we were made to camp a good league from their tents,[2] and before we were taken to his court we were told we would have to pass between two fires, which we refused to do under any consideration. But they told us: "Fear not, we only make you pass between these two fires lest perchance you think something injurious to our lord, or if you carry some poison, for the fire will remove all harm." We answered them: "Since it is thus we will pass through, so that we may not be suspected of such things." When we came to the *orda* we were questioned by his procurator, who is called Eldegai, as to what we wanted to make our obeisance with, that is to say, what gifts we desired to give him; we answered him as we had previously answered Corenza, that the Lord Pope had sent no presents, but that we ourselves, of those things which we had by the grace of God and the Lord Pope for our

---

1 D'Avezac (485) justly remarks: "We may feel surprise at the geographical ignorance of the friar, who, though he might have known the truth by the testimony of his own eyes, remained imbued with ancient errors, and confounds in a single sea the Pontus, the Palus Mæotis, the Caspian sea, or sea of the Khazars, and also the great lake of Aral." Rubruck's geographical knowledge was much superior on all these points. He does not mention the Aral lake, and may have taken it to be part of the Caspian; I am inclined to think, however, that he passed some distance north of it.

2 *Stationes*, which the friar says (616) were "*rotundas in modum tentorii.*" In another part of his work (770) Friar John says that he found at Batu's camp the son of the Duke of Yaroslaw, who had with him a Russian knight called Sangor, a Coman by birth, but then a Christian. The friar's interpreter at Batu's camp was a Russian from Susdal.

expenses, desired to show him our respect as best we could. Presents having been given and accepted, the procurator called Eldegai questioned us as to our coming; and to him we gave the same reasons as we had previously given to Corenza.

(745) XI. Having been informed of our reasons, they led us into the dwelling, after having made a bow, and heard the caution about the threshold, which has been mentioned. Having entered then we said what we had to say on bended knees, and then we presented him the letters (of the Pope), and requested that interpreters be given us able to translate them. These were given us on Good Friday (6th April), and we carefully translated the letters into the Ruthenian, Saracenic, and Tartar languages, and this latter interpretation was given to Bati, who read it and noted it carefully. After that we were taken back to our dwelling, but no food was given us, save once on the night of our arrival a little millet in a bowl.

XII. This Bati holds his court right magnificently, for he has door-keepers and all the other officials like unto their Emperor. He sits also in a raised place, as on a throne, with one of his wives; but every one else (of his family), as well his brothers and his sons as others of lesser degree, sit lower down on a bench in the middle (of the tent). All the other people sit behind them on the ground, the men to the right, the women to the left. He has tents made of linen (*pannis lineis*). (746) They are large and quite handsome, and used to belong to the King of Hungary. And no outsider save a servant dare enter the tent, no matter how great and mighty he may be, unless he is called, unless perchance he knows he is wanted. When we had stated our object, we took a seat to the left,[1] for thus do all

[1] With the women, placing them in a position of inferiority; the women sat on the right of the chief, the traveller's left when facing

ambassadors in going, but on coming back from the Emperor they always placed us on the right. In the middle of the dwelling near the door is a table, on which is placed drink in gold and silver vases; and Bati never drinks, nor does any prince of the Tartars, especially when they are in public, without there being singing and guitar playing. And when he rides out, there is always carried over his head on a pole an umbrella or little awning; and all the very great princes of the Tartars do likewise. This Bati is kind enough to his own people, but he is greatly feared by them. He is, however, most cruel in fight; he is very shrewd and extremely crafty in warfare, for he has been waging war for a long time.

XIII. On Holy Saturday (7th April) we were called to his tent and that same procurator of Bati's came out to us, and told us from him that we were to go to the Emperor Cuyuc in their country, and that some (747) of our party would be kept there (with Bati) in the expectation that they would want to send them back to the Lord Pope. We gave them letters concerning all we had done to carry back (to the Pope), but when they had got as far as Mauci, he detained them until our return. As for ourselves, on the day of the Resurrection of the Lord (8th April), having said mass and settled everything, accompanied by the two Tartars who had been detailed to us at Corenza's, we started out most tearfully, not knowing whether we were going to life or death.[1] We were furthermore so feeble that we could hardly ride; during the whole of that lent our only food had been millet with salt and water; and likewise on the

him. The left side of the host is the place of honour in China, but not so in Mongolia and Tibet, where guests sit to the right of the host.

[1] Benedict (*infra*, 35) says they started on Tuesday after Easter, *i.e.*, 10th April.

other fast days; nor had we anything else to drink but snow melted in the kettle./

XIV. Comania hath to the north of it, immediately after Ruscia, the Morduins, the Bilers, or great Bulgaria, the Bascarts or great Hungary; after the Bascarts, the Parrosits (748) and the Samogeds, after the Samogeds those who are said to have dog-faces, who live in the deserts along the coasts of the Ocean. To the south it (*i.e.*, Comania) has the Alans, the Circasses, the Gazars, Greece and Constantinople; also the land of the Ibers, the Cachs, the Brutaches, who are said to be Jews and who shave their heads, the country of the Zicci, of the Georgians and of the Armenians, and the country of the Turks.[1] To the west it has Hungary and Ruscia. And this country (of Comania) is extremely long, for we were riding through it at great speed, having every day fresh horses, five or seven times a day, except, as I have said, when we were riding through desert tracts when we got better and stronger horses (749) able to stand more work, and we

---

[1] The Bilers are the *Belar* of mediæval Mahommedan writers, the Bulgars of the Volga (d'Avezac, 490); Schiltberger (49) speaks of the city of *Bolar*. The country of the Bascarts is Rubruck's *Pascatir*; Friar John uses the Russian form of the name, *Bashkurt*. The Parossits are the *Borassyts* of Edrisi, the Permiaks of modern writers (d'Avezac, 492). The Samogeds are the Samoyeds, the inhabitants of "the country of darkness" of Mohammedan mediæval writers; Rubruck refers to them (266), but does not name them. Friar John, in another part of his work (678), says "the Samogeds live by the chase, and make their dwellings and clothing of the skins of animals." The dog-faced people, or *Cynocephalæ*, as Benedict (*infra*, 36) calls them, are a classical reminiscence (see *infra*, 36, and d'Avezac, 493). King Heythum of Armenia speaks of a country beyond Khatai, where the men were shaped like dogs (Dulaurier, 472). On the Alans, Circasses (or Kerkis) and Gazars, see *infra*, 42, note 1. On the Ibers, or Georgians, see *infra*, 46. In another passage of his work (709) Pian de Carpine identifies the Georgians with the *Obesi*, the Abazes or Abkhases (d'Avezac, 497). Friar John's Cachs appear to be the people of Kakhethi in Georgia (d'Avezac, 495). The Brutaches may be the inhabitants of the *Berdagj* of mediæval Mohammedan writers (d'Avezac, 496). Rubruck refers (382) to Jews living in this district. On the Zicci, a western branch of the Cherkess, see *infra*, 45, note 4.

kept this up from the beginning of lent to the eighth day after Easter (16th April).[1] The Tartars killed these Comans; some fled from before them, and others were reduced to slavery. Most of those who fled have come back to them.

XV. After that we entered the country of the Cangitae,[2] which in many places suffers from a great scarcity of water, and in which but few people remain on account of this deficiency of water. And so it happened that the men of Ieroslav, Duke of Ruscia, who were going to join him in the country of the Tartars, lost some of their number who died of thirst in this desert. In this country and also in Comania, we found many human skulls and bones scattered about on the ground like cattle-dung.[3] We travelled through this country (of the Cangitae) from the eighth day after Easter to nearly the Ascension of our Lord.[4] These people are pagans, and the Comans as well as the Cangitae do not till the soil, but only live on the produce of their animals; nor do they build houses, but live in tents. The Tartars have also annihilated them, and now occupy their country; those of them who were left they have reduced to slavery.

XVI. Leaving the country of the Cangitae we entered that of the Bisermins.[5] These (750) people used to speak the

---

[1] Benedict (*infra*, 35) says it only took them two weeks to ride through Comania, but he counts merely from the time they left Batu's camp. To this we must add the "five weeks and more" he says they took to ride from the Dnieper to Batu's camp, near Sarai, on the Volga. The two narratives agree perfectly.

[2] Rubruck (274) calls them *Cangle*, and says they were Comans. Benedict uses the same name for them as John.

[3] Conf. the Constable of Armenia's remarks in Introductory Notice, *supra*.

[4] *I.e.*, from the 16th April, 1246, to the middle of May: Ascension day falling that year on the 17th May.

[5] *Bisermin* is a corrupt form of Mussulman. *P'u-su-man kuo*, "country of the Pusuman," occurs in Chinese works of the Mongol period. In the Russian annals the name *Bussurman* is also found (Bretschneider, *Med. Travel.*, 33; also his *Med. Geog.*, 120). D'Avezac,

Coman language, and do still speak it; but they hold the religion of the Saracens. We found in that country innumerable ruined cities, overthrown villages, and many deserted towns. There is a great river in that country whose name I do not know, and on which stands a city called Ianckint, and also another called Barchin, and still another called Ornas, and many more whose names I do not know.[1] This country used to have a lord who was called

(523) thinks Friar John used it to designate Turkestan; it seems to me, however, that he applies it more particularly to the Khorazmian empire. Benedict (*infra*, 37) calls this country *Turkya* (*i.e.*, Turkestan). He says they travelled through it for ten days, or roughly 350 miles. Anthony Jenkinson (79) uses the word *Bussarmans* to designate the Moslem, and says it means circumcised. See also *infra*, p. 48, note 3.

[1] The "great river" is the Syr daria. The traveller must have followed it up from its mouth to perhaps Chimkent, which may be the town of *Lemfinc* he mentions in another part of his work (771). D'Avezac, (512) and Bretschneider (*Med. Geog.*, 135) identify Ianckint with *Yenguikend*, and Barchin with the *Pa-erh-chen* of the Chinese, the *Barkhalikend* of the Persians. As to Ornas, Fraehn (*Ibn Fozlan*, 162) thinks it is Urghendj; d'Avezac, (505-511) tries to prove that it was the ancient Tanais, the mediæval Tana at the mouth of the Don. I accept as much more probable Bretschneider's suggestion (*Med. Geog.*, 236) that it was Otrar, the ruins of which famous place have been found on the right bank of the Syr daria, to the east of Fort Perowsky. In another part of his work (672-674), Friar John says that after the election of Ogodai as Emperor, Batu was sent against the Alti-Soldan and the country of the Bisermins (*i.e.*, the Khorazm Shah and the Khorazmian empire). In the latter country "a certain city called Barchin resisted them for a long time. . . . But the people of another city called Ianckint hearing (of the capture of Barchin), went out and surrendered themselves into his hands, and so their city was not destroyed. . . . And then they (*i.e.*, the Mongols) marched against a city called Ornas (also written in some MSS. *Ornac* and *Orpar*), and this city was a very populous one, for there were there not only many (kinds of) Christians—Gazars. Ruthenians, and Slavs, and others—but also Saracens, and these latter had dominion over the city. And this city was full of riches, for it is situated on a river which flows by Ianckint and the land of the Bisermins, and which flows into a sea (or lake, *mare*), so it is as it were a (sea) port, and all the other Saracens had a very great market in that city. And as (the Mongols) could not capture it otherwise, they cut the river which flowed by the town, and flooded it with all its things and people." It is quite true that these details of the siege of Ornas agree with what Mohammedan writers tell us of the siege of Urghendj by the Mongols in 1221 (see d'Ohsson, ii, 265, *et seq.*), and for that matter with what Vincent of Beauvais (bk. xxix, ch. lxxxix) says of the siege of Bagdad in 1258; but the siege of Otrar in 1219 was also one of the longest and most difficult the Mongols had undertaken in this famous campaign, and the inundating

the Great Soldan,[1] and he was put to death by the Tartars with all his progeny, but I am ignorant of his name. The country has very high mountains; to the south of it is Jerusalem, Baldach, and the whole country of the Saracens. Near its borders are stationed the chiefs Burin and Cadan, who are uterine brothers.[2] To the north of it is a part of the country of the Black Kitayans and an Ocean, and in that quarter is stationed Sitan, a brother of Bati.[3] We travelled through this country from the feast of the Ascension (17th May) to about eight days before the feast of Saint John the Baptist (24th June).

(751) XVII. After that we entered the country of the Black Kitayans, in which they (*i.e.*, the Mongols) have built anew, as it were, a city called Omyl, in which the Emperor has erected a house where we were invited to drink; and he who was there on the part of the Emperor

---

of Urghendj may have been done on account of the success of this expedient in the siege of Ornas. As to the identity of Ornas with Tana, we have no knowledge even that the latter place existed in the thirteenth century; in fact, we learn from Rubruck that in his time the trade of the Sea of Azow was carried on at Matriga, and that only small flat boats went to the mouth of the Don for fish and salt. Had any trading port existed there at the time, he would surely have mentioned it. The Russian bishop Peter (1245) speaks of a very great city called *Ernac*, or *Ornachi*, which had been captured by Bathatarcan (Matth. Paris, *Op. cit.*, iv, 387). Mohammedan mediæval writers say that Juchi in 1219 captured Ozkend, Barkhalikend and Eschnars (d'Ohsson, i, 222). It is just possible that Eschnars, wherever it was on the Syr daria, is Peter's *Ernas* or *Ornachi*, and that this place is the same as Friar John's *Ornas* and Benedict's (*infra*, 36) *Ornarum*. Sir John Maundevile (255) refers to the city of *Octorar*.

1 *Altisoldanus*: in some MS. *Altisoldam* and *Alti-Soldanus*. I have followed d'Avezac (504) in translating it as if it were *Altus Soldanus*. The Sultan here referred to is Alayeddin Mohammed. According to Mohammedan writers, he died a fugitive from the Mongols, in a little island in the Caspian, in 1220 (d'Ohsson, ii, 255).

2 Burin is the same as Rubruck's Buri; Kadan, according to Rashideddin, was not a son of Chagatai, as Friar John states (666), but of Ogodai (d'Avezac, 584).

3 Sitan is the Schiban of Mohammedan writers. Friar John (666) says that he and Batu were sons of Tossuc-can, by which name he designates Juchi, the eldest son of Chingis.

made the nobles of the town and also his own two sons clap their hands before us (when we drank).[1] Leaving this place we found a not very large lake, and as we did not ask its name, we do not know it. On the shore of this lake was a little hill, in where there is said to be an opening, whence in winter there issue out such great tempests of wind that people can barely and at great danger pass by.[2] In summer, however, though one always hears the sound of the winds, but little comes out of the opening, according to what the inhabitants told us. We travelled along the shore of this lake for several days ; it has several islands

---

[1] Conf. Rubruck, 225. The original town of Imil, on the river which still bears that name, and which flows into the Ala Kul, passing south of the town of Chuguchak, was built by the Kara-Khitai somewhere about 1125. Imil was Kuyuk's appanage (*ulus*) (Bretschnieder, *Med. Geog.*, 109, 221, 305). In another passage (648), Friar John says that Ogodai rebuilt the city. He adds that "to the south of it lies a great desert (evidently the Takla-makan), in which it is credibly asserted that wild men live. They have no speech, nor joints in their limbs. If they fall down they cannot get up without assistance. They have, however, enough instinct (*discretionem*) to make felt of camels' (wild camels?) wool, with which they clothe themselves and make shelters against the wind. If any Tartars chase them and wound them with arrows, they put grass in the wound and flee swiftly before them." The presence of wild men somewhere in the deserts of Central Asia has been reported by many travellers, from Heythum, of Armenia, to Sir Douglas Forsyth and P. K. Kozloff, of Roborowsky's expedition in 1893-95. The latter heard of them living in the valley of the Urungur (not far from Omyl, by the way)—see Rockhill, *Land of the Lamas*, 150, 256 ; also his *Diary*, 144, and *Geog. Jour.*, ix, 554. Chinese annals of the sixth century make mention of a race or tribe called K'o-lan, living probably between Sa-chou and the Lob nor, which they describe as the most degraded and unsightly of all savage tribes. They could not distinguish colours or sounds ; they were stupid and weak, knew not how to fight, or even quarrel ; in every respect they were like brute beasts (Ma Tuan-lin, bk. 334, 4).

[2] Either the traveller's memory served him badly, or else the text is here wrong. The lake, it would seem, is the Ala Kul, and the wind, that which blows through the Ala Tau coming from the Ebi nor and the desert beyond (see note to p. 294 of Rubruck). If this be the case, he cannot have come to the lake after leaving Omyl, but must have passed it before getting there, or else he passed it on his return journey. If the text is at fault, the only correction necessary would be to change the first word "leaving," and read "before reaching." That he passed the Ala Kul on his way east, seems clear from the fact that he states, a few lines further on, that he travelled along it, "having it on his left."

in it, and it lay upon our left hand. This country has great abundance of streams, not large ones, however; on either bank of these rivers are woods, but of no great width.[1] Ordu lives in this country;[2] he is older than Bati, in fact, older than any (752) of the other chiefs of the Tartars, and the *orda* or court is that of one of his wives who rules over it. For it is a custom among the Tartars that the courts of their princes and nobles are not broken up (on their death), but some women are always appointed who govern them, and the same proportion of presents are given them that their lord had been in the habit (during his life) of allowing them. After this we came to the first *orda* of the Emperor,[3] in which was one of his wives; but as we had not yet seen the Emperor they would not invite us nor let us come into her *orda*, though they had us well served in our own tent, according to Tartar fashion; and they kept us there for a whole day, so that we might rest.

XVIII. Proceeding thence on the eve of the feast of Saint Peter (28th June), we entered the country of the Naiman, who are pagans.[4] On the day of the feast of the apostles Peter and Paul (29th June) there fell in that place a great snow, and we experienced great cold. This country is exceptionally mountainous and cold, and (753)

---

1 Conf. what Rubruck says (281) of the country of the Kara-Khitai.

2 Urda or Orda of Mohammedan writers. Little is said of this prince in the works to which I have had access. He took part in the great wars in Europe and Asia, and seems to have been a faithful adherent of Kuyuk, as it was he who made the report to that Emperor on Ujugen's conspiracy to seize the throne before Kuyuk's election (d'Ohsson, ii, 194, 203).

3 This must have been in the Imil country, as the Emperor here referred to is clearly the then deceased Ogodai.

4 Rubruck says the Naiman were Christians. Supposing they professed the Uigur creed, which Rubruck states to have been a jumble of Manichæism and Buddhism, with perhaps a slight tinge of Nestorianism, they might be classed among his idolaters (as he, in fact, sometimes does the Uigurs), or among Christians. Conf. Ney Elias (*Tarikhi-rashidi*, 290), where, translating from Jiwani, he speaks of the Naiman as *Tarsa*, which he renders by "Christians."

there is very little plain in it. These two nations[1] do not till the soil, but like the Tartars live in tents. These latter have nearly exterminated them. We travelled through this country many days.

XIX. After that we entered the country of the Mongals, whom we call Tartars. And we journeyed through that country for three weeks, I think riding hard, and on the day of the feast of blessed Mary Magdalen (22nd July) we arrived at Cuyuc's, the present emperor. Along all this (part of the) route we travelled very fast, for our Tartars had been ordered to take us quickly to the solemn court which had already been convened for several years for the election of an emperor,[2] so that we might be present at it. So we had to rise at dawn and travel till night without a stop; often we arrived so late that we did not eat at night, but that which we should have eaten at night was given us in the morning; and we went as fast as the horses could trot, for there was no lack of horses, having usually fresh horses during the day, those which we left being sent back, as I have stated previously; and in this fashion we rode rapidly along without interruption.

---

## II.

Concerning the arrangement of the Emperor's court and of his princes.

(754) I. When we reached Cuyuc's camp, he caused us to be given a tent and allowances such as the Tartars are in the habit of giving; but they treated us better than they did the other ambassadors. We were not called (before Cuyuc) however, for he had not yet been elected, nor had they

---

[1] *I.e.*, the Kara-Khitai and the Naiman.

[2] Ogodai died in 1241, but the parliament (*kuriltai*) which elected Kuyuk only met in the spring of 1246 (d'Ohsson, ii, 195, *et seq.*).

settled about the succession; the translation of the letters of the Lord Pope, and what else we had said (to Corenza and Batu), had been sent him by Bati. And when we had been there five or six days, he sent us to his mother,[1] where the solemn court was being held. When we got there they had already erected a great tent (755) made of white purple, which in our opinion was large enough to hold more than two thousand persons; and around it a wooden paling had been made, and it was ornamented with divers designs.

On the second or third day we went with the Tartars who had been assigned to guard us (to this tent); and all the chiefs met there, and each one was riding around in a circle over hill and dale with his men. On the first day they were all dressed in white purple; on the second day, and then it was that Cuyuc came to the tent, they were dressed in red (purple); on the third day they were all in blue purple, and on the fourth day in the finest baldakins.[2] In the paling near the tent were two big gates: one through which only the Emperor could pass, and at which there was no guard though it was open, for no one would dare to go in or out by it; and the other way by which all those who had admittance went in, and at this one were guards with swords, bows and arrows, and if anyone came near the tent outside of the set bounds, he was beaten if caught, or shot at with headless arrows if he ran away. The horses were kept at about two arrow-flights, I should say, from the tent. The chiefs went about everywhere with a number of their men all armed; but nobody, unless a chief, could go to the horses, without getting badly beaten for

---

[1] The Empress Turakina, who was Regent from the time of Ogodai's death to the election of Kuyuk.

[2] Conf. Benedict's account (*infra*, p. 37), and Rubruck (230); also d'Avezac (524). *Purpura* may have been a velvet stuff, but its meaning remains uncertain. *Baldakinus* was a silk brocade (Heyd, ii, 697).

trying to do so. And many (of the horses) there were which (756) had on their bits, breast-plates, saddles and cruppers quite twenty marks worth of gold[1] I should think. And so the chiefs held counsel beyond[2] the tent, and discussed the election, while all the rest of the people were far away from the tent. And there they remained till about noon, when they began drinking mare's milk, and they drank till evening so plentifully that it was a rare sight.

III. They called us inside (the tent), and gave us mead, for we would not drink mare's milk at all; and this was a great honor they showed us; and they kept on urging us to drink, but not being in the habit of it, we could not do so, and we let them see that it was distasteful to us, so they stopped pressing us. In the great square was the duke Jeroslav of Susdal in Ruscia, and several princes of the Kitayans and Solanges, also two sons of the King of Georgia,[3] a soldan, the ambassador of the Calif of Baldach, and more than ten other soldans of the Saracens,[4] I believe, and as we were told by the procurators. For there were more than four thousand envoys, as well those bringing tribute as those offering presents, soldans and other chiefs who had come to present themselves (757) in person, those who had been sent by their (rulers), and those who were governors of countries. All these were put together outside the paling, and drink was given to them at the same time; as for ourselves and the duke Jeroslav, whenever we were outside with them they always gave us a higher place. I think, if I remember rightly, that we

[1] About £10 10*s.* of our money.

[2] *Infra*, or "outside the paling," in the space reserved for them, and which is called a little farther on *magnum forum*, or "great square."

[3] These two princes were David, son of Giorgi Lascha, and David, son of Queen Rusudan, his cousin. Kuyuk decided that the latter should succeed the former on the throne of Georgia on his death (Dulaurier, 451).

[4] Conf. d'Ohsson, ii, 196.

were at that place for a good four weeks; and I am under the impression that the election was made there, though it was not proclaimed. It was for the following reason that it was generally believed (that Cuyuc had been chosen): whenever Cuyuc came out of the tent, they sang to him, and as long as he remained outside of it they inclined before him certain fine staffs on the ends of which were (tufts of) red wool, which was done to no other chief. They called this tent (*statio*) or court the Sira-Orda.[1]

IV. Coming out of the tent, we all rode together to another place some three or four leagues distant, where there was a fine large plain near a river flowing between

---

[1] Simon of St. Quentin (Vincent of Beauvais, bk. xxxi, ch. xxxii, 452a) describes as follows the ceremonial of raising a new Mongol emperor to the throne. He did not witness himself such a ceremony, and it may well be that he got the details from Benedict the Pole, who was back in Asia Minor in 1248, at about the time of the return of Ascelin's mission from Baidju's camp (see Introductory Notice). "All the Barons being assembled, they placed a gilded seat in their midst, and made this Gog (chan, *i.e.*, Khakan) sit on it, and they put a sword before him and said, 'We want, we beg, and we command that you shall have dominion over all of us.' And he said to them: 'If you want me to reign over you, are you ready each one of you to do what I shall command, to come whenever I call, to go wherever I may choose to send you, to put to death whomsoever I shall command you?' They replied that they were. Then he said to them, 'My command shall be my sword.' To this they all agreed. They then placed a piece of felt on the ground, and put him on it, saying: 'Look upwards and recognize God, and downward and see the felt on which you sit. If you reign well over your kingdom, if you make largess, and rejoice in justice, and honour each of your Princes according to his rank, you shall reign in glory, all the world shall bow to your rule, and God will give you everything your heart can desire. But if you do otherwise, you shall be miserable, lowly, and so poor that this felt on which you sit shall not even be left you.' After saying this, the Barons made the wife of Gog sit on the felt; and with both of them seated there, they lifted them up from the ground, and proclaimed them with a loud voice and cries Emperor and Empress of all the Tartars" (conf. Schiltberger, 48). The Sira Orda, Friar John states in another passage (608), was half a day's journey from Karakorum. We learn from other sources that it was situated at a place called Ormektua. The emperor Ogodai used to pass the summer there (d'Ohsson, ii, 84). The staffs with tufts of red wool on the ends were *tughs*. Baber, i, 217, says the Khan of the Mongols in his time had nine *tughs*.

mountains,[1] where another tent was set up, and it is called by them the Golden Orda: and here it was that Cuyuc was to have been placed on the throne on the day of the Assumption of our Lady (15th August); but it was deferred on account of the hail which fell, to which I have referred previously. This tent (758) rested on pillars covered with gold plates, fastened with gold nails and other woods, and the top and sides of it were covered with baldakins; the outside, however, being of other kinds of stuff. Here we remained until the feast of Saint Bartholomew (24th August), when there assembled a great multitude, and they all stood with their faces turned to the south, some of them a stone's throw from others, going ever farther and farther away, making genuflexions towards the south. As for us, not knowing whether they were making incantations or bending their knees to God or what else, we would not make any genuflexions.[2] After doing this for a long while they went back to the tent, and placed Cuyuc on the imperial seat, and the chiefs knelt before him; and after that the whole people did likewise, except ourselves who were not his subjects. Then they began drinking, and as is their custom, they kept on drinking till evening. After that they brought in carts of cooked meat, without salt, and to each four or five they gave a quarter.

---

[1] This river must be the Orkhon, unless we identify the Sira Orda, or Ormektua, with the modern Urmukhtin, about 60 miles south of Kiakhta, on the road to Urga, in which case the river would be the Shara ossu. In Mongol, "Golden Orda" is *Altan ordu*.

[2] As shown in the next paragraph, the friar made the prescribed genuflexion to the living emperor. See on this subject in general *Amer. Hist. Review*, ii, 42, *et seq.*, 627 *et seq.*; also Pauthier, *Cérémonial à la Cour de Khoubilai*. It is interesting to note that in A.D. 981 the Chinese envoy, Wang Yen-tê, sent to the Uigur Prince of Kao-chang, refused to make genuflexions (*pai*) to him, as being contrary to the established usages as regards envoys. The prince and his family, however, on receiving the envoy, all faced eastward (towards Peking) and made an obeisance (*pai*) on receiving the imperial presents (*shou tz'ŭ*) (Ma Tuan-lin, Bk. 336, 13).

To those who were inside (the tent) they gave meat and salted broth for sauce; and in this fashion they passed days in feasting.

V. It was at this place (the Golden Orda) that we were called into the Emperor's presence; after that Chingay[1] (759) the prothonotary had written down our names and the names of those who had sent us, and also those of the chief of the Solanges and of the others, he repeated them all, shouting with a loud voice before the Emperor and all the chiefs. When this had been done each of us had to bend the left knee four times,[2] and they cautioned us not to touch the threshold, and having searched us carefully for knives, and not having found any, we entered the door on the east side, for no one dare enter that on the west side save the Emperor; and the same rule applies if it is the tent of a chief; but those of low rank pay little attention to such matters. And when we entered his tent, it was the first occasion since he had been made Emperor (that he had given an audience). He received likewise the ambassadors, but very few persons entered his tent. Here also such great quantities of presents were given him by the ambassadors, silks, samites, purples, baldakins, silk girdles worked in gold, splendid furs and other things, that it was a marvel to see. Here also it was that a kind of umbrella or awning (760) that is carried over the Emperor's head was presented to him, and it was all covered with precious stones.[3] Here also a certain governor of a province brought

---

[1] Chingai was a Uigur; he had been minister of Ogodai, but during the regency of Turakina he was deprived of his office (d'Ohsson, ii, 189).

[2] Probably an error for three times. Baber (i, 224) mentions the fact of one of his uncles bending the knee nine times before his elder brother, but this is very unusual.

[3] One of the insignia of royalty in the East from the earliest times. Such umbrellas are called *chattra* in Sanskrit, *chatta* or *chhatr* in Hindustani. Ibn Batuta (iii, 228) speaks of a *chhatr* raised over the elephant of the Sultan of Sindh, which was of silk set with precious stones, and had a handle of pure gold.

to him many camels covered with baldakin and with saddles on them, and a kind of arrangement inside of which people could sit, I think there were forty or fifty of them ; and (he also gave him) many horses and mules covered with armour, some of hide, others of iron.[1] They asked us if we wished to make any presents; but we had already used up nearly everything we had, so we had nothing at all to give him. It was while here that on a hill some distance from the tent there were more than five hundred carts, all full of gold and silver and silken gowns, all of which was divided up between the Emperor and the chiefs ; and the various chiefs divided their shares among their men as they saw fit.

VI. Leaving this place, we came to another where there was a wonderful tent, all of red purple, a present of the Kitayans. We were taken into it also, and here again when we entered they gave us mead or wine to drink, and offered us cooked meat, if we wanted it. There was a high platform of boards[2] in it, on which was the Emperor's throne (761): and the throne was of ebony, wonderfully sculptured ; and there were also (on it) gold, and precious stones, and, if I remember rightly, pearls ; and one went up to it by steps, and it was rounded behind. There were benches placed around the throne, on which the ladies sat in rows on the left side ;[3] on the right side no one sat on raised seats, but the chiefs sat on seats of lesser height placed in the middle (of the tent), and the other people sat behind them, and the whole day there came there a great concourse of ladies. These three tents of which I have spoken[4] were

---

[1] On the armour in use among the Mongols, see Rubruck, 381.

[2] *Solarium de tabulis.* Conf. Rubruck's description of the palace at Karakorum.

[3] From this it would seem that the seats occupied by the wives of the Emperor were on a level with his throne. Conf., however, Benedict, *infra*, p. 38.

[4] The tent of white purple, the Sira Orda, and the Golden Orda.

very big; but his wives had other tents of white felt, and they were quite large and handsome. It was here also that they separated: the mother of the Emperor went in one direction, the Emperor in another, for the purpose of rendering justice. The paternal aunt of the Emperor was in prison, for she had killed his father in the time when their army was in Hungary, and it was for this that the army had retreated from those countries. She and a number of others were tried for this, and put to death.[1]

VII. At this same time Jeroslav, grand-duke in a part of Ruscia called Susdal, died at the Emperor's *orda*. It happened that he was invited by the mother of the Emperor (to her tent), and she gave him to eat and drink with her own hand, as if to honour him; and he went back to his lodgings (762) straightway and fell ill, and after seven days he was dead, and all his body became livid in strange fashion; so that everyone believed that he had been poisoned, that they might get free and full possession of his lands. As an argument in favour of this (supposition, the Empress) sent at once, without the knowledge of any of her people who were there, an envoy in all haste to his son Alexander in Ruscia to come to her, for she wished to give him his father's lands; but he would not go, but remained there (at home); in the meanwhile (the Empress) sent also letters for him to come and receive his father's lands. It was believed by all that he would be put to death if he should come, or imprisoned perpetually.[2]

---

[1] I cannot trace this story. After Kuyuk's election he had an inquiry made into the conspiracy of Ujugen to seize the throne after the death of Ogodai. A number of Ujugen's officers were, as a result, put to death (d'Ohsson, ii, 203). All accounts agree that Ogọdai died a natural though sudden death, which overtook him after a hunt and a night of drinking.

[2] Yaroslaw II, Vsevolodvitch, Grand Duke of Russia, reigned from 1238 to 1247. He went to the Mongol Court in 1245 or 1246. Karamsin (iv, 38) refers to the rumour that he had been poisoned there, but dismisses it as highly improbable. He says that the Duke died on his

VIII. It was after this death (of Jeroslav) that our Tartars took us to the Emperor, if I remember correctly the time; and when the Emperor heard from our Tartars that we had come to him, he ordered us to go back to his mother, for he wanted two days after that to unfurl his standard against the whole of the western world, as was emphatically told us by those who knew, as has been previously stated, and he wished us not to know it. When we had returned (to the Empress), we remained there a few days, when we were sent back again to him; and we remained with him for quite a month, in such hunger and thirst that we were barely able to keep alive, for the allowances which they gave the four of us were scarcely enough for one; and we could find nothing to buy, the market being too far away. Had not the Lord sent us a certain Ruthenian called Cosmas, a goldsmith, and a great favourite of the Emperor,[1] who helped us a little, I verily believe we should have died, unless the Lord (763) had helped us in some other way. He showed us before putting it in place the throne of the Emperor which he himself had made, and also the seal he had manufactured for him, and he told us the superscription on his seal.[2] We also learnt many private details (*secreta*) about

way back to Russia, and that his body was carried back to Vladimir. Alexander did visit the Mongol Court, with his brother Andrew, but was lucky enough to get back to Russia in 1249 (Karamsin, iv, 78-80). This Alexander is the famous St. Alexander Nevsky.

[1] Rubruck's best friend at the Court of Mangu was the French goldsmith, Guillaume Buchier.

[2] In another passage (715) he says the seal of the Emperor bore the words: "God in Heaven, and Cuyuc-Can on earth. Might of God. The seal of the Emperor of all men." The letter of Kuyuk to Pope Innocent IV begins by "*Dei fortitudo Cuyuc Can, omnium hominum imperator*, which in Mongol would be *Möngkä Tängri Kuchundur, Kuyuk Khakhan.* "By the power of eternal Heaven, Kuyuk, Khakhan." This, I take it, was the inscription on the seal, which in all probability was written in Mongol and in Chinese seal characters (conf. Devéria, *Notes d'épigraphie Mongole*, 31, and Sir John Maundevile, 231).

the Emperor, from those who had come with other chiefs, several Ruthenians and Hungarians who knew Latin and French, also Ruthenian clerks and others who had been with them, some as long as thirty years, in war and in other events, and who knew all about them as they understood the language, having been continually with them some twenty, others ten years, more or less. From these we were able to learn about everything: they told us most freely of all things without our having to question them, for they knew of our desire.

IX. After these things had happened the Emperor sent his prothonotary Chingay to tell us to write down what we had to say and our business, and to give it to him; this we did, writing down all we had previously said at Bati's, as has been stated above. After an interval of several days, he had us again called, and told us, through Kadac, the procurator of the whole empire, and in the presence of the prothonotaries Bala and Chingay, (764) and of many others of his secretaries, to say all we had to say; and this we did right willingly. Our interpreter on that occasion, as well as on the other, was Temer, a knight of Jeroslav's, now a clerk with him, and another clerk of the Emperor's.[1] And he (*i.e.*, Kadac) asked us on the latter occasion if there were any persons with the Lord Pope who understood the written languages of the Ruthenians or Saracens or Tartars. We replied that we did not use either the Ruthenian, Tartar, or Saracenic writing, and that though there were Saracens in the country, they were far distant from the Lord Pope. We added that it appeared to us the best plan for them to write in Tartar, and to have it translated to us, and that we would carefully write it down

---

[1] In another passage (771) he gives the name of this clerk as Dubarlaus, and says he was also in the service of Duke Yaroslaw. He also mentions two servants of the Duke's called Jacob and Michel.

in our language, taking both the (original) letter and the translation to the Lord Pope. On this they left us and went back to the Emperor.

X. On the feast of Saint Martin (11th November) we were again summoned, and Kadac, Chingay, Bala and several others of the secretaries came to us, and the letter was translated to us word for word; and as we translated it into Latin[1] they made us explain each phrase, wishing to ascertain if we had made a mistake in any word; and when (765) the two letters were written they made us read them together and separately for fear we had left out anything, and they said to us: "Be sure you understand it all, for it must not be that you do not understand everything, when you have reached such very distant lands." And having told them: "We understand it all," they re-wrote the letter in Saracenic, so that it might be read to the Lord Pope if he could find any one in our part of the world able to do so.

XI. It is the custom of the Emperor of the Tartars never to address in person a stranger, no matter how great he may be; he only listens, and then answers through the medium of someone, as I have explained. Whenever they explain any business to Kadac, or listen to an answer of the Emperor, those who are under him (*i.e.*, his own subjects), remain on their knees until the end of the speech, no matter how great they may be. One may not, for it is not the custom, say anything more about any question after it is disposed of by the Emperor.[2] This Emperor has a procurator, prothonotaries and secretaries, and also all the other officers for public as well as private affairs, except advocates, for they carry out without a murmur all judgments according to the Emperor's decision. The

---

[1] This translation is given in d'Avezac, 594. The letter contains nothing of importance or interest.

[2] Conf. Rubruck, 360, 396.

other princes of the Tartars do in like manner as regards those things which pertain to their offices.

XII. This Emperor may be forty or forty-five years or more old; he is of medium stature, very prudent and extremely shrewd, and serious and sedate in his manners; (766) and he has never been seen to laugh lightly or show any levity, and of this we were assured by Christians who were constantly with him. We were also assured by Christians who were of his household that they firmly believed that he was about to become a Christian. As signal evidence of this he keeps Christian clerks and gives them allowances, and he has always the chapel of the Christians in front of his great tent, and (these priests) chant publicly and openly and beat (a tablet) according to the fashion of the Greeks at appointed hours, just like other Christians, and though there may be ever so great a multitude of Tartars and of other people. And the other chiefs do not have this.

XIII. Our Tartars who were to come back with us told us that the Emperor proposed sending his ambassadors with us. He wished, however, I think, that we should ask him to do so, for one of our Tartars, the elder of the two, told us to ask it; but it not seeming to us good that they should come, we replied that it was not for us to ask it, but that if the Emperor of his own will sent them, we would with God's help guide them safely. There were various reasons, however, for which it seemed to us inexpedient that they should come. The first reason was that we feared they would see the dissensions and wars among us, and that it would encourage them to march against us. The second reason was that we feared they were intended to be spies. The third reason was that we feared lest they be put to death, as our people for the most part are arrogant and hasty: thus it was that when the servants who were with us (767) at the request of the

Cardinal Legate in Germany were going back to him in Tartar dress, they came near being stoned by the Germans on the road, and were forced to leave off that dress.[1] And it is the custom of the Tartars never to make peace with those who have killed their envoys till they have wreaked vengeance upon them. The fourth reason was that we feared they would carry us off, as was once done with a Saracen prince, who is still a captive, unless he is dead. The fifth reason was that there was no need for their coming, for they had no other order or authority than to bring the letters of the Emperor to the Lord Pope and the other princes (of Christendom), which we (already) had, and we believed that evil might come of it. Therefore it pleased us not that they should come. The third day after this, which was the feast of Saint Brice (13th November), they gave us permission to leave (*licentiam*) and a letter of the Emperor signed with his seal, and then they sent us to the Emperor's mother, who gave to each of us a fox-skin gown with the fur outside and wadding inside, and also a piece of purple—of which our Tartars stole a palm's length from each, and also more than half of another piece which was given to our servant; but though it was no secret to us, we did not choose to make any ado over it.

---

## III.

Concerning the route we travelled in coming back.

(768) I. So we started on our way back, and we were travelling the whole winter, resting most of the time in the snow in the desert, save when in the open plain where there

---

[1] Hugh of Santocaro, the Pope's Legate in Germany, had sent some of his servants with the mission to assist it—probably as far as Kiew (Wadding, *Annales*, iii, 119, and d'Avezac, 481). Conf. Rubruck's remarks (312) about the danger of allowing Mongol envoys to visit Europe.

were no trees we could scrape a bare place with our feet; and often when the wind drifted it we would find (on waking) our bodies all covered with snow.[1] And so we travelled along till we came to Bati, on the Ascension of our Lord (9th May), and to him we told what (the Emperor) had answered the Lord Pope. He replied that he had nothing to ask other than what the Emperor had written; but he said that we must carefully tell the Lord Pope and the other lords everything the Emperor had written. Safe conducts having been given us we left him, and reached Mauci on the Saturday after the octave of Pentecost (2nd June), where were our companions and servants who had been detained, and whom we caused to be brought back to us. Thence we went to Corenza, who again begged presents of us, but not having (anything) we gave nothing. He gave us two Comans, who were accounted of the Tartars, as far as Kiew (769) in Ruscia.[2] Our own Tartar did not leave us till we had left the last Tartar camp. The others who had been given us by Corenza led us in six days from the last camp to Kiew.

II. We reached (Kiew) fifteen days before the feast of Saint John the Baptist (9th June). The Kiewians who had heard of our arrival all came out to meet us rejoicing, and congratulated us as if we had risen from the dead, and

---

[1] The only detail concerning the route followed by the mission on its return journey is a brief reference (771) to its having passed through a town of the Bisermins called Lemfinc. Although I am unable to identify this town (it may, however, be Chimkent), it was in all probability in the Syr daria valley; and it seems likely that the route followed from Kuyuk's camp to this point was practically the same as in going, and from there to Batu's also very nearly the same: though on the 9th May, when the mission arrived at that Prince's camp, he may have been somewhat farther north than the neighbourhood of Sarai, his winter quarters.

[2] In another passage (771) he notes that he met on the border of Comania the Duke Roman (of Russia), then on his way to the Tartars; also the Duke Aloha and the Duke of Cherneglove (Chernigow), who accompanied him back through Russia.

so they did to us throughout Ruscia, Poland and Bohemia.[1] Daniel and Vassilko his brother received us with great rejoicing, and kept us, against our will, for quite eight days; during which time they held counsel between themselves and the bishops and other notables about those things on which we had spoken to them when on our way to the Tartars. And they answered us jointly, saying, that they wished to have the Lord Pope for their particular lord and father, and the holy Roman Church as their lady and mistress, and confirming likewise all they had previously transmitted on the matter through their abbot; and after that they sent with us to the Lord Pope their letters and ambassadors.

---

[1] He notes (772) that he met at Kiew a number of Constantinople traders who had come there through the Tartar country; all of them were Italians. He mentions among others Michel of Genoa, Manuel of Venice, and Nicolas of Pisa.

A

NARRATIVE OF

# FRIAR JOHN OF PIAN DE CARPINE'S MISSION;

DERIVED FROM AN ORAL STATEMENT OF HIS COMPANION,

## FRIAR BENEDICT THE POLE.[1]

(774)

IN the year of Our Lord one thousand two hundred and forty-five, Friar John of the order of Minor Friars, and of Pian de Carpine, despatched by the Lord Pope to the Tartars in company with another friar,[2] left Lyons in France, where the Pope was, on Easter day (16th April), and having arrived in Poland he took at Breslau a third friar of the same order, Benedict by name, a Pole by nationality, to be the companion of his labour and tribulations and to act as his interpreter. Through the assistance of Conrad, Duke of the Poles, they reached Kiew, a city of Ruscia, now under the dominion of

[1] The text was published for the first time by d'Avezac (*op. cit.*, 774-779). It was found in MS. No. 2477 of the Colbert Collection in the Bibliothèque Nationale at Paris.

[2] Stephen of Bohemia was his name, as we learn from Wadding (*Scriptores*, 221).

the Tartars. The headman of the city gave them an escort for a distance of six days thence to the first camp of the Tartars, near the border of Comania.[1]

(775) II. When the chiefs of this camp heard that they were envoys of the Pope they asked for and received presents from them. Friars John and Benedict, having by their order left behind the third friar, who was too feeble, also their horses and the servants they had brought with them, set out for a second camp on the Tartars' own horses and with pack animals provided by them; and so, after changing horses at several camps, they came on the third day to the chief of an army of eight thousand men,[2] and his attendants (*ministri*), having asked for and received presents, conducted them to their chief Curoniza. He questioned them as to the motive of their journey and the nature of their business. This having been stated, he gave them three of his Tartars, who got them supplied with horses and food (*expensis*) from one army to another, till finally they came to a prince, Bati by name, who is one of the greatest princes of the Tartars, and the same that ravaged Ungaria.

III. On the route thither they crossed the rivers called Nepere and Don. They spent five weeks and more on the road, to wit, from the Sunday, *Invocavit*, to the Thursday, *Cenae Domini*, on which day they reached Bati,[3] finding him beside the great river Ethil, which the Ruscians call Volga, and which is believed to be the Tanais.[4] The

---

[1] Apparently the town governed by the greedy Alan Micheas, mentioned by Pian de Carpine (*supra*, p. 4).

[2] Pian de Carpine (*supra*, p. 5) refers to this camp as "the first camp of the Tartars."

[3] The Sunday, *Invocabit*, is the first Sunday in Lent (26th February, 1246). Thursday, *Coena Domini*, is Holy Thursday, *i.e.*, 5th April, 1246. Friar John says they reached Batu's on the 4th April.

[4] All classical geographers believed that the Volga joined the Don not far from its mouth, and that the combined streams flowed into the sea of Azow. Even Ptolemy appears to have held this view. Conf. Rubruck (252) who gives the course of the Volga correctly.

attendants of Bati having asked for and received presents, consisting of forty beaver skins and eighty badger skins,[1] these presents were carried between two consecrated fires; and the Friars were obliged to follow the presents, for it is a custom among the Tartars to purify ambassadors and gifts by fire. Beyond the fires there was a cart with a golden statue of the Emperor, which it is likewise customary to worship.[2] But the Friars refusing positively to worship it, were nevertheless obliged to bow their heads (before it). Bati, having heard the letter of the Pope (*legatione*), and examined every word of it, sent them (776) after five days, that is to say on the Tuesday after Easter,[3] together with his letters which he gave to one of their own Tartar guides, to the son of the great Emperor,[4] which son's name is Cuyuc Kan, in the fatherland of the Tartars.

IV. Leaving therefore Prince Bati, (the Friars), having wrapped their legs with bandages, so as to be able to bear the fatigue of riding, left Comania behind after two weeks. In this country they found a great deal of wormwood (*absincium*),[5] for this country was once called Pontus, and Ovidius says of Pontus:

"*Tristia per vacuos horrent absinthia campos.*"[6]

While the Friars were travelling through Comania they

---

[1] *Pelles taxorum.*

[2] Conf. Pian de Carpine's remarks (620) on the subject.

[3] April 10th, 1246. Pian de Carpine (747) states they left Batu's camp on April 8th.

[4] Ogodai, son of Chingis Khan, died in 1241; his son Kuyuk was only elected in 1246.

[5] Saksaul, or *Anabasis Ammodendron.* On the time taken to traverse Comania, see *supra*, p. 13, note 1. Clavijo (104) states that he was made to travel day and night in order to reach Timur's court more promptly.

[6] Ovid., *Epist.*, 1, iii.

had on their right the country of the Saxi,[1] whom we believe to be Goths, and who are Christians; after them the Gazars, who are Christians.[2] In this country is the rich city of Ornarum,[3] which was captured by the Tartars by means of inundations of water. After that the Circasses, and they are Christians; after that the Georgians, and they too are Christians. Prior to that, while in Ruscia, they had the Morduans on their left, and they are pagans, and for the most part they shave the backs of their heads. After them were the Bylers, and they are pagans; and after that the Bascards, who are the ancient Ungari; then the Cynocephales, who have dogs' heads; and then the Parocitæ,[4] who have a small narrow mouth, who can masticate nothing, but who live on liquids and sustain themselves on the odours of meats and fruits.

(777) V. On the border of Comania they crossed a river called Jaiac, and there begins the country of the Kangitæ. They travelled through this for twenty days, and they found few people there, but many swamps and vast salt marshes and salt rivers,[5] which we take to be the Maeotide

---

[1] The Goths of the Crimea (conf. Rubruck, 219).

[2] Contemporary Mohammedan writers state that the Ghozz or Khazar Turks lived to the east of the sea of Tabaristan or Caspian (Ibn Khaldun, *Not. et extr.*, xix, i, Pt. 1, 156). They may have occupied the country around the Lake Aral, which the Kankali (the friars' *Cangitae or Cangle*) had evacuated in the early part of the thirteenth century (d'Ohsson, i, 196). The Khazars were mostly Jews, but Christians and Mohammedans were also numerous amongst them.

[3] Pian de Carpine (674) calls it *Ornas* (see Schuyler, *Turkestan*, i, 401, and *supra*, p. 14, note 1).

[4] Solinus (*op. cit.*, 207) speaks, on the authority of Megasthenes, of a dog-headed people of India, without speech, and also of a people which fed solely on the odour of wild apples (conf. Pliny vii, 2, 282, 283; McCrindle, *Ancient India*, 83; also *supra*, p. 12, note; and Schiltberger, 35). The Chinese annals of the sixth century (*Liang shu*, bk. 54; *Nan shih*, bk. 79) tell of a kingdom of dogs (*Kou kuo*) in some remote corner of north-eastern Asia. The men had human bodies but dogs' heads, and their speech sounded like barking. The women were like the rest of their sex in other parts of world.

[5] *Salsas, et flumina salsa.* The salt marshes and lakes near the river Ural (Jaiac), the largest of which is the Indersky, into which

swamps. For eight days they went through a vast desert, barren and sandy. After the country of the Kangitae they came to Turkya, where they for the first time[1] found a big city (called) Janckynt, and they travelled for about ten days in this Turkya.[2] Now Turkya professes the religion of Machomet. After Turkya they entered a country called Kara-Kytai, which meaneth Black Kytai ; and these people are pagans, and they found no town there. These were once the masters of the Tartars.[3] After that they entered the country of the Tartars on the feast of Mary Magdalen.

VI. They found the Emperor in that country in a great tent which is called Syra-Orda, and here they remained for four months, and they were present at the election of Cuyuc Kan, their Emperor. And the same Friar Benedict the Pole told us orally that he and the other friar saw there about five thousand great and mighty men, who on the first day of the election of the king all appeared dressed in baldakin ; but neither on that day nor on the next, when they appeared in white samites, did they reach an agreement. But on the third day, when they wore red samites, they

---

flow two salt springs. There are some thirty salt lakes in the Ural province. The remark that these swamps may be the Maeotide swamps is probably the editor's. Benedict and his companion did not, however, know of the existence of the Aral, nor did William of Rubruck, nor Marco Polo either, for that matter. Friar William passed probably a considerable distance to the north of it ; the two first-named took it for a part of the Caspian, which in turn they believed to be a portion of the Black Sea.

[1] *Primo*, *i.e.*, since leaving the right bank of the Dnieper. By *Turkya* we must understand Turkestan. Friar John (680) calls the Seldjuk empire of Asia Minor *Urum*, i.e., Rum. This Turkya he calls (672) the country of the Bisermins.

[2] The part of Turkestan (*Turkya*) through which they travelled was the valley of the Syr daria. They probably went from near Yengui-kend or Yanikent (*Janckynt*, Pian de Carpine's *Ianckint*) to near the modern town of Turkestan, or perhaps considerably to the east of it (see Schuyler, i, 401).

[3] This phrase seems to me to show some knowledge on the part of Benedict of the story of Unc Khan and Prester John.

came to an agreement and made the election. This same friar declared also that about three thousand envoys, coming from different parts of the world, were present at that same court with messages, letters, tribute or presents of divers kinds and in great numbers. These same friars, who were counted among them, had to put on, (778) as of necessity bound, baldakin over their gowns, for no ambassador may appear in the presence of the chosen and crowned sovereign unless he be properly dressed.[1]

VII. Having been taken into the Syra-Orda, that is to say, the tent (*statio*), of the Emperor, they saw him there crowned and gorgeous in splendid attire seated on a raised dais (*tabulatum*), richly ornamented with gold and silver, and above it was trellis-work (*cancellatum*), and around the edge four separate flights of steps led up to the platform. Three of these flights were in front of the dais; by the middle one the Emperor alone goes up or comes down, by the two side ones the nobles and others (pass), but by the fourth, which is behind (the Emperor), his mother, his wife, and his relatives ascend. The Syra-Orda had three openings in guise of doors; the middle one, which far exceeded the others in size, was always left without any guard, the King alone entering by it. And if anyone else should have entered by it, he would have been without a doubt put to death. The two other side doors were closed with silk (hangings), and had very rigid guards, who watched them in arms, and through these everyone else passed with signs of reverence for fear of the established punishment.

VIII. On the third day the letter of the Lord Pope was carefully listened to and gone over through (the medium of) officials and interpreters. After that the Friars were sent to the mother of the Emperor, whom they found in another

---

[1] Rubruck (268) refers to this remark of Benedict.

locality, seated in like fashion, in a large and most beautiful tent. After receiving them with great courtesy and friendliness, she sent them back to her son. While they were stopping there, they used frequently to have with them some of the Georgians living among the Tartars. They are quite respected by the Tartars, because they are a strong and warlike people. They are called Georgians because Saint George aids them in their fights; and he is their patron and they honour him (779) above all other saints.[1] They use the Greek idiom in their Holy Scriptures, and they have crosses over their tents and carts. The customs of the Greeks are observed in divine service among the Tartars.

IX. The business on which the Friars had come having been settled, they took their leave of the Emperor, carrying back with them letters of his signed with his seal to the Lord Pope; and they went their way back, travelling westward with the ambassadors of the soldan of Babylon,[2] who after accompanying them for fifteen days then left them and turned southward. The Friars continued on their journey westward, and after passing the Rhine at Cologne, got back to the Lord Pope in Lyons, and presented to him the letters of the Emperor of the Tartars.

---

[1] Conf. Rubruck (383) where he derives the name from that of the river Cur.

[2] The Ayubite Sultan of Egypt, whose capital, Cairo, was then called Babylon.

THE

# JOURNEY TO THE EASTERN PARTS OF THE WORLD, OF FRIAR WILLIAM OF RUBRUCK,

OF THE ORDER OF MINOR FRIARS,

IN THE YEAR OF GRACE MCCLIII.

---

(213)

TO the most excellent lord and most Christian Louis, by the grace of God illustrious King of the French, from Friar William of Rubruck, the meanest in the order of Minor Friars, greetings, and may he always triumph in Christ.

It is written in Ecclesiasticus of the Wise man: "He shall go through the land of foreign peoples, and shall try the good and evil in all things."[1] This, my lord King, have I done, and may it have been as a wise man and not as a fool; for many do what the wise man doth, though not

---

[1] Ecclesiasticus, xxxix, 5. The Vulgate has: "*In terram alienigenarum gentium pertransiet: bona enim et mala in hominibus tentabit,*" whereas our monk has: "*In terram alienarum gentium transiet, bona et mala in omnibus temptabit.*" I fancy he quotes here from memory, as he does (391) in another passage of the Bible, which he also misquotes.

wisely, but most foolishly; of this number I fear I may be. Nevertheless in whatever way (214) I may have done, since you commanded me when I took my leave of you that I should write you whatever I should see among the Tartars, and you did also admonish me not to fear writing a long letter, so I do what you enjoined on me, with fear, however, and diffidence, for the proper words that I should write to so great a monarch do not suggest themselves to me.

Be it known then to your Sacred Majesty that in the year of our Lord one thousand CCLIII, on the nones of May (7th May), I entered the Sea of Pontus, which is commonly called Mare Majus, or the Greater Sea,[1] and it is one thousand CCCC miles in length,[2] as I learnt from merchants, and is divided as it were into two parts. For about the middle of it there are two points of land, the one in the north and the other in the south. That which is in the south is called Sinopolis, and is a fortress and a port of the Soldan of Turkia; while that which is in the north is a

---

[1] The name Pontus, or Pontus Euxinus, was used by all classical authors to designate the Black Sea, and is also found in the early Mohammedan writers (Masudi and Edrisi). The earliest use of the name "Black Sea" would seem to be in Constantine Porphyrogenitus (*De administrando*, 152); he there refers to it as Σκοτεινή θαλάσση, though throughout the rest of the work he invariably uses the name "Pontic Sea" (Ποντική θαλάσση), or Pontus (Πόντος). Friar Jordanus (53) uses the name *Mare Nigrum*. His *Mare Maurum* seems to designate the eastern part of the Euxine. Some of the early Arab geographers use the name "Sea of Nitoch," and "Sea of the Khazars."

[2] This is greatly in excess of the truth. Hakluyt has "1008 miles in length." The classical writers had very erroneous ideas about the size of the Black Sea (see Pliny, iv, 24, and Tchihatcheff, *Asie Mineure*, i, 34, *et seq.*). The greatest length of the Black Sea is about 550 geographical miles, its greatest width about 325 (Rawlinson, *Herodotus*, iii, 65).

[3] Sinopolis, or Sinope, was captured by the Turks in 1215 (Hammer, *Hist.*, i, 34). Strabo (xii, 3, 467) says it was a colony of the Milesians. The city stood on a rocky peninsula, and had two ports. It was noted from early times for its powerful fleet and its tunny-fish (πηλαμυδεῖα) fisheries (see also Ibn Batuta, ii, 348, and Heyd, i, 298, 551). The Seldjuk kingdom of Rum, with its capital at Iconium, comprised most

certain province now called by the Latins Gazaria,[1] but by the Greeks who inhabit along its sea coast it is called Cassaria, which is Cesaria. And there are certain promontories projecting out into the sea to the south toward Sinopolis; and there are three hundred miles between Sinopolis and Cassaria, and so there are seven hundred miles from these points to Constantinople in length and breadth, and seven hundred to the east, which is Hyberia, that is to say, the province of Georgia.

So we made sail for the province of Gazaria, or Cassaria, which is about triangular in shape, having on its west side a city called Kersona,[2] where Saint Clement was martyred.

---

of Asia Minor. It was formed from the Seldjuk empire in 1084, and lasted to 1300 (Hammer, *op. cit.*, i, 11, *et seq.*). Pian de Carpine (680) speaks of "the soldan of Urum," but nowhere uses the word Turkia.

[1] This name was given to the Crimea, probably in the eighth century, on account of the Khazars who then occupied it as part of their domain, which extended from north of the Caucasus to the Don. This nation, which seems to have been of Turkish stock, though some writers say of Finnish, is first mentioned by Priscus in A.D. 626. He writes their name Ἀκατζίροι and Ἀκατίροι. Menander calls them Κατζίροι, and Jornandes uses the form *Agazirri*. The form Χαζάροι is also used. Rashideddin says that when the descendants of Oguz entered Persia, one of their tribes, having fixed its residence amidst forests, received the name of *Agacheris*. Quatremère (53) identifies the Khazars with the Agacheris, or "Men of the Woods," but the latter name would seem to have been applied to many Turkish tribes. Pian de Carpine (674) refers to the Khazars as Gazari, and Friar Jordanus (54) speaks of "the empire of Osbet (Uzbeg), which is called Gatzaria."

[2] The city of Sevastopol. Jornandes (428) says the Scythians allowed the Greeks (of Heraclea) to found this town of Chersonesus to trade with them. He speaks of the Aulziagri Huns who lived in the neighbourhood of Cherson, "where the greedy trader brought the rich products of Asia." In the earliest times, as in those of our traveller and Ibn Batuta, the export trade of this place consisted principally in furs and slaves. Jornandes, in fact, speaks (*loc. cit.*) of the Hunuguri as noted for the sable skins with which they supplied the market; the "rich products of Asia" referred to above only means the silk and other fabrics of western Asia, which were imported into Cherson by the Greek traders. The exact nature of the trade at this place may probably be determined by what Strabo (xi, 2, 423) states in reference to that of the town of Tanais, at the mouth of the Don (Tanais). He says that the nomads brought there slaves, furs, and various products of native industry, while the Greeks imported principally tissues and wine—a real west coast trade! (see also Heyd, i, 11, 48; and *infra*, p. 43, note 2, on the trade of Soldaia).

And as we were sailing past it we saw (215) an island on which is a temple said to have been built by angelic hands.[1] In the middle, at the summit of the triangle as it were, on the south side, is a city called Soldaia,[2] which

---

[1] Berthier de la Garde says that this passage of Rubruck applies very exactly to a point (or headland) in the harbour of Sevastopol, and corroborates the legend which connects it with the martyrdom of St. Clement and the construction of a church dedicated to him on this spot. This headland would seem to have been at one time an island, and it would at all events look like one to a ship sailing by. The church on it is marked on Russian maps of as late a date as 1772. It is about 12 *versts* from the monastery of St. George, and the relics of St. Clement were found there by Constantine the Philosopher. Bacon (i, 357), after quoting this passage of Friar William, adds "in this temple the body of the saint was buried." Some writers have located the place of St. Clement's martyrdom at Inkerman, but Berthier thinks this inadmissible (*Materials for the Archæology of Russia*, No. 12; *The Antiquities of Southern Russia, Excavations in the Chersonesus*, by A. L. Berthier de la Garde, 1893, 61, *et seq.*). St. Clement is said to have been the immediate successor of Peter the Apostle. He was exiled to the Chersonesus during the persecution of Diocletian, and was martyred in about A.D. 100, during the persecution of Trajan. Whether our traveller referred to this spot or to another in the neighbourhood must remain doubtful, for traditions are also connected with Cape Chersones and Cape Fioraventi; on the latter now stands the monastery of St. George, but it is believed by some archæologists that the famous temple of Artemis of the Thracians, or Parthenon, occupied the same place, though other authorities say it was on Cape Chersones.

[2] The modern Sudak. The earliest mention I have found of this place dates from the twelfth century; then, as now, it was known to Oriental writers as Sudak; while western mediæval authors write the name *Sodaia*, *Soldachia*, *Soltadia*, *Sholtadia*, but more frequently *Soldaia*. The Greeks transcribed the name *Σουγδαια*. As Friar William justly remarks, it was in his time the emporium for Western Asiatic and Russian trade, monopolising that which in former centuries had been carried on at Kherson and Tanais—for Tana hardly existed in his time, at least we find no mention of it anywhere. Ibn Alathir (xiv, 456) says it was the capital of the Kipchak, and that the inhabitants of the country drew their supplies from it, for it was situated on the sea of the Khazars, and ships came there laden with stuffs. The Kipchaks bought from them, selling them young girls, slaves, black fox, beaver, grey squirrel skins, and other products of their country. Ibn Batuta tells us (ii, 415) that when he visited this town "its port was among the largest and finest known. Outside the city are gardens and streams. Turks inhabit it, with a corps of Greeks, who live under their protection and are artizans; most of the houses are built of wood. This city was formerly very large, but the greater part was destroyed in a civil war between the Greeks and the Turks." Sudak was first captured by the Mongols in 1223, but lost shortly after, being recaptured in 1239 Hammer *Golden. Horde*, 87;

looketh across towards Sinopolis; and thither come all the merchants arriving from Turkia who wish to go to the northern countries, and likewise those coming from Roscia and the northern countries who wish to pass into Turkia. The latter carry vaire and minever, and other costly furs;[1] the others (the former) carry cloths of cotton or bombax,[2] silk stuffs and sweet-smelling spices.[3] To the east of this province is a city called Matrica,[4] where the river Tanais

---

Antoninos, *Zametki xii-xv veka*, etc., 595; Heyd, i, 299, *et seq*.). Friar William thought—and in this he but followed the opinion of classical writers—that the coasts of the Crimea ran due east and west, north and south, Sudak occupying the south-east angle on the coast.

[1] *Varium et grisium*. There is some uncertainty as to the exact species of furs called by these names. "Vair et griz," "vaire and minever," are constantly used in mediæval works. Ducange (iii, 961) says they are commonly synonymous terms, but sometimes they are used to indicate distinct kinds of furs. *Vaire* is supposed to be squirrel; *minever* is also a kind of squirrel skin, possibly the same as vaire, but with the white fur of the belly left on it. Others, however, say that *minever* was an inferior quality of ermine. Ibn Batuta (ii, 401), speaking of the Russian furs, ranks ermine first and, sable or marten second. Pegolotti (Yule's *Cathay*, 306) speaks of the "Sclavonian squirrel." In another passage (329), Rubruck says that skins, *varii et grisii*, formed the currency of the Russians. Hakluyt renders these words by "ermines and gray furres." Purchas (34) translates this, "little spotted and grisel'd skins." Karamsin (i, 307), quoting Russian annalists, says the skins used as currency were those of marten and squirrel. I am inclined to believe that, whatever the correct interpretation of these words may be, as used by Friar William they designate marten and grey squirrel skins.

[2] Heyd (ii, 614) says that the most ancient name given to cotton in western works is *bombacium*, though, from the end of the thirteenth century, one occasionally finds the word *cottonum*, derived from the Arabic *rotn*. Rubruck uses the word *cottone* in several passages; Joinville also speaks of *telle de coton*.

[3] On the spice trade of the Levant in the thirteenth century, see Heyd, ii, 611, 693, *et seq*.

[4] Matrica, also called *Matracha*, *Matica*, and *Matrega*, was situated on the Taman peninsula, near the straits of Kertch, and on a branch of the Kuban river, called by Edrisi the Sakir. I have not been able to ascertain the date of its foundation, but in the tenth century it was already an important political and commercial centre of the Khazars. It is mentioned by Constantine Porphyrogenitus (*De administr.*, 181), who calls it Ταμάταρχα (possibly τα Μάταρχα). In A.D. 966 it was captured by the Russians under Sviatoslaw, and formed part of a Russian principality, which derived its name, Tmutorkan (Constantine's Tamatarcha?), from it, down to the time of the Coman invasion in the early part of the twelfth century, when it seems to have regained its

falls into the sea of Pontus, through an opening xii miles wide. For this river, before it enters the sea of Pontus, forms a kind of sea to the north which has a width and breadth of seven hundred miles, with nowhere a depth of over six paces,[1] so large vessels do not enter it, but the merchants of Constantinople who visit the said city of Matrica send their barks as far as the River Tanais[2] to buy dried fish, such as sturgeon, barbel and tench,[3] and other fishes in infinite varieties. The said province of Cassaria is therefore encompassed by the sea on three sides: to wit, on the west, where is Kersona, the city of Clement, and to the south where is the city of Soldaia, to which we were steering, and (216) which makes the apex of the province, and to the east by the sea of Tanais. Beyond this opening is Zikuia,[4] which does not obey the

---

independence (Karamsin, i, 214). In 1230 we hear of Matrica as having a Greek prince, people and clergy. In the middle of the fifteenth century Matrica was occupied by the Genoese, who held it for a long time under the suzerainty of one of the Cherkess princes (Antoninos, 829; Heyd, i, 206; ii, 180, 379).

[1] Friar William's view that the real mouth of the Don (Tanais) is at the Straits of Kertch, and that the Sea of Azov (*Palus Maeotis*) is properly but part of the river, meets with the approval of modern geographers. Réclus (*Géographie*, v, 792) says that "the Maeotide Gulf is a river and a sea at the same time." Conf. our author's further remarks on the subject, 252. The views of the ancients regarding the Palus Maeotis, which Rubruck here only refers to as "a kind of sea," were rather hazy. Strabo (vii, 5, 258) gives its circumference as 9,000 stadia. Pliny (iv, 24, 197) says that some authors state it is 1,406,000 paces in circumference, others 1,125,000. Jornandes (428) gives its circumference as 1,400,000 paces, and adds that its depth nowhere exceeds eight ells.

[2] Had the town of Tanais, or Tana, still existed at the time, it is hardly credible that our traveller would have omitted to mention it.

[3] *Hosas* (or *thosas*) *barbotas*. I have translated the terms conjecturally. Tench is *tinca* in Latin, *tenche* in Old French. In another passage, 249, our traveller refers to a *barbota* given him on the Don. Hakluyt has "Sturgeon, Thosses, Barbils, etc."

[4] Strabo (ii, 31, 107; xi, 12, 45; xvii, 24,712) refers to the *Zygi*, *Zygoi*, or *Zygioi*, among the tribes living between the Sea of Hyrcania (Caspian) and the Pontus. He also mentions (xi, 11, 446) a tribe of *Siginnoi* living near the Caucasus, probably in the plains north of it, as he refers to the women being expert chariot-drivers. Constantine

Tartars, and to the east (of that) are the Suevi[1] and Hiberi,[2] who do not obey the Tartars. After that, to the south, is Trapesund, which hath its own lord, Guido by name, who is of the family of the emperors of Constantinople, and he obeyeth the Tartars.[3] After that is the country of

---

Porphyrogenitus (*De admin.*, 181) says : "18 or 20 miles from Tamatarcha (Matrica) is the river Ucruch (Ουκρουχ) which separates Zichia (Ζιχίας) from it ; from the Ucruch (probably a branch of the Kuban) to the river Nicophin (Νικόψιν) was Zichia." Pian de Carpine (748) speaks of the *terra Ziccorum*. See also d'Avezac, 497, and Douglas W. Freshfield, *Proc. Roy. Geo. Soc.*, x, 328, *et seq.*

[1] The *Suanians* of Pliny (vi, 4), or *Soanes* (Σοάναι) of Strabo (xi, 14, 425). They are a people of Karthwelian race, and still occupy in the western Caucasus the country (Suanetia) they did in classical times (de Morgan, ii, 182, 189 : Finlay, iv, 339).

[2] By Hiberi our author has already told us he understands Georgians. He would have stated the case more correctly if he had said that the Georgians did not quietly submit to the Tartar yoke, for Georgia had been subdued by the Mongols in 1239 or thereabouts.

[3] This is one of the very few errors into which our traveller has fallen. The Emperor Andronikos Ghidos (his Guido) of Trebizonde only reigned to 1235. From 1238 to 1263, Manuel I, surnamed "the Great Captain," was on the throne. Joinville (167) says : "Tandis que le roy fermoit Sayete (*i.e.*, was fortifying Sidon, in 1252), vindrent à li les messages à un grant seigneur de la profonde Grèce, lequel se fesoit appeler le grant Commenie et sire di Trafentesi (the Great Comnenus, lord of Trebizonde) . . . . Au roy requistrent que il li envoaist une pućelle de son palais, et il la prenroit à femme. Et le roy respondi que il n'en avoit nulles amenées d'outre-mer, et leur loa que ils alassent en Constantinoble à l'empereur, qui étoit cousin le roy, et li requeissent que il leur baillast une femme pour leur seigneur, tele que feust du lignage le roy et du sien." Had not Friar William left on his journey before the time of the arrival of this important mission at Sidon, it cannot be conceived that he should have committed this mistake as to the reigning emperor. The empire of Trebizonde was founded in 1204 by Alexis Komnenos, son of Manuel, the eldest son of Andronikos. He took the title of "Great Comnenus," which was also borne by his successors. He died in 1222, and was succeeded by Andronikos Ghidos, his son-in-law, who became a vassal of the Seldjuk sultan of Iconium. When the Mongols, in 1240 or thereabouts, had driven the Queen of Georgia, Rusadan, from Tiflis, and her son David had been elected King of the Iberian and Lazian tribes, Trebizonde threw off the yoke of allegiance to the Turks, and united itself with the new Iberian kingdom. Andronikos was succeeded in 1235 by Joannes I (Axuchos), who was killed while playing *tzukanion*, a game resembling polo, in 1238, and was succeeded by Manuel I, "the Great Captain," a son of the founder of the empire, who reigned until 1263. He was in the early part of his reign a vassal of the Seldjuks, and after the battle of Konsadac in 1244, of the Mongols (Finlay, iv, 317-339). The name Trebizonde is written *Trapezounta* by Byzantine authors, *e.g.*, Const. Porphyro., *De Adminis*, 226.

Vastacius, whose son is called Ascar after his maternal grandfather,[1] and who is not subject (to them). From the opening (of the sea) of Tanais to the west as far as the Danube all is theirs (*i.e.*, the Tartars'), even beyond the Danube towards Constantinople, Blakia,[2] which is the land of Assan,[3] and minor Bulgaria as far as Sclavonia, all pay them tribute; and besides the regular tribute, they have taken in the past few years from each house one axe and all the iron which they found unwrought.[4]

We arrived then in Soldaia on the 12th of the calends of June (May 21st), and there had preceded us certain

---

[1] John Ducas Vataces, or John III, was the Greek emperor at Nicca from 1222 to 1255. He had by his first wife, Irene Lascaris, daughter of the Emperor Theodore Lascaris, whom he succeeded, a son called also Theodore Lascaris, our author's *Ascar* (see Gibbon, vii, 358, *et seq.*; Lebeau, xvii, 326, *et seq.*; and on this emperor's character and administration, *ibid.*, xvii, 413-415). Though Vataces was not a vassal of the Mongols, he paid them tribute.

[2] The Vlachs or Vallachians of Thessaly (our author's Blakia) called themselves, as do the modern Greeks, by the name of Romans. The name of Vlachs, or Vallachians, appears to have been given them by the Sclavonians who colonized their depopulated country. This country became known as Great Vlachia, or Vallachia (Finlay, iii, 227).

[3] Or rather "the kingdom of the Asanides." This Bulgo-Vallachian kingdom was founded in the latter part of the twelfth century by three brothers, Peter, Asan (or Yusan), and John. Asan first mounted the throne in 1186, and on his death in 1196 he was succeeded by Peter, who shortly afterwards was murdered and succeeded by John. This state seems to have been quite as much Vallachian as Bulgarian. The old Bulgarian language had completely died out, the language of the court was Vallachian, and Asan and his successors affected to regard themselves as descendants of the Romans (Finlay, iii, 229, *et seq*, iv, 28). After the first Asan, several monarchs of Bulgaria bore this name; but from 1246 to 1277 the reigning sovereign was named Michel (Lebeau, xvii, 348, *et seq.*).

[4] *In massa.* Hakluyt's text reads *frumentum*, "corn," instead of *ferrum*, as in all the other MSS. In his translation (1102) the passage is rendered: "exacted of every household an axe, and all such corne as they found lying in heapes." Such tribute of iron seems to have been commonly levied by the Mongols, a people little able to produce the quantity of that metal needed by them. To cite only a few cases, we read that Hulagu demanded from each person on the capitation lists of Armenia the payment, among other things, of one arrow and one horseshoe (Dulaurier, 483). We are told in the *Chronicle of Nestor* (12) that the Drevlians of Russia paid the Khazars a tribute of one sword for each household (see also Karamsin, i, 50, 314).

merchants of Constantinople, who had said that envoys from the Holy Land were coming who (217) wished to go to Sartach.[1] I had, however, publicly preached on Palm Sunday (April 12th) in Saint Sophia that I was not an envoy, neither yours nor anyone's, but that I was going among these unbelievers according to the rule of our order. So when I arrived these said merchants cautioned me to speak guardedly, for they had said that I was an envoy, and if I said I was not an envoy I would not be allowed to pass. So I spoke in the following way to the captains of the city, or rather to the substitutes of the captains, for the captains had gone to Baatu during the winter bearing the tribute, and had not yet returned: "We have heard say in the Holy Land that your Lord Sartach is a Christian,[2] and greatly were the Christians rejoiced thereat, and chiefly so the most Christian lord the King of the French, who has come thither on a pilgrimage and is fighting against the Saracens[3] to wrench the holy places from out

---

[1] This Mongol chief was son of Batu. His name is variously written in the MSS., *Sartach*, *Sartath*, *Sarhat*, *Sarcath*, *Sarchac*, *Sarthac*, *Sarcach*, *Sarchat*, *Serttah*, and *Salcath*. I have uniformly written it Sartach, a transcription which closely approximates that adopted by Mohammedan contemporary writers (Bretschneider, *Med. Geog.*, 298).

[2] The belief that Sartach was a Christian was general at the time; most contemporary writers, Mohammedan as well as Christian, refer to it. The Armenian chronicles say that Sartach had been brought up by the Russian (or Syrian) Christians, was baptized, and lived as a Christian; Bar Hebraeus states that not only had he been baptized, but that he became a deacon (Klaproth, *Journ. Asiat.*, xii, 211, 277; Dulaurier, 452; see also Friar William's opinion of his Christianity, 263). In 1254, Pope Innocent IV wrote to him congratulating him on his conversion, which he had learnt from a presbyter named John, who had come to him from Sartach. On this mission of John to the Pope, see Rémusat, 61. He thinks it was a self-imposed one.

[3] The Mongols called the Mohammedans *Sartol*, the *Sarti* of Pian de Carpine (710). This word, the same as our *Saracen*, comes from the Arabic *sharki*, "Oriental." The earliest use I have found of it in a western writer is in Eusebius (*Hist. Eccles.*, vi, 42, 288), who there speaks of the Βάρβαροι Σαρακηνοί. Constantine Porphyrogenitus (*De Ceremon.*, i, 739) refers to the Εσπέριοι, or the Saracens of the

their hands: it is for this I wish to go to Sartach, and carry to him the letters of the lord king, in which he admonisheth him of the weal of all Christendom." And they received us right favourably, and gave us lodgings in the episcopal church. And the bishop of this church had been to Sartach, and he told me much good of Sartach, which I later on did not discover myself.

Then they gave us the choice whether we would have carts with oxen to carry our effects, or sumpter horses. (218) And the merchants of Constantinople advised me to take carts, and that I should buy the regular covered carts such as the Ruthenians carry their furs in,[1] and in these I could put such of our things as I would not wish to unload every day; should I take horses it would be necessary to unload them at each stopping-place and to load other horses; and furthermore I should be able to ride more slowly following the gait of the oxen. Then I accepted their advice, unfortunately, however, for I was two months on the way to Sartach, which I might have travelled in one had I gone with horses.

I had brought with me from Constantinople, on the advice of merchants, fruits, muscadel wine and dainty biscuits to present to the first captains (of the Tartars), so that my way might be made easier, for among them no one is looked upon in a proper way who comes with empty hands. All these things I put in one of the carts, since I had not found the captains of the city, and I was told they would be most acceptable to Sartach if I could carry them to him that far. We set out on our journey

West (*El Magreb*). Pian de Carpine's *Bisermins* (*i.e.*, Mussulmans) seems to have applied more particularly to the Mohammedan states of Turkestan (see Bretschneider, *Med. Geog.*, 120).

[1] Probably in all points similar to the high two-wheeled Tartar carts used in south-east Russia and Central Asia, and still called *arba*: a name which Ibn Batuta (ii, 361, 362), who travelled in one from Soldaia to the Kipchak court in the fifteenth century, gives to this conveyance.

about the calends of June (1st June) with our four covered carts and two others which were lent us by them and in which was carried bedding to sleep on at night. And they gave us also five horses to ride, for us five persons, myself, and my companion Friar Bartholomew of Cremona, and Gosset the bearer (219) of the presents, and Homo Dei the dragoman,[1] and the boy Nicholas whom I had bought at Constantinople by means of your charity.[2] They gave us also two men who drove the carts and looked after the oxen and horses.

Now from Kersona all the way to the mouth of the

---

[1] *Homo Dei Turgemannus.* The name of Friar William's interpreter has puzzled former translators, and I confess that I do not feel sure that the explanation I have to offer of it is acceptable. Hakluyt has "the man of God, Turgemanus." Bergeron translates it by "*le bonhomme*," while da Civezza and F. M. Schmidt retain the Latin name. Assuming that this man was a half-bred Arabic-speaking Syrian, a language with which the Friar was almost certainly familiar, and that he was also a Mohammedan, it occurs to me that he may have been called Abd-ullah, "the servant or slave of Allah," and that our traveller preferred to give him a name which had not such a strong Mohammedan *cachet* about it. In mediæval Greek and Latin, ἄνθρωπος and *homo*, and in French *homme*, had the meaning of "liegeman, bondsman, slave."

*Turgemannus* is the Arabic *tarjuman*, the Turkish *terguman*, the mediæval and modern French *truchement* or *trucheman*. The form *terciman* also occurs, as in the letter of Arghun to the Pope, dated 1285 (Chabot, 190). The word *dragoman* was also in use, even before the time of Friar William. It occurs in Byzantine Greek under the form δραγομάνος (Codinus, 40), and Joinville (101) says, "Il avoit gens illec qui savoient le sarrazinnois et le françois, que l'on appele drugemens." William Thomas (1550), in his translation of Barbaro's *Travels*, uses (51) the word *trouchman*.

[2] Very likely a native of the Kipchak, for his familiarity with the anguages of the country through which Friar William was about to travel would have made him a valuable addition to the party. The slave-markets of the Levant were supplied at this time principally from the Kipchak. A little later on, the Mameluks of Egypt were mostly recruited among these Kipchak slaves. The *Mesalek al-absar* (269) says that "notwithstanding the superiority of the inhabitants of the Kabdjak over the troops of the Djerkes, Russians, Madjar, and As, these people carried off their children, which they sold to traders." On the slave trade of the Levant in the Middle Ages, see Heyd, ii. 555, *et seq.* Nicholas only accompanied Friar William as far as Batu's camp on the Volga. He was detained there, and sent back to Sartach to await the Friar's return.

Tanais there are high promontories along the sea, and there are forty hamlets between Kersona and Soldaia, nearly every one of which has its own language; among them were many Goths, whose language is Teutonic.[1]

Beyond these mountains to the north is a most beautiful orest,[2] in a plain full of springs and rivulets, and beyond this forest is a mighty plain which stretches out for five days to the border of this province to the north, where it contracts, having the sea to the east and the west, so that there is a great ditch from one sea to the other.[3] In this plain used to live Comans[4] before the Tartars came, and they forced the cities referred to and the forts to pay them

---

[1] Friar Benedict (*supra*, p. 36) speaks of the "country of the Saxi, whom we believe to be Goths," which he says lay to the south of his route when travelling through Comania. It would seem from the following passage of Barbaro (27) that "forty villages" was the name of a place. He says, speaking of the Isle of Capha, as he calls the Crimea, that it has "twoo places walled, but not stronge, the one whereof is called Sorgathi (Sudak?), which they also called Incremin, that signifieth a fortresse; and the other Cherchiarde, which signifieth xl places." I am rather inclined to believe, however, that Barbaro slightly misunderstood his informant. The word *castella*, used by Friar William, is old French *kasel*, or *cazal;* the modern French equivalent is "*bourg*." William of Tyr (1111, 1112) has "*quicumque . . . casalia habent*," which in the old French version is rendered "cil qui auront les viles champestres que l'on apele casiaus." Hakluyt renders *casalia* by "cottages or granges" (107); *castella* he translates "castles" (103). Barbaro (30), speaking of these Goths of the Crimea, says: "The Gothes speake dowche, which I knowe by a dowcheman, my servunt, that was with me there: for they understode one an other well enough, as we understande a furlane (*i.e.*, a man of Forli) or a florentine. Of this neighborhode of the Gothes and Alani, I suppose the name Gotitalani to be deryved, for Alani were first in this place. But than came the Gothes and conquered these cuntreys, myngleng their name with the Alani, and so being myngled togither called themselfs Gotitalani, who, in effect, folowe all the Greekish facions, and so also do the Circassi." Busbeck, in the middle of the sixteenth century, while at Constantinople conversed with two of these Goths, one of whom, he says, looked like a man from Flanders. He took down a vocabulary in their language, some seventy-five words and phrases, about two-thirds of which are pure Teutonic, if not English (*Epistolæ*, 383, *et seq.*; see also Heyd, ii, 208; Yule, *Cathay*, 200; d'Avezac, 49?).

[2] The southern Crimea is still noted for its beautiful and varied orest growth (Réclus, v, 824).

[3] The ditch at the Isthmus of Perekop.

[4] On the Comans, see *infra*, note to p. 253 of text.

tribute; but when the Tartars came[1] such a multitude of Comans entered this province, all of whom fled to the shore of the sea, that they ate one another, the living the dying, as was told me by a certain merchant who saw it, the living devouring and tearing with their teeth the raw flesh of the dead, as dogs do corpses. Toward the end of this province are many and large lakes, on whose shores are brine springs, the water of which as soon as it enters the lake is turned into salt as hard as ice. And from these brine springs Baatu and Sartach derive great revenues, for from all Ruscia they come thither for salt, and for each cart-load they give two pieces of cotton worth half an yperpera. There come there also by sea many ships for salt, and all contribute according to the (220) quantity (they take).[2]

After having left Soldaia we came on the third day across the Tartars, and when I found myself among them it seemed to me of a truth that I had been transported into another century. I will describe to you as well as I can their mode of living and manners.

---

[1] The Mongols invaded the Crimea for the first time in 1222. D'Ohsson (i, 339) says: "On the news of the unexpected invasion of the Mongols, the Kipchacs (Friar William's Comans) retired from all sides towards the extremities of their territory, abandoning their best pasture lands to the enemy's army, which took up its winter quarters in the heart of the country. Ten thousand Kipchac families passed the Danube and entered the territory of the Roman empire; the Emperor, John Ducas, took them in his service . . . . A great number also took refuge on Russian territory."

[2] Strabo (vii, 4, 258) already refers to the great quantity of salt the Greeks were in the habit of getting from the Palus Maeotis. At the present day the salt lakes of Perekop yield annually as much as 23 millions of poods, or 759 millions of pounds. There are four other groups of salt lakes in the Crimea, but the Perekop group yields the most (E. Stanton, *Salt Production of Russia*; U.S. Consular Reports, vol. iv, 477; see also Tott, 358, and Clarke, 112). The *yperpera* appears to have been worth about ten shillings sterling (see *infra*, note to p. 244 of text, for the value of the *yperpera*).

NOWHERE have they fixed dwelling-places, nor do they know where their next will be. They have divided among themselves Cithia,[1] which extendeth from the Danube to the rising of the sun; and every captain, according as he hath more or less men under him, knows the limits of his pasture lands and where to graze in winter and summer, spring and autumn. For in winter they go down to warmer regions in the south: in summer they go up to cooler towards the north. The pasture lands without water they graze over in winter when there is snow there, for the snow serveth them as water.[2] They set up the dwelling in which they sleep on a circular frame of interlaced sticks

---

[1] Isidorus, to whom Friar William frequently refers as an authority, says (xiv, 500) that formerly Scythia extended from India to the confines of Germany and the Danube, but that later on this term was applied to a region of smaller extent, beginning in the east at the Seric Ocean, and extending westward to the Caspian, while to the south it reached to the Caucasus. Hakluyt (104) renders the first phrase: "They have in no place any settled citie to abide in, neither knowe they of the celestiall citie to come." Clavijo (112) says: "The Zagatays have no other dwellings than tents, moving from the banks of the rivers in summer to the warm districts in winter. Timur with all his host wanders in the same way over the plains, winter and summer."

[2] Strabo (vii, 3, 254) says of the Scythians: "The tents of the Nomads are of felt, and fixed on carts, and in these they live; all around them are the flocks which supply them with the milk, cheese, and meat on which they feed. They follow them in their pasturages, changing all the time for new places with grass. In winter they live in the marshes near the Mæotis, in summer in the steppes (ἐν τοῖς πεδίοις)." The custom of dividing the pasture lands, or assigning certain limits to the annual migrations of each band or tribe, existed from the earliest times among the Turks; as it does, in fact, among all pastoral tribes, or those living by the chase, as the Indians of North America. In the Annals of the Chin dynasty of China (A.D. 557-581), we read of the Turks that "though they wander about, each of the tribes has its separate land" (*Chou shu*, bk. 50, 3; conf. also Marco Polo, i, 244; Radloff, *Aus Siberien*, i, 414; and Sven Hedin, *Through Asia*, i, 419). The latter, speaking of the Kirghiz of the Pamirs, says: "They spend the summer on the *yeylaus* (summer pasture-grounds) . . . . and in winter . . . . they seek the pastures (*kishlaks*) in the valleys. The members of the same aul are, as a rule, kinsmen, and always graze the same yeylaus and the same kishlaks. No other aul is permitted to encroach upon pastures thus appropriated without previous agreement."

converging into a little round hoop on the top, from which projects above a collar as a chimney, and this (framework) they cover over with white felt. Frequently they coat the felt with chalk, or white clay, or powdered bone, to make it appear whiter, and sometimes also (they make the felt) black. The felt around this collar on top they decorate with various pretty designs. Before the entry they also suspend felt (221) ornamented with various embroidered designs in color. For they embroider the felt, colored or otherwise, making vines and trees, birds and beasts.[1]

---

[1] The round felt-covered tent common to the Tartar, Turki, and Mongol tribes has been described in about the same terms by every writer on this part of Asia (see Herodotus, iii, 35; Marco Polo, i, 244; Ibn Batuta, ii, 361, 377-379, 387; Bergmann, ii, 82, *et seq.*; Pallas, *Voyages*, i, 503). I will only give Pian de Carpine's description of it (616): "They (*i. e.*, the Mongols) have round tent-like dwellings (*stationes*), made of twigs and small sticks. In the top they have a round opening which admits the light, and by which the smoke can escape, for they keep a fire always in the centre. The sides and roof are covered over with felt, and the doors are also made of felt. Some dwellings are large, some small, according to the importance or poverty of the people. Some of them can be taken down and put up in a moment, and are always carried on pack animals; while others cannot be taken apart, and are carried on carts; one ox hitched to the cart could haul the smaller ones: the larger require three, four, or more, according to their size; and wherever they go, either to war or elsewhere, they take them along with them."

The custom of carrying set-up tents on carts, which at one time or another has obtained among various peoples and tribes of Northern Asia, is noted by Hesiod (Goettling's ed., 33); by Herodotus (iv, 46); by Hippocrates (*De aere, aqua et locis*, 44, 353) (this last-named author mentioning a detail not found elsewhere, that the Scythian carts had four and even six wheels); Strabo (i, 104, 249, *et pas.*); Pomponius Mela (i, 619); and many other classical writers also speak of them. Ammianus Marcellinus, xxii, 176, tells us the Alans had their cart-tents covered with bark (*corticibus tectis*).

Chinese annals state that a great branch of the Turkish nation was known to them in the first centuries of the Christian era as the *Kao-ch'ê*," or "High carts;" on account, it is said, of the high-wheeled felt-covered carts in which they lived, but the characters with which the name is written are purely phonetic. These Kao-ch'ê, who at a later period were called by them T'ieh-lê, or K'i-lê, comprised the Kirghiz, the Uigurs, the Alans, the Karluks, nearly all the tribes, in fact, called Oguz Turks by Mohammedan writers (*T'ang shu*, bk. 257; Ma Tuan lin, bks. 344, 347). In the twelfth and early part of the thirteenth centuries, a branch of these Kao-ch'ê lived to the north-east of the Caspian, around the Aral lake. They were known to mediæval Mohammedan writers as the Kankalis, or Kankly, a name

And they make these houses so large that they are sometimes thirty feet in width. I myself once measured the width between the wheel-tracks of a cart xx feet, and when the house was on the cart it projected beyond the wheels on either side v feet at least. I have myself counted to one cart xxii oxen drawing one house, eleven abreast across the width of the cart, and the other eleven before them. The axle of the cart was as large as the mast of a ship, and one man stood in the entry of the house on the cart driving the oxen.[1]

Furthermore they weave light twigs into squares of the size of a large chest, and over it from one end to the other they put a turtle-back also of twigs, and in the front end they make a little doorway; and then they cover this

---

which Abulghazi (41) says was derived from the Turki word *kang*, "cart," their first father having invented carts. Friar William (265) refers to the Cangle.

*Pei shih* (bk. 94) says that the Kitan tribes of Shih-wei, to the east of Lake Baikal used ox-carts, on which they had straw-covered huts like the felt-covered ones of the Turks (see also Marco Polo, i, 244; Ibn Batuta, ii, 361; Barbaro, 13; Anthony Jenkinson, 52, 55).

In modern times Pallas (*Voyages*, v, 154) notes that he met, near the lower Volga, a band of Tartars or Mankates, who called themselves Kunduran, "like most of the people inhabiting the Kuban, whence they came." "Their Jurts, or Jurtens," he says, "differ in shape and construction from those of the Kalmuks and other Nomadic peoples of Asia. They are not susceptible of being taken to pieces, but they are also lighter, and of a size to be on a cart, that is to say, they are only 8 ft. or 9 ft. in diameter. . . . When they go from one place to another, they put this tent, or cabin, on a two-wheeled cart (*Arba*), so that it rests in front and behind on the shafts, and reaches beyond the wheels on the sides . . . . The rich have two or three cabins, according to the size of their families. These have, besides, a private cart carrying a little kind of house in wood, something like the moveable huts of our shepherds. In these they sleep with their wives. In summer, when they are stopping for any length of time in any one spot with their flocks, they do not take the trouble to take the cabins off the carts . . . . They harness bulls to their carts, usually two, with a third sometimes as leader" (see also Le Bruyn, *Voyages*, i, 305).

Mongol tents of the present time have usually designs in stitchwork on the felt which covers the entry, and Kirghiz tents have broad ornamental bands in fringe and stitchwork around the sides.

[1] These carts must have been exceptionally large ones. Conf. Pian de Carpine's remarks in the preceding note.

coffer or little house with black felt coated with tallow or ewe's milk, so that the rain cannot penetrate it, and they decorate it likewise with embroidery work. And in such coffers they put all their bedding and valuables, and they tie them tightly on high carts drawn by camels, so that they can cross rivers (without getting wet). Such coffers they never take off the cart.

When they set down their dwelling-houses, they always turn the door to the south,[1] and after that they place the carts with coffers on either side near the house at a half stone's throw, so that the dwelling stands between two rows of carts as between two walls. (222) The matrons make for themselves most beautiful (luggage) carts, which I would not know how to describe to you unless by a drawing, and I would depict them all to you if I knew how to paint. A single rich Moal or Tartar has quite c or cc such carts with coffers. Baatu has xxvi wives, each of whom has a large dwelling, exclusive of the other little ones which they set up after the big one, and which are like closets, in which the sewing girls live, and to each of these (large) dwellings are attached quite cc carts.[2] And

---

[1] The tents faced south because the prevailing winds of Northern Asia are westerly. I have often seen Mongol tents facing east and south-east. When camped, as in the narrow valleys south of the Ts'aidam and around the Koko nor, the tents always face down the valley (conf. Bergmann, ii, 96, and Yule, *Marco Polo*, i, 245). It is interesting to find it noted in the *Chou Shu* (bk. 50, 3) that the Khan of the Turks, who lived always on the Tu-kin mountain, had his tent invariably facing south, "so as to show reverence to the sun's rising place."

[2] Ibn Batuta (ii, 413) tells us that one of the wives of the Tartar Khan of the Kipchak, when on a short visit to her father, Andronicus II the Younger, Emperor of Constantinople, though she had left in the Khan's camp most of her women and baggage, had still with her nearly 400 carts, 2,000 horses, 300 oxen, 200 camels, 500 horsemen, 200 young slave-girls, and 20 pages. The Chinese traveller, Ch'ang-chun (1221-1224), speaking of the camp of Ochigin, the younger brother of Chingis Khan, says that it was composed of "several thousands of black carts and felt tents standing in rows." The same traveller tells us of the camp (*ordu*) of one of Chingis' consorts, which was composed of "more than a thousand carts and tents" (Bretschneider, *Med. travel.*, 21, 24).

when they set up their houses, the first wife places her dwelling on the extreme west side, and after her the others according to their rank, so that the last wife will be in the extreme east; and there will be the distance of a stone's throw between the *iurt* of one wife and that of another. The *ordu*[1] of a rich Moal seems like a large town, though there will be very few men in it. One girl will lead xx or xxx carts, for the country is flat, and they tie the ox or camel carts the one after the other, and a girl will sit on the front one driving the ox, and all the others follow after with the same gait. Should it happen that they come to some bad piece of road, they untie them, and take them across one by one. So they go along slowly, as a sheep or an ox might walk.

---

WHEN they have fixed their dwelling, the door turned to the south, they set up the couch of the master on the north side. The side for the women is always the east side, that is to say, on the left

---

[1] *Curia.* Friar William states (267) that he uses this word to render the Mongol term *orda*, a word now usually transcribed *ordu* or *ordo*. Pian de Carpine (609) says, "*orda* means the dwellings (*stationes*) of the emperor and the princes." This interpretation of the word is confirmed by contemporary Mohammedan writers (Quatremère, 21, 23, 98). Chinese writers of the Mongol period translate the word by *hsing kung*, or "moveable palace" (Bretschneider, *Med. travel.*, 25). Palladius (40) says the term *ordo* is, properly speaking, a separate palace of the Khan, under the management of one of his wives. Bergmann (ii, 83) states that among the Kalmuks the word *oergo* (*ordu*) is used to designate either a collection of tents or else the dwelling of a prince or high lama. The Kalmuk terms *oergo*, *garr*, and *kosh*, he adds, correspond to our "palace, house, hut." The *Jihan Kushai* (Quatremère, 54) says the Mongols used the word *iurt* to designate a camp or a dwelling (see also d'Ohsson, i, 83). Friar William, however, is not very careful in the use of the word *curia*; he applies it alike to the camp of a prince, to a single tent—he does not use the word *tentorium* more than two or three times—to the imperial court, as court and as building, in which it is being held. I have therefore translated *curia*, sometimes by the Mongol term *ordu*, sometimes by *iurt*, and other times by *court*. Quatremère (101) is of opinion—and Friar William's use of the word *curia* seems to justify his belief—that the word *ordu* designated originally those tents of the Mongols which were always set up and carried about on ox-carts.

of the house of the master, he sitting on his couch with his face turned to the south. (223) The side for the men is the west side, that is, on the right. Men coming into the house would never hang up their bows on the side of the women.[1]

And over the head of the master is always an image of felt, like a doll or statuette, which they call the brother of the master; another similar one is above the head of the mistress, which they call the brother of the mistress, and they are attached to the wall; and higher up between the two of them is a little lank one (*macilenta*), who is, as it were, the guardian of the whole dwelling. The mistress

---

[1] So firmly established were these rules of etiquette that they were strictly adhered to by the Mongol emperors in their palaces. The same rules still obtain throughout Mongolia, and among the Tartar and Tibetan tent-dwellers. The annexed plan of the interior of a

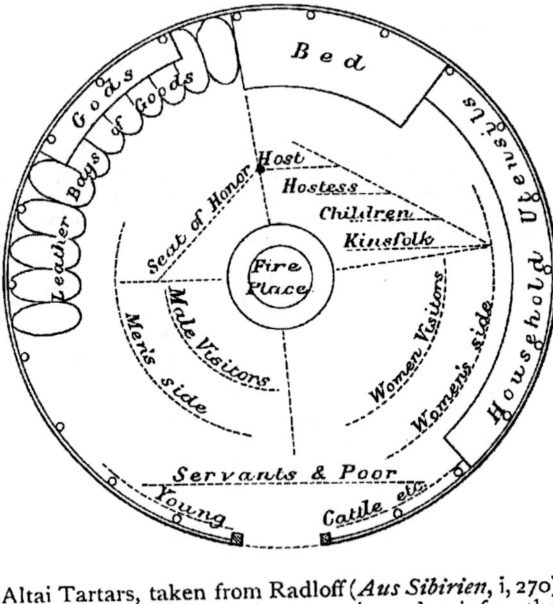


*urt* of Altai Tartars, taken from Radloff (*Aus Sibirien*, i, 270), explains this interior arrangement of the tents (see also *infra*, the description of the ceremonies in the palace at Karakorum, and conf. Pian de Carpine, 745).

places in her house on her right side, in a conspicuous place at the foot of her couch, a goat-skin full of wool or other stuff, and beside it a very little statuette looking in the direction of the attendants and women. Beside the entry on the women's side is yet another image, with a cow's tit for the women, who milk the cows; for it is part of the duty of the women to milk the cows. On the other side of the entry, toward the men, is another statue with a mare's tit for the men who milk the mares.[1]

---

[1] Pian de Carpine (618-620) says: "They have certain idols made of felt in the image of a man, and these they place on either side of the door of their dwelling; and above these they place things made of felt in the shape of tits, and these they believe to be the guardians of their flocks, and that they insure them increase of milk and colts. They make yet others out of silk stuffs, and these they honour greatly. Some persons put these in a handsomely-covered cart before the door of their dwelling, and whoever stealeth anything from that cart is without mercy put to death. Now, when they want to make these idols, all the noble ladies in the camp meet together, and make them with due reverence; and when they have made them they kill a sheep and eat it, and the bones they burn in the fire. And when any child falls ill, they make in this same fashion an idol and tie it over its couch. The chiefs, chiliarchs, and centurions have always a he-goat in their dwellings. To these said idols they offer the first milk of every flock and of every herd of mares; and when they begin to eat or drink, they first offer them of their food or drink. And when they kill any animal, they offer the heart in a bowl to the idol in the cart, and leave it there till the morrow, and then they take it away, cook it and eat it.

"They also make an idol of their first emperor, which they place in a cart in a place of honour before the dwelling, as I saw before the *orda* of the emperor (Kuyuk Khan), and they offer it many gifts; and they offer it also horses, which none may ride till their death. They offer it likewise other animals, and if they kill any of these to eat they break none of their bones, but burn them in the fire. And they bow to it facing the south, as they bow to God" (conf. *supra*, 35, Benedict's account).

Marco Polo (i, 249, ii, 478) informs us that the chief of these "gods" of felt is called *Natigay*, and that the image on his left hand is his wife, and his children those in front of him.

Barbaro (34) says: "The Tartariens worship Images that they carie in their carts, though some there be that use daylie to worship that beast that they happen first to meete whan they go foorthe of their doores."

Passing to modern times, Pallas (*Voyages*, iii, 433, iv, 511) tells us of the "idols dressed like dolls" found in the iurts of the Buriats. These idols, he says, are also found among the Beltire Tartars of the Abakan. When sacrifices are made, their magicians take these idols and bless them. The same traveller (*op. cit.*, iv, 579) speaks of the *Tus*, or

And when they have come together to drink, they first sprinkle with liquor this image which is over the master's head, then the other images in order. Then an attendant goes out of the dwelling with a cup[1] and liquor, and sprinkles three times to the south, each time bending the knee, and that to do reverence to the fire; then to the east, and that to do reverence to the air; then to the west to do reverence to the water; to the north they sprinkle for the dead. When the master takes (224) the cup in hand and is about to drink, he first pours a portion on the ground.

---

household gods of the Tartars of Krasnoyarsk, which they also call *Aimae*. They sacrifice to them little animals, and offer them the skins of the victims, meat, or such other objects as they value or wish to obtain. The idol placed on the east side of the entry of the tent, but outside it, is the representative of an evil deity which they have to propitiate by sacrifices. There is another idol, that of the good deity. On the day of its feast they hold it over the fire, perfuming it with absinth, when it turns red. This idol is kept inside the iurt.

Radloff (*Aus Sibirien*, i, 363), speaking of the Kumandin Tartars, says that on entering one of their huts he found hanging over the window opposite the door five idols. The first with its head upwards was said to be *Sary-kan*, the next one, which resembled it closely, was called *Kyrgys-kan*. The third figure was called *Tös-kanym*, and its head was downwards, while the second had its upwards. The fourth figure was that of *Kudy-kan*, and it was a little larger than the previous ones. As to the fifth, it was called *Kop-kälgän*. The two last-named were provided with moustaches. The owner of the hut did not show any special reverence to these idols, though he asked Radloff not to touch them.

Palladius (15), quoting the *Hei-lung chiang wai chi*, or "Records of the foreign tribes of the Amur country," says: "The Dahurs and Barhus have in their dwellings, according to the number of the male members, puppets made of straw, on which eyes, eyebrows, and mouths are drawn; these puppets are dressed up to the waist. When some one of the family dies his puppet is taken out of the house, and a new puppet is made for every newly-born member of the family. On New Year's Day offerings are made to the puppets, and care is taken not to disturb them by moving them, etc., in order to avoid bringing sickness into the house."

The word *ongot*, *ongon*, or *ongotui*, by which these idols are usually designated among the Tungusic people, appears to be the original of Marco Polo's *Natigay* (Yule, *Marco Polo*, 250; see also Cordier, *Odoric*, 486; d'Ohsson, i, 16; Gombojew, 652).

[1] *Ciphum*. Wooden cups were then as now in general use among all the tribes of northern Asia. Ibn Batuta (ii, 392) refers to "the pretty and light wooden cups" used by the people of the Kipchak in his time.

If he were to drink seated on a horse, he first before he drinks pours a little on the neck or the mane of the horse.[1] Then when the attendant has sprinkled toward the four quarters of the world he goes back into the house, where two attendants are ready with two cups and platters to carry drink to the master and the wife seated near him upon the couch. And when he hath several wives, she with whom he hath slept that night sits beside him in the day, and it becometh all the others to come to her dwelling that day to drink, and court is held there that day, and the gifts which are brought that day are placed in the treasury of that lady.[2] A bench with a skin of milk, or some other drink, and with cups, stands in the entry.[3]

---

[1] The custom of making oblations towards the cardinal points, the zenith and the nadir, is still adhered to by many Mongols and Tibetans. It is noted by the Russian archbishop Peter in 1245 (Matth. Paris, *op. cit.*, iv, 388), and by Pian de Carpine (622) who says they specially reverenced and worshipped the sun, the moon, fire, water, and the earth; in the morning especially they made these libations.

[2] *Mesalek al-absar* (264) referring to the Turks of the Kipchak, has: "Each of the princesses his wives (*i.e.*, of the Khan of Kipchak) collects a portion of the taxes. Each day of the year this prince goes to the house of one of his wives, with whom he passes the day and takes his meals. She presents him with a full suit of clothes, and he gives the clothes he takes off to some favourite courtier." Pian de Carpine (642) says: "When a Tartar has several wives, each has her own tent and household, and he drinks and eats and sleeps with one of them one day, and another day with another. One of them, however, is the greatest among them, and he stops more frequently with her than with the others; and though they are so many they do not often wrangle among themselves."

[3] Pallas (*Voyages*, i, 698) remarks: "The principal piece of furniture of the dirty cabins of the Bashkirds is a big skin or vase of leather in the form of a bottle; it is placed on a wooden stand, and is always full of sour milk, which they call *arjan*." See on *arjan* or *airan*, Rubruck, p. 240 of text.

IN winter they make a capital drink of rice, of millet, and of honey; it is clear as wine: and wine is carried to them from remote parts. In summer they care only for *cosmos*.[1] There is always *cosmos* near the house, before the entry door, and beside it stands a guitar-player with his guitar. Lutes and vielles (225) such as we have I did not see there, but many other instruments which are unknown among us.[2] And when the master begins to drink, then one of the attendants cries with a loud voice, "Ha!" and the guitarist

---

[1] These three kinds of drinks, which Friar William in another passage (335) calls cervoise (beer) of rice, or *terracina*, cervoise of millet, and *boal*, were imported probably from China and the Kipchak, but were certainly not manufactured by the Mongols. The wine they probably got from Persia and from Turkestan. Pian de Carpine (640) states the facts more accurately. He says: "They (the Mongols) drink great quantities of mare's milk, if they have it; they drink also sheep's, goat's, cow's, and camel's milk. Wine, cervoise, and mead (*medonem*, Friar William's *bal*, or *boal?*) they have not, unless it is sent from other nations or is given to them." Ibn Batuta (ii, 408) says of the Kipchak: "The principal drink of the Turks is a wine prepared with honey, for they belong to the hanefite sect and consider the use of wine permissible. When the Sultan wants to drink, his daughter takes the cup in her hand; she salutes her father by bending her knee, then she hands him the cup. When the Sultan has drunk, she takes another cup and hands it the great khatun, who drinks, then she presents it to the other khatuns according to their rank . . . . Finally the inferior emirs rise and serve drink to the sons of the Sultan, and during all the time they sing *nawaliyah* (short songs)" (see also Quatremère, 356). Chinese travellers in the Kipchak in the thirteenth century also refer to the use there made of a "fermented beverage from honey" (Bretschneider, *Med. travel.*, 118). The *cervoise of rice* (*cervisia de risio*) is, of course, Chinese rice wine. *Cosmos* is Marco Polo's *kemiz*, our *kumiz* or *kumiss* (see Yule, *Marco Polo*, i, 250).

[2] The most ancient and commonly-used musical instruments of the Turkish tribes appear to have been the reed-pipe, drum, and several kinds of guitars with four, five, or nine strings (*Pei shih*, bk. 94). Bergmann (ii, 175) says the Kalmuks use the drum, a kind of zither, the flute, and a violin. Radloff (*Aus Sibirien*, i, 381) states that the Tartars of the Altai have a reed-pipe, a guitar, a kind of violin called *kobys*, a horizontal harp (zither?) called *tyattagan*. I have never seen an instrument of the latter description used by Mongols, though instruments of this description are employed in China, Japan, and Korea. See also F. Grenard (*Haute Asie*, ii, 136, *et seq.*); and Clarke (53), who says the commonest instrument among the Kalmuks is a two-stringed lute (*balalaika*).

strikes his guitar, and when they have a great feast they all clap their hands, and also dance about to the sound of the guitar, the men before the master, the women before the mistress. And when the master has drunken, then the attendant cries as before, and the guitarist stops. Then they drink all around, and sometimes they do drink right shamefully and gluttonly.[1] And when they want to challenge anyone to drink, they take hold of him by the ears, and pull so as to distend his throat, and they clap and dance before him. Likewise, when they want to make a great feasting and jollity with someone, one takes a full cup, and two others are on his right and left, and thus these three come singing and dancing towards him who is to take the cup, and they sing and dance before him ; and when he holds out his hand to take the cup, they quickly draw it back, and then again they come back as before, and so they elude him three or four times by drawing away the cup, till he hath become well excited and is in good appetite, and then they give him the cup, and while he drinks they sing and clap their hands and strike with their feet.[2]

Of their food and victuals you must know that they (226) eat all their dead animals without distinction, and with such flocks and herds it cannot be but that many animals die.[3] Nevertheless, in summer, so long as lasts

---

[1] Pian de Carpine (637) goes so far as to say that drunkenness was honourable among the Mongols. At all events, now, as in old times, this people has shown a strong taste for drink. Friar William, in the course of his narrative, frequently refers to this fact.

[2] Gombojew (664) says it is still customary among the Mongols to sing when bringing a guest wine.

[3] Pian de Carpine (638) says : "Their food is everything that can be eaten ; for they eat dogs, wolves, foxes and horses, and when pushed by necessity, human flesh. They also eat *abluviones quae egrediuntur de iumentis cum pullis*. I have also seen them eat lice, saying : "Why should I not eat them that eat my son's flesh and drink his blood?" I have seen them also eat rats. They use neither tablecloths nor napkins. They have no bread nor oil nor vegetables, nothing but

their *cosmos*, that is to say mare's milk, they care not for any other food. So then if it happens that an ox or a horse dies, they dry its flesh by cutting it into narrow strips and hanging it in the sun and the wind, where at once and without salt it becomes dry without any evil

---

meat, of which, however, they eat so little that other people could scarcely exist on it.

"They get their hands covered with the grease of the meat, but when they have finished eating they wipe them on their boots, on the grass, or something else, though the more refined among them have some little bits of cloth with which they wipe their hands when they have finished eating. One of them takes the food (out of the kettle), and another takes the pieces of meat from him on the point of a knife, and gives to each one: to some more, to others less, as they wish to show them more or less honour" (see also Gombojew, 659).

The habits of the Mongols are to-day exactly what they were in Friar William's time. I may add that it is usual when one has finished eating anything out of the little wooden bowl each one carries with him, to lick it clean and put it back in the folds of one's gown.

The charge of cannibalism was frequently made against the Mongols by mediæval writers. The Russian Archbishop, Peter, stated, in 1245, before the Council of Lyons, that the Mongols "eat the flesh of mares, and dogs, and other abominations, and even when necessary human flesh, not raw, however, but cooked; they drink blood, or water, or milk" (Matth. Paris, iv, 386-389). See also the letter of Ivo of Narbonne in 1243 to the Archbishop of Bordeaux (*ibid.*, iv, 273), and the Introductory Notice, *supra.*

Joinville (147) states that the Mongols carried their uncooked meat "entre leurs celles et leur paniaus (horse blankets), quant le sanc en est bien hors; si la manjuent toute crue." This idea that the Mongols cooked their meat under their saddles is as old as Ammianus Marcellinus at least. He says (xxxi, 347), speaking of the Huns, "they are satisfied with wild roots for food, or with the flesh of the first animal they find; they mortify it for a while on their horse between their thighs" (conf. Schiltberger, 48). Coming down to more recent times, we read in Busbeck (*Epistolæ*, 385) that some Goths of the Crimea told him that the Tartars ate the raw flesh of dead horses, and that they put bits under the saddles of their horses, which they ate with delight when it had become heated by the bodies of the horses (see also Gombojew, 657; and Clarke, 52, 70).

While there is no doubt that the Mongols, like the Chinese, will eat horses, camels, or cattle which have died naturally, I doubt whether they ever do it except *faute de mieux*. Bergmann (ii, 116) agrees with this view; see, however Tott (i, 349). Pallas (*Voyages*, i, 512) says they have the greatest aversion for wolf's flesh, and in fact for that of all other small carnivorous animals.

I may note here, in connection with the Mongols' way of eating, that they never take the scum off the pot in which meat is boiling, but eat it with the meat, holding it to be the choicest juice and essence of the meat. This custom I find noted by John de Luca in his *Relation des Tartares* (Thevenot, i, 28; and also Rockhill, *Diary*, 207).

smell.[1] With the intestines of horses they make sausages[2] better than pork ones, and they eat them fresh. The rest of the flesh they keep for winter. With the hides of oxen they make big jars, which they dry in admirable fashion in the smoke.[3] With the hind part of the hide of horses they make most beautiful shoes. With the flesh of a single sheep they give to eat to L men or C; for they cut it up very fine in a platter with salt and water,[4] for they make no other sauce; and then with the point of a knife or a fork which they make for the purpose, like that which we use to eat coddled pears or apples, they give to each of the bystanders a mouthful or two according to the number of the guests. Prior to this, before the flesh of the sheep is served, the master takes what pleases him; and furthermore if he gives to anyone a special piece, it is the custom that he who receives it shall eat it himself, and he may not give it to another; but if he cannot eat it all he carries it off with him, or gives it to his servant if he be present, (227) who keeps it; otherwise he puts it away in his *captargac*, which is a square bag which they carry to put such things in, in which they store away bones when

---

[1] Sun-dried meat is used in Mongolia and among the nomads of Tibet. It is usually eaten without any other preparation.

[2] *Andulges*, in French *andouilles*. Bergmann (ii, 129) says that the Tartar horse-sausages surpass all others. They are made of blood or pieces of the intestines (*mangenstücken*). *Andouille* is made in the same way.

[3] Pallas (*Voyages*, i, 516) describes in detail the manufacture of these leather vessels, which are made both of horse and of ox hides, the latter being the better. "They leave them in the smoke," he says, "two, three, or even four days, when they become as translucid as horn." Radloff (*Aus Sibirien*, i, 425) says that among the Kirghiz they are called *saba*, and that they hold four to six buckets (see also Rockhill, *Diary*, 172). Those I have there described are of a more primitive make.

[4] Ibn Batuta (ii, 407) describing a feast given by the Khan of the Kipchak, says that a golden or silver ladle containing salt dissolved in water was put on each table. Salt dissolved in a little pot-liquor is, at the present day, placed before the guests at a Mongol meal. The most honoured guest will receive the brisket or the tail of the sheep, these being the choicest pieces (conf. Bergmann, ii, 128).

they have not time to gnaw them well, so that they can gnaw them later and that nothing of the food be lost.[1]

This *cosmos*, which is mare's milk, is made in this wise. They stretch a long rope on the ground fixed to two stakes stuck in the ground, and to this rope they tie toward the third hour the colts of the mares they want to milk. Then the mothers stand near their foal, and allow themselves to be quietly milked; and if one be too wild, then a man takes the colt and brings it to her, allowing it to suck a little; then he takes it away and the milker takes its place. When they have got together a great quantity of milk, which is as sweet as cow's as long as it is fresh, they pour it into a big skin or bottle, and they set to churning it with a stick prepared for that purpose, and which is as big as a man's head at its lower extremity and hollowed out; and when they have beaten it sharply it begins to boil up like new wine and to sour or ferment, and they continue to churn it until they have extracted the butter. Then they taste it, and when it is mildly pungent,

---

[1] Joinville (148) speaking of the way of eating of the Tartars, remarks: "Ce que il ne peuent manger jetent en un sac de cuir; et quant il ont fain, si oevrent le sac, et manguent touzjours le plus viex devant: dont je vi un Coramyn (Korasmian) qui fu des gens l'empereour de Perse, qui nous gardoit en la prison, que quant il ouvroit son sac nous nous bouchions (le nez), que nous ne pouvions durer, pour la puueisie (puanteur) qui issoit du sac." The Dutch envoys to Peking, in 1654, having been at an imperial banquet at which Mongol chiefs were also present, noted that "it was a pleasure to see these famished Tartars filling their leather pouches or skins with the hair still on" (Nieuhoff, *Embassy*, 53-59). It is still customary among the Mongols for the guests to dispose of all the food placed before them. If one cannot eat all that is given him, he may give it to the bystanders, or else he will store it away in his gown. I have never seen them use a bag of the description referred to. *Kabtaga*, or *kabtagan*, means "pouch or bag" in Mongol; and Mr. F. Grenard has kindly informed me that in Turki works of the fifteenth or sixteenth centuries he has found the word *K'aptorghai*, meaning "pouch, large purse," and sometimes "cartridge case." Pian de Carpine (640) notes that "it is a great sin among them to allow any portion of drink or food to be lost: so they may not give a bone to the dogs unless they have previously taken the marrow out of it." The same habit obtains to-day among the Mongols and Kirghiz.

they drink it.[1] It is pungent on the tongue like rapé wine when drunk, and when a man has finished drinking, it leaves a taste of milk of almonds on the tongue, and it makes the inner man most joyful and also intoxicates weak heads (228), and greatly provokes urine. They also make *caracosmos*,[2] that is "black *cosmos*," for the use of the great lords. It is for the following reason that mare's milk curdles not. It is a fact that (the milk) of no animal will curdle in the stomach of whose fetus is not found curdled milk.[3] In the stomach of mares' colts it is not found, so the milk of mares curdles not. They churn then the milk until all the thicker parts go straight to the bottom, like the dregs of wine, and the pure part remains on top, and it is like whey or white must. The dregs are very white, and they are given to the slaves, and they provokes much to sleep.[4] This clear (liquor) the lords drink, and it is assuredly a most agreeable drink and most efficacious. Baatu has XXX men around his camp at a day's distance, each of whom sends him every day such milk of a hundred mares, that is to say every day the milk of three thousand mares, exclusive of the other white milk which they carry to others.[5] As in Syria the peasants give a

---

1 On the preparation of *kumiss*, Friar William's *cosmos*, conf. Yule (*Marco Polo*, i, 249); Pallas, (*Voyages*, i, 506, 511); and Atkinson (*Western Siberia*, 287).

2 Yule (*Marco Polo*, i, 252) says that "black kumiss" is mentioned in Wassaf. Bretschneider (*Med. Geog.*, 249) says Chinese mediæval writers sometimes call the Kipchak *Ha-la-chih* (Turkish, *kalladj*, "black"), because the people sent black mare's milk as a present to the Mongol emperors. I have found no other references to this beverage, nor is it, I think, known at the present day. An alcoholic drink called *araka*, or *areki*, is distilled by the Mongols from kumiss (Pallas, *Voyages*, i, 510).

3 *Regula enim est quod nullius animalis in cujus fetus ventre lac non invenitur coagulum coagulatur.* Previous translators have all failed to understand this passage.

4 These dregs are called *bossa* by the Kalmuks; they are also used in tanning skins (Pallas, *Voyages*, i, 511).

5 Pian de Carpine (671) refers to the Emperor's herds of mares for milking; and Marco Polo (i, 291) says: "the Khan keeps an immense

third of their produce, so it is these (Tartars) must bring to the *ordu* of their lords the milk of every third day. As to cow's milk they first extract the butter, then they boil it down perfectly dry, after which they put it away (229) in sheep paunches which they keep for that purpose; and they put no salt in the butter, for on account of the great boiling down it spoils not. And they keep this for the winter.[1] What remains of the milk after the butter they let sour as much as can be, and they boil it, and it curdles in boiling, and the curd they dry in the sun, and it becomes as hard as iron slag, and they put it away in bags for the winter. In winter time, when milk fails them, they put this sour curd, which they call *gruit*, in a skin and pour water on it, and churn it vigorously till it dissolves in the water, which is made sour by it, and this water they drink instead of milk.[2] They are most careful not to drink pure water.

The great lords have villages in the south, from which millet and flour are brought to them for the winter. The poor procure (these things) by trading sheep and pelts. The slaves fill their bellies with dirty water, and with this they are content. They catch also rats, of which many kinds

---

stud of white horses and mares; in fact more than 10,000 of them, and all pure white without a speck. The milk of the mares is drunk by himself and his family, and by none else."

[1] The Mongols of the present day prepare and keep their butter in the same way. Bergmann (ii, 121) remarks that they make butter of cow's, ewe's or mare's milk, but the soft mare's milk butter does not keep as well as the other two kinds.

[2] In another passage Friar William more correctly transcribes the name *grut*. It is the *kurt* of the Kirghiz (Radloff, *Aus Sibirien*, i, 428), the *kurut* of the Afghans, the *chura* of the Tibetans. Marco Polo (i, 254) says of it: "They also have milk dried into a paste to carry with them, and when they need food they put this in water and beat it up till it dissolves, and then drink it." This drink is called *shuurmik* among some of the Tartars (Pallas, *Voyages*, i, 511, 699; see also Radloff, *op. cit.*, i, 298; Yule, *Marco Polo*, i, 257; and Tott, i, 333). In the Koko nor country and Tibet, this *krut* or *chura* is put in tea to soften, and then eaten either alone or mixed with parched barley meal (*tsamba*).

abound here. Rats with long tails they eat not, but give them to their birds.[1] They eat mice and all kinds of rats which have short tails. There are also many marmots, which are called *sogur*, and which congregate in one hole in winter, XX or XXX together, and sleep for six months; these (230) they catch in great numbers.[2] There are also conies,[3] with a long tail like a cat's, and on the end of the tail they have black and white hairs. They have also many other kinds of small animals good to eat, which they know very well how to distinguish. I saw no deer there. I saw few hares, many gazelles. Wild asses I saw in great numbers, and these are like mules. I saw also another kind of animal which is called *arcali*,[4] which has quite the body of a sheep, and horns bent like a ram's, but of such size that I could hardly lift the two horns with one hand, and they make of these horns big cups. They have hawks and peregrine falcons[5] in great numbers, which they all carry on their right hand. And they always put a little thong around the hawk's neck, which hangs down to the middle of its breast, by which, when they cast it at its

---

1 Here, of course, their hawks, eagles (*barkut*), and other hunting birds are meant. The best hawks appear to have come from the Upper Yenisei and the Lower Amur (d'Ohsson, i, 104).

2 Probably the *Mus citillus*, the *suslik* of the Russians, which Pallas says the Mongols are very fond of eating. He says also that they like the flesh of badgers and marmots (*Voyages*, i, 197, 512). Mr. Grenard tells me that *soghur*, more usually written *sour* in Turki, is the ordinary name of the marmot.

3 *Cuniculi.* Marco Polo (i, 244) states that the Mongols are very fond of "Pharaoh's rats," which is supposed to be some variety of gerboa.

4 On p. 278 he gives the correct Mongol name, *culan* (*khulan*), of this animal. He is the first western traveller to mention it by that name, and the same remark applies to the *argali*, the *Ovis Poli*. Marco Polo (i, 181) speaks of the wild sheep of Badakshan, whose horns were "good six palms in length" (see Yule's remarks, *op. cit.*, i, 185).

5 *Falcones, girfaus erodios* (or *herodios*). Bergeron has rendered the latter term by "herodiens et faucons." The same words occur, however, in Marco Polo; and Yule (i, 262), renders them, no doubt correctly, by "peregrine falcons" (see Ducange, 1131, s. v. *Herodius*).

prey, they pull down with the left hand the head and breast of the hawk, so that it be not struck by the wind and carried upward. So it is that they procure a large part of their food by the chase.[1]

Of their clothing and customs you must know, that from Cataia, and other regions of the east, and also from Persia and other regions of the south, (231) are brought to them silken and golden stuffs and cloth of cotton, which they wear in summer.[2] From Ruscia, Moxel, and from greater Bulgaria and Pascatir, which is greater Hungary, and Kerkis,[3] all of which are countries to the north and full of forests, and which obey them, are brought to them costly furs of many kinds, which I never saw in our parts, and which they wear in winter. And they always make in winter at least two fur gowns, one with the fur against the body, the other with the fur outside exposed to the wind and snow; these latter are usually of the skins of wolves or foxes or papions;[4] and while they sit in the dwelling they have

---

[1] Falconry is still a favourite amusement among the Mongols, Kirghiz, and the Manchus of China. At the present day hawks are carried on the left hand, if small, or on the left forearm if the birds are large (see Marco Polo, i, 384, 388; Yule, *Cathay*, 135; Bergmann, ii, 187; Radloff, *Aus Sibirien*, i, 466; and Rockhill, *Diary*, 13). Anthony Jenkinson (73) says the Tartars used to kill wild horses with their hawks.

[2] *Panni serici et aurei et tele de wambasio.* The first is probably the same as the stuff called *nacchetti di seta e d'oro* by Pegolotti, which, he says, western traders went all the way to China to get (Heyd, ii, 698); and which Friar William in another passage (317) calls *nasic.* The *tele de wambasio* (or *bombasio*) is called elsewhere by our traveller *tele de cotone*; Joinville (107) also speaks of "*telle de coton.*" Heyd (ii, 612) mentions the cotton of Asia Minor, Persia, India, and Egypt as the most esteemed in the Middle Ages; the cotton fabrics of Persia and India were especially fine.

[3] Kerkis in this passage designates the Kirghiz; elsewhere our author uses the same word as the name of the Cherkess.

[4] *Papionibus.* In another passage (315) he says Mangu Khan sent him three gowns, *de pellibus papionum.* The *papion*—for the word is still used in French—is a baboon, the *cynocephalus papion.* I cannot imagine, however, that monkey skins were ever much used as furs among the Mongols; the supply must have been small, the cost considerable. There is a species of baboon, I believe, found in the

another lighter one. The poor make their outside (gowns) of dog and kid (skins).

When they want to chase wild animals, they gather together in a great multitude and surround the district in which they know the game to be, and gradually they come closer to each other till they have shut up the game in among them as in an enclosure, and then they shoot them with their arrows.[1] They make also breeches with furs.[2] The rich furthermore wad their clothing with silk stuffing, which is extraordinarily soft, light and warm. The poor line their clothes with cotton cloth, or with the fine wool which they are able to pick out of the coarser. With this coarser they make felt to cover their houses and coffers, and also for bedding. With wool and a (232) third of horse hair mixed with it they make their ropes. They also

---

mountains north of Peking, and another kind of monkey, with long reddish hair on parts of its body, in Eastern Tibet and Ssŭ-ch'uan. The skin of the latter is used as a fur by the Chinese, though not commonly. I am inclined to thind that the papion of Friar Rubruck was a badger, or some variety of fox. Ibn Batuta (ii, 401) says the most prized fur in the Kipchak was ermine, next sable, then grey squirrel. Ibn Alathir (xiv, 456) speaks of the Kipchak selling at Sudak *borthasi* or black fox, beaver, grey squirrel, or other furs.

[1] On the great hunts of the Mongols, see Marco Polo (i, 384, 386-388); Yule (*Cathay*, i, 135); and d'Ohsson (i, 321).

[2] The Mongols of the present day commonly wear in winter trousers of sheep or lamb skins, with the wool on the inside. The Kirghiz wear in riding huge baggy trousers called *chimbar*, into which they tuck their gowns. Pian de Carpine (614) thus describes the Mongol dress: "The clothes of the men and women are of one pattern. They do not use capes, cloaks, hoods, or skins (*pellibus*); but they wear tunics of bukeran, purple or baldakin, made in the following fashion. They are open from top to bottom, and double over the breast; on the left side they are fastened with a tape, and on the right with three, and furthermore on the left side they are open to the armpit. They make fur gowns of all kinds after the same pattern; but they wear the outside fur gown with the fur outside, and it is open behind, with a tail down to the knees."

The purple, baldakin, and bukeran, of Friar John are probably, as pointed out by d'Avezac (525), Rubruck's "silk and gold stuff, and cloth of cotton." Though there seems little doubt that *bukeran* was a light cotton or stuff, muslin our author (290) speaks of a stiff bukeran (*stamina rigidata*). (See also Yule *Marco Polo*, i, 48, and *supra*, p. 19).

make with felt covers, saddle-cloths and rain cloaks; so they use a great deal of wool.[1] You have seen the costume of the men.

The men shave a square on the tops of their heads, and from the front corners (of this square) they continue the shaving to the temples, passing along both sides of the head. They shave also the temples and the back of the neck to the top of the cervical cavity, and the forehead as far as the crown of the head, on which they leave a tuft of hair which falls down to the eyebrows. They leave the hair on the sides of the head, and with it they make tresses which they plait together to the ears.[2]

And the dress of the girls differs not from the costume of the men, except that it is somewhat longer. But on the day following her marriage, (a woman) shaves the front half of her head, and puts on a tunic as wide as a nun's

---

[1] Felt is still applied to all these and many other purposes by the Mongols. They mix horse-hair with the wool in making ropes, so that they may not stretch when wet, and to prevent them from getting kinkled. On the manufacture of felt, see Atkinson (*Upper and Lower Amoor*, 42), and Rockhill (*Ethnology*, 700).

[2] Vincent of Beauvais (bk. xxix, ch. lxxi, 420*a*) says: "They shave across the top of the head and both temples to the ears, so that the shaved part of the head has the shape of a horseshoe. They also shave the back part. The rest of the hair they wear long and make into plaits behind the ears. And all those among them shave their heads in this fashion, whether they be Romans (*i.e.*, Greeks), Saracens, or others." Pian de Carpine (611) describes the Mongols as follows: "They differ in their appearance from all the rest of mankind, for they are broader between the eyes and cheeks than other men, and their cheekbones stand out a good deal from the jaws. Their noses are flat and small; they have small eyes, with lids drawn up to the eyebrows. They are usually small in the waist, a few only excepted; nearly all are of short stature. Nearly all of them have but very little beard; a few have some hairs on their upper lip and as a beard, and this they never shave. They wear crowns (of hair) on the tops of their heads, like clerks (among us), and from one ear to the other, for a width of about three fingers, they shave it all as a general thing, right round the crown. On their foreheads they shave off all (the hair) for a space of two fingers in breadth; the hair left behind the crown and the shaven part (on the forehead) they let grow down to the eyebrows, while they let the hair on either side grow longer than in front. The rest of their hair they let grow like women, making two plaits of it, tying them each behind the ear. They have also small feet."

gown, but everyway larger and longer, open before, and tied on the right side. For in this the Tartars differ from the Turks; the Turks tie their gowns on the left, the Tartars always on the right.[1] Furthermore they have a head-dress, which they call *bocca*, made of bark, or such other light material as they can find, and it is big and as much as two hands can span around, and is a cubit and more high, and square like the capital of a column. This *bocca* they cover (233) with costly silk stuff, and it is hollow inside, and on top of the capital, or the square on it, they put a tuft of quills or light canes also a cubit or more in length. And this tuft they ornament at the top with peacock feathers, and round the edge (of the top) with feathers from the mallard's tail, and also with precious stones. The wealthy ladies wear such an ornament on their heads, and fasten it down tightly with an amess, for which there is an opening in the top for that purpose, and inside they stuff their hair, gathering it together on the back of the tops of their heads in a kind of knot, and putting it in the *bocca*, which they afterwards tie down tightly under the chin.[2] So it is that when several ladies are riding together,

---

[1] The Mongols, Chinese, Japanese, Tibetans, and I believe most of the other nations of northern Asia of the present day, fold their gowns to the right across them. The Chinese annals of the sixth century note the peculiar habit of the Turkish tribes, of folding their gowns across them to the left. "They button to the left (*tso jên*)," the *Chou shu*, bk. 50, 3, says of them.

[2] Vincent of Beauvais (bk. xxix, ch. lxxxv, 421*b*), describes the *bogtak*, but does not mention it by its name. Plan de Carpine (614) says: "Married women wear a very full gown, open in front down to the ground. On their heads they wear a round thing made of twigs or bark, and it is an ell in height, and finishes on top in a square; and it grows in size all the way up to the top, and on the summit of it is a long slender rod of gold, silver or wood, or else a feather. And it is fastened on to a felt cap (*pillolum*) which reaches to the shoulders: and the cap as well as this thing is covered with bukeran or purple or baldakin; and they never go before men without this thing (*instrumentum*) on, and by it they are distinguished from other women. The maidens and young women can be distinguished from the men with great difficulty, for in all respects they are dressed like them. They

and one sees them from afar, they look like soldiers, helmets on head and lances erect. For this *bocca* looks like a helmet, and the tuft above it is like a lance. And all the women sit their horses astraddle like men. And they tie their gowns with a piece of blue silk stuff at the waist and they wrap another band at the breasts, and tie a piece of white stuff below the eyes which hangs down to the breast.[1] And the women there are wonderfully fat, and she who has the least nose is held the most beautiful. They disfigure themselves horribly by painting their

---

(*i.e.*, the men) have caps which are not like those of other nations, but we are unable to clearly describe their shapes."

Quatremère (102) quotes a number of Persian authors who use the word *bogtak* to distinguish the head-dress worn exclusively by Mongol princesses (see also Ibn Batuta, ii, 379, 388 ; Cordier, *Odoric*, 369, 409 ; Yule, *Cathay*, 131 ; and Clavijo, 154). Such high head-dresses seem to have been worn at various times by many Asiatic peoples or tribes ; whether they were quite like the Mongol *bogtak* or not I am unable to say. *Wei shu* (bk. 102, 13), speaking of an Uigur people called the Yen-ta, says : "It was the custom of the Yen-ta for brothers to have the same wife : if a man had no brothers, his wife wore a head-dress (or cap) with but one horn. If he had brothers, she added as many points (or horns) as he had brothers." Yüan-chuang describes in about the same terms the head-dress of the women of Himatala, who may, by the way, be the Yen-ta of the Wei shu (Julien, *Voyages*, ii, 197). The nearest modern approach to the Mongol *bogtak* seems to me to be the high head-dress, covered with bark or red cloth, of the Votiak women of Kasan (Pallas, *Voyages*, v, 32). We find another head-dress of like description, which may owe its origin to the *bogtak*, worn at the present time by the Christian women of Urfah, between Diarbekir and Aleppo (Percy Badger, i, 329). The head-dress of the Kirghiz women, and the high Flemish head-dress called *hennin*, introduced into France by Isabeau de Bavière, should not be omitted in this enumeration.

[1] Vincent of Beauvais (bk. xxix, ch. lxxxv, 421*b*) describes the gorgeous harness of the big stout palfreys the rich Mongol ladies rode. "All the wives of great Barons," he says, "are dressed in samites or golden purples (*purpuris deauratis*), as are their husbands. Usually, however, all women are clothed in boqueram (gowns) made with many plaits at the waist . . . . They have also another kind of gown of white woollen stuff (*panno laneo albo*), which all Tartars put on over their clothes when it rains and in winter." Vincent is here quoting from Friar Simon of St. Quentin. The Mongols referred to lived in Asia Minor or Persia. The Kirghiz women still cover their faces when riding and exposed to the cutting wind.

faces.[1] They never lie down in bed when having their children.[2]

(234) It is the duty of the women to drive the carts, get the dwellings on and off them, milk the cows, make butter and *gruit*, and to dress and sew skins, which they do with a thread made of tendons. They divide the tendons into fine shreds, and then twist them into one long thread. They also sew the boots, the socks and the clothing.[3] They never wash clothes, for they say that God would be angered thereat, and that it would thunder if they hung them up to dry.[4] They will even beat those they find washing them. Thunder they fear extraordinarily; and

---

[1] Conf., *infra*, his description of Scatay's wife. The custom of rubbing the face with unguents, usually black, to protect the skin from the effects of the wind, has been practised in northern Asia for a long time. As early as the seventh century, we hear of it obtaining in Tibet (Rockhill, *Land of the Lamas*, 214).

[2] The Kalmuk women have their children in a crouching position; the Kirghiz bring forth theirs kneeling (H. Ploss, *Das Weib.*, ii, 276). In China, Japan, Mongolia and Tibet, a crouching position is, I believe, the rule. Pallas (*Voyages*, i, 570), says that when a Kalmuk woman is in childbirth, a lama is called in who reads prayers, while the husband stretches a net round the outside of the tent, and beats the air with a club till the child is born; crying the while *gart chetkir*, "be off, devil!"

[3] Pian de Carpine (643) says: "The maids and women ride and race on horseback as skilfully as the men; we saw them also carrying bows and arrows. The women are able to stay on horseback for a very long time as well as the men; they ride with very short stirrups. They take good care of their horses, but then they are careful of all their things. Their women do all the work: they make the fur gowns, the clothes, the shoes and boots, and everything else that is made of leather. They drive the carts and load *(reparant)* them, they load the camels, and they are most active and strong in all their work. All the women wear trowsers *(femoralia)*, and some of them shoot with the bow like men." All writers of the period state that the Mongol women accompanied the men into the battles, were fine archers, and fought as bravely as they (Matth. Paris, iv, 388; d'Ohsson, i, 329). The domestic duties of the Mongol women are the same to-day as they were in Friar William's time (see Bergmann, ii, 165-167, and Radloff, *Aus Sibirien*, i, 295-297).

[4] Conf. d'Ohsson, i, 409; ii, 93. The Mongols of the present day still have this superstition (Rockhill, *Diary*, 154, 207). Rashideddin says that they believed any liquor spilt in the tent, or wet boots put to dry in the sun, would attract lightning (d'Ohsson, ii, 618).

when it thunders they will turn out of their dwellings all strangers, wrap themselves in black felt, and thus hide themselves till it has passed away.[1] Furthermore, they never wash their bowls, but when the meat is cooked they rinse out the dish in which they are about to put it with some of the boiling broth from the kettle, which they pour back into it.[2] They also make the felt and cover the houses.[3]

The men make bows and arrows, manufacture stirrups and bits, make saddles, do the carpentering on (the framework of) their dwellings and the carts; they take care of the horses, milk the mares, churn the *cosmos* or mare's milk, make the skins in which it is put; they also look after the camels and load them. Both sexes look after the sheep and goats, sometimes the men, othertimes the women, milking them.[4]

They dress skins with a thick mixture of sour ewe's

---

[1] Pian de Carpine (632) says: "If anyone is killed by thunder, all the people who were in the camp (at the time) must pass through fire. The tent, bed, cart, felt and clothing, and everything of the kind they have will be touched by no one till they have been purified." Schiltberger (50) says that among the Tartars a man killed by lightning was held to be a saint.

[2] Pian de Carpine (639) says: "They never wash their bowls, and if sometimes they rinse them out with the pot liquor, they pour it back into the pot on the meat. In like fashion they wash their pots and cooking utensils." The Mongols still follow this expeditious plan. They never wash the pails in which they keep milk or curd: it would bring bad luck; but they leave on the inside a thick crust of hardened curd, mixed with hair and dung (conf. Atkinson, *Western Siberia*, 286; see also *supra*, p. 64).

[3] *Cooperiunt domos.* By this, I take it, is to be understood that the women put the sheets of felt in place over the framework of the tents each time they were set up. I have not noticed that this work was exclusively reserved to the women among the Mongols of the present day.

[4] Pian de Carpine (643) says: "The men look after nothing at all but their arrows, though they give a little attention to the flocks. They hunt and practise archery: for all of them from the smallest to the biggest are good archers, and as soon as their children are two or three years old they begin to ride, to manage horses, and to race. And they give them bows according to their age, and teach them to shoot: they are very agile and daring."

milk and salt.[1] When they want to wash their hands or head, they fill their mouths (235) with water, which they let trickle on to their hands, and in this way they also wet their hair and wash their heads.[2]

As to their marriages, you must know that no one among them has a wife unless he buys her; so it sometimes happens that girls are well past marriageable age before they marry, for their parents always keep them until they sell them. They observe the first and second degrees of consanguinity, but no degree of affinity; thus (one person) will have at the same time or successively two sisters.[3] Among them no widow marries, for the following

---

[1] *Lacte ovium acetoso inspissato et salso.* Pallas (*Voyages*, i, 514) says that the Kalmuk women tan skins with the residuum of milk left after the distillation of *araka* and a little salt. The skins are afterwards softened and smoked. "Sometimes," he adds, "they use a mixture of ashes and salt water, and after the skins have been dried and smoked, they are rubbed with a mixture of putrid sheep or ox liver and milk." The Mongols and Tibetans of the Koko nor country soften the skins with sour cream.

[2] This mode of washing the face and hands is still in vogue in Mongolia and northern China. Persian authors say that the *Yassak*, or Ordinances of Chingis Khan, ordered all Mongols not to put their hands in any water, but to take it up in their mouths to wash with (Quatremère, *op. cit.*, 436).

[3] Vincent of Beauvais (bk. xxix, ch. lxxvi, 420*b*) states that a Tartar did not consider a woman his wife till she had conceived or borne a child. If she proved barren, he might send her away. Furthermore, a husband did not get the wife's dower till she had borne him a son, nor did the woman receive it from her father and mother till she had a child.

Pian de Carpine (612) says of the Mongols' marriage customs: "Each one hath as many wives as he can support; some have a hundred, some fifty, some ten, some more, others fewer. And as a general rule they marry all their relatives except their own mother, their daughters and sisters by the same mother. They may however marry their sisters through their father, and also their father's wives after his death. A younger brother, or some other younger member of the family, is expected on the death of his elder to take the brother's wife. All other women without any distinction they take as wives, and they buy them right dearly from their parents. After the death of their husbands (the women) do not easily make second marriages, except some one wishes to take his step-mother as a wife" (see also Marco Polo, i, 222, 245; Radloff, *op. cit.*, i, 476; and Rockhill, *Diary*, 156). The Chinese annals attribute the above customs to a number of tribes of northern Asia, to the Turks, to the Tu-ku-hun, a people probably of

reason : they believe that all who serve them in this life shall serve them in the next, so as regards a widow they believe that she will always return to her first husband after death. Hence this shameful custom prevails among them, that sometimes a son takes to wife all his father's wives, except his own mother; for the *orda* of the father and mother always belongs to the youngest son, so it is he who must provide for all his father's wives who come to him with the paternal household, and if he wishes it he uses them as wives, for he esteems not himself injured if they return to his father after death.[1] When then anyone has made a bargain with another to take his daughter, the father of the girl gives a feast, and the girl flees to her relatives and hides there. Then the father says: "Here, my daughter is yours: take her wheresoever you find her." Then he searches for her with his friends till he finds her, and he must take her by force and carry her off with a semblance of violence to his house.[2]

---

Kitan (or Moho) descent, to the T'ang-hsiang, a Tibetan people, and to others (*Chou shu*, bk. 50; *T'ang shu*, bk. 221). Of the Turks the *Chou shu* says they could marry in the ascending lines of affinity, but not in the descending. These customs still prevail among the Kafirs (Robertson, *Kafirs of the Hindu Kush*, 535; see also Elias, *Tarikh-i-rashidi*, 251).

[1] To cite but one example of this custom among the Mongols: Tutukai (or Budugai), fourth daughter of Hulagu, married in the first place Tenker Kurkan, then his son Sulamuh, then his son Jijak Kurkan (Howorth, *History*, iii, 213). Conf. Gombojew, p. 652, and Quatremère, *op. cit.*, 89, 92. Clarke (*Travels*, 52) says that in his time (1799) a Kalmuk widow became the property of her husband's brother, if he chose to claim her (see also Haxthausen, *Transcaucasia*, 403, who notes this custom among the Orsethes). Pian de Carpine (642) notes that there was no difference between the sons of the first wife and those of concubines as to inheritance and other rights. It is stil customary among the Kirghiz for the youngest son to receive as his inheritance, besides a portion of the flocks and herds, his father's winter camp with its pasturages (*kishlak*) (Radloff, *op. cit.*, i, 416). Blackstone (*Commentaries* ii, 83) says this custom once prevailed in Scotland.

[2] Clarke (*op. cit.*, 70), speaking of the marriage customs of the Kalmuks, says: "A girl is first mounted, who rides off at full speed. Her lover pursues, and if he overtakes her she becomes his wife." *Wei*

(236)

As to their justice you must know that when two men fight together no one dares interfere, even a father dare not aid a son; but he who has the worse of it may appeal to the court of the lord, and if anyone touches him after the appeal, he is put to death. But action must be taken at once without any delay, and the injured one must lead him (who has offended) as a captive. They inflict capital punishment on no one unless he be taken in the act or confesses.[1] When one is accused by a number of persons, they torture him so that he confesses. They punish homicide with capital punishment,[2] and also co-

---

*shu*, (bk. 103, 15) speaking of the Kao-ch'ê (Turks or Uigurs), says the man brought cattle and horses to the camp in which he wished to choose a wife, and took the one who could sit a horse which he tried to make throw her. This may be a survival of an older custom, in which the bride fled with—or was carried off by—her lover. *Tang shu* (bk. 219, 7) says of Kitan (or Sien-pi) of Shih-wei, probably of the same stock as the Mongols, that the man began by serving the family of the woman for three years; then a portion of her property was given to the woman he had chosen for a wife, and he carried her off to the sound of drums and with dancing. When the husband died, the woman did not marry again. On the social organisation of the Mongols of the present day, see Kopernicki (*Journ. Anthrop. Inst.*, i, 413, *et seq.*); Grenard (*op. cit.*, ii, 249, 250) states that in Chinese Turkestan, especially among the Kazak, the idea of abduction of the bride is still clearly observed in the marriage ceremonies.

[1] According to the Chinese code of the present dynasty, the death penalty cannot be applied unless the criminal confesses. Torture is permitted, however, to extract it.

[2] Chingis Khan's *Ulag yassak*, or Great Ordinances, punished with death homicide, robbery, adultery, fornication, sodomy; also him who lost for the third time money entrusted to him, him who received stolen goods or runaway slaves, him who picked up a weapon in battle and did not restore it to its owner, him who used sorcery to another's injury, him who interfered in a duel (d'Ohsson, i, 408). Haithon (*Hist. Orient.*, 72) says the Mongols considered it a mortal sin to leave the bit in a horse's mouth when he was feeding. Pian de Carpine (641) mentions capital punishment for adultery, brigandage, and open larceny. He also remarks (635): "Their women are chaste and nothing is heard among them of lewdness; but some of the expressions they use in joking are very shameful and coarse." They have not changed since then. Marco Polo (i, 259) says that for "horse-stealing or some other great matter, they cut the thief in two with a sword. Howbeit, if he

habiting with a woman not one's own. By not one's own, I mean not his wife or bondwoman, for with one's slaves one may do as one pleases. They also punish with death grand larceny, but as for petty thefts, such as that of a sheep, so long as one has not repeatedly been taken in the act, they beat him cruelly, and if they administer an hundred blows they must use an hundred sticks :[1] I speak of the case of those beaten under order of authority. In like manner false envoys, that is to say persons who pass themselves off as ambassadors but who are not, are put to death. Likewise sorcerers, of whom I shall however tell you more, for such they consider to be witches.

When anyone dies, they lament with loud wailing, then they are free, for they pay no taxes for the year. And if anyone is present at the death of an adult, he may not enter the dwelling even of Mangu Chan for the year. If it be a child who dies, he may not enter it for a month. (237) Beside the tomb of the dead they always leave a tent if he be one of the nobles, that is of the family of Chingis, who was their first father and lord. Of him who is dead the burying place is not known.[2] And always

---

be able to ransom himself by paying nine times the value of the thing stolen, he is let off." Ibn Batuta (ii, 364), referring to the Kipchak, says : "He in whose possession is found a stolen horse, must return it to its owner, and give him nine like it ; if he cannot do this, his children are seized ; but if he has no children, he is slaughtered like a sheep."

[1] Marco Polo (i, 259) says : "When anyone has committed a petty theft, they give him, under the orders of authority, seven blows of a stick, or seventeen, or thirty-seven, or forty-seven, and so forth, always increasing by tens in proportion to the injury done, and running up to one hundred and seven."

[2] Vincent of Beauvais (bk. xxix, ch. lxxxvi, 421*b*) says : "If the dead Tartar has been a rich and mighty man, he is buried in his most costly robes, and in some hidden place remote from all, so that he be not despoiled of his raiment." He goes on to say that the friends of the deceased kill his horse and skin it, fill the skin with straw, and suspend it by poles over his tomb. They eat the flesh, and keep up their lamentations over the deceased for 30 days, more or less. "There are some Tartars," he adds, "and some Christians also

around these places where they bury their nobles there is a camp with men watching the tombs. I did not understand that they bury treasure with their dead. The Comans

---

but very bad ones, among whom the sons, on the father getting old and worn out by age, give him a certain fatty substance (*pinguia*) like sheep's tail to eat, which oppresses him and he is easily suffocated. When the father is dead, they burn the body and collect the ashes, which they keep as something precious. And every day when they eat they sprinkle their food with this powder" (see Gombojew, 658).

Pian de Carpine (628) says: "When a person is dead, if he is of the nobles, he is buried secretly in the steppe wherever it pleaseth them: he is buried however with his tent (*statio*) and seated in the middle of it, and they put a table before him, and a bowl full of meat, and a jar full of mare's milk; and a mare with her foal is buried with him, also a horse with bit and saddle. And another horse they eat, and fill the skin with straw and put it on two or four poles over him, so that he may have a dwelling in the other world, and a mare to give him milk, and that he may increase his horse herd, and have horses on which to ride. And the bones of the horse which they eat they burn for the good of his soul. And often the women come together to burn bones for the souls of the men, as I have seen with my own eyes, and have been told by others. I saw also that Occodai-can, the father of the present Emperor (Kuyuk), had let a small tree grow for his soul, and he ordered that no one was to cut a branch of it, and whoever did, as I found out myself, was beaten, despoiled and badly treated. So it was that though I was greatly in need of something to whip my horse with, I did not dare cut a switch there. Furthermore they bury gold and silver with a person. They break up the cart on which he was carried, destroy his dwelling, and his name may not be pronounced by anyone for three generations." D'Ohsson (ii, 60) states that when Tului, son of Chingis, died, a mirror (*tului*) was called *gueuzugu*, the use of the word *tului* having been tabooed. Various other cases might be cited (see Rockhill, *Diary*, 160).

Friar John adds (630): "Some of their great people are buried in another fashion. They go secretly into the steppe (*campo*), and having removed the grass in a certain spot together with its roots, they make a great pit, and in the side of this pit they make a grave underground; and the slave which he loved best they put under him, and he lies there so long under him that he is about to draw his last breath, when they take him out to let him breathe; and this they do three times, and if he escapes alive he is free thereafter, and does what he pleases, and is a great man in the camp, even among the relatives (of his dead master). The dead man they place in the grave made in the side of the pit as explained above; then they fill up the pit which is in front of the grave, and put back the grass as it was before, so that no one may find the place afterwards. There is another mode of burial similar to the above, except that they leave a tent above the grave on the steppe.

"In their country there are two cemeteries. The one in which they bury the emperors, chiefs and all the nobles: and wherever they may be, whenever it is possible, they carry them thither; much gold and silver is buried with them. The other is that in which were buried all those who were killed in Hungary; for a great many were killed there.

raise a great tumulus over the dead, and set up a statue to him, its face to the east, and holding a cup in its hand at the height of the navel. They make also pyramids to the rich, that is to say, little pointed structures, and in some places I saw great tiled covered towers, and in others stone houses, though there were no stones thereabout. Over a person recently dead I saw hung on long poles the skins of xvi horses, four facing each quarter of the world; and they had placed also *cosmos* for him to drink, and meat for him to eat, and for all that they said of him that he had been baptised. Farther east I saw other tombs in shape like great yards covered with big flat stones, some round, some square, and four high vertical stones at the corners facing the four quarters of the world.[1] When anyone sickens he lies on his couch, and places a sign over his dwelling

---

To that cemetery no one dare come except the guardians who are placed there to watch it; and if anyone should come there, he would be laid hold of, despoiled and beaten and very badly treated. It happened that we ourselves in ignorance of this entered the bounds of the cemetery of those who had been killed in Hungary, when they came on us and wanted to shoot us with their arrows; but as we were ambassadors and did not know the customs of the country, they let us go."

The appellation of "first father" applied to Chingis is but the translation of his Chinese dynastic title of *T'ai tsu*, "the great ancestor. Most founders of dynasties in China since the third century, B.C., have either borne this title or that of *Kao tsu*, "Exalted ancestor." In the letter of Arghun to the Pope in 1285, he refers to "Gingiscam primo patri omnium Tartarorum" (Chabot, *Hist. de Mar-Jabalaha*, 190).

See also, on the burial customs of the Mongols and Comans, Ibn Batuta, iv, 301; Lebeau, *Bas Empire*, xvii, 397; and Palladius, 11, 12. The Kirghiz still bury their dead in a recess dug in the side of the grave (Sven Hedin, *op. cit.*, i, 420). Conf. *Journ. Roy. Asiat. Soc.*, n. s., xii, 443.

[1] The tumuli of Southern Russia and of Northern Asia, the tombs of Comans, Turks and of other peoples who have at various times occupied these vast regions, have been described by most travellers who have visited these countries (Atkinson, *West. Siberia*, 168, 235; also his *Upper and Lower Amoor*, 39, 157, 179, 191, etc.) One dome-shaped tomb he describes (p. 191) was 37 ft. high. In a place near Kopal the tombs covered an area of four miles by one. Radloff (*Aus Sibirien*, ii, 104 *et seq*), gives a detailed description of similar tombs, and of the interior arrangement and contents of a number which he opened.

The *Chou shu* (bk. L) says that it was customary among the ancient Turks to place around a tomb as many upright stones as the deceased had killed persons in his lifetime.

that there is a sick person therein, and that no one shall enter. So no one visits a sick person, save him who serves him.[1] And when anyone from the great *ordu* is ill, they place (238) guards all round the *ordu*, who permit no one to pass those bounds. For they fear lest an evil spirit or some wind should come with those who enter. They call, however, their priests, who are these same soothsayers.

---

WHEN therefore we found ourselves among these barbarians, it seemed to me, as I said before, that I had been transported into another world. They surrounded us on their horses, after having made us wait for a long while seated in the shade under our carts. The first question was whether we had ever been among them before. Having answered that we had not, they began to beg most impudently for some of our provisions. We gave them some of the biscuit and wine that we had brought with us from the city,[2] and when they had drunk one flagon they asked for another, saying that a man enters not a house with one foot only; but we gave it not, excusing ourselves on the score of the smallness of our stock. Then they asked whence we came and where we wanted to go. I told them what I have already said: that we had heard that Sartach

---

[1] Pian de Carpine (628) says: "When any one of them sickens unto death, a spear is put in his tent and around it they wrap a black felt; and thenceforth no one who is a stranger dare enter the bounds of his dwelling. And when he begins to agonize, nearly all leave him, for no one of those who have witnessed his death can enter the *orda* of any chief or of the emperor until the new moon" (conf. Rubruck, p. 344 of text).

[2] *Villa*, Constantinople, ἡ πόλις, is of course meant. We usually derive the Turkish name Stambul from την πόλιν, but I am inclined to believe that Pears (*Fall of Constantinople*, 177) is right in thinking that the Turkish name is but an abbreviation of Constantinople, just as *Skenderun* is of Alexandretta, *Isnik* of Niceaea, etc.

was a Christian, and that I wanted to go to him, for I had your letters to deliver to him. They made most diligent inquiry whether I was going of my own free will, or whether I was sent. I answered that no one forced me to go, nor would I go if I did not want to, so I was going of my own free will (239), and also of the will of my superior. I was most careful never to say that I was your ambassador. Then they asked me what was in the carts, whether it was gold or silver or costly clothing that I was taking to Sartach. I answered that Sartach would see for himself what we were bringing to him when we reached him, but that it was none of their business to ask: they should have me shown to their captain, and that he, if it so pleased him, should have me taken to Sartach, otherwise I would go back.

Now there was in that province a relative of Baatu, a captain by the name of Scatay,[1] to whom the lord emperor of Constantinople was sending (by me) letters that I be allowed to pass. So they agreed (to do as I asked), supplying us with horses and oxen, and two men to guide us; and those who had brought us went back. Before, however, giving us all this, they kept us waiting for a long time, begging of our bread for their little ones, admiring everything they saw on our servants, knives, gloves, purses and belts, and wanting everything. I excused myself on the plea that we had a long journey before us, and that we could not at the start deprive ourselves of necessary things. Then they called me an impostor. It is true that they took nothing (240) by force; but they beg in the most importunate and impudent way for whatever they see, and if a person gives to them, it is so much lost, for they are

---

[1] The name is variously written *Scatai*, *Scatay*, *Scatatai*, *Scatatay* and *Scatanay*. It may be that the chief is the same as the Cadan, Cartan, or Catan, mentioned by Pian de Carpine (667), and *supra*, p. 8, and whose wife, he says (743) was Batu's sister.

ungrateful. They consider themselves the masters of the world, and it seems to them that there is nothing that anyone has the right to refuse them :[1] if he refuses to give, and after that has need of their service, they serve him badly. They gave us to drink of their cow's milk, from which the butter had been taken ; it was very sour, and is what they call *aira*.[2] And thus we left them, and it seemed to me that we had escaped from the midst of devils. On the next day we came to their captain.

For two months, from the time we left Soldaia to when we came to Sartach, we never slept in a house or tent, but always in the open air or under our carts ; and we never saw a city, but only Comans' tombs in very great numbers.[3]

That evening the man who was guiding us gave us *cosmos* to drink, and at the taste of it I broke out in a sweat with horror and surprise, for I had never drunk of it. It seemed to me, however, very palatable, as it really is.

---

[1] Pian de Carpine (636) says : "They are haughtier than any other people, and despise all the rest of the world, holding them as less than nothing, be they high or low. . . . They are greater liars than other men, and there is hardly any truth in them. At first some of them are quite bland, but they bite like the scorpion. They are astucious and deceitful, and where they can, they get around everyone by trickery."

[2] The ordinary drink of the Kirghiz is boiled milk mixed with water, and allowed to get sour. It is called *airan* (see Pallas, *Voyages*, i, 618 ; Radloff, *Aus Sibirien*, i, 439). Atkinson, *Upper and Lower Amoor* (42), calls it *hyran*.

[3] Ibn Batuta (ii, 363) remarks that it is the custom of the people of the Kipchak to travel in the same way as the pilgrims on the Hedjaz road. They start after the morning prayer, camp towards nine or ten o'clock in the morning, start again in the afternoon, and camp again in the evening. Bergmann (ii, 182) says that the usual distance travelled daily by a Kalmuk is estimated by them at from 20 to 25 versts, or about 13¼ to 16½ statute miles. In Mongolia and Central Asia, the length of the stage is regulated to a great extent by the supply of grass and water ; the average distance, however, is, I think, from 20 to 30 miles when travelling on horseback, and 14 to 15 with camels. Friar William probably went at about this latter rate, or even more slowly, with his ox carts.

IN the morning then we came across the carts of Scatay carrying the dwellings, and it seemed to me that a city was coming towards me.[1] I was also astonished at the size of the herds of oxen and horses and flocks of sheep, though I saw but few men to manage them. So I asked how many men (Scatay) had under him, and I was told that there were not (241) over five hundred, of whom we had passed half at another camp. Then the man who guided us began telling me that I must give something to Scatay, and he made us stop while he went ahead to announce our coming. It was already past the third hour, so they set down their dwellings near some water, and (Scatay's) interpreter came to us, and as soon as he learnt that we had never been among them before he begged of our provisions, and we gave him some. He wanted also a gown, for he was to act as translator of our words in the presence of his master. We excused ourselves. He asked what we were bringing to his master, so we got a flagon of wine and filled a small basket[2] with biscuits and a plate with apples and other fruit, but he was not pleased because we were not taking some costly tissue. However we went with this in fear and trembling. (Scatay) was seated on

---

[1] Ibn Batuta (ii, 380) thus describes his first view of the camp of the Khan of Kipchak: "Then the imperial cortège, which the Turks call *ordu*, arrived. We saw a great city moving with its inhabitants, containing mosques and markets, with the smoke of kitchens rising in the air; for the Turks cook their food during the march. Carts drawn by horses transport these people, and when they have come to the camping place they unload the tents which are on the *arbas*, and put them up on the ground; for they are very light. They do the same with the mosques and the shops."

[2] *Veringal.* Yule (*Marco Polo*, i, 371) says there is a Venetian sea-term, *Vernegal*, applied to a wooden bowl in which the food of the men is put. I have not found this word in any dictionary at my disposal, but as Friar William in another passage (254) uses the word *cophinum*, the old French word *coffin*, meaning "a small basket," I have no hesitation in translating it as I have done. It was probably a round flat basket, in shape and size like a plate. Hakluyt (p. 111) renders it by "maund." See also Pauthier, *Marco Polo*, 280.

his couch, with a little guitar in his hand, and his wife was beside him ; and in truth it seemed to me that her whole nose had been cut off, for she was so snub-nosed that she seemed to have no nose at all ; and she had greased this part of her face with some black unguent, and also her eyebrows, so that she appeared most hideous to us. Then I spoke to him in the terms previously used, for it was essential that we should everywhere say the same thing ; about this we had been well cautioned by those who had been among them, never to change what we said. Then I begged him to be pleased to accept these trifles of us, excusing myself, being a monk and not allowed by my order to own gold or silver or costly robes (242) : so I had nothing of the sort to give him, only of our food to offer him for a blessing. Then he had the things accepted, and at once distributed among his men who had gathered there to drink. I also gave him the letters from the emperor of Constantinople. This was on the octave of the Ascension (5th June). He at once sent them to Soldaia, to be translated there, for they were in Greek, and he had no one with him who knew the Greek language. He asked us if we would drink *cosmos*, or mare's milk ; for the Christians, Ruthenians, Greeks and Alans who live among them, and who wish to follow strictly their religion, drink it not ; for of a truth they consider themselves to be no longer Christians if they drink it, and the priests have to bring them back into the fold as if they had denied the faith of Christ.[1] Then I made answer that we had had enough of our own to drink so far, but that if that liquor

---

[1] Greek priests whom I have consulted on this point have assured me that such used to be in the twelfth century the general belief of the Christians inhabiting among the Tartars. They have, however, been unable to produce any documentary evidence. The Armenian chronicles say that the Georgians would not partake of the Mongol feasts nor drink their kumiss, "because they were Christians" (Dulaurier, 236, 238).

should give out, we should have to drink what he gave us. He asked about the contents of the letters we were sending to Sartach. I told him that the sealed ones were our bulls but that there was naught in them but good and friendly words. He then asked what we would say to Sartach. I answered: "Words of the Christian faith." He asked which, for he would be pleased to hear them. Then I expounded to him as well as I could through my interpreter, who was neither over intelligent nor fluent, the symbol of the faith. When he had heard it, he remained silent, but wagged his head. Then, having made choice of two men to watch over us, and over the horses and oxen, he made us drive about[1] with him until the return of the messenger whom he (243) had sent to have the letters of the emperor translated, and we went about with him until the day after Pentecost (8th June).

---

ON Pentecost eve (6th June) there came to us certain Alans, who are there called Aas, and they are Christians according to the Greek rite, and use the Greek writing and have Greek priests.[2]

---

[1] *Bigare.* Friar William seems to use this word to designate the moving about of the camp with the big tents on carts.

[2] The Alans or Aas appear to be identical with the An-ts'ai or A-lan-na of the *Hou Han shu* (bk. 88, 9), of whom we read that "they led a pastoral life N.W. of Sogdiana (K'ang-chü) in a plain bounded by great lakes (or swamps), and in their wanderings went as far as the shores of the Northern Ocean" (Ma Tuan-lin, bk. 338). *Pei shih* (bk. 97, 12) refers to them under the name of Su-tê and Wen-na-sha (see also Bretschneider, *Med. Geog.*, 258, *et seq*). Strabo (xi, 2, 422, and 5, 434), refers to them under the name of Aorsi living to the north but contiguous to the Albani, whom some authors confound with them, but whom later Armenian historians carefully distinguish from them (De Morgan, *Mission*, i, 232). Ptolemy (vi, 14) speaks of this people as the "Scythian Alans" (Ἀλανοὶ Σκύθαι); but the first definite mention of them in classical authors is, according to Bunbury (ii, 486), found in Dionysius Periergetes (305), who speaks of

They are not however scismatics like the Greeks,[1] for without any respect to persons they honour all Christians. And they brought us cooked meats, begging us to eat of their food, and to pray for one of theirs who had died. Then I told them that it was the eve of a great festival, and that on that day we did not eat meat, and I told them of the festival, at which they were much pleased, for they were in ignorance of what concerned the Christian rite, the name of Christ alone excepted. And they and many other Christians, Ruthenians and Hungarians asked whether they could be saved, for they had to drink *cosmos* and eat carrion and beasts slaughtered by Saracens and infidels, which those Greek and Ruthenian priests consider about the same as

---

the ἀλκήεντες Ἀλανοί (see also De Morgan, i, 202, and Deguignes, ii, 279, *et seq.*).

Ammianus Marcellinus (xxxi, 348) says the Alans were a congeries of tribes living E. of the Tanais (Don), and stretching far into Asia. "Distributed over two continents, all these nations, whose various names I refrain from mentioning, though separated by immense tracts of country in which they pass their vagabond existence, have with time been confounded under the generic appellation of Alans." Ibn Alathir, at a later date, also refers to the Alans as "formed of numerous nations" (Dulaurier, xiv, 455).

Conquered by the Huns in the latter part of the fourth century, some of the Alans moved westward, others settled on the northern slopes of the Caucasus; though long prior to that, in A.D. 51, they had, as allies of the Georgians, ravaged Armenia (see Yule, *Cathay*, 316; Deguignes, i, pt. ii, 277, *et seq.*; and De Morgan, i, 217, *et seq.*).

Mirkhond, in the *Tarikhi Wassaf*, and other Mohammedan writers speak of the Alans *and* As. However this may be, it is thought that the Oss or Ossetes of the Caucasus are their modern representatives (Klaproth, *Tabl. hist.*, 180; De Morgan, i, 202, 231). See also on the subject of the Alans, Yule, *Cathay*, 373, and *Marco Polo*, ii, 164, 492; Vivien de St. Martin, *Nouv. Ann. des Voyages*, Aug.-Sept., 1848, 164; Devéria, *Journ. Asiat.*, ixe série, viii, 431; and Haxthausen, *op. cit.*, p. 385, *et seq.*

[1] In the tenth century, we find the Emperor of Constantinople addressing the Alan chiefs as his "spiritual sons" (Const. Porphyrogenitus, *De adminis.*, i, 688). Bar Hebræus also states that the Alans admitted the unity of persons in the Trinity, but not the unity of nature; in other words, that they belonged to the church of Rome (Quatremère, 80; see also Mosheim, *Hist. Tart. Eccles.*, Appendix, 167, *et seq.*).

carrion, or sacrifices to idols; and because they did not know the facts, neither could they keep them if they did know. Then I explained to them as well as I could, teaching them and comforting them in the faith. The meat which they had brought (244) we kept for the feast day, for we could find nothing to buy with gold and silver, but only with linen or other tissues, and of those we had none. When our servants showed the yperpera, they rubbed them with their fingers, and put them to their noses to smell if they were copper.[1] Neither did they (*i.e.*, the Mongols) give us food, but only cow's milk, very sour and bad-smelling. Our wine was about exhausted, and the water was so muddy from the horses that it was not drinkable; had it not been for the biscuits we had, and God's mercy, we should probably have perished.

---

ON the day of Pentecost (7th June) a certain Saracen came to us, and while in conversation with us, we began expounding the faith, and when he heard of the blessings of God to man in the incarnation, the resurrection of the dead and the last judgment, the washing away of sins in baptism, he

---

[1] This proves that the Mongols had a pretty good idea of Byzantine coins of the period. Pachymeres (*Andron. Paleol.*, vi, 343) says that in the reign of John Ducas Vataces (Friar William's Vatacius) the gold coins (*aurea* or *hyperpera*) contained one-third alloy. Even at a later date, Ibn Batuta (ii, 444) says that one of the wives of the Khan of Kipchak "gave me three hundred dinars in gold of the country, which is called *alberberah* (iperpera); but this gold is not good."

Pian de Carpine (707) speaks of "yperpera or besants." Gibbon (*History*, vii, 341) "guesses" from a corrupt passage of Guntherus that "the Perpera was the *nummus aureus*, the fourth part of a mark of silver, or about ten shillings sterling in value." Friar John uses the word yperpera as synonymous with bezant, as did Joinville, Marco Polo, and others (Yule, *Marco Polo*, ii, 535). It cannot be estimated at less than 10*s*. 6*d*. or 11*s*.

said he wished to be baptised; but while we were making ready to baptise him he suddenly jumped on his horse saying he had to go home to consult with his wife. And the next day talking with us he said he could not possibly venture to receive baptism, for then he could not drink *cosmos*. For the Christians of these parts say that no true Christian should drink, but that (245) without this drink it were impossible to live in these deserts. From this opinion I could not possibly turn him. So you will see how far they are astray from the true faith through this opinion, which has been implanted among them by the Ruthenians, of whom there are great numbers there.

On this same day (7th June) this captain (Scatay) gave us a man to guide us to Sartach, and two to take us to a camp which was five days off, as oxen travel. And they gave us also a goat for food, and several skins of cow's milk, but only a little *cosmos*, for it is held very precious among them. And so we set out due north,[1] and it seemed to me that we had passed through one of the gates of hell. The men who conducted us began robbing us in the most audacious manner, for they saw that we took but little care. Finally, after losing a number of things, vexation made us wise.

We came finally to the end of this province (of Gazaria), which is closed by a ditch (running) from one sea to the other,[2] and outside of it was the camp of these (Mongols);

---

[1] *Recte in aquilonem.* Friar William's bearings are always off a great many points. In the present case, travelling from Sudak to Perekop, he was going in a general N.W. by N. direction.

[2] There is to my mind little doubt that the ditch, which Herodotus (iii, 2, 15) states was built by the blind slaves of the Scythians to close the Chersonesus, was at the isthmus of Perekop; though some writers think that it, like the wall mentioned by Strabo (vii, 4, 258), ran across the Kertch peninsula from the bay of Kaffa to that of Arabat. That there was a ditch at Perekop in ancient times is demonstrated by the fact that Strabo (vii, 3, 255) places a tribe of Taphrioi (from Τάφρος,

and when we came among them they were such horrible-looking creatures that they seemed like lepers. They were stationed there to collect the tax from those who get salt from the salt lakes of which I have already spoken. From this point we should have to travel xv days, they said without seeing anyone. We drank *cosmos* with them, and gave them a basket full of biscuits; and they gave the eight of us (246) a goat for the whole long journey, and I know not how many skins of cow's milk. So having changed horses and oxen we set out, and in ten days we covered the distance to the next camp; and along the whole route we only found water in holes made in hollows, with the exception of two small streams. And we were travelling due east from the time we left this province of Gazaria,[1] having the sea to the south and a vast wilderness to the north, which extends in places over xxx days in breadth; and in it is neither forest, nor hill, nor stone, but only the finest pasturage. Here the Comans, who are called Capchat,[2] used to pasture their flocks; the Teutons,

---

"ditch") immediately north of the isthmus. The word Perekop, I may also remark, means "a cutting," "a ditch." The old ditch of our traveller's time was repaired somewhere about 1470 by the Khan of the Crimea, Mengli Girai. Traces of it still remain, but the forts and redoubts erected by the Russians at the time of the Crimean War have taken the place of the old ramparts (Réclus, *Géographie*, v, 835). The word *Krim*, the same author (v, 826) says, has the meaning of "fortress," a most appropriate name for the Crimea, which by the cutting and fortifying of the isthmus of Perekop could be turned into an impregnable stronghold.

[1] *Recte in orientem*. Again the bearing given by our traveller must be wrong; he travelled in all probability during the first ten days after leaving the isthmus of Perekop, E.N.E. After reaching the first camp beyond Perekop, his route lay probably nearly due N.E. till he came to the Volga.

[2] The Comans, or Kipchak Comans, as our author also calls them, are identical with the Polovtses, or "dwellers of the Plain," of the early Russian annalists (Nestor, *Chronique*, 12, 19, *et pas.*), the Turks of the Desht (or "Plain") Kipchak of Mohammedan contemporary writers. Under the name of Kumam or Comans, they are frequently mentioned by Byzantine writers. The origin of this name is not known. Some writers, as Adelung (*Mithridates*, i, 479), think they may have taken

however, call them Valans, and the province Valania. It is stated however by Isidorus that Alania extends from the river Tanais to the Palus Maeotis and the Danube; and this country which extends from the Danube to the Tanais (which is the boundary between Asia and Europe), and which it takes two months hard riding, as ride the Tartars, to cross, was all inhabited by the Capchat Comans, as was also that beyond the Tanais to the Etilia, between which two rivers are x (247) good days. To the north of this province lies Ruscia, which is everywhere covered with

---

it from the river Kuma, which discharges in the Caspian; but as d Avezac (487) remarks, the name already occurs in Xenophon (*Anabasis*, vii, 8, 15), under the form Comania (Κομανιά). Assyrian inscriptions of the eighth century, B.C., speak of an expedition of Tiglath Pileser (B.C. 747-727) against the *Comani*, who lived at that time in the present Kurdistan. The king is there said to have defeated their army of 20,000 men, captured and destroyed their castles and towns, and laid waste "the far spreading country of the Comani" (Rawlinson, *Five Ancient Monarchies*, ii, 67). It would, therefore, seem more likely that the river Kuma took its name from the Comani. Pomponius Mela (i, 603) mentions the Comani among the nations of the interior of Western Asia. Rashideddin gives the following legend concerning the origin of the Kipchak: "Oghuz Khan having been defeated by the tribe of the Itbarak, was forced to retire to an island between two rivers. At that time it happened that a woman, whose husband had been killed in the battle, was delivered of a child in the hollow of a large tree. When Oghuz heard of this he said: 'As this woman has no husband, I will adopt her son.' The child received the name of *Kipchak*, a word derived from the Turkish *kubuk*, meaning 'a decayed tree.' All the people of Kipchak are descended from this adopted son of Oghuz. After seventeen years, Oghuz succeeded in gaining the superiority over the Itbarak. He conquered Iran, and returned to his original home. Afterwards, when the Itbarak revolted, Oghuz settled the Kipchak between their country and the river Jaik (Ural). Since that time the Kipchak have remained, both in summer and winter, in the same country." The country is frequently called "the Desht" by Mohammedan writers, but the name is usually written Deshti-Kapchak (Quatremère, 67; *Mesalek al-absar*, 281, 284; Burnes, *Travels in Bokhara*, i, 322, ii, 267). Ibn Alathir (xiv, 456) says the Mongols claimed the Kipchak as of their race. Ibn Batuta (ii, 356) describes the country in about the same terms as Friar William: "This plain is covered with grass and flowers, but one sees in it neither mountain, tree, hill nor slope." See also d'Ohsson, i, 338; Yule, *Marco Polo*, i, 52, ii, 491; Bretschneider, *Med. Geog.*, 162; *Mesalek al-absar*, 268. Rubruck (274) says the Cangle were a branch of the Comans. Radloff (*Aus Sibirien*, ii, 10) and Sven Hedin (*op. cit.*, i, 259) mention a tribe of Kirghiz called Kipchak still living in the eastern Pamirs.

forests, and extends from Poland and Hungary to the Tanais, and it was all ravaged by the Tartars, and is still being ravaged every day. For the Tartars prefer the Saracens to the Ruthenians, who are Christians, and when the latter can give no more gold or silver they drive them off to the wilds, them and their little ones, like flocks of sheep, there to herd their cattle.[1] Beyond Ruscia to the north is Pruscia, which has all been recently conquered by the Teutonic knights;[2] and of a truth they might readily acquire Ruscia, if they would put their hand to it, for should the Tartars hear that the great priest, that is the Pope, was about to make a crusade against them, they would all flee to their deserts.

---

WE travelled eastward, seeing nothing but the sky and the earth, only now and then to our right the sea which is called Sea of Tanais,[3] and tombs of Comans visible two leagues off, on account of

---

[1] Pian de Carpine (700) says that when he was in Russia "there was a certain tax-gatherer sent there by Kuyuk Khan and Batu who took from each man one child out of every three, and all the men who had no wives. And as to the women he took all those who had no husbands, and in like manner all paupers. Those left were counted, and of each, down to the new-born babe, whether rich or poor, was exacted the following tribute: a skin of a white bear (or) one black beaver (or) one black sable (*zabulus* or *sabulus*), one skin of a black animal they have in the north, the name of which I know not in Latin, but which in German is called *iltis* (pole-cat), and which the Poles and Ruthenians call *dochori* (*choreke* in Russian), (or) one black fox skin. And whoever paid not this was led off to the Tartars and made a slave."

[2] The Teutonic order began the conquest of Prussia and Livonia in 1230, but it was not until about 1310 that the whole country was subdued (Karamsin, iii, 167-172).

[3] Friar William more frequently gives the sea of Azov its classical name of *Palus Mæotis*, by which it was also known to many of the Mohammedan writers: Masudi calls it *Maitus*, and Abulfeda *Matych*. Abulmahasen, Quatremère says (*Not. et Extr.*, xiii, 272), gives it the name of Sea of Sudak, and Ibn Alathir (xiv, 457) calls it Sea of the

the custom of burying the whole of a family in one spot. As long as we were in the desert it fared well with us, but such misery as I had to suffer when we came to inhabited places, words fail me to express. For our guide wanted (248) me to meet every captain with a present, but our supplies sufficed not for that, for daily we were eight persons eating our bread, without counting those who came by hazard, who all wanted to eat with us. There were five of us, and the three who were conducting us, two driving the carts and one going with us to Sartach. The meat they had given us was insufficient, and we could find nothing to buy with money.[1] To add to this, when we were seated in the shade under our carts, for the heat was intense at that season, they pushed in most importunately among us, to the point of crushing us, in their eagerness to see all our things. If they were seized with a desire to void their stomachs, they did not go away from us farther than one can throw a bean: they did their filthiness right beside us while talking together, and much more they did which

---

Khazars, a name applied to the Caspian by Mohammedan writers, but intelligible here, as some Mohammedan geographers of his time believed that the Caspian communicated by the Sea of Azov with the Black Sea. Barbaro (4, *et passim*) calls it "Sea of Tabacche," which may be for "Sea of Tanais."

[1] Friar Ascelin and Simon of St. Quentin had similar experiences (see Vincent of Beauvais bk. xxxi, ch. xl-lii, 453*a*-454*b*). Pian de Carpine (670) remarks: "No matter whence the ambassadors come, they are (on arriving among the Mongols) in dire distress as to victuals and clothing; for their allowances are poor and small, especially when they reach (the camp) of any of the princes and are forced to wait there; for then they give so little to ten men that two could barely live on it. Nor while at the courts of the princes nor on the road do they give to eat but once a day, and little enough then; and if they insult one, it cannot be resented, but must be borne in patience. Great numbers of presents are asked for among them, as well by the princes as the great and the small, and if they are not given, they abuse one and hold him as nothing; and if (the envoys) are sent by a great personage, they will not receive a moderate present, but say: 'You come from a great personage, and you give so little?' So they scorn to receive it, and if the ambassadors want to do their work satisfactorily, they must give larger ones."

was vexatious beyond measure.[1] Above all this, however, I was distressed because I could do no preaching to them; the interpreter would say to me: "You cannot make me preach, I do not know the proper words to use." And he spoke the truth; for after awhile, when I had learned something of the language, I saw that when I said one thing, (249) he said a totally different one, according to what came uppermost in his mind. So, seeing the danger of speaking through him, I made up my mind to keep silence.

We travelled along then in great distress from stage to stage till a few days before the feast of blessed Mary Magdalen (22nd June) we came to the great river Tanais, which separates Asia from Europe,[2] just as the river of Egypt divides Asia from Affrica. At the place where we came to it Baatu and Sartach had established a village of Ruthenians on the east bank, who ferried envoys and merchants across on small boats. They first passed us across, then the carts; putting one wheel in one boat and the other in another and tying the boats together they rowed them across.[3] At this place our guide did a most

---

[1] Pian de Carpine (637) remarks: "they are a filthy people in eating and in drinking, and in all their other doings."

[2] The south-eastern boundary of Europe appears to have been fixed at the Tanais or Don from very ancient times. Herodotus (iii, 32) refers to it, but says he cannot conceive why it should have been adopted as the boundary (see Rawlinson's note on the subject). The opinion that the Nile separated Africa from Asia was also adopted by classical geographers (Pomponius Mela, i, 603). On the sources of the Tanais, see *infra*. Rubruck tells us that after leaving Perekop he travelled in an easterly direction till he came to the Don, and that when he left that river it took him nine days to reach Sartach's camp, which was three days W. of the Volga. The first three or four days he had to travel on foot, and so did not probably cover more than thirty to forty miles. The point where he came on the Don was therefore in all likelihood not over 200 miles from the Volga by the route he followed, which was N.E. (see also F. M. Schmidt, 178-179).

[3] These boats were probably canoes. Barbaro (31) speaks of the boats dug out of great trees growing along the Volga, and used by the Russians on that river.

foolish thing; thinking that the people had to supply us with horses, he sent back to their owners from the near bank the animals which had brought us; but when we asked for animals they replied that they were exempted by Baatu from any other service than ferrying across those who came and went. From merchants even they collect much money. So we remained there on the river bank for three days. The first day they gave us a big barbel[1] just out of the water, the second day some rye bread and a little meat which the headman of the village (250) collected from the different houses; the third day we got dried fish, of which they have great quantities here. That river at this point was as broad as the Seine at Paris. And before we came there, we passed many fine sheets of water full of fish, but the Tartars do not know how to catch them, nor do they care for fish unless they can eat it as they would mutton. This river is the eastern boundary of Ruscia, and takes its rise in the Mœotide fens, which extend to the ocean in the north.[2] The river, however, flows southward, forming a big sea of

---

[1] *Borbata.* Pallas (*Voyages*, i, 202), enumerating the various kinds of fish found in the Volga, speaks of the "barbue" or *rhombus piscis.* This may be our traveller's *borbota*, or *barbata* as some of the MSS. write it (see *supra*, p. 45).

[2] *Oritur de paludibus Meotidis.* Hakluyt's MS. wrongly reads *mergitur* on p. 120, where this statement is repeated; all the other MSS., however, have *oritur.* In the present phrase Hakluyt's text omits the word *Meotidis.* The copyist was evidently disinclined to accept as correct Friar William's statement, which was at variance with the notion concerning the sources of the Don then universally held. Even Roger Bacon (*op. cit.*, i, 357), who has incorporated in his review of the geography of eastern Europe and Asia all Rubruck's remarks, adheres to the classical views on the sources of the Don, and places them in the Rhipæan mountains. Our traveller was the first, since Herodotus, to locate correctly the sources of the Don, which flows out of Ivan Lake in Tula. Herodotus (iii, 42) had said that the Tanais "is a stream which has its source far up the country, in a lake of vast size, and which empties itself into another still larger lake, the Palus Mæotis." The name Don was already used by the Slavs in Rubruck's time; both Pian de Carpine (*supra*, p. 8) and Friar Benedict (*supra*, p. 34) call it by that name (see also F. M. Schmidt, 184).

seven hundred miles before it reaches the Sea of Pontus, and all the streams we passed flow also in that direction. This same river has a forest on its west bank. Beyond this point the Tartars go no farther north, for at that season, about the beginning of August, they commence going back southward; so there is another village lower down (the river), where envoys pass over in winter. We found ourselves here in great straits, for we could procure neither horses nor oxen for money. Finally, when I had proved to them that we were working for the common good of all Christendom, they obliged us with oxen and horses; but we ourselves had to go on foot.

It was the season (251) when they were cutting the rye. Wheat thrives not there; but they have great abundance of millet. The Ruthenian women arrange their heads as among us, but their outside gowns they trim from the feet to the knee with vaire or minever. The men wear capes like the Germans; on their heads they wear felt caps, pointed and very high.

We trudged along for three days without seeing anyone, and just as we and the oxen were well worn out, and unable to find any Tartars, two horses came running towards us; we took them with great delight, and our guide and the interpreter got on them, in the hope of being able to find some people. Finally on the fourth day[1] we found some people, and we were as happy as shipwrecked mariners on reaching port. Then we got horses and oxen and went along from stage to stage till we reached the camp of Sartach on the second day of the Calends of August (July 31st).

---

[1] Since leaving the ferry across the Don.

THE country beyond the Tanais is most beautiful, with rivers and forests. To the north are great forests, inhabited by two races of men: to wit, the Moxel,[1] who are without any religion, a race of pure pagans. They have no towns, but only little hamlets in the forest. Their chief and the greater part of them were killed in Germany; for the Tartars (252) took them with them to the borders of Germany, and so they have formed a high opinion of the Germans,[2] and they hope that through them they may finally be freed of the Tartar yoke. If a trader comes among this people, he with whom he first puts up must provide for him as long as he sees fit to stay among them. If one sleeps with another's wife the husband cares not, unless he sees it with his own eyes; so they are not jealous.[3] They have swine, honey and wax, precious furs and hawks.

---

[1] The Moxel and Merdas form the two branches of the Finnish Mordwin people. These names, according to Pallas (*Voyages*, i, 104), correctly transcribed are *Mokshad* and *Ersad*, the first name being applied by them to their race in general. The earliest mention I have found of this people is in Jornandes (444), where he speaks of the *Mordensimnis* among the peoples of Hermanaric's empire. Constantine Porphyrogenitus (*De Adminis.*, 166) refers also to the *Mordia* country. Nestor (*Chronique*, 2) calls them *Mordwa*. Pian de Carpine (676) speaks of them as *Morduani*, and in another passage (709) as *Mordui*. Barbaro (33) calls this people the *Moxii*, and adds that they were mostly pagans. Some of their customs, as described by him, are purely Tartar, especially that of sacrificing horses at burials and setting up the stuffed skin over the grave (see also Castren, *Ethnolog. Vorlesungen*, 134, and especially Smirnow, *Populations Finnoises*, i, 260, *et seq.*). This latter author (264, *et seq.*) shows that the identification of the Merdas with the *Burtas* or *Bartas* of the early Mohammedan geographers cannot be accepted.

[2] Referring to the conquests being made at the time by the Teutonic Order, and to the possibility of their extending them to the Volga.

[3] Smirnow (*op. cit.*, i, 337) says: "In the beginning the Mordwin family was only the association of several persons living together. . . . There is no question of marriage in the proper sense of the word." The same author, speaking of the Mordwins of the present day, says (*loc. sup. cit.*): "The girls do not generally marry before twenty or twenty-five; but when barely at the age of puberty, that is to say at the age of fourteen, they have relations with the boys of their village. . . . . Liaisons between cousins are frequent; they are not unknown between brothers and sisters."

After them are the others called Merdas, whom the Latins call Merdinis, and they are Saracens. Beyond them is the Etilia, the largest river I have ever seen, and it comes from the north, from Greater Bulgaria and flows south, and it falls into a certain lake which has a circumference of iiii months journey, and of it I shall tell you later.[1] So these two rivers, the Tanais and the Etilia, in the north where we crossed them, are only distant the one from the other x days; but to the south they are far remote from one another. For the Tanais flows down into the Sea of Pontus, while the Etilia forms with many other rivers which flow into it from Persia, this sea or lake. To the south we had very high mountains, inhabited, on the side facing this desert, by the Kerkis[2] and the Alans or Aas, who are Christians and still fight the Tartars. Beyond them, along the sea or lake of Etilia, live certain Saracens called Lesgi,[3] who likewise owe them no allegiance. Beyond them are the Iron Gates, which Alexander made to keep the barbarous nations out of Persia; of these I

---

[1] On Friar William's views concerning the Caspian, see *infra*, p. 118.

[2] The Cherkesses or Circassians are of course meant. Here, as on p. 70, our traveller writes the name *Kerkis*. In the present passage, however, MSS. D and E give the correct reading, *Cherkis*. Pian de Carpine (659) also writes *Kergis* for *Cherkis*. The only detail he gives concerning them (679) is their habit of taking a strip of skin off their faces from ear to ear as a sign of mourning for their deceased fathers. The Cherkesses, who descend from the ancient Sarmatian tribes of classical authors, have occupied for the last two thousand years the Caucasian slope of the Black Sea and the Sea of Azov, the Kuban steppes (De Morgan, *Mission*, ii, 277).

[3] Strabo (xi, 5, 432) speaks of the *Legai* (Λῆγαι) and *Gelai* (Γῆλαι) two Scythic nations living between Albania (*i.e.*, E. Caucasus) and the Aorsi (the Alans). Latin authors called this people *Legæ*. In the seventh century, Jornandes (432) refers to them as occupying the same country, and calls them *Lazi*. Ibn Alathir (455) speaks of them as the *Lekz*, and says that in his time (tenth century) they were partly Mohammedan, partly Christian. The country occupied at the present time by the Lesgians is called Daghestan. De Morgan (ii, 278) does not think this people can be classed, on the vague statement of Strabo, in the Turanian race, but sees in it an inextricable mixture of all the races and tribes which have successively overrun this country (see also *infra*, 380, 381).

shall tell you later, for I passed through this place on my way back, and between these two (253) rivers in this country through which we were travelling used to live Comans Capchac before the Tartars occupied it.

---

SO we found Sartach three days from the Etilia, and his *ordu* seemed to us very big, for he has six wives, and his eldest son who was beside him had two or three, and every one of them had a big dwelling and perhaps two hundred carts. Our guide went to a certain Nestorian, Coiac[1] by name, who is one of the most important men of his *ordu*. This latter made us go a long way to an officer who is called the *Jamiam*, for thus they call him whose duty it is to receive envoys.[2] In the evening this Coiac had us told to come to him. Then our guide asked us what we were going to take to him, and he was greatly scandalized when he saw that we were getting nothing ready to take to him. We stood in front of him seated in all his glory, striking a guitar and making people dance before him. Then I repeated what I had previously said elsewhere as to the reason for which we had come to his master, begging him to assist us that his lord might see our letters. I also excused myself, being a monk, for neither having, receiving nor carrying with me gold or silver or any precious thing,

---

[1] The name is variously written in the MSS. *Caiac*, *Coiat* and *Coiac*.

[2] In another passage (298) the name is correctly written *Iam*. Marco Polo (i, 420) says: "And the messengers of the Emperor in travelling from Cambaluc, be the road whichsoever they will, find at every 25 miles of the journey a station which they call *Yamb*, or, as we should say, the 'Horse Post-House.'" Pallas (*Voyages*, i, 698) speaks of the *Jami*, or "relais de poste," of Asiatic Russia when he visited it in 1769 (see also Yule, *Cathay*, 131; Cordier, *Odoric*, 374, 416; d'Ohsson, i, 406; and Yule, *Marco Polo*, i, 423). These post-stations were established by Ogodai in 1234 throughout the Mongol empire (d'Ohsson, ii, 63).

but only books and the chapel,[1] with which we served God, so we were not offering presents to either him or his lord, for having put away all worldly goods I could not be the bearer of those of others. Then he replied right pleasantly that (254) I did well, being a monk, to keep my vows; that he did not want of our things, but would rather give us of his own if we were in want; and he caused us to sit down and drink of his milk, and after awhile he besought us to say a blessing for him, which we did. He also asked us who was the greatest lord among the Franks. I said: "The Emperor, if his land were in peace." "No," he said, "it is the King of France." For he had heard of you from Messire Baldwin of Hainaut.[2] I also found there one of the companions of David,[3] who had been in Cyprus (with him), and who had told him of all he had seen. Then we went back to our lodgings.

The next day (1st August) I sent him (Coiac) a flagon of muscadel wine, which had kept perfectly good during the

---

[1] *Capella in qua serviebamus Deo.* The word *capella* in mediæval Latin, and also in modern French, is used to designate both the place in which mass is celebrated, and by extension the chalice, candlesticks, censors, and other objects used in church worship. Friar William uses it in the latter sense. See Ducange, *Glossarium*, ii, 221, and Littré, *Dictionnaire*, s. v. *chapelle*.

[2] Baldwin of Hainaut, a knight in the service of the Emperor Baldwin of Constantinople, had married, in 1240, a Coman princess, daughter of Soronius, on the conclusion of a treaty of peace between that Prince's horde and Baldwin II (Lebeau, *Histoire*, xvii, 392). We learn from our traveller (326) that Baldwin had travelled through northern Asia, going as far, it would seem, as Karakorum. I know no other mention in any contemporary record of this journey.

[3] *Unum de sociis David.* The David referred to is he who in 1248 came to St. Louis, when at Nicosia in Cyprus, on a mission from the Mongol general Ilchikadai. For some inexplicable reason all translators have misunderstood the reference, and have translated these four words by "a Knight of the Temple," supposing, I take it, that it that *socius David* was for *socius* or *miles Salomonis* (Hakluyt, 116, 117; Purchas, 13; Bergeron, 32; Karamsin, iv, 73; da Civezza, *Storia Universalle*, i, 433; Devéria, *Notes d'épigraphie*, 45). William of Nangis (360) says David's companion when at St. Louis' camp was called Marchus. This may be the person here referred to.

whole long journey, and a hamper[1] of biscuits which pleased him very much; and that evening he kept our servants with him. The next day he sent me word to come to the court, bringing with me the king's letters, the vestments and the church ornaments and the books, fo his master wished to see them. We did accordingly, putting in one cart the books and the chapel, and in another bread, wine and fruit. Then he caused us to explain all about the books and vestments, and many Tartars and Christians and Saracens looked on seated on their horses. When he had finished examining them, he asked if I would give all these things to his master. When I heard this I was shocked, and his words displeased me. Dissimulating, however, I replied: " My lord, we beg that your lord will deign receive this bread, wine and fruit, not as a present, for it is too trifling, but for a blessing, and so that we appear not before him with empty hands. He shall see the letters of the lord King, (255) and by them he shall know why we come to him, and then we will await his pleasure, we and all our belongings. As to these vestments they are holy, and may not be touched except by priests." Then he told us to put them on to go in unto his lord, and this we did. I put on the most costly of the vestments, with a most beautiful cushion (*pulvinar*) against my breast, and took the Bible which you had given me, and the beautiful Psalter which my lady the Queen had presented me with, and in which were right beautiful pictures. My companion took the missal and the cross, while the clerk (Gosset) put on a surplice and took the censer. And so we came before his (*i.e.*, Sartach's) dwelling, and they raised the felt which hung before the entry,

---

[1] *Cophinus*, which I take to be the same as the *veringal* used on p. 86. Isidorus (xx, 720) says *cophinus* is "*vas ex virgulis aptum mundare stercora, et terram portare.*" The French word *coffin* is still sometimes heard.

so that he could see us. Then they made the clerk and the interpreter to bow the knee (three times):[1] of us they did not demand it. Then they enjoined us earnestly to be most careful in going in and coming out not to touch the threshold of the dwelling,[2] and also to chant some blessing for him. So we went in chanting, "*Salve, regina!*" In the entry of the dwelling there was a bench with *cosmos* and cups, and all Sartach's wives had come thither and the Moal came crowding in around us.

Then this Coiac handed him the censer with the incense, and he examined it, holding it in his hand most carefully. After that he handed him the Psalter, at which he took a good look, as did the wife who was seated beside him. Then he handed him the Bible (256), and he asked if the Gospels were in it. I said that it contained all the Sacred writings. He also took in his hand the cross, and asked if the image on it were that of Christ. I replied that it was. Those Nestorians and Hermenians never make the figure of Christ on their crosses; they would thus appear to entertain some doubt of the Passion,[3] or to be ashamed of

---

[1] This additional detail is only found in MS. A. The cushion called *pulvinarium* is used to carry the Gospels on, but in this case the Bible was probably placed on it.

[2] Pian de Carpine, Marco Polo, Friar Odoric, all mention this point of Mongol etiquette. At a later date, when the Mongol emperors occupied palaces, it was extended to the threshold of the audience hall (Yule, *Cathay*, 132; and *Marco Polo*, i, 370, 372). The prohibition extended to the tent ropes. The same custom existed among the Fijians, I believe. I may note that it also prevailed in ancient China. It is said of Confucius "when he was standing he did not occupy the middle of the gate-way; when he passed in or out, he did not tread on the threshold" (*Lun-yü*, bk. x, ch. iv, 2).

[3] *Male sentire de passione.* "The Nestorians have no images or pictures in their churches, and are very much opposed to the use of them, even as ornaments, or as barely representing historical facts illustrative of sacred scriptures. They will not even allow of a crucifix, and regard the mere exhibition of such an emblem, to say nothing of adoration, as a monstrous iniquity. . . . The only symbol in use among them is the plain Greek cross" (Badger, ii, 132, 414). Father Alishan tells me that the Armenians will not have the image of the Christ on their crosses, so as not to expose Him to the scoffing of

it. Then he caused the bystanders to withdraw so that he could better see our ornaments. Then I presented to him your letter, with translations in Arabic and Syriac, for I had had them both translated and written in these languages at Acon.[1] And there were there (at Sartach's camp) Hermenian priests who knew Turkish and Arabic, and that companion of David who knew Syriac, Turkish, and Arabic. Then we went out and took off our vestments, and some scribes and this Coiac came, and they translated the letters (into Mongol). When he (Sartach) had heard them, he caused our bread and wine and fruit to be accepted, and our vestments and books to be carried back to our lodgings. All this took place on the Feast of Saint Peter in chains (1st August).

---

THE next morning (2nd August) came to us a priest, the brother of that Coiac, who begged for a little vase with holy oil,[2] for Sartach wanted to see it, he said; and we gave it to him. Toward vespers (257) Coiac called us, and said to us: "The lord King hath written good words to my lord; but they contain certain difficulties, concerning which he would not venture to do anything without the advice of his father: so you must go to his father. And the two carts which you brought here, with the vestments and books, leave them to me, for my lord wishes to examine them carefully." I at once suspected

---

unbelievers. Crosses with the image of the Saviour on them are sometimes used by them, he adds, and some are known to have been in use even before our traveller's time.

[1] Or Acre, from which port I think it probable that Friar William sailed to Constantinople.

[2] *Crismate.* The Nestorians do not use holy oil or chrism, but only pure olive oil. The Chaldeans, however, use chrism in baptisms (Badger, ii, 212, 213, 408). The Armenians make a great use of holy oil, which they call *mieron* (Tournefort, *Voyage*, ii, 163).

evil of his greed, and said to him: "My lord, not only these, but the two other carts which we have, will we leave under your care." "No," he said; "leave these, but do what you wish with the others." I told him this was quite impossible, but that we would give everything over to him. Then he asked us if we wished to remain in the country. I said: "If you have well understood the letters of the lord King, you can see that that is the case." Then he said that we must be very patient and humble; and with this we left him that evening.

The next morning he (Coiac) sent a Nestorian priest for the carts, and we brought all four of them. Then the brother of this Coiac came up, and separated all our belongings from the things which we had taken the day before to the court, and these, to wit the books and the vestments, he took for himself; notwithstanding that Coiac had ordered us to take with us the vestments we had worn before Sartach, so that, should occasion arise, we might put them on before Baatu; but the priest took them from us by force, saying: "What, you have brought these to Sartach, and now you want (258) to take them to Baatu!" And when I sought to reason with him, he answered me: "Say no more, and be off with you." So I had to bear it in patience, for we were not allowed to go in unto Sartach, nor was there anyone to do us justice. I was afraid also of the interpreter, lest he say something differently from what I should speak, for he used to be eager for us to make presents to everyone. I had one comfort; as soon as I discerned their greed, I abstracted the Bible from among the books, also the sentences and the other books of which I was specially fond.[1] I did not

---

[1] *Sentencias et alios libros quos majis diligebam.* In another passage (272) he says the only books he had were a Bible and a breviary; perhaps by *Sentencias* he refers to the latter book. Among the books which Sartach kept, we are told (380), there were a copy of the

dare abstract the Psalter of my lady the Queen, for it had been too much noticed on account of the gilded pictures in it. And so we were sent back with the two remaining carts to our lodgings. Then came he who was to guide us to Baatu, and he wanted to start at once. I told him that on no account would I take the carts, and this he reported to Coiac, who ordered that we should leave them and our servant with him, and this we did.

Travelling then due east toward Baatu, we came on the third day (5th August) to the Etilia,[1] and when I saw its waters, I wondered from where away up in the north (259) so much water could come down.

Before we left Sartach, the above mentioned Coiac and a number of scribes of the court said to us: "You must not say that our lord is a Christian. He is not a Christian, but a Moal." For the name of Christian seems to them that of a nation. They have risen so much in their pride, that though they may believe somewhat in the Christ, yet will they not be called Christians, wishing to exalt their own name of Moal above all others, nor will they be called Tartars. The Tartars were another people of whom I have heard as follows.

---

Bible in verses, and a work in Arabic worth thirty bezants, or about £16 10*s*. These two books, together with the Psalter, were permanently kept by Sartach, but all the others were given back to the traveller when he stopped at Sartach's camp on his way back to Syria.

[1] Ptolemy was the first classical writer to mention the Volga, which he calls *Rha*. Menander (229) calls it *Attila*, Constantine Porphyrogenitus (*De Adminis.*, 105) uses the two forms *Atel* ('Ατήλ) and *Etel* ('Ετέλ), while Theophanes (*Chronologia*, i, 545) calls it *Atal* ('Αταλ). The original of these names is the Turkish *atel* or *itil*, meaning "river." The name Volga was already employed by the Russians in Rubruck's time; both Pian de Carpine (*supra*, p. 8) and Friar Benedict (*supra*, p. 34) use it, but they thought this river emptied into the Black Sea. The name Volga is derived, I think, from that of the Bulgars, who lived on its banks, in the present government of Kazan; though it has been commonly supposed they took their name from the river.

AT the time when the Franks took Antioch[1] the sovereignty of these northern regions belonged to a certain Con cham. Con was his proper name, *cham* his title, which means the same as soothsayer. All soothsayers are called *cham*, and so all their princes are called *cham*, because their government of the people depends on divination. Now we read in the history of Antioch, that the Turks sent for succor against the Franks

---

1 The Crusaders captured Antioch in A.D. 1098. The original of our traveller's Con cham is Gur Khan, "the Universal Khan," a title taken in 1125 by Yeh-lü Ta-shih, the founder of the Kara-Khitai dynasty. In 1126 he established his capital at Belasagun, on the Chu (or Ili) river (Bretschneider, *Med. Geog.*, 101, 109; d'Ohsson, i, 165). The title *Khan*, Rubruck's *Cham*, though of very great antiquity, was only used by the Turks after A.D. 560, at which time the use of the word *Khatun* (Rubruck's *caten*, 315) came in use for the wives of the Khan, who himself was termed *Ilkhan*. The older title of *Shan-yü* did not, however, completely disappear among them, for Albiruni says that in his time the chief of the Ghuz Turks, or Turkomans, still bore the title of *Jenuyeh*, which Sir Henry Rawlinson (*Proc. Roy. Geo. Soc.*, v, 15) takes to be the same word as that transcribed *Shan-yü* by the Chinese (see *Ch'ien Han shu*, bk. 94, and *Chou shu*, bk. 50, 2).

Although the word *Khakhan* occurs in Menander's account of the embassy of Zemarchus, the earliest mention I have found of it in a western writer is in the *Chronicon* of Albericus Trium Fontium, where (571), under the year 1239, he uses it in the form *Cacanus*. The proper use of the works *Khan* and *kaân* is thus stated by Quatremère, 10, 84, *et seq.*: "We find in the historians two different names to designate the Mongol monarchs, that of *khan* and that of *kaân*. The first, which is common to the Mongol language and to the other Tartar dialects, was the title that Chinghiz took, passed since to a portion of the princes of his family, and is given still in our days to the sovereigns of the different peoples of Northern Asia. As to the name *kaân*, the first monarch who bore it was Oktai, who transmitted it to his successors, to the exclusion of all the other Mongol princes. This title was doubtless higher than that of *khan*, since the emperors of the principal dynasty had adopted it to distinguish themselves from the other *khans*, over whom they exercised the right of sovereignty . . . . I do not hesitate to admit that *kaân* is only due to the slightly-altered pronunciation of the (Mongol) word *Kkakan*;" see also Lacouperie, *Khan, Khakan and other Tartar Titles*.

The title *Khakhan* is used by Simon of St. Quentin (Vincent of Beauvais, bk. xxxi, ch. xxxii, 452*a*) under the form *Gogcham*, which means, he says, "Emperor, King." The title Khakan being once transcribed Gog-cham, it was but natural for Simon to give to Mangu, whom he takes for the brother of Kuyuk, the bearer of the title, the name of Magog, as he, in common with most Europeans of his time,

to King Con cham; for from these parts came all the Turks.[1] That Con (260) was of Caracatay. Now *Cara* means black, and *Catay* is the name of a people, so Caracatay is the same as "Black Catay."[2] And they are so called to distinguish them from the Cathayans who dwell by the ocean in the east, and of whom I shall tell you hereafter. Those Caracatayans lived in highlands (*alpibus*) through which I passed, and at a certain place amidst these alps

---

believed that the Mongols were the people of Gog and Magog spoken of by Ezekiel the Prophet (xxxviii, 1-5, 15, 16; xxxix, 6, 11-16). He also uses the word *Chan*, or *Chaam*, which means, he says, "King or Emperor, magnificent or magnified" (*magnificus sive magnificatus*).

The word *Kham*, meaning a sorcerer, a shaman, which our traveller takes to be the same as *Khan* or *Khakan*, has not even an etymological connection with it; see *infra*.

[1] The earliest mention of the Turks is found in the *Chou shu* (A.D. 557-581), bk. 50. The customs of this people resembled closely those which Rubruck and his contemporaries ascribe to the Tartars in their times, especially as regards the funeral rites and the rules governing marriage, the worship of Heaven and Earth, etc. Menander refers to them in his account of Zemarchus' mission; he calls them (227) "the Turks who used to be called Sacae." Theophanes Byzantius (*Frag. Hist. Graec.*, iv, 270) speaks of "the Turks who used to be called Messagetae in olden times, and who are called by the Persians in their language Kermichiones (Κερμιχίωνα)," while Theophylactus (124) refers to the "Huns who live in the north and east, and whom the Persians call Turks." The same author (286) confirms what the *Chou shu* says about their cult. Pian de Carpine does not mention the Turks, and only once Turkia, though he in one passage (680) refers to the "Soldan of Urum," the Seldjuk kingdom of Rum, Friar William's *Turkia*. Our author would seem to be well aware of the racial affinities between the Turks and the Mongols. Benedict (*supra*, p. 37) uses the word *Turkia* to designate Turkestan (see also William of Tyr, 22, 24).

[2] The dynasty of the Khara-Khitai, called Hsi (or Western) Liao by the Chinese, was founded in A.D. 1224 by Yeh-lü Ta-shih, a prince of the Khitan dynasty of Liao, which had just been destroyed in northern China by the Nü-chen Tartars. No satisfactory explanation of the origin of the name "Black Khitai" has been given; Bretschneider has given a complete translation of the article on the Hsi Liao found in the History of the Liao (*Liao shih*), followed by other translations drawn from the annals of the Kin and Yuan dynasties (*Med. Geog.*, 96, *et seq.*; see also d'Ohsson, i, 165; and Yule, *Cathay*, 178, *et seq.*). Bretschneider states that the explanation given by d'Herbelot (*Bibl. Orient.*, ii, 203) of the name Kara-Khitai is absurd; its name is there derived from the people who bore it living in the woods; d'Herbelot explains the name *Kara Mongol* in a like manner.

dwelt a certain Nestorian, a mighty shepherd and lord over a people called Nayman,[1] who were Nestorian Christians. When Con cham died, that Nestorian raised himself to be king (in his stead) and the Nestorians used to call him King John, and to say things of him ten times more than was true. For this is the way of the Nestorians who come from these parts: out of nothing they will make a great story, just as they have spread abroad that Sartach is a Christian, and so of Mangu chan and Keu chan,[2] because they show more respect to Christians than to other people; though of a truth they are not Christians. So great reports went out concerning this King John; though when I passed through his pasture lands,[3] no one knew anything of him save a few Nestorians. (261) On those pasture lands lived Keu chan, to whose court went Friar Andrew, and I also passed through them on my way back. This John had a brother, also a mighty shepherd, whose name was Unc;[4] and he lived beyond the alps of the

---

1 Pian de Carpine (752) states that the Naiman were heathens. It was not when the first Gur-Khan of the Kara Khitai died that the Naiman prince seized the throne, but in 1211 or 1212, when the last Gur-Khan was dethroned by Guchluk Khan (Rubruck's King John) of the Naimans. Mohammedan and Chinese authorities agree on this point (d'Ohsson, i, 167, *et seq.*; Bretschneider, *Med. Geog.*, 113). The Naiman were a Turkish tribe (Howorth, *History*, i, Pt. 1, 20, 691). Sven Hedin, *op. cit.*, i, 316, ii, 672, mentions a tribe of Naiman Kirghiz living on the Eastern Pamirs. The word *Naiman* means "light" in Turki. Ney Elias (*Tarikh-i-rashidi*, 74, 93) says the name of this people must have been Naiman-Uighurs.

2 Kuyuk Khan. The MSS. usually write this *Kencham*, but in some passages we find the form *Keu chan*, which is a much better transcription.

3 *Pascua*, which our author seems to use as synonymous with *alpes*.

4 Unc chan is the Togrul of Rashideddin, a son of Gurkhan Khan of the Keraits (d'Ohsson, i, 51). Marco Polo (i, 227) speaks of "Unc Can, the same that we call Prester John." Palladius (*op. cit.*, 23) has shown how some of the confusion concerning Ung Khan has arisen, the title of Wang Khan (Ung Khan) being transferred from Prester John, already dead at the time, to the Turkish tribe of Wang-Ku

Caracatayans, some three weeks journey from his brother, and he was lord of a little town called Caracarum,[1] and the people he had under his rule were called Crit and Merkit,[2] and they were Nestorian Christians. But that lord of theirs had abandoned the worship of Christ, and had taken to idolatry, having about him priests of the idols, who are all invokers of demons and sorcerers. Beyond those pasture lands, some x or xv days, were the

---

(Ongu, Raschideddin's Ongot). The whole subject of Prester John has been so admirably discussed by Yule (*Marco Polo*, i, 229, *et seq.*) that nothing remains to be said about it.

1 *Villule que dicitur Caracarum.* The name of this famous town is variously written in the MSS., *Caracarum*, *Caracaron*, *Carecarum*, *Caratorum*, *Caratharum.* I have everywhere used the first form, which is also that most frequently found in the MSS. Pian de Carpine (608) is the first western traveller to mention it by name. He writes it *Caracaron* ; he did not visit the city, though he got to within half a day's journey of it.

2 D'Avezac (*op. cit.*, 534) has suggested that Friar William's *Crit* and *Merkit* should be corrected to *Crit* and *Mecrit*, so as to agree with Pian de Carpine's statement (645). D'Avezac takes Crit, Merkit for a double word like Longa and Solanga, Chin and Machin, etc., and identifies them with the Keraits. Howorth (*History*, i, Pt. 1, 699) agrees with d'Avezac's views. That our traveller should have grouped the two names together on account of the similarity of sound is probable, but that he meant to refer the two names to one people is very doubtful. Yule (*Marco Polo*, i, 231) thinks Friar William's Crit and Merkit are the Keraits and Mekrits, the latter already mentioned by Pian de Carpine (645) under the form *Merkit.* While the Keraits were undoubtedly Nestorian Christians (see Quatremère, 93), our traveller is, it would seem, wrong in thinking that the Mekrits had been converted to Christianity. The Keraits lived on the Orkhon and the Tula, S.E. of Lake Baikal ; Abulfaraj relates their conversion to Christianity in 1007 by the Nestorian Bishop of Merv. Rashideddin, however, says their conversion took place in the time of Chingis Khan (d'Ohsson, i, 48 ; Chabot, *op. cit.*, 14). D'Avezac (536) identifies, with some plausibility, I think, the Keraits with the K'i-lê (or T'ich-lê) of the early Chinese annals. The name K'i-lê was applied in the third century, A.D., to *all* the Turkish tribes, such as the Hui-hu (Uigurs), Kieh-ku (Kirghiz) Alans, etc., and they are said to be the same as the Kao-ch'ê, from whom descended the *Cangle* of Rubruck (*Tang shu*, bk. 217, i ; Ma Tuan-lin, bk. 344, 9, bk. 347, 4). As to the Merkits, or Merkites, they were a nomadic people of Turkish stock, with a possible infusion of Mongol blood. They are called by Mohammedan writers Uduyut, and were divided into four tribes. They lived on the Lower Selinga and its feeders (d'Ohsson, i, 54 ; Howorth, *History*, i, Pt. 1, 22, 698).

pasture lands of the Moal,[1] who were very poor people, without a chief and without religion except sorcery and soothsaying, such as all follow in those parts. And next

[1] *Moal.* Friar William's transcription of the word Mongol seems to be taken from the Turki form of that word, *Mogal.* The earliest mention I have found of the name Mongol in oriental works occurs in the Chinese annals of the After T'ang period (A.D. 923-934), where it occurs in the form *Meng-ku.* In the annals of the Liao dynasty (A.D. 916-1125) it is found under the form *Meng-ku-li.* The first occurrence of the name in the *Tung chien kang-mu* is, however, in the 6th year Shao-hsing of Kao-tsung of the Sung (A.D. 1136). It is just possible that we may trace the word back a little earlier than the After T'ang period, and that the *Meng-wa* (or *ngo,* as this character may have been pronounced at the time), a branch of the Shih-wei, a Tungusic or Kitan people living around Lake Keule, to the east of the Baikal, and along the Kerulun which empties into it, during the seventh and subsequent centuries, and referred to in the *T'ang shu* (bk. 219), is the same as the later Meng-ku. Though I have been unable to find, as stated by Howorth (*History*, i, pt. 1, 28), that the name *Meng-ku* occurs in the T'ang shu, his conclusion that the northern Shih-wei of that time constituted the Mongol nation proper, is very likely correct. "On tracing the Mongols to the Shih-wei," he says (*op. sup. cit.*, 31) "we connect them to some extent with the Kitan who were descended from the Shi-wei; and if this be well grounded, we connect them further with the Sian-pi and Uhuan, who were of the same stock as the Khitans, and also with the Yuan-yuan."

I. J. Schmidt (*Ssanang Setzen*, 380) derives the name *Mongol* from *mong*, meaning "brave, daring, bold," while Rashideddin says it means "simple, weak" (d'Ohsson, i, 22). The Chinese characters used to transcribe the name mean "dull, stupid," and "old, ancient," but they are used purely phonetically. Simon of St. Quentin (Vincent of Beauvais, bk. xxxi, ch. xxxiv, 452*a*) says that the Tartars called themselves *Mongli* or *Mongol*, and Pian de Carpine (645) transcribes the name *Mongal.* In Byzantine works the only mention I have found of the name is in Pachymeres (i, 344), who speaks of "the Tochari who call themselves Muguls (Οὓς αὐτοὶ Μουγουλίους λέγουσιν)."

The Mongols of the present day are commonly called by the Chinese *Ta-tzŭ*, but this name is resented by the Mongols as opprobious, though it is but an abbreviated form of the name *Ta-ta-tzŭ*, in which, according to Rubruck, they once gloried.

Pian de Carpine (645) thus describes the country occupied by the Mongols at the time of the birth of Chingis Khan. "There is a certain country in the East which, as previously stated, is called Mongal. That country had once four nations: one called Yeka Mongal, or the Great Mongals, the second called Su-Mongal, or Aquatic-Mongals, though they called themselves Tartars from a certain river which flows through their country and which is called Tatar (or Tartar); another was called Merkit; the fourth Mecrit. All these nations had the same physical appearance and spoke one language, though they were divided among themselves into provinces and principalities" (conf. Haithon, *Hist. Orient.*, 26; see also *supra*, p. 111, note 2, and *infra*, p. 115, note 2).

to the Moal were other poor people, who were called Tartars.[1] Now King John being dead without an heir,

---

[1] *Tartari.* The earliest date to which I have been able to trace back the name Tartar is A.D. 732. We find mention made in a Turkish inscription found on the river Orkhon and bearing that date, of the *Tokuz Tatar*, or "Nine (tribes of) Tatars," and of the *Otuz Tatar*, or "Thirty (tribes of) Tatars." It is probable that these tribes were then living between the Oguz or Uigur Turks on the west, and the Kitan on the east (Thomsen, *Inscriptions de l'Orkhon*, 98, 126, 140). Mr. Thos. Watters tells me that the Tartars are first mentioned by the Chinese in the period extending from A.D. 860 to 874: the earliest mention I have discovered, however, is under date of A.D. 880 (*Wu tai shih*, bk. 4). We also read in the same work (bk. 74, 2) that "The Ta-ta were a branch of the Mo-ho (the name the Nû-chēn Tartars bore during the Sui and T'ang periods: Ma Tuan-lin, bk. 327, 5). They first lived to the north of the Kitan. Later on they were conquered by this people, when they scattered, a part becoming tributaries of the Kitan, another to the P'o-hai (a branch of the Mo-ho), while some bands took up their abode in the Yin shan in southern Mongolia, north of the provinces of Chih-li and Shan-hsi, and took the name of *Ta-ta.*" In 981 the Chinese ambassader to the Prince of Kao-chang (Karakhodjo, some twenty miles south-east of Turfan) traversed the Ta-ta country. They then seem to have occupied the northern bend of the Yellow River. He gives the names of some nine tribes of Ta-ta living on either side of the river. He notes that their neighbours to the east were Kitan, and that for a long time they had been fighting them after the occupation of Kan-chou by the Uigurs (Ma Tuan-lin, bk. 336, 12-14). We may gather from this that these Tartars were already settled along the Yellow River and the Yin shan (the valley in which is now the important frontier mart of Kuei-hua Ch'eng) at the beginning of the ninth century, for the Uigurs, driven southward by the Kirghiz, first occupied Kan-chou in north-western Kan-su, somewhere about A.D. 842.

Turning to western sources of information, we find that Byzantine writers have all classed the Tartars among the Sacae or Scythic nations, which included all the tribes, without any regard to ethnic or linguistic affinities, which at one time or another had occupied northern and western Asia. Thus George Acropolita, in his *Annals*, calls the Tartars by the name of *Tachari* (Ταχάρι), or *Tacharioi* (Ταχάριοι), though in one passage (Bonn edit., 58) he uses the name *Tatars* (Ταтάρι). Pachymeres invariably calls these people *Tochari* (Τοχάρι), though in one place he uses the name *Muguls.* Among the writers of the thirteenth century in Western Europe the name is uniformly written *Tartari* in Latin, and *Tartarins* in French. In one case only, in the letter of Ivo of Narbonne, dated 1243 (see *supra*, Introduction), have I found the form *Tatar*, or *Tattar*, used.

Howorth (*History*, i, Pt. I, 702) derives, on the authority of Wolff, the name Tartar from a Tungusic word, *tartar* or *tata*, "to drag, to pull," and thinks it is equivalent to our word "nomad." Some Western contemporary writers derived the name Tartar from a river

his brother Unc was brought in (*ditatus est*), and caused himself to be proclaimed chan, and his flocks and herds were driven about as far as the borders of the Moal. At that time there was a certain Chingis, a blacksmith,[1] among the people of Moal (262), and he took to lifting the cattle of Unc chan whenever he could, so that the herdsmen complained to their lord Unc chan. So he got together an army, and made a raid into the land of the Moal, seeking for this Chingis, but he fled among the Tartars and hid himself there. Then this Unc chan having got great booty from the Moal and the Tartars went back. Then that Chingis spoke to those Tartars and to those Moal, saying: "'Tis because we are without a chief, that our neighbours oppress us." And they made him chief and captain of

---

called *Tar* or *Tartar*, which flowed through their early home (Matth. Paris, *Chron. Maj.*, iv, 78). Others thought the name was taken from the great island of *Taraconta* in their country, while others again imagined it was taken from "the broad country of *Tharsi*" (Matth. Paris, *op. cit.*, iv, 109. The Russian archbishop, Peter, who visited Lyons in 1245, thought the Tartars descended from the Midianites, who, fleeing before Gideon, had hidden themselves in the farthest corners of the north in a vast desert called *Etreu*, where they lived in high and impenetrable mountains, in caves and dens, whence they had driven the lions and dragons, their first denizens. The English captive among the Mongols, who supplied Ivo of Narbonne with most of the details contained in his letter previously referred to, had also a vague notion of the remote eastern origin of the Mongols. William of Nangis (365) says that David, the messenger of Ilchikadai to St. Louis in 1248, stated that the name Tartar was derived from that of the country where the great Khan lived, and which was called *Tarta*.

Whatever the opinion concerning the origin of the name, nearly all Christians in the first half of the thirteenth century believed that the Tartars were of the lost tribes of Israel. So strong was this belief that the Tartars were of Jewish descent, that we are told that the Jews of Europe, especially those of Germany, thinking that the Mongols were sent by God to free them from the oppression of the Christians, endeavoured in 1241 to smuggle arms and provisions to them (Matth. Paris, *op. cit.*, iv, 131-133).

[1] The name is variously written in the MSS. *Chingis*, *Cyngis*, and *Cingis*. I have preferred the first mode of transcription, the one which Pian de Carpine (646 *et seq.*) invariably uses. This writer makes no mention of the legend giving to Chingis the trade of a blacksmith, on the origin of which see *infra*; he only says (646) that he was "a mighty hunter before the Lord."

the Tartars and the Moal. Then he secretly got together an army and fell upon Unc chan and defeated him, so that he fled to Cathay. And it was there that his daughter was captured, and Chingis gave her to wife to one of his sons, who by her had Mangu, who now reigneth.[1]

Now this Chingis used to despatch the Tartars in every direction, and so their name spread abroad, for everywhere was heard the cry: "The Tartars are coming!" But through the many wars they have been nearly all killed off, and now these Moal would like to extinguish even the name and raise their own in its stead.[2] The country in which they first lived, and where is still the *ordu* of Chingis

---

[1] Dokuz Khatun, a daughter of Iku, *son* of Unc chan, married Tului, and at his death his son Hulagu (Quatremère, 93). Chaur Bigui (or Beighi), daughter of Unc chan, was to have married Chingis' son Juchi in 1202, but Unc chan at the last moment refused his consent to the marriage. Mangu Khan was son of Siurkukteni, or Siurkukiti Beighi (Pian de Carpine, 666, calls her Seroctan), daughter of Djagambo, *brother* of Unc chan, and his father was Tului, Chingis' son. Chingis himself married a daughter of this same brother of Unc chan; her name was Abgah Beighi (Quatremère, 91; d'Ohsson, i, 67; ii, 59, 267; Yule, *Cathay*, 147).

[2] Rashideddin says: "The name of *Tatar* has been celebrated the world over from most ancient times. The Tatar nation, divided into a great many branches, comprised (at the time of Chingis Khan) about seventy thousand huts. Its territory was near the Chinese territory and lake Buyir . . . The Tatars were most of the time subjects or tributaries of the emperor of Khitai . . . notwithstanding their internal discords, they made in old times great conquests; they became so powerful and feared that the other Turkish peoples passed themselves off as Tatars, and held themselves honoured by this name; just as to-day the Chelairs, Tatars, Uirats, Unguts, Keraits, Naiman, Tanguts and others glory in the name of Mongol, rendered illustrious by Chinguiz Khan and his descendants; a name they would before that have spurned. The young men of all these nations believe at present that their ancestors always bore the name of Mongol; it is not so, for anciently the Mongols were only one of the Turkish nations. It is only since Alankua, that is to say three centuries, that the name exists. It was given to the descendants of that princess, who had become very numerous" (d'Ohsson, i, 428). Rashideddin brought his history of the Mongols down to the year 1303; therefore, according to him, the name of Mongol had first appeared in the eleventh century. The Chinese authorities cited (*supra*, p. 112, note) take it back to the first half of the tenth.

(263) chan, is called Onankerule.[1] But because Caracarum is the district where their power first began to spread, they hold it their royal city, and near there they elect their chan.

---

OF Sartach I know not whether he believes in the Christ or not. This I do know, that he will not be called a Christian, and it even seemed to me that he mocked the Christians. For he is on the road of the Christians, to wit, of the Ruthenians, Blacs, Bulgarians of Minor Bulgaria, Soldaians, Kerkis and Alans, all of whom pass by him when going to his father's *ordu* carrying presents to him, so he shows himself most attentive to them. Should, however, Saracens come along carrying more presents than they, they are sent along more expeditiously. He has Nestorian priests around him who strike a board and chant their offices.[2]

---

[1] *Onankerule*, the country watered by the Orkhon and Kerulun rivers, *i.e.*, the country to the south and south-east of Lake Baikal. The headquarters (*ya-chang*) of the principal chief of the Uigurs in the eighth century was 500 *li.* (about 165 miles) south-west of the confluence of the Wen-kun ho (Orkhon) and the Tu-lo ho (Tura). Its ruins, sometimes but wrongly confounded with those of the Mongol city of Karakorum, some twenty miles from it, built in 1235 by Ogodai, are now known by the name of Kara balgasun, "Black City." The name *Onankerule* seems to be taken from the form *Onan-ou-Keloran*, which occurs in Mohammedan writers (Quatremère, 115 *et seq.*; see also *T'ang shu*, bk. 43*b*).

[2] *Pulsant tabulam.* A board or bar of iron suspended to a rope has, from apparently the earliest times, been used by the Greek and Eastern Christians in church worship instead of bells. This board or bar is called *semantron* (σήμαντρον) or *simandro* (σιμανδρο) in Greek, the Armenians call it *jamahar*. The mallet used to strike it is called *roptron* (ρόπτρον) (Constantine Porphyrogenitus, *De Ceremo.*, ii, 235; Chardin, *Voyages*, i, 224 and Tournefort, i, 45). Pian de Carpine (766) says the Nestorians at the court of Kuyuk Khan "beat (the *semantron*) at the hours, according to the fashion of the Greeks." Bells were not, however, unknown among the Nestorians. Rashideddin says that the Christians at the chapel before the tent of Dokuz Khatun —the Kerait Christian wife of Hulagu—"rang the bells" (Quatremère, 94, 95). The Constable of Armenia, Sempad, also states that

And there is another one called Berka, a brother of Baatu,[1] who has his pasture lands toward the Iron Gate, where passes the road followed by all the Saracens coming from Persia and Turkia, and going to Baatu, and who when passing through bring him presents; and he has made himself a Saracen, and he does not allow (264) pork to be eaten in his *ordu*. When we came back Baatu had ordered him to move from that place to beyond the Etilia to the east, not wanting Saracens to pass by where he was, it appearing to him harmful. During the iiii days we were at Sartach's *ordu*, we were not once furnished with food, and only once with a little *cosmos*.

On the road between him and his father we were in great fear, for the Ruthenians, Hungarians and Alans, their slaves, of whom there are very great numbers among them, are in the habit of banding together xx or xxx in number, and run off at night (armed) with arrows and bows, and whomsoever they find at night they kill. During the day they hide, and when their horses are tired, they come by night to the herds of horses in the pastures and change their horses, and take one or two with them to eat when necessary. Our guide greatly feared some adventure with them.[2] On this part of the road we should have died of

---

the Christians in the Mongol camps *pulsant campanas et percutiunt tabulas*" (Will. of Nangis, 362; see also Mosheim, *Hist. Eccles. Tartar.*, Appendix 50). Tibetan lamas also use on some occasions, and to summon the monks to attend certain ceremonies, a board about six feet long and a foot broad, which is struck with a piece of hard wood. This board is called *ganti*. It is very likely that they originally got this contrivance from the Nestorians.

[1] This Mongol prince's name is also written *Bercai*, *Berekeh* and *Berekai*. He was the third son of Juchi. His brothers were Batu, Urda, Shiban, Tangkute, Bergachar and Tuka-Timur (d'Ohsson, ii, 8). Pian de Carpine (668) writes his name *Berca*. Sartach, dying shortly after Batu, was succeeded in his command by his young son Ulagchi; but he also died after a few months, and was succeeded by Berka in 1256. This prince died in 1265, and was buried at Sarai on the Volga (d'Ohsson, iii, 377, 419; Hammer-Purgstall, *Goldenen Horde*, 144-181).

[2] Conf. *supra*, p. 3, Friar John's account.

hunger, had we not carried with us a small supply of biscuit.

So we came to the Etilia, the greatest of rivers, for it is four times greater than the Seine, very deep, coming from Greater Bulgaria, which is (265) in the north, flowing southward, and emptying into a certain lake, or sea, which is now called Sea of Sirsan, from a certain city on its coast in Persia.[1] Isidorus, however, calls it the Caspian sea,[2] for it has the Caspian mountains and Persia to the south, the Mulihec mountains, that is the mountains of the Axasins to the east,[3] which touch the Caspian mountains; to the north is this wilderness in which are now the Tartars, though at first there were here certain Comans

---

[1] *Mare Sirsan.* One MS. reads *Sirtan*, and two others *Sircan.* This may be a copyist's error for *Mare Servanicum* or "Sea of Shirwan," which Vincent of Beauvais uses (bk. xxx, ch. xcvii, 440*b*) to designate the Caspian. Sirsan may also be for (Taba)ristan, the Caspian being known as "Sea of Tabaristan" by the early Mohammedan writers (Masudi, i, 263; Ibn Khaldun, 156). Both of these suppositions are open to the objection that there was no town of Shirwan or Tabaristan. The only other suggestion I have to make, is that "Sea of Sirsan" is the "Sea of Kegham," or "Lake of Sevan," names the Armenians used in the thirteenth century to designate the Caspian (Dulaurier, 235). Sea of Kegham is the same as Marco Polo's (i, 54) "Sea of Ghel or Ghelan." Polo calls the Caspian in another passage (ii, 495) "Sea of Sarain" (Sarai?). Friar Odoric calls it "Sea of Bacuc," and the Catalan map (*Not. et Extr.*, xiv, 126), "*Mar del Sarra e de Bacu*," a combination of the two preceding names.

[2] *Etymologiarum*, 486, where he classes it among "the gulfs of the sea."

[3] Also written in the MSS. *Muliech* and *Musihet.* The correct reading is *Mulidet*, from the Arabic *molhid*, "impious, a heretic." This famous sect of *Melahideh*, or *Hachichihs*, whence our word Assassin, is also known as the Ismaelians and Bathenis, or "partisans of the inner cult." They were exterminated by Hulagu. Joinville (138, 139) gives some interesting details concerning them. He writes their name *Assacis* (see Hammer, *Hist. of the Assassins*, 41 *et seq.*; Michaud, *Histoire*, i, 472 *et seq.*; Quatremère, 122; Bretschneider, *Med. Travel.*, 63, 78; Cordier, *Odoric*, 473, *et seq.*). Friar William is, of course, wrong in placing the Ismaelians to the east of the Caspian. They were scattered through Syria, Irak, Dilem and Khorasan. Their stronghold, Alamut, was north-east of Kasvin, south of the Caspian. It was taken and destroyed by Hulagu in 1256 (see also *infra*).

called Cangle.[1] And on that side (*i.e.*, the north) it receives the Etilia, which rises in summer as does the Nile of Egypt. To the west of it are the mountains of the Alans, the Lesgians, the Iron Gate and the mountains of the Georgians. So this sea has mountains on three sides, but on the north it has this plain. Friar Andrew went himself along two sides of it, the southern and the eastern, and I along the other two, the northern in going from Baatu to Mangu chan, and again in coming back; and along the western side in coming back from Baatu to Syria. One can go around it in iiii months,[2] and it is

---

[1] The *Cangle* of our traveller are called by Pian de Carpine (749) *Cangitae*. They are called *K'ang* (or *Hang*)*li* or *Kanglin* by Chinese writers of the Mongol period, and *Kankali Turks* by contemporary Mohammedan writers, who say that in the beginning of the thirteenth century they lived to the east of the Jaik river (Ural), which is the location assigned them by Friars John, Benedict and William (Bretschneider, *Med. Geog.*, 147; d'Ohsson, i, 197). Constantine Porphyrogenitus (*De Adminis.*, 164, 167) speaks of a tribe of *Kagcar* (Κάγκαρ) or *Kangar* (Κάγγαρ), which word, he adds, means "noble, strong," living between the Volga and the Jaik (Ural), and who were a branch of the Patzinakitae (the Bejnak of the Arabs, the Petchenegs of the Turks). Abulghazi, as previously remarked, derives the name Kankali from *kang*, "a cart." The western Turks were also at one time known as *Kao-ch'ê*, "High carts," by the Chinese. These characters, which happily describe a peculiar feature of Turkish life at the time, were, however, used phonetically, and transcribe an original which must have closely approximated to the name given this people by Mohammedan writers. Deguignes (*Histoire*, i, pt. 2, 389), and since then W. Schott, have endeavoured to identify the Kang-li with the people of Kang-chiu or Sogdiana; but, as pointed out by Bretschneider (*Med. Geog.*, 150), similarity of sound is the only ground for the identification. Klaproth (*Tabl. de l'Asie*, 279) says that several Nogai Tartar tribes still bear the name of *Qangly*, and Radloff (*Türkstämme Sibiriens*, 22) mentions a small branch of the Usbeks living in the Sarafstan valley called *Kangly* (see Bretschneider, *Med. Geog.*, 147, and d'Ohsson, i, 197).

[2] This was the view held by classical authors. Dionysius Periegetes says it has a circumference of three months' journey (Müller, *Geog. Graeci Minores*, ii, 344). Herodotus (i, 276) had stated that the Caspian had no connection with any other sea, and that its length was fifteen days in a row-boat, its greatest breadth an eight-days' voyage; but all his successors down to Ptolemy believed that the Caspian was connected by a long and narrow gulf with the Ocean. Isidorus simply followed Pliny (vi, 36), who believed in the gulf theory (Bunbury, ii, 593). Marco Polo (i, 54) gives the length of the Caspian as 700 miles (conf. Bacon, *Opus Majus*, i, 354, and Sir John Maundevile, 266).

not true, as stated by Isidorus, that it is a gulf of the Ocean. It nowhere reaches the Ocean, but is everywhere surrounded by land.

---

ALL this country on the west side of this sea, (266) from where are the Iron Gates of Alexander and the mountains of the Alans, to the northern Maeotide marshes where rises the Tanais, used to be called Albania. Isidorus says of it that it has dogs in it so big and fierce that "they seize bulls and kill lions": the truth is, as I have heard tell, that toward the Northern ocean they make dogs to drag carts like oxen, so great is their size and strength.[1]

At this place where we reached the Etilia, the Tartars have made a new village with a mixed population of Ruthenians and Saracens,[2] and they ferry across the

---

[1] Friar William takes this definition of Albania from Isidorus (*Etymolog.*, xiv, 501). He there says : "*Albania*, thus called from the colour of the people, who are born with light (*albo*) hair : this begins in the East at the Caspian sea, and extends through deserts and wilds along the coast of the Northern Ocean to the Palus Maeotis. There are great dogs in this country, and so ferocious that they seize bulls and pull down lions." Sir John Maundevile (143) refers to "Albanye" and its "gret Houndes so stronge that they assaylen Lyouns and slew hem." Strabo (xi, 4, 431) had already spoken of the excellence of the hunting dogs of Albania, but Albania for him was the north-eastern slope of the Caucasus, the country of the Alans of our traveller (380, 381), to the north-west of Derbend. Isidorus, however, had copied from Solinus (93), who in turn had taken his information from Pliny (viii, 51, 343). Hakluyt's text wrongly reads *mergitur*, "it empties into," the Palus Maeotis, or Sea of Azov (see *supra*, p. 97, note 2).

Our traveller, assuming the limits assigned to Albania by Isidorus to be correct, has naturally enough supposed that the dogs he heard of as used by the Samoyed and other tribes of the far north to draw their sledges, were those spoken of by Pliny and others. Ibn Batuta (ii, 399. 402) speaks of the dog-sledges used in the "Country of darkness" to the north of Bulgar, where the dogs are the traveller's only guides (see also Marco Polo, ii, 479).

[2] This would seem to be the town of Ukek, Marco Polo's *Ucaca*. Our traveller says it took over thirty days to go from the town of

envoys going to and coming from the *ordu* of Baatu; for Baatu is on the farther bank to the east, neither does he go beyond this point we had reached when he comes north in summer, and he had begun moving southward (when we arrived). From January to August he goes up to the cool country, as do all of them, and in August they begin moving back.

So we went down the river in a boat from this village to his (Baatu's) *ordu*, and from that place to the cities of Greater Bulgaria[1] to the north there are five days. I

---

Bulgar to Derbend, and he tells us further on that it took him fifteen days to go from Sarai to Derbend, so the village in question must have been about ten days north of Sarai. This corresponds well with the position of Ukek. Yule (*Encycl. Britan.*, xxi, 47) seems to adopt this view. Ibn Batuta (ii, 414) says that Ocac (Ukek) was ten days from Sarai, and that the mountains of the Russians were distant one day from it. The present village of *Uwek*, about six miles south of Saratov, occupies probably the same position as the Mongol town (Yule, *Marco Polo*, i, 8; and F. M. Schmidt, 182).

[1] *Villas majoris Bulgarie.* I have no doubt that "The Great City" is meant, called *Bulgar* by Mohammedan writers. It was situated between Kazan and Simbirsk, below the confluence of the Kama and the Volga, near the left bank of the latter. The present village of *Bolgary* or *Uspenskoye* occupies the site of the Bulgar of the Mongol period. Nicolas and Maffeo Polo visited Bulgar, or *Bolgara* as Marco Polo calls it, in 1261 (Yule, *Marco Polo*, i, 4, 6). Pian de Carpine (747) calls the Bulgars *Bilers* (the *Belar* of Abulfeda and Rashideddin). See also d'Avezac (490); Ibn Batuta (ii, 398). On the commerce of Bulgar in the Middle Ages, see Heyd (i, 61), and Quatremère (404). The question of the early religion of the people of Bulgar is mixed. The *Mesalek al-absar* (270) says: "Formerly, as stated by Masudi and other writers, Islam had spread among the Bulgars; but for a long time past this people has renounced the true faith, and is governed by princes worshippers of the cross." Masudi states that it was in the beginning of the tenth century that Islam penetrated to this country, prior to which time the people were fire-worshippers, but Prof. Berezin says this event took place as early as the ninth year of the Hegira (Bretschneider, *Med. Geog.*, 255-257). Yule (*Marco Polo*, i, 7) says that prior to their conversion to Islam, the people had probably professed Christianity. He cites no authority for this opinion, and I can find no mention of this fact in either Nestor's *Chronicle* nor in Russian history, where such an important fact would surely have been mentioned. The statement in *Mesalek al-absar* that Islam had lost its hold on the people at the end of the thirteenth century, seems to be confirmed by a statement made by the Arab historian Makrizi, that in A.H. 780 the sheikh Amineddin Mohammed Nasifi came to Egypt, and stated that he had been to the Bulgar country, where he

wonder what devil carried this religion of Machomet thither. From the Iron Gate, which is the door out of Persia, there are more than thirty days through the desert, going up (267) along the Etilia, to this Bulgaria, along which route there is no city, only some villages near where the Etilia falls into the sea; and these Bulgarians are the worst kind of Saracens, keeping the law of Machomet as no others.

When I saw the *ordu* of Baatu, I was astonished, for it seemed like a great city stretched out about his dwelling, with people scattered all about for three or four leagues. And as among the people of Israel, where each one knew in which quarter from the tabernacle he had to pitch his tents,[1] so these know on which side of the *ordu* they must place themselves when they set down their dwellings. A court (*curia*) is *orda* in their language, and it means "middle,"[2] for it is always in the middle of the people, with the exception, however, that no one places himself right to the south, for in that direction the doors of the court open. But to the right and left they may spread out as they wish, according to the lay of the land, so long as they do not bring the line of tents down right before or behind the court.

We were first taken to a certain Saracen, who gave us no food. The next day we were taken to the court, and they had a great awning spread, for the dwelling could not hold all the men and women who had come thither. Our guide cautioned us to say nothing until Baatu[3] should have bid

---

had preached Islam to the people, who were plunged in the deepest ignorance, and had converted a number (Quatremère, 404; see also *infra*).

[1] See *Numbers*, i, 51-53; ii, 1-31. [2] See *supra*, p. 57, note 1.

[3] Simon of St. Quentin writes the name *Batoth*, Pian de Carpine *Bati*. Batu, the conqueror of the Kipchak, the commander-in-chief of the army which had ravaged Hungary, was son of Tului, son of Chingis Khan. Sir John Maundevile (129) refers to "Bathol who duellethe at the Cytee of Orda."

us speak, and then to speak briefly. He asked also (268) whether you had already sent ambassadors to the Tartars. I said that you had sent to Keu chan,[1] but that you would not even have sent envoys to him and letters to Sartach if you had not believed that they were Christians. Then they led us before the pavilion, and we were warned not to touch the ropes of the tent, for they are held to represent the threshold of the door. So we stood there in our robes and barefooted, with uncovered heads, and we were a great spectacle unto ourselves. Friar John of Policarp[2] had been there; but he had changed his gown, fearing lest he should be slighted, being the envoy of the lord Pope. Then we were led into the middle of the tent, and they did not require us to make any reverence by bending the knee, as they are used to do of envoys. We stood before him the time to say: "*Miserere mei, Deus,*" and all kept profound silence. He was seated on a long seat as broad as a couch, all gilded, and with three steps leading up to it, and a lady was beside him.[3] Men were seated about on his right, and ladies on his left: and where the room on the women's side was not taken up by them, for there were only present the wives of Baatu, men occupied it. A bench with *cosmos* and big cups of gold and silver, ornamented with precious stones, was in the entry of the tent. He looked at us intently, and we at him, and he seemed to me to be about the height of my lord (269) John de Beaumont,[4] may his soul rest in peace. And his face was all covered at that

---

1 Referring to the Mission of Friar Andrew in 1249.

2 All the MSS. read Policarp. Of course, Friar John of Pian de Carpine is referred to. The detail concerning the change of dress is not mentioned in Friar John's work; it is only found in that of his companion, Friar Benedict the Pole (*supra*, p. 38).

3 Probably his first wife, whose name was Borakchin (d'Ohsson, ii, 337).

4 Jean de Beaumont accompanied St. Louis to the Holy Land. Joinville calls him "le bon chevalier." His nephew was Guillaume de Beaumont, marshal of France, and he also was on this crusade.

time with reddish spots.[1] Finally he bid me speak, and our guide told us to bend the knee and speak. I bent one knee as to a man, but he made sign to me to bend both, which I did, not wishing to dispute over it.[2] Then he bid me speak, and I, thinking I was praying God, having both knees bent, began my speech by saying: "Oh lord, we pray God from whom proceedeth all good things, and who gave you these worldly goods, to give you hereafter celestial ones, for the former without the latter are vain." And as he listened attentively, I added: "You must know for certain that you shall not have the celestial goods unless you have been a Christian; for God saith: 'He who shall have believed and have been baptized, shall be saved, but he who shall not have believed shall be condemned'." At this he quietly smiled, and the other Moal began clapping their hands, laughing at us, and my interpreter stood dumbfounded, and I had to reassure him that he be not afraid. Then silence being reestablished, I said: "I came to your son, because we had heard that he was a Christian, and I brought him letters from the lord King of the French. He (*i.e.*, Sartach) it is who has sent me here to you. You must know the reason why." Then he caused me to rise, and he asked your name and mine, and that of my

---

[1] *Perfusus gutta rosea.* Ducange says *gutta rosea* is for *gutta rosacea*, and that it means "*rubido in facie.*" I can offer no explanation, unless Batu was then recovering from small-pox or some other eruptive disease. Hakluyt renders this by "he had a fresh ruddie colour in his countenance."

[2] The etiquette of the Mongol court appears to have exempted those who belonged to clerical orders, whether Christian, Buddhist, Taoist or Mohammedan, from performing some at least of the genuflexions and prostrations required of laymen. The Taoist Ch'ang-ch'un, when received in 1222 by Chingis Khan, remarks: "It must be said here that the professors of the *Tao* when presented to the Emperor were never required to fall upon their knees or to bend their heads to the ground (*kotow*). On entering the imperial tent they only made a bow and placed their hands together" (Bretschneider, *Med. travel.*, 47; see also Du Halde, *Déscription*, iv, 269, and *infra*).

companion and (270) of the interpreter, and he had it all written down, and he also asked against whom you were waging war, for he had heard that you had left your country with an army.[1] I replied: "Against the Saracens who are profaning Jerusalem, the house of God." He also asked whether you had ever sent envoys to him. "To you," I said, "never." Then he made us sit down, and had us given of his milk to drink, and they hold it to be a great honour when anyone drinks *cosmos* with him in his dwelling.[2] While sitting there I was looking down, but he bid me turn my face up, either wishing to see me better, or on account of their sorcery, for they hold it to be a bad omen or sign, or as portending evil, if one sits before them with face turned down as if in sorrow, and especially so if he rest his chin or his cheek in his hand. Then we went out, and after a little while our guide came to us, and while conducting us to our lodging said to me: "The lord

---

[1] As showing the care with which the rules of etiquette of the Mongol courts were observed, it is not amiss to cite the following description of the audience granted in 1262 by Berka (Sartach's successor) to the envoys of the Sultan of Egypt, Beibars. The ambassadors were brought into the Khan's tent on the left side of the throne, but after presenting their letters they passed to the right side. (Pian de Carpine, 746, says that when on his way to the court of Mangu, he was placed on the left side of Batu, when received by him, while on his return he was seated on his right side.) They knelt on both knees; no one was allowed to enter the royal tent with arms, or even strung bows. They were told not to touch with the foot the threshold of the tent, not to eat snow, not to wash their clothes within the precincts of the royal residence. The tent within which Berka was seated was covered with white felt, and lined with silk stuffs, ornamented with pearls and precious stones. It was large enough to hold five hundred persons. The Khan was seated on a throne, and his first wife was beside him; fifty or sixty of his officers were seated on stools. When Berka's vizir had read the letter of Beibars, the ambassadors passed with their suite to the right of the throne (d'Ohsson, iii, 387-389; conf. also *infra*).

[2] Quatremère (354-359) cites many passages from contemporary Mohammedan writers, showing that it was a custom of the Mongol princes to offer a cup of kumiss or wine to honoured guests. Batu would appear to have been of rather pleasing manners. Pian de Carpine (746) says he was *satis benignus*. The Mongols called him *Suin Khan*, or "The Good Prince" (d'Ohsson, ii, 334).

King requests that you remain in this country, but Baatu may not do this without the permission of Mangu chan. So you and your interpreter must go to Mangu chan. As to your companion and the other man, they will go back to Sartach, where they will await your return." Then the interpreter Homo Dei began to lament, deeming himself lost, and my companion to declare that they might sooner cut off his head than separate him from me; and I said that without a companion I could not go, and moreover that we really required two servants (271), for should one happen to fall ill, I could not be left alone. So he went back to the court and told Baatu what I had said. Then he commanded; "Let the two priests and the interpreter go, and the clerk return to Sartach." He came back and told us the decision; but when I wanted to speak about the clerk, that he might come with us, he said: "Say no more about it, for Baatu has settled it, and I dare not go again to the court." The clerk Gosset had xxvi yperpera of your alms and no more;[1] of these he kept x for himself and the boy, and he gave the xvi others to Homo Dei for us; and so we parted from each other with tears, he going back to Sartach, and we remaining there.

---

ON the eve of the Assumption (14th August) he (Gosset) reached the *ordu* of Sartach, and the next day the Nestorian priests were dressed in our vestments in the presence of Sartach. As for us, we were taken to another host who was to provide us with lodgings, food and horses, but as we had nothing to give him he did it all meanly. We drove about (*bigavimus*) with Baatu for v weeks, following the Etilia

---

[1] Twenty-six yperpera would make about £14 12*s*. The boy (*puer*) was the slave called Nicholas, bought at Constantinople.

down its course.[1] Sometimes my companion was so hungry that he would say to me, almost with tears in his eyes: "It seems to me I shall never get anything to eat." (272) The market always follows the *ordu* of Baatu, but it was so far away from us that we could not get there, for from lack of horses we had to travel afoot.[2] Finally some Hungarians who had been clerks found us out, and one of them still knew how to sing with much expression, and was looked upon by the other Hungarians almost as a priest, and was called to the burial of their dead; and another of them was well versed in grammar, for he understood accurately all we said to him, though he could not reply. These men were a great consolation to us, bringing us *cosmos* to drink and sometimes meat to eat. I was greatly distressed when they asked me for some books, as I had none to give them, having only a Bible and a breviary. So I said to them: "Bring us tablets (*cartas*), and I will write for you as long as we are here." And this they did, and I wrote on both sides of them the hours of the Blessed Virgin and the office for the dead. One day a Coman joined us, who saluted us in Latin, saying: "*Salvite, domine!*" Much astonished, I returned his salutation, and asked him who had taught it him. He said that he had been baptized in Hungary by the brethren of our order,[3] who had taught it to him. He said, furthermore,

---

[1] The rate of progress of these great camps must have been very slow, probably not over six or eight miles a day, often less. In the thirty-five days Friar William was with Batu, they did not, in all likelihood. travel 150 miles. This is the more likely since the Friar, who was a very stout man, travelled on foot (see *infra* and F. M. Schmidt, 189).

[2] Conf. what Pian de Carpine says on his treatment at Kuyuk's court, *supra*, p. 26. Simon of St. Quentin says that when at Baiju's court he and his companions were reduced to bread and water, with now and then a little milk once a day.

[3] I have not been able to find out the date of the first establishment of the Franciscans in Hungary. The Dominicans were there as early as 1221, working at the conversion of the Comans (Mamachio,

that Baatu had asked him a great deal about us, and that he had told him of the condition of our order.

I saw (273) Baatu riding with all his horde (*turba*); and all the heads of families were riding with him, but according to my estimate there were not over five hundred men. At last, about the feast of the Elevation of the Holy Cross (14th September), there came a rich Moal to us, whose father was a chief of a thousand, which is a high rank among them,[1] and he said: "I am to take you to Mangu chan. The journey is a four months one, and it is so cold on it that stones and trees are split by the cold. Think it over whether you can bear it." I answered him: "I trust that, by the grace of God, we may be able to bear what other men can bear." Then he said: "If you cannot bear it, I shall abandon you on the road." I replied: "That is not right; we are not going of ourselves, but are sent by your lord, so, being entrusted to your care, you should not abandon us." Then he said: "All will be well." After that he made us show him all our clothing, and what seemed to him of little use he made us leave with our host. The next day they brought each of us a sheepskin gown, breeches of the same material, boots according to their fashion, felt stockings, and hoods such as they use. The day after the Elevation of the Holy Cross (15th September) (274) we started on our ride,[2] with two pack horses for the three of us, and we rode constantly eastward until the feast

---

*Annalium*, 646). The Franciscans were established in Bohemia in 1232 (*Annalecta*, ii, 56); they may have sent missionaries from there to Hungary.

[1] In Mongol *mingatan*. There were five classes of Mongol officers bearing this title; they managed certain administrative districts. Over them were chiefs of ten thousand, and under them chiefs of hundreds and of tens (see *Yuan shih*, bks. 91, 98, and Devéria, *Journ. Asiat.*, ixe série, viii, 104).

Yule (*Ency. Brit.*, xxi, 47) thinks the point where the traveller left the Volga must have been between 48° and 50° N. lat.; that is to say, less than 150 miles S. of the point where he had come upon the Volga. F. M. Schmidt accepts this view, which is also mine.

of All Saints. And through all that country and beyond, the Cangle used to live, and they were a branch (*parentela*) of the Comans. To the north of us was Greater Bulgaria, and to the south the Caspian Sea.

---

AFTER travelling xii days from the Etilia,[1] we found a great river which they call Jagac,[2] and it comes from the country of Pascatir in the north, and falls into this previously-mentioned sea (*i.e.*, the Caspian). The language of Pascatir is the same as that of the Hungarians,[3] and they are shepherds without any towns whatever, and on the west this country confines on Greater Bulgaria.[4] From this country eastward, and on that side to the north, there are no more towns; so Greater Bulgaria is the last country with towns. 'Twas from this country of Pascatir

---

1 *I.e.*, on the 26th September.

2 The river Ural. We find this river already called by this name, under the form *Daich* (Δαίχ), in Menander (229); while Constantine Porphyrogenitus (*De Admin.*, 151) writes it *Geich* (Γεήχ). Pian de Carpine (743) transcribes the name *Jaic*, and Friar Benedict (777) *Jaiac* (see also Bretschneider, *Med. Geog.*, 151).

3 The Bashkirds. Pian de Carpine (708) speaks of "Bascart, which is Great Hungary," and Friar Benedict (776) of "the Bascarts, who are the ancient Ungari." Mohammedan authors called them *Bashguird*. On their conquest by Batu, says d'Ohsson (ii, 620), quoting the *Tarikh Djihankushai*, they were a very considerable and Christian nation. They are of Finnish stock, and now speak a Turkish dialect; but Yule (*Ency. Brit.*, xxi, 47) thinks it quite possible they formerly spoke a language akin to Magyar. Mussulman historians of that period identified the Bashkirds with the Hungarians. E. D. Butler (*Ency. Brit.*, xii, 374) says: "The Magyar or native Hungarian language is of Asiatic origin, belonging to the northern or Ural-Altaic (Finnic Tartaric) division of the Turanian family, and forming along with the Ugro-Ostiakian and Vogul dialects the Ugric branch of that family" (conf., however, Bretschneider, *Med. Geog.*, 164).

4 Constantine Porphyrogenitus (*De Admin.*, 46) calls it "Black Bulgaria" (μαύρη λεγουμένη Βουλγαρία), and says the people used to be called Onogunduroi (Ονογουνδούροι), a name which connects them with the Huns. Theophanes (*Chronographia*, i, 545) uses, however, the name Great Bulgaria (μεγάλη Βουλγαρία) (see *supra*, p. 107, note 1).

that went forth the Huns, who were afterward the Hungarians ; hence it is the same as Greater Bulgaria. Isidorus says[1] that with their fleet horses they crossed the barriers which Alexander had built among the rocks of the Caucasus to confine the savage tribes, and that as far as Egypt all the country paid them tribute. They ravaged all the world as far as France, so that they were a greater power than are now the Tartars. With them also came the Blacs (275), the Bulgars and the Wandals. For from that Greater Bulgaria come the Bulgars, who are beyond the Danube near Constantinople. And beside Pascatir are the Illac, which is the same word as *Blac*, but the Tartars do not know how to pronounce (the letter) B, and from them come those who are in the land of Assan.[2] They call both of them Illac, the former and the latter. The language of the Ruthenians, Poles, Bohemians and Sclavons is the same as that of the Wandals,[3] and the hand of all of them was with the Huns, as now is that of the greater part of them with the Tartars, whom God has raised up out of the remote parts of the earth, a mighty people but a stupid race, according to what the Lord saith : "I will move them to jealousy (that is, those who do not keep his law) with those which are not a people ; I will provoke them to anger with a foolish nation."[4] This is fulfilled to the letter as to all the nations who do not keep the law of the Christ. That which I have told of

---

[1] I have not found the passage referred to in Isidorus's writings ; but they are so bulky that it may easily have escaped me.

[2] A branch of the Volga Bulgars occupied the Moldo-Vallach country in about A.D. 485, but it was not until the first years of the sixth century that a portion of them passed the Danube under the leadership of Asparuk, and established themselves in the present Bulgaria, Friar William's "land of Assan" (see also p. 47, note 3).

[3] This observation as to the connection of these languages is perfectly correct ; this is probably the earliest notice of the fact by any western writer.

[4] Deuteronomy, xxxii, 21 (conf. Romans, x, 19).

the land of Pascatir I know from the preaching-friars who went there before the advent of the Tartars,[1] but since then (276) it has been subjugated by the neighbouring Saracen Bulgars, and some of the people have become Saracens. The rest may be learned from the chronicles, for it is a well established fact that those provinces from Constantinople (westward) and which were called Bulgaria, Blackia and Sclavonia were provinces of the Greeks, and that Hungary was Pannonia.

So we rode through the country of the Cangle from the feast of the Holy Cross (15th September) to the feast of All Saints (1st November), and nearly every day we went, as well as I could estimate, about the distance from Paris to Orleans, and sometimes more, according to the supply of horses.[2] For sometimes we changed horses two or three times in a day, while at others we went for two or three days without finding anyone, so we had to go slower. Out of xx or xxx horses we, as foreigners, always got the worst, for they invariably took their pick of horses before us. They always gave me a strong horse, on account of my

[1] This early mission of the Dominicans seems to have been entirely overlooked by the historians of the Order. The only reference I have found to it is in Albericus Trium Fontium (*Chronicon*, 564), where, under the date of 1237, he records that "Rumors having got abroad (in western Europe) that the Tartar nation wished to invade Comania and Hungary, four preaching friars travelled for an hundred days as far as Old Hungary, and they on their return stated that the Tartars had already invaded Old Hungary and reduced it to their rule."

[2] It probably appeared quite this distance to the portly Friar, but it is highly improbable that his party travelled sixty miles a day, which is about the distance from Paris to Orleans. When we take into consideration what he says a few lines farther on about tired horses, poor mounts, and riding he and Friar Bartholomew on one horse, I doubt very much if the average rate was much over twenty-five to thirty miles a day. It must be noted that our traveller does not mention the Sea of Aral. He either passed considerably to the north of it (and this supposition is the more likely since he says (279) that he had crossed the mountains beyond the Volga), or he took it for the Caspian. It was unknown to the ancients.

great weight;[1] but I dared not inquire whether he rode easily or not, nor did I venture to complain if he proved hard, but I had to bear it all with equal good grace. Consequently we used to have to endure extreme hardships; ofttimes the horses were tired out before we had reached the stage, and we had to beat and whip them, put our clothing on other pack horses, change our saddle horses for pack horses, and sometimes even the two of us ride one horse.

---

(277)

TIMES out of number we were hungered and athirst, cold and wearied. They only gave us food in the evening; in the morning we had something to drink or millet gruel,[2] while in the evening they gave us meat, a shoulder and ribs of mutton, and some pot liquor. When we had our fill of such meat broth, we felt greatly invigorated; it seemed to me a most delicious drink and most nourishing. On Fridays I fasted without drinking anything till evening, when I was obliged, though it distressed me sorely, to eat

---

[1] *Ponderosus valde.* This is the only personal detail in the whole narrative.

[2] *Sorbere milium.* Parched millet is still a favourite food of many Mongol tribes; it is either eaten dry and washed down with a gulp of tea, or else it is put in the tea and softened. Boiled millet with mutton is also often eaten. Ibn Batuta (ii, 364), speaking of the food of the Tartars of the Kipchak, says: "They prepare a dish in that country with an ingredient found there like millet, and called *addughy*. They put water on the fire, and when it boils they put a little *dughy* (millet) in it. If they have meat, they chop it up and cook it with the grain. Then they serve some to each person in his cup; they pour a little curdled milk over it, and swallow it down." Pian de Carpine (640) says of the Mongols' food that in winter "they cook millet in water, and make it so thin that they cannot eat it but have to drink it. And each one of them drinks a bowl or two, and eats nothing else the day long. In the evening they give to each a little meat, and they drink the broth from the meat." This was the ordinary diet of the Mongols in his day, and at the present day it is practically the same. Mongols, Tibetans, and Chinese when travelling do not eat in the morning: the one meal of the day is taken in the evening.

meat. Sometimes we had to eat half-cooked or nearly raw meat, not having fuel to cook it; this happened when we reached camp after dark, and we could not see to pick up ox or horse dung. We rarely found any other fuel, save occasionally a few briars.[1] In a few spots along the banks of some of the streams were woods, but such spots were rare. At first our guide showed profound contempt for us, and was disgusted at having to guide such poor folk; but after awhile, when he began to know us better, he would take us to the yurts (*curia*) of rich Moal, where we had to pray for them, and if I had had a good interpreter, I had opportunities for bringing about much good. This Chingis, the first Chan, had four sons,[2] whose descendants are very numerous; and these all have big *ordus*, and they multiply daily and are scattered all over this vast sealike desert. Our guide took us (278) to many of these, and they would wonder greatly at our not receiving gold, silver, or costly clothing. They inquired also of the great pope, if he were as old as they had heard, for they had heard that he was five hundred years old. They asked about our countries, if there were many sheep, cattle and horses there. As to the Ocean sea, they were quite unable to understand that it was endless, without bounds.

The eve of All Saints (31st October) we left the road to the east,[3] for the people had already moved a good deal to

---

[1] These briars were saksaul, with which Friar Benedict, who calls it (*supra*, p. 35) *absincium*, says this country was covered.

[2] Juchi, Chagatai, Ogodai, and Tului. The eldest died during his father's lifetime.

[3] It is, of course, impossible to determine with any great degree of exactitude the point where our traveller took a southerly course. Assuming, as I have done, that he did not make over thirty miles a day, he had probably not travelled, in the thirty-four days since passing the Ural river, a thousand statute miles. Allowing for the windings in the trail followed, he would seem to have changed his direction somewhere about E. long. 69°. Yule (*Cathay*, ccxii) thinks he struck south at about long. 67°; and F. M. Schmidt on his map—for in the body of his work he does not attempt to settle the question—

the south, and we made our way by some alps due south continually for viii days.[1] In that desert I saw many asses called *culam*,[2] and they greatly resemble mules; our guide and his companion chased them a great deal, but without getting one, on account of their great fleetness. The seventh day we began to see to the south some very high mountains, and we entered a plain irrigated like a garden, and here we found cultivated land. On the

---

places this point at about 70° 30'. It must not be thought that the direction then taken was *due* south. Our traveller throughout his narrative uses this term (*recte*). In the present case he probably travelled S.E. (see *supra*. p. 91, note 1; p. 92, note 1).

[1] *Direximus iter per quosdam alpes recte in meridiem.* Peschel (p. 166) understands this passage to mean that the traveller travelled *in the direction of* (*per*) certain Alps; and F. M. Schmidt (p. 192), misunderstanding, I take it, Yule's translation, accepts this interpretation. Yule (*Cathay*, ccxi) translates as I have done. I have followed Yule's interpretation, first, because Friar William speaks of entering a plain after travelling seven days south, when he came in sight of a high range of mountains; and second, because he uses in other passages the preposition *per*, in the usual sense of "through"; at p. 260 of the text he speaks of the mountain pasture lands (*alpes*) of the Kara-Kitayam "*per quas transive*"; and on p. 390 he says, "*tendebamus per altissima montana et per maximas nives in occidentem.*" Furthermore, if we accepted Peschel's and Schmidt's translation, we should have to imagine that Rubruck travelled over a plain for seven days in the direction of these alps without perceiving "the very high mountains to the south of them"; how this could be done I fail to see. Yule (*Cathay*, ccxii) supposes that our traveller crossed the "Alps" of the Kara tau, S.E. of the town of Turkestan, and then entered the valley of the Talas. This seems much more likely to me than that he should, as indicated on Schmidt's map, have gone straight through the desert to the north and south of the river Chu, until near the present Aulié-ata, and then have turned eastward. Pian de Carpine's route—which ran probably not far from the right bank of the Syr-daria—joined that followed by Rubruck, I should think, not far from the latter's Kinchat.

[2] See *supra*, p. 69. The Mongols call the wild ass *kulan*—often pronounced *hulan*. This animal is also found in Persia (where it is known as *ghor khar*), in parts of western India, Turkestan, and Tibet. Strabo (vii, 4,259) states that the Scythians of southern Russia used to hunt there *ὀνάγροι*; and Herodotus (iv, 61) says that the Indians in Xerxes' army had wild ones harnessed to their chariots. This I think is untrue, for I do not believe that the wild ass has ever been domesticated. On the wild ass hunting by the Mongols in the thirteenth century, see d'Ohsson (i, 322). I have often chased them on horseback, but even when wounded they could get away from the best pony I have ever seen.

octave of All Saints (8th November) we entered a certain town of Saracens called Kinchat,[1] and its captain came out of the town to meet our guide, bearing mead (*cervisia*) and cups. For it is their custom that in all towns subject to them, they come out to meet the messengers of Baatu and Mangu chan with food and drink. At that season of the year there was ice on the roads in those parts, and even earlier, from the date of the feast (279) of Saint Michel (29th September) we had had frost in the desert. I inquired the name of this province; but as we had already passed into another territory, they were unable to tell me anything beyond the name of the town, which was a very small one. And there came a big river down from the mountains,[2] which irrigated the whole country wherever they wanted to lead the water, and it flowed not into any sea, but was absorbed in the ground, forming many marshes. There (at Kinchat) I saw vines, and twice did I drink wine.[3]

---

THE next day we came to another village nearer the mountains, and I inquired concerning these mountains, which I understood to be those of the Caucasus, which confine at either extremity on the sea, from the west to the east, and which we had already crossed at the sea

---

[1] This town is mentioned under the name of Kendjek in the *Mesalek al-absar* (224) as one of the cities of the Talas valley (see note on next page; and F. M. Schmidt, p. 193).

[2] The Talas river, which is finally lost in the sands of the Muyum Kum (Yule, *Cathay*, ccxii; Bretschneider, *Med. Travel*, 34; F. M. Schmidt, p. 194).

[3] Grapes have been raised and wine made in this part of Turkestan for at least two thousand years. At Vernoye, for example, which is in the foot-hills of the Trans-Ili Ala tau, and at an altitude of 2,430 ft., grapes are successfully grown (Petermann, *Mittheilungen*, xix, 402 and F. M. Schmidt, p. 193).

previously mentioned into which the Etilia flows.[1] I asked also concerning the town of Talas[2] in which were Teuton slaves of Buri, of whom Friar Andrew had spoken (to me),[3] and concerning whom I had made much inquiry at the *ordus* of Sartach and Baatu. I was unable to learn anything concerning them, only the following circumstances of the death of their master Buri. Not finding his pasture lands good, one day while drunk he spoke to his men, saying: "Am I not of the race of Chingis chan as well as Baatu? (for he was the nephew or brother of Baatu).[4]

---

[1] The mountains he had in view were those of the Ala tau, those nearest him being what is now designated as the Alexander range. Classical geographers, whom our traveller follows in this, thought the Caucacus traversed Asia from east to west, and conceived the Ural mountains to be a branch of this great range (conf. F. M. Schmidt, p. 195, and *infra*).

[2] The town of Talas appears to have been situated on the river of the same name. It is first mentioned by Menander (228), in his account of the mission of Zemarchus. Its position is not known, but it was on the highroad from eastern to western Turkestan. The Chinese pilgrim, Yuan-chuang (Julien, *Pèlerins*, i, 14), visited it, and states that it was an important trading point. It is also referred to by Chinese travellers in the thirteenth century (Bretschneider, *Med. Travel*, 34, 75, 114; and *Med. Geog.*, 111). The *Mesalek al-absar* (224) says it was frequently called Jenghi-Talas: "From Samarkand to Jenghi they count twenty days' march. Jenghi is composed of four towns, separated the one from the other by the distance of a parasang (about four miles). Each one of them has a particular name; one is called Jenghi, the second Jenghi-bâlik, the third Kendjek (Rubruck's Kinchat?), and the fourth Talas." If this Talas is the same as the one referred to by our traveller—which seems hardly possible—he must, on leaving Kinchat, have taken an easterly direction with a little southing, which would have brought him nearer the mountains, as required by his narrative, but still Talas would have been a great deal nearer than was told him. See also F. M. Schmidt, pp. 195-200. He places Talas near the present Aulie-ata. Conf. also N. Elias, *op. cit.*, p. 79.

[3] There is no mention made of these Teuton slaves in the brief accounts which have reached us of Friar Andrew's mission; but there is every reason to suppose that Friar William had often seen Andrew after his return from Mongolia to Syria (see *supra*, Introductory notice).

[4] Buri was, according to d'Ohsson (ii, 111), a grandson of Chagatai, and therefore a second cousin of Batu. Bretschneider, however (*Med. Geog.*, 169), says he was Chagatai's son, and Pian de Carpine (666) agrees with this, thus making him Batu's first cousin.

Why should I not go to the banks of the Etilia like Baatu, to graze there?" Now these words were reported to Baatu, and he wrote to Buri's men, telling them to bring him their lord in chains, and this they did. Then Baatu asked if he (280) had spoken such words, and he confessed that he had, though he sought to excuse himself as being drunk, for they usually condone the offences of drunken men. But Baatu replied: "How dare you mention my name in your drunkenness!" and he had his head cut off.[1]

As to those Teutons I was unable to learn anything concerning them all the way to Mangu chan's *ordu*, but in the village just referred to I gathered that Talas was beyond us in the direction of the mountains, vi days' travel. When I reached the *ordu* of Mangu chan I gathered that Mangu had transported these Teutons, with Baatu's permission, the distance of a month's travel to the east of Talas, to a certain town called Bolat, where they are digging for gold and manufacturing arms,[2] so I could neither go nor come

---

[1] The origin of the quarrel between Batu and Buri is thus stated in the "Secret history of the Mongol dynasty" (*Yuan chao pi shih*), in Batu's report of the event to the Emperor Ogodai: "When the army returned (in 1243, after the conquest of eastern Europe), a banquet was arranged, at which all the princes were present. Being the eldest, I drank one or two cups of wine before the others. Buri and Guyuk were incensed, left the banquet and mounted their horses, at the same time reviling me. Buri said: 'Batu is not superior to me; why did he drink before I drank? He is an old woman with a beard. By a single kick I could knock him down and crush him!' Guyuk said: 'He is an old woman with bow and arrows. I shall order him to be thrashed with a stick!' Another proposed to fasten a wooden tail to my body. Such is the language that was used by the princes when, after the war with the different nations, we had assembled to deliberate on important matters; and we were obliged to break up without discussing the affairs. Such is what I have to report, O Emperor, my uncle" (Bretschneider, *Med. Geog.*, 169). After Shiramun's conspiracy (see *infra*, p. 164) Buri was in 1252 delivered to Batu by Mangu Khan and put to death, probably to avenge the old insult. The Mongols did not, when putting to death any of their princes, spill their blood: they were wrapped in felt and crushed to death, or else drowned (d'Ohsson, ii, 269, 458; iii, 243).

[2] The Mongols and Tartars have never been able to extract iron from the ore, except in a very primitive way, and must always have

back their way. However, in going I passed quite near that town (of Bolat), perhaps three days from it, but I was unaware of it, nor could I have turned from my route if I had known it.

From the village I have mentioned we went eastward, close to the mountains above referred to, and from that point we entered among the subjects of Mangu chan, who everywhere sang and clapped their hands before our guide, because he was an envoy of Baatu. For they show each other this mark of honor; the subjects of Mangu receive in this fashion the envoys of Baatu, and those of Baatu the envoys of Mangu. The subjects of Baatu, however, are the stronger, so they do not observe the custom so carefully. A few days later we entered the alps in which the Caracatai used to live, and there we found a great river which we had to pass in a boat.[1] After that we entered

---

been largely dependent for the supply necessary for the manufacture of their arms and domestic utensils on what they could import or levy as tribute. Our traveller has referred to the tribute of iron they had exacted from the people of north-eastern Europe (*supra*, p. 47). We can easily imagine how useful these Germans must have been to them, smelting iron and manufacturing weapons. Bolat is the *Pulad* of Persian mediæval writers, the *Po-lo* or *Pu-la* of Chinese travellers of the thirteenth century, the *Phulat* of King Heythum, who mentions it between Dinka-balekh (which Bretschneider, *Med. Geog.*, 300, thinks may perhaps be traced in the modern Tsing-ho, a river and town east of Lake Sairam on the road between Urumtsi and Kuldja) and the Sut Kul (Lake Sairam) (Klaproth, *Jour. Asiat.*, xii, 282). It is worthy of note, in connection with what we are told of the occupation at Bolat of these Germans, that the name *Pulad* is said to mean "steel"—I know not in what language (Klaproth, *loc. sup. cit.*). The Chinese traveller Ch'ang-tê, who passed through this town, which he calls *Po-lo*, in 1253, says that wheat and rice were raised there, that the houses were built of clay, and the windows furnished with glass (Bretschneider, *Med. Travel*, p. 70). It would seem highly probable that this use of glass—which then, as now, was practically unknown in this part of the world—had been introduced by these same Germans. Quatremère (*Not. et Extr.*, xiii, 229) makes the extraordinary mistake of identifying Rubruck's Bolat with Balkh (see also Bretschneider, *Med. Geog.*, 221, 300).

[1] Leaving Kinchat our traveller followed in an easterly direction along the northern base of the Alexander range, then crossing the Chu, which at that season of the year was probably an insignificant stream—for he does not mention it—he took an E.N.E. direction

a (281) valley, where we saw a ruined camp, whose walls were nothing but mud, and the soil was cultivated there. And after that we found a goodly town, called Equius,[1] in which were Saracens speaking Persian, though they

---

through the hills which separate the Chu from the Ili, and in which he says the Kara-Khitai had their summer pasturages (*alpes*). Leaving these hills he came on the Ili river, which he had to pass in a boat. Yule had (in *Cathay*, ccxiii) identified the "great river" of our traveller with the Chu, but in a later study on Rubruck (*Ency. Brit.*, xxi, 47), he accepts the view that it was the Ili, as does F. M. Schmidt (202). From here our traveller probably followed the great military road up the broad valley, in which are the feeders of the south branch of the Kara-mal. This road, then as now, passed by the modern town of Kopal. Thence Friar William went along the foot-hills of the Ala tau, to the present Lepinsk, from which point, probably by a rather circuitous trail, he came to the head of the Ala kul. The Chinese traveller, Ch'ang-tê, who travelled through this country south of Lake Baikal little more than a year before Rubruck, speaks of it as being thickly inhabited: "The country was intersected in all directions by canals, which irrigated the fields. Numerous ancient walls and other ruins were seen. The people said that in former times the Ki-tan dwelt there." Four days after passing this place, he reached the Talas (river?) (Bretschneider, *Med. Travel*, 74; see also F. M. Schmidt, 203).

[1] The identification of Rubruck's "great river" with the Ili obliges us to reject Yule's identification of Equius with the *Aspareh* of Shah Rokh's mission, which was on the Chu, somewhere near the present Pishpek, or Tokmak (*Cathay*, ccxiii). Likewise, we must consider as unlikely Howorth's identification of Equius with the Chinese mediæval traveller Ch'ang-tê's Yi-tu, which was in the neighbourhood of a river "*flowing eastward*" called the Yi-yün; and which place Howorth thinks he finds in the modern It-kīyu or Sari Kurgan on the Chu (Howorth, *History*, i, pt. 1, 282). The Yi-tu of Ch'ang-tê might be Rubruck's Equius, if we could identify his Yi-yün river with, say, the Borotala mal, which flows eastward into the Ebi nor, and suppose that the Chinese traveller had followed along the southern slope of the Ala tau up the course of the Bŏrotala, and then crossed over into the valley of the Kok su. This would have brought him exactly to the place where F. M. Schmidt places Equius on his map, a position which I think may be provisionally accepted as at least possible. Schmidt (203) says that Equius was only one day's travel from Kailac, which all writers on the subject agree upon placing a little to the west of the modern Kopal. The text does not bear out Schmidt's statement, although I am fain to admit that our author has succeeded in conveying that idea to his readers. See, however, Yule (*Ency. Brit.*, xxi, 47), where he thinks Schmidt misapprehends the text. Quatremère (*Not. et Extr.*, xiii, 288, 234) identifies the Isigheul of the *Mesalek al-absar* with Equius, but this does not help matters, for we do not know where Isigheul was.

were a very long way off from Persia. The next day, having crossed these alps which project from the high mountains in the south, we entered a beautiful plain with high mountains to the right, and a sea or lake which is xxv[1] days in circumference to the left. And all this plain is well watered by the streams which come down from the mountains, and all of which flow into this sea. In the summer time we came back along the north shore of this sea, and there likewise were great mountains. In this plain there used to be many towns, but most of them were destroyed, so that the Tartars might graze there, for there were most excellent pasturages in that country. We found there a big town called Cailac,[2] where there was a market, and many traders frequented it. Here we rested xii days,[3] waiting for a certain secretary of Baatu, who was to be associated with our guide in the matters to be settled at Mangu's *ordu*. This country used to be called Organum,[4] and the people used to have a language and letters of their own; (282) but now it is all occupied by Turcomans.[5]

---

[1] Hakluyt's MS. reads "fifteen."

[2] As pointed out by Yule (*Cathay*, ccxii, 576), Rubruck's Cailac is the *Kayalik* of Persian mediæval writers, and probably the *Kaligh* of Sadik Isfahan, the *Haulak* or *Khaulak* of Edrisi (d'Ohsson, ii, 246, iii, 516). Chinese writers of the Mongol period call it *Hai-va-li* (*Med. Travel*, 70). F. M. Schmidt (204), as well as all other writers on the subject, places Cailac a little to the west of the modern Kopal (N. Elias, *op. cit.*, 288).

[3] Some of the MSS. read xv. Yule (*Cathay*, ccxiv) has suggested that these figures are possibly a clerical error for vii, as otherwise we are obliged to suppose that the traveller covered the distance from Kinchat to the head of the Ala kul in fourteen days. The distance between these two points is about five hundred miles; this supposes an average progress of over thirty-five miles a day, which is—especially in a hilly country, as was part of this—an excess over what Friar William appears to have done in any other part of his journey.

[4] As pointed out by Yule (*Cathay*, 522), the name of Organa, the widow of Kara Hulagu, grandson and successor of Chagatai, and regent of his *ulus* on his death, has been transferred to the country itself. She lived at Almalik, at or near the modern Kuldja (Bretschneider, *Med. Travel*, 62; and *Med. Geog.*, 217).

[5] Benjamin of Tudela (36) speaks of the *Thogarmans* or Turks, and Haithon, *Hist. Orient.* (21), refers to the *Turquians*. Pian

Moreover, the Nestorians of those parts used to perform their services in that language, and write books in those letters,[1] and perhaps it was by them that those people were called Organa on account, as was told me, of their having been excellent guitar players (or *organiste*).[2] 'Twas here I first saw idolaters, of whom you must know there are many sects in the east.

The first are the Iugurs, whose country confines on this said country of Organum, being situated among the mountains to the east of it;[3] and in all their towns is found a mixture of Nestorians and Saracens, and they are also scattered about towards Persia in the towns of the Saracens.

---

de Carpine (701) mentions the Turcomans among the nations conquered by the Mongols. D'Ohsson (i, 196) tells us that the name Turcman, or "resembling Turks," was given by the Persians to the Kankalis (Rubruck's *Cangle*), when at the beginning of the thirteenth century they migrated to the Kharizm. Some authors, however, derive the name from the Turki *tir*, "to draw, to shoot," and *oman*, "arrow" (Pears, *Fall of Constantinople*, 15). William of Tyr (22, 24) says: "The people of the Turks, or of the Turcomanns (for they have the same origin) was at first a northern one. The Seldjuks took the name of Turks; those who continued to lead a pastoral life, that of Turcomanns."

[1] On the introduction of writing among the Uigurs and Mongols by the Nestorians, see *infra*.

[2] *Organiste* in mediæval Latin, French and Greek (ὀργανάριος) means a musician, a player on any kind of instrument.

[3] The position here assigned to the country of the Uigurs is quite correct. In the thirteenth century they occupied Urumtsi, Turfan, Karakhodjo and adjacent localities, all situated S.E. of the Kuldja (Organum) country (Bretschneider, *Med. Geog.*, 194). Chinese writers say the Uigurs (called by them at various epochs *Yuan-ho*, *Hui-ho*, *Hui-hu*, and *Hui-hui*) were at one time known as *Kao lun ch'ê* or "high-wheeled carts" and as *Kao ch'ê*, "high carts." They descended from the ancient Hsiung-nü, who became later on the Tu-küeh (Turks) (*Wei shu*, bk. 103; *T'ang shu*, bk. 217a; Ma Tuan-lin, bk. 344, *s.v.*, *T'ieh-lê;* see also Bretschneider, *Med. Geog.*, 189-211, where the subject is fully treated from Chinese sources). Mohammedan historians agree with Chinese in putting the Uigurs with the Kankalis (Kao-ch'ê of the Chinese), Kipchaks, Karluks, etc., among the Oguz Turks (d'Ohsson, i, 423, 429 *et seq.;* Howorth, *History*, i, pt. 1, 21, 694, and *J.R.A.S.*, 1898, 809-838). Vilh. Thomsen (*op. cit.*, 147) suggests that the name Uigur is but a corruption of the Turkish Oguz; if this can be accepted, it might be the original of the Chinese name Kao-ch'ê. Pian de Carpine (650) writes the name *Huiurs.*

In the said city of Cailac they had three idol temples, two of which I entered to see their foolishness. In the first one I found a person who had a little cross in ink on his hand,[1] whence I concluded he was a Christian, and to all that I asked him he replied that he was a Christian. So I asked him: "Why have you not here the Cross and the figure of Jesus Christ?" And he replied: "It is not our custom." So I concluded that they were Christians, but had omitted this through some doctrinal error. I noticed there behind a chest which served in the place of altar (283) and on which they put lamps and offerings, a winged image like Saint Michel, and other images like bishops holding their fingers as if blessing.[2] That evening I could

---

[1] Theophylactus (225) tells us of some Turks, sent in the sixth century as prisoners to Constantinople, who bore the sign of the cross pricked in black dots on their foreheads. They said that, many years before, when a pestilence was ravaging their country, Christians (Nestorians) had suggested to them to do this, and that by this means the pestilence had been averted. The cross seen by our traveller may have been a hooked cross or *swastika*, which I have sometimes seen tattooed on the hands of Mongols and Tibetans. Tattooing is not common among the people of central and northern Asia (omitting, of course, such tribes as the Chuckches and others of the far north-east). Pomponius Mela (622) says the Agathyrsi, a Scythian tribe living N. of the Sea of Azov (probably the same as the Khazars, see *supra*, p. 42, note 1), tattooed their faces and hands, the amount of tattooing increasing with the social rank (conf. Herodotus, iii, 179). Chinese annals tell us that among the Kirghiz in the third or fourth century, the men had tattoo marks on their hands, and the women when they married had them made on the nape of their necks (Ma Tuan-lin, bk. 348). The Chinese pilgrim Yuan-chuang states that the people of Kashgar (*Kieh-sha*) were in the habit of compressing the heads of their new-born children between boards—a custom attributed also by classical authors to the Huns, Sidonius Apoll. *Panegyr. Anthem.*, 245 *et seq.*)—and "decorated their bodies with bluish-green designs." Julien (*Pélerins*, ii, 220) and Beal (*Records*, ii, 307) have mistranslated this passage, having read *ching* "eye" instead of *ch'ing* "blue."

[2] This idol temple was, I take it, a Buddhist one. I am, however, quite unable to say whether the Buddhist monks of Cailac professed the Tibetan or the Indian form of that religion, for Buddhism was first introduced there directly from India, or rather from Khotan, though Tibetan Buddhism may have spread there in the thirteenth century. The winged figure would seem to be one of the *yi-dam* or patron saints of the Lamaist's pantheon, many of whom are represented with

find out nothing more, for the Saracens shun these (idolaters) so much that they will not even speak of them, and when I asked Saracens concerning the rites of these people, they were scandalised. The day following was the first of the month and the Easter of the Saracens,[1] and I changed my host and was lodged near another idol temple, for the people entertain envoys each as he may and according to his ability. Going into this idol temple I found the priests of the idols there, for on the first of the month they throw open the temples and put on their sacerdotal vestments, offer (incense, hang up lamps and offer) the oblations of bread and fruit of the people.[2] Now, in the first place, I will tell you of the rites common to all idolaters, and after that of those of the Iugurs, who form as it were a sect distinct from the others. They all worship to the north, with joined hands, prostrate themselves to the ground with bended knees, placing their foreheads on their hands. As a result of this, the Nestorians in those parts never join their hands in praying, but pray with their hands held extended before the breast.[3]

They (the idolaters) place their temples east and west;

---

wings. The images with hands held in the position of blessing are seen in all Buddhist temples, but they represent the Buddha or Bodhisattwas in the act of preaching.

[1] I suppose that the feast of *Bairam* is meant. Schiltberger (70) also refers to "the Infidels' Easter-day," and to "another Easter-day" which is the feast of *Kurban Bairam*.

[2] Buddhists have always kept the first and fifteenth of each month as special church feasts, on which the monks make general confession. The eighth and twenty-fifth are also religious feasts. These four days are called *dus bzang*, "good days," by the Tibetans. (Rockhill, *Land of the Lamas*, 100.) The first of the month is the most important, the ceremonies lasting during the whole day; incense is burnt, and offerings made of bread, fruit, water, and lamps lit before all the images.

[3] At the present day, at all events, I am quite sure that there is no special orientation observed by Buddhists in praying, though—as wherever possible the temples have a southern exposure—they do usually face to the north. Nor do they clasp their hands, but hold them together with opened palms.

on the north side they make an alcove projecting out like a choir, or sometimes, if the building is square, it is in the middle of the building. So they shut off on the north side an (284) alcove in place of a choir, and there they put a coffer as long and as broad as a table,[1] and after that coffer to the south they place the chief idol, and that which I saw at Caracarum was as large as we paint Saint Christopher.[2] And a Nestorian who had come from Cathay told me that in that country there is an idol so big that it can be seen from two days off.[3] And they place other idols around about (the principal one), all most beautifully gilt. And on that coffer, which is like a table, they put lamps and offerings. Contrary to the custom of the Saracens, all the doors of the temples open to the south. They also have big bells like ours: 'tis for this reason, I think, that the eastern Christians do not have

---

[1] The text is rather confused, and there is a useless repetition, perhaps the result of hasty dictation. The meaning is, that the altar is either placed in front of the apsis of the temple, or in the centre of the building when it is square. The arrangement as indicated by Friar William applies perfectly to Lama temples and Chinese Buddhist (*hoshang*) temples of the present day, in which there is a long table in front of the images on which lamps and offerings are placed.

[2] In the Christian legend Saint Christopher was a giant. Many of the early representations of him are more than life-size.

[3] Colossal statues of Buddhas are numerous in China, Mongolia and Tibet. Marco Polo (i, 221) speaks of "the great stone statues ten paces in length" at Campichu (Kan-chou in N.W. Kan-su), and King Heythum mentions a very large clay image of *Shakemonia* (Shakyamuni) and an enormous one of *Madri* (Maitreya, the coming Buddha), also of clay, in a fine temple which he saw, or heard of, in China (Klaproth, *Journ. Asiat.*, xii, 289). The largest stone image I have seen is in a cave temple at Yung-kán, about ten miles N.W. of Ta-t'ung Fu in Shan-hsi. Père Gerbillon says the Emperor K'ang-hsi measured it himself and found it to be 57 *chih* high (61 ft.) (Duhalde, *Description*, iv, 352). I have seen another colossal statue in a cave near Pin chou in N.W. Shan-hsi; and there is another about forty-five miles S. of Ning-hsia Fu, near the left bank of the Yellow River (Rockhill, *Land of the Lamas*, 26 and *Diary*, 47). The great recumbent figure of the "Sleeping Buddha" in the Wo Fo ssŭ, near Peking, is of clay.

any. The Ruthenians, however, have them, and so do the Greeks in Gazaria.[1]

All the priests (of the idolaters) shave their heads, and are dressed in saffron colour, and they observe chastity from the time they shave their heads, and they live in congregations of one or two hundred.[2] On the days when they go into the temple, they place two benches, and they sit in the region of the choir but opposite the choir,[3] with books in their hands, which they sometimes put down on these benches; and they keep their heads uncovered as long as they are in the temple, reading in silence and keeping silence. And when I went into one of their temples at (285) Caracarum, and found them thus seated, I tried every means of inducing them to talk, but was unable to do so. Wherever they

---

[1] Bells were, however, used among the Christians living with the Mongols. Trigault (*Exped. Chrét.*, i, 87), in the early part of the seventeenth century, mentions having seen one of these early Christian bells, which he says was in cast-iron (see also *supra*, p. 116, note 2).

[2] Saffron colour was that prescribed for all monks by Buddhist canon law (*Vinaya*), and is still worn by the southern Buddhists, and since the fifteenth century by a large part of the Lamas of Mongolia and Tibet. The absence of any reference to red garments, which in the thirteenth century were, I think, universally worn by all the Tibetan clergy, is interesting, as it would tend to show that the Buddhism professed at the time among the Mongols was not entirely of either Tibetan or Chinese origin, but retained probably many of the customs derived from the early Indian Buddhism of Central Asia. The use of high church hats, of the formula *Om mani padme hûm*, and other details noticed in subsequent pages, show, however, that Tibetan Buddhism had already begun to exercise a considerable influence in the country. On Buddhist monasteries in the Mongol times, see Palladius (*op. cit.*, 29), and Yule (*Marco Polo*, i, 293). Rubruck makes reference in one passage to a priest wearing red clothes. He had come from Cathay, but was probably a Mongol or Tibetan.

[3] *Sedent e regione corus contra corum.* At the present day, as apparently in Rubruck's time, the Lamas when holding church services sit in rows on either side of the temple from the altar to the doors. They have low benches or tables before them, on which they place the heavy, cumbrous volumes they read. They wear while in the temple, on occasions of ceremony, their high yellow hats (*ser dja*), but on ordinary occasions they go through their devotions bareheaded. It is customary for all laymen to take off their hats in Lama temples.

go they have in their hands a string of one or two hundred beads, like our rosaries, and they always repeat these words, *on mani baccam*, which is, "God, thou knowest," as one of them interpreted it to me, and they expect as many rewards from God as they remember God in saying this.[1] Around their temple they make a fine courtyard, well surrounded by a wall, and in the side of this facing the south, they make the main gate where they sit and talk. And over this gate they set up a long pole, which, if it be possible, rises above the whole city, and by this pole it may be known that this building is an idol temple.[2] This practice is common to all idolaters. When I went into the idol temple I was speaking of, I found the priests seated in the outer gate, and when I saw them with their shaved faces they seemed to me to be Franks, but they had barbarian mitres on their heads.[3] These Iugur priests have the following dress: wherever they go they are always dressed in rather tight saffron-coloured tunics, over which is a girdle like the Franks, and they have a stole (*pallium*) over their left shoulder, passed round the chest and the

---

[1] The rosaries used by the Lamas and people of Mongolia and Tibet at the present day have 108 beads, corresponding to the "108 doors of the Law." Their varieties are endless. (See Waddell, *Jour. Asiat. Soc. Bengal*, lxv, 24, *et seq.*; Rockhill, *Ethnology*, 736). This is the earliest reference I know of to the famous formula *Om, mani padme hûm*: "Om, the jewel in the Lotus, hûm." It appears, however, to have been in use as early as the tenth century, for it is found in a Chinese translation of the *Vyuha ratnaradja sûtra*, made between A.D. 980 and 1001 (Sensho Fujii, *Hansei, Zasshi*, xiii, No. 2, etc.; see also Rockhill, *Land of the Lamas*, 326 *et seq.*).

[2] Such poles, often topped with a big black bundle to resemble a yak tail, and so identifying these poles with the Turkish *tughs*, an emblem of authority used in Asia from remote times, are always placed before Lama temples. Somewhat similar ones are placed before Chinese temples.

[3] The variety of hats and caps worn at the present day is very great. Waddell (*Buddhism in Tibet*, 196) shows twenty styles of Lama hats and coats; see also Cunningham, *Ladak*, 238, and Rockhill, *Ethnology*, 731.

back to the right side, like (286) the chasuble (*casula*) worn by a deacon in Lent.[1]

The Tartars have adopted their (*i.e.*, the Uigurs') letters. They begin writing at the top, and run the line downward; and in like manner they read it, and they make the lines to follow each other from left to right.[2] They make great use of drawings and letters for their sorcery, so their temples are full of short sentences (*brevibus*) hung up there.[3] The letters which Mangu chan sends us are in the Moal language, but in their script.

They burn their dead according to the custom of the ancients, and put the ashes in the top of pyramids.[4]

---

[1] This dress is a purely Buddhist one: the *pallium* or shawl thrown round the body is worn as well in southern Buddhist countries as in northern. Friar William does not, I think, wish it to be understood, though he mixes them in his account somewhat, that the Uigur priests were identical with the Buddhists, or "idolaters" as he styles them; though it would seem that not only did they dress like them, but that their temples had images in them similar to those of the Buddhists. The Friar's discussion with these Uigur priests about the soul could not have been held with Buddhists, who neither believe in a soul nor in a personal God. Apparently, as stated a little farther on by our traveller, the only article of Christian faith these Uigurs believed was that of one God. Pian de Carpine (650) says, "the Huiurs are Christians of the sect of the Nestorians." This may well be; from Friar William's account of the tenets of this latter sect as professed among the Mongols, they were no more Christians than the Uigurs (see *supra*, page 17, note 4).

[2] On the origin of the Mongol script, see *infra*, p. 150, note 1.

[3] *Cartis et caracteribus pro sortilegio.* A considerable source of profit for Lamas and Chinese *hoshang* of the present day is stamping on bits of paper or cotton magic formulas or prayers, usually surrounding a central figure of some God or guardian saint (*ch'ös-chyong*). Over the houses and tents of the people, as well as around the temples, or attached along the high poles which Rubruck has mentioned in front of the temples, are innumerable bits of white cotton stamped with such sentences. The interior walls of the temples are also covered with most elaborately-finished charms or pictures, often beautifully illuminated. Like charms are worn on the person, tied to guns, or fastened around the necks of horses, and vast quantities of them are frequently scattered about for the benefit of whoever may find them (Rockhill, *Land of the Lamas*, 77, 98; *Diary*, 93, 153, and *infra*, p. 162).

[4] It is not quite clear whether the author refers to a custom of the Uigurs, or of both them and the Buddhists The Chinese *hoshang* and the southern Buddhists always burn their dead. Sung-yun, a Chinese pilgrim who passed through Khotan in A.D. 518, states that it was

When then I had sat down beside these priests, after having been in the temple and seen their many idols, great and small, I asked them what they believed concerning God. They answered: "We only believe that there is one God." Then I asked: "Do you believe he is a spirit, or something corporeal?" "We believe that he is a spirit," they said. "Do you believe that he has never taken upon him human nature?" They said: "Never." "Then," said I, "if you believe that he is one and a spirit, why do you make him bodily images, and so many? Furthermore, if you do not believe that he became man, why do you make him in human shape rather than in that of some animal?" Then they replied: "We do not make these images to (of) God,[1] but when some rich person among us dies, his son, or wife, or someone dear to him, has made an image of the deceased, and puts it here, and we revere it (287) in memory of him." Then I said: "Then you only make these out of flattery for man." "Only," they said, "in remembrance."

Then they asked me, as if in derision: "Where is God?" To which I said: "Where is your soul?" "In our body," they said. I replied: "Is it not everywhere in your body, and does it not direct the whole of it, and, nevertheless, is invisible? So God is everywhere, and governs all things, though invisible, for He is intelligence and wisdom." Then, just as I wanted to continue reasoning with them, my interpreter got tired, and would no longer express my words, so he made me stop talking.

The Moal or Tartars who are of this sect, though they

---

customary there to burn the dead, and collecting the ashes build towers over them (Beal, *Records*, i, lxxxvii). Perhaps a similar custom was in vogue in Rubruck's time among the Uigurs.

[1] *Non figuramus istas ymaginas Deo*, which may be "we do not make these images to God," but the context seems to require that we should read *Dei*, though all the MSS. have *Deo*. The images referred to must be the felt ones spoken of by Pian de Carpine (*supra*, p. 59, note 1), and mentioned again in the next paragraph.

believe in one God, make nevertheless images of their dead in felt, and dress them in the richest stuffs, and put them in one or two carts, and no one dare touch these carts, which are under the care of their soothsayers, who are their priests, and of whom I shall tell you further on. These soothsayers are always before the *ordu* of Mangu and of other rich people, for the poor have none, but only those of the family of Chingis. And when they are on the march, these (soothsayers) precede them as the pillar of a cloud did the children of Israel, and they decide where to pitch the camp, and when they have set down their dwellings, all the *ordu* follows them. And when a feast day comes about, or the first of the month, they take their images and arrange them (288) in a circle in their house. Then the Moal come, enter the house, and bow before the images and do them reverence. And no stranger may enter that house. I tried to force my way into one hut, but was most rudely treated.

---

THOSE Iugurs who live interspersed with the Christians and Saracens, through frequent disputations, as I believe, have reached the point of having no belief but that in a single God. These Iugurs used to inhabit the cities which first obeyed Chingis chan, who therefore gave his daughter to their king.[1] And Caracarum is as it were

---

[1] Friar William would seem to have been misinformed on this point, for I can find no record of Chingis having given one of his daughters in marriage to an Uigur prince. He did, however, give his daughter Chichegan as wife to Turalji, son of Kutuke Bigni, chief of the Uduyut or Merkites (d'Ohsson, i, 419). The positions here assigned to the people of Prester John (the Keraits) and to the Uigurs (prior to their overthrow in the ninth century by the Kirghiz) is correct. The Merkites lived on the Selinga, just to the north of the Keraits, and the confusion is thus easily explained. Howorth (*History*, i, pt. 1, 698) does not understand this passage of the text as I have. It was not at the time when the Uigurs were living near Karakorum that the Mongols borrowed their script and applied it to their

in their territory, and all the land of the king or the Prester John and of Unc his brother, was round about this country, though they occupied the pasture lands to the north, while the Iugurs lived amidst the mountains to the south. So it happened that the Moal adopted their letters, and they are their best scribes, and nearly all the Nestorians know their letters.[1] Beyond them to the east among those mountains are the Tanguts, most valiant men, who captured Chingis in war; and he, peace being made, and once freed by them, subdued them.[2] These people have very

---

language, but at a much later date. There is, so far as I know, no information available as to the date of the introduction of Nestorianism among the Uigurs, and of the adaptation of the Syriac-estrangelo alphabet to their language; but, prior to its spread among them, Manichæism appears to have taken strong hold of them; and that its tenets were still believed in the thirteenth century is clearly evidenced in the theological discussion which Friar William had with one of the *tuins* (possibly an Uigur, but at all events evidently professing their creed), and related in a subsequent chapter. Manichæism was introduced among the Uigurs about A.D. 762, as we learn from the famous inscription of Kara Balgasun published by Radloff (*Atlas Alterthümer der Mongolei*, xxxi-xxxv). See also Chavannes (*Le Nestorianism* , 16, 45, 47) and Devéria (*Musulmans et Manichéens Chinois*, 454).

[1] In 1204, after the defeat of the Naiman by Chingis Khan, he caused the first minister of that kingdom, an Uigur called T'a-ta-tung-o, to teach the language of his native land to his sons, and to apply his script to the Mongol language (d'Ohsson, i, 89; Drouin, *Journ. Asiat.*, ixe série, vii, 488). Pian de Carpine (650) says that the Uigurs "have adopted their (*i.e.*, the Nestorians') alphabet, for they did not before that have any script; but now they call it the script of the Mongals (*litteram Mongalorum*)." (See also Isaac Taylor, *The Alphabet*, i, 29 *et seq.*)

[2] The kingdom of Tangut, or Hsi Hsia, as the Chinese called it, ruled over the present province of Kan-su and adjoining country, from A.D. 1004 to 1226, when it was finally destroyed by Chingis Khan (d'Ohsson, i, 370 *et seq.*). The founder of this dynasty was Li Tê-ming of the To-pa clan of the Táng-hsiang, a Tibetan people of N.E. Tibet. It is supposed by some writers that the name Tangut is derived from Táng-hsiang. Chinese authorities tell us that the name was originally borne by a people living in the Altai, and that the word is Turkish (Howorth, *J.R.A.S.*, xv, Pt. IV, 4; Rockhill, *Land of the Lamas*, 73; and *J.R.A.S.*, 1891, 6). At all events, the population of Tangut was a mixture of Tibetans, Turks, Uigurs, Tukuhuns, Chinese, etc. I cannot find any reference to the capture of Chingis by the Tangut. In his campaign of 1209-1210, he was forced to raise the siege of Ning-hsia on the Yellow River, by the Tanguts inundating the surrounding plain. This may be the event which gave rise to our author's story (d'Ohsson, i, 106).

strong cattle, with very hairy tails like horses, and with bellies and backs covered with hair. They are lower on their legs than other oxen, but much stronger. They draw the big (289) dwellings of the Moal, and have slender, long, curved horns, so sharp that it is always necessary to cut off their points. The cows will not let themselves be milked unless sung to. They have also the temper of the bull, for if they see a man dressed in red they throw themselves on him to kill him.[1]

Beyond these are the Tebet,[2] a people in the habit of eating their dead parents, so that for piety's sake they should not give their parents any other sepulchre than their bowels. They have given this practice up, however, as they were held an abomination among all nations. They still, however, make handsome cups out of the heads

---

[1] Yaks are here referred to. The first western author to refer to them was Cosmas Indicopleustes, in his *Christian Topography* (360), where he calls them *agriobous*. The average load carried by a yak is about 250 lbs. The wild yak bull is an enormous animal, and the people of Turkestan and North Tibet credit him with extraordinary strength. Mirza Haidar, in the *Tarikhi Rashidi* (416), says of the wild yak or *kutás*: "This is a very wild and ferocious beast. In whatever manner it attacks one it proves fatal. Whether it strikes with its horns, or kicks or overthrows its victim. If it has no opportunity of doing any of these things, it tosses its enemy with its tongue twenty *gaz* into the air, and he is dead before reaching the ground. One male *kutás* is a load for twelve horses. One man cannot possibly raise a shoulder of the animal" (see also Marco Polo, i, 266, 268).

[2] The natives call Tibet *Bod*, pronounced *Beu*, and Central or Upper Tibet was, and still is, called *Stod Bod*, pronounced *Teu-Beu*, whence the name *Tibet*, *Tebet*, *Tobbat*, and the other forms of the name. Pian de Carpine (658) calls Tibet *Burithabet*, which d'Avezac (565) thinks may be the Mongol *Baron-Tala*, by which name the Mongols designate Tibet. Rashideddin (d'Ohsson, i, 82) also uses the word *Buri Tibet*. I am inclined to think it is a hybrid word, composed of the native appellation *Bod* and of the word *Tibet*. Pian de Carpine (*loc. sup. cit.*) says of the people of Tibet: "They are pagans. They have a most astonishing, or rather horrible, custom, for when anyone's father is about to give up the ghost, all the relatives meet together, and they eat him, as was told to me for certain. They have no hairs in their beard; for they carry an iron (pincher) in their hand, as I saw myself, with which they always pluck out their beard, if some hair grows out in it: and they are very ill-shapen." Tibetans and Mongols still pluck out their beards as here described.

of their parents, so that when drinking out of them they may have them in mind in the midst of their merry-making. This was told me by one who had seen it.[1] These people have much gold in their country, so that when one lacks gold he digs till he finds it, and he only takes so much as he requires and puts the rest back in the ground; for if he put it in a treasury or a coffer, he believes that God would take away from him that which is in the ground.[2] I saw many misshapen individuals of this people. Of the Tanguts I have seen big men, but swarthy. The Iugurs are of medium size, like us. Among the Iugurs the Turkie Coman language has its source and root.[4] After Tebet are Longa and Solanga,[5] whose (290) envoys

---

[1] As shown in the preceding note, Pian de Carpine makes this same charge of cannibalism against the Tibetans; and Marco Polo (i, 292) says of the people of Tibet (or Kashmir, for the text is not clear) that they ate all those who had been put to death by lawful authority. So far as I am aware, this charge is not made by any oriental writer against the Tibetans, though both Arab travellers to China in the ninth century and Armenian historians of the thirteenth century say the Chinese practised cannibalism. The Armenians designate China by the name *Nankas*, which I take to be Chinese *Nan kuo*, "southern country," the *Manzi* country of Marco Polo (Reinaud, *Relations*, i, 23, 52, 68; Dulaurier, 486). Chinese writers say that the Liu-chiu islanders in the southern portion of the group ate their dead (Ma Tuan-lin, bk. 327). The Tibetans still make libation bowls out of human skulls, and some of the lamas use such bowls to eat out of. The ancient Turks and the Naiman made drinking bowls out of their enemies' skulls (see d'Ohsson, i, 82; Rockhill, *Ethnology*, 727; Yule, *Cathay*, clii, 151, and Marco Polo, i, 292; conf. Herodotus, iii, 46; and Strabo, xi, 7, 439, 11, 445.

[2] Gold is found in most of the streams and rivers of Tibet, from the sands of which the people wash it with pans or wooden cradles. The belief referred to by our author is still general in the country, and mining is not allowed, under the impression that if nuggets of gold are removed from the earth no more gold will be found in the river gravels: the nuggets being held to be the plants which produce the dust gathered in the rivers (Rockhill, *Land of the Lamas*, 209).

[3] The Tibetans, with their huge sheepskin gowns forming a big bag at the waist, in which half the wearer's goods are stored, their long matted locks, their bare legs with small calves, look misshapen enough. The dress this people wore in the thirteenth century, we learn from Chinese sources, was the same as they still have.

[4] This is an interesting and perfectly accurate statement.

[5] Longa and Solanga are the Churches and Sulangka of the mediæval Mohammedan writers. The country of these two peoples

I saw at court, and they had brought with them more than ten big carts, each of which was drawn by six oxen. They are little men and swarthy like Spaniards, and they wear tunics like the chasuble (*supertunicale*) of a deacon, except with narrower sleeves. On their heads they wear a mitre like a bishop's, except that in front it is slightly lower than behind, and it does not terminate in a point, but is square on top, and is of stiff black buckram, and so polished that it shines in the sun's rays like a mirror or a well-burnished helmet.[1] And at the temples are long strips of the same stuff, which are fastened to the mitre, and which stand out in the wind like two horns projecting from the temples. When the wind strikes it too violently, they fold them up across the mitre over the temples, where they remain like a hoop across the head; and a right handsome ornament it is. And whenever the principal envoy came to court

formed one of the twelve governments of the Mongol empire. The Churches are called *Nu-chên* by the Chinese, but they called themselves, we are told, *Lu-chên* or *Lu-chih.* This may be the original of our traveller's *Longa.* The name *Solanga* is still borne by some of the Manchus, the Solons. The country of Longa and Solanga comprised probably a large part of northern and eastern Manchuria, and even northern Korea. According to mediæval Mohammedan writers, Sulangka comprised the cultivated part of the Churches' country—that which contained towns and villages (d'Ohsson, ii, 478, 638). Some writers have supposed that Longa and Solanga was one of those "double jumbles," as Yule calls them, like Gog-Magog, Chin-Machin, Koli-Ukoli, etc. Chinese annals also refer to the fact that the carts of the Nu-chên were drawn by oxen. Pian de Carpine (*supra*, p. 20) speaks of the *Solanges.*

[1] The dress and head-dress of these envoys is very similar to that still worn by the Koreans. Chinese histories inform us that this Korean head-dress was worn by many of the nation's neighbours of Korea (see Ma Tuan-lin, bks. 326, 1, 327, 17). Our traveller says this cap was made of *stamina rigidata per coloram nigram.* As a matter of fact, it is made of horsehair and very fine strips of bamboo, dyed black, and very highly varnished. I may note here that, after the Mongol occupation of Korea, the official classes adopted for a while the Mongol dress and coiffure (*Korean Repository*, v, 179). The wings of these Korean caps do not project from in front, but from behind; those worn by the envoys seen by Friar William must have differed slightly from those of the Koreans.

he carried a highly-polished tablet of ivory about a cubit long and half a palm wide. Every time he spoke to the chan or some great personage, he always looked at that tablet as if he found (291) there what he had to say, nor did he look to the right or the left, nor in the face of him with whom he was talking. Likewise, when coming into the presence of the Lord, and when leaving it, he never looked at anything but his tablet.[1]

Besides these people there is another, as I was assured, called Muc,[2] who have towns, but who take no animals for themselves. There are, however, many herds and flocks in their country, but no one herds them; when anyone wants some, he goes to a hill and calls, and all the animals hearing the call come around him, and let him treat them as if they were tame. If an ambassador or any foreigner come to that country, they put him in a house, and give him all he requires, until his business has been settled; for should a foreigner go about the country, his odour would

---

[1] These tablets are called *hu* in Chinese, and were used in China and Korea; in the latter country down to quite recent times. They were made of jade, ivory, bamboo, etc., according to the rank of the owner, and were about three feet long. The *hu* was originally used to make memoranda on of the business to be submitted by the bearer to the Emperor, or to write the answers to questions he had had submitted to them. Odoric also refers to "the tablets of white ivory which the emperor's barons held in their hands as they stood silent before him" (Yule, *Cathay*, 141; Cordier, *Odoric*, 378).

[2] One MS. has *Nunc*, but this is no help in solving the question. F. M. Schmidt (218) thinks *Muc* may be the *Mouky*, or *Moho*, of north-east Asia. This is quite out of the question. Chinese histories tell us that the Nu-chên Tartars were called Mo-ho only during the Sui and T'ang periods (A.D. 589-905), but that in the tenth century the name Nu-Chih, or Nu-chên, was assumed as the national name (Ma Tuan-lin, bk. 327, 5). I am inclined to think that aboriginal populations of Ssŭ-ch'uan and Kan-su, often called *Man*, or *Man-tzŭ*, by the Chinese, are referred to, or perhaps even the Mosso of Yun-nan. These people lived in fortified villages on hill-tops, and then, as now, had the village flocks herded together in the adjacent valleys. I may note that it is still a custom among Tibetan and Mongol chiefs to keep traders who may visit them more or less in seclusion, so as to retain all the trading in their own hands. This, and not the danger of the cattle running away on account of the peculiar odour of the foreigners, may have originated the story told Friar William.

cause the animals to run away and they would become wild.

There is also great Cathay, whose people were anciently, as I believe, called Seres. From among them come the best silk stuffs (which are called *seric* by that people), and the people get the name of Seres from one of their cities.[1] I was given to understand that in that region there is a city with walls of silver and towers of gold. In that land are many provinces, the greater number of which do not yet obey the Moal, and between them and India there is a sea. These Cathayans are small men, who

---

[1] Friar William was the first western writer to identify Cathay with the classical country of the Seres. Yule (*Cathay*, xliv, cxxv) thinks that Rubruck's *seric* is probably derived from the Mongal *sirkek*, which in turn is the Chinese *ssŭ*, silk; and that the name *Ser*, and *Seres* may have been formed by inverse analogy from the word *sericum*, taken as an adjective. I can find no better authority for our traveller's statement that the name Seres is derived from that of a city than Isidorus (*op. cit.*, 500), who says "Seres is a fortress of the Orient, from which the people of the Seres and the country take their name." He probably quoted from some earlier writer, but I have not been able to trace his remark (see also Yule, *Cathay*, cxxv). Our author writes the name *Cataya*, or *Cathaia*. Sempad, of Armenia, writes it *Chatha*; Will. of Nangis (360) and Pian de Carpine, *Kitaia*. This latter traveller's remarks (653) on Cathay supplement our author's so well that I will give them in full. "The Kitayans," he says, "are pagans, and have a special script; and they have a New and Old Testament, it is said, and they have Lives of the Fathers, and hermits and houses made like churches, in which they pray at appointed times; and it is said they have some saints. They worship one God, they honour the lord Jesus Christ, and believe in a life eternal, but do not baptize at all. They honour and revere our Scriptures, are fond of Christians, and do many acts of charity: they seem to be quite a kind-hearted and humane people. They have no beard, and in the shape of their face they resemble a good deal the Mongals, but they are not so broad in the face; they have a tongue of their own; no better artizans are to be found in the whole world, in all the works which men are wont to perform. Their country is very rich in corn, wine, gold, silver and silk, and in all those things on which human beings depend for subsistence." The Old Testament I take to be the "Five Classics" (*Wu Ching*), the New Testament the "Four Books" (*Ssŭ Shu*). The Lives of the Fathers are probably the Confucian Analects and the works of Mencius; and Confucius, Mencius and Lao-Tzŭ are in all likelihood the saints referred to. The one God they worship is either *T'ien*, "Heaven," or *T'ien Chu*, "the Lord of Heaven." The other points in his remarks are too well known to require comment.

in speaking aspirate strongly through the nose, and in (292) common with all Orientals, have small openings for the eyes. They are most excellent artisans in all manners of crafts, and their doctors know full well the virtues of herbs, and diagnose very skilfully the pulse; but they do not use diuretics, nor do they know anything about the urine: this I have seen myself.[1] There are a great many of them at Caracarum, and it is their custom for all sons to follow the same trade as their fathers. 'Tis for this reason that they pay such a great tribute; for they give the Moal daily a thousand five hundred *iascots* or cosmos; an *iascot* is a piece of silver weighing ten marks; so this is XV thousand marks, exclusive of the silk tissues and the provisions which they receive from them, and the other servitudes which are put on them.[2]

---

[1] Yule (*Cathay*, cxxv) says Martin Martini, in his *Atlas Sinensis*, alludes to a popular Chinese saying about the golden walls of Hsi-an Fu. "This passage," he adds, "is remarkable with reference to the remark of Ptolemy about the metropolis *Thinae*, that there was no truth in the stories of its brazen walls." It was in all probability a poetical figure of the Chinese to give an idea of the magnificence of the great city, with its yellow-tiled palaces and walls. Mr. Watters tells me that he thinks something of the kind was also written about Lo-yang in the T'ang period.

At the time Rubruck wrote, China south of the Yellow River was still independent.

As regards the statement about the Chinese doctors not using diuretics (*urinalibus non utuntur*), our author is certainly wrong, as Chinese botanical works and their pharmacopeia contain frequent mention of diurectics, and the examination of the urine is an important part of their diagnoses. Yule (*Cathay*, cxxv) has misunderstood this phrase; he translates it: "but they don't examine the urine or know anything on the subject." See the interesting remarks on this subject by the Arab travellers to China in the ninth century (Reinaud, *op. cit.*, i, 118).

[2] I have no explanation to offer of the word *iascot*, but agree with Yule (*Cathay*, cxxv) in thinking that the *cosmos* is the *sommo* of Pegolotti, which I may add is the *saum* of Ibn Batuta (ii, 412, 414). Pegolotti estimates the *sommo* at five gold florins (47*s.* 6*d.*), while Ibn Batuta says the *saum* weighed five ounces. The value assigned to the *iascot* would be about £5 5*s.*, assuming, as I have done (*supra*, p. 90), that the mark was worth 10*s.* 6*d.* The difference in the values assigned to the *sommo* of Pegolotti, and to the *cosmos* of Rubruck, is not

ALL these nations are in the mountains of the Caucasus,[1] but on the north side of these mountains, and (they extend) as far as the eastern Ocean, and (this is) also to the south of that Sithia which the pastoral Moals inhabit, and whose tributaries they all are. And all of them are given to idolatry, and tell fables of a host of gods, and of deified human beings, and of the genealogy of the gods, as do our poets.

Living mixed among them, though of alien race (*tanquam advene*), are Nestorians and Saracens all the way to Cathay. In xv cities of Cathay there are Nestorians, and they have an episcopal see in a city called Segin,[2] but for the rest they

---

material, as neither were coins, but simply lumps of bullion, what are now known in China as *yuan pao*, and in Turkestan and Tibet as *yambu*. According to our author, the Chinese paid the Mongols a daily tribute of about £7,875. or £2,876,375 a year. On p. 329, speaking of the *Manse*, he says they paid the Mongols an annual tribute, by which they bought peace from them, of two thousand *tuman* of iascots, or 200 millions of iascots! These sums must be greatly in excess of what we have reason to believe the people of northern and southern China (for Rubruck's *Manse* must be the Sung empire, Marco Polo's *Manze*) paid the Mongols. Under the reign of Ogodai, China, subject to the Mongols, was assessed at about 500,000 ounces of silver, 80,000 pieces of silk, and 400,000 sacks of grain. The population was reported at the same time to be 1,100,000 families (d'Ohsson, i, 372 ; ii, 69). Asiatics, Chinese and Mongols especially, are never very particular about figures, and I fancy these were given our traveller off-hand by some person who had but a very vague notion of the subject.

[1] *Inter montes Caucasi*. Classical geographers thought the Caucasus extended from the Indian Ocean to Asia Minor, its branches covering all Asia. Jornandes (432) says "it begins in the Indian Ocean. Its southern slope is arid and burnt by the sun, while its northern is swept by violent winds and snows. This mountain chain makes a bend towards Syria, and after that it trends northward and extends towards Scythia, where it makes long loops, advancing as far as the Rhipæan mountains." Isidorus, who is Rubruck's geographical guide, says (*op. cit.*, xvi, 521): "The Mons Caucasus extends from India to the Taurus; and on account of the diversity of peoples and languages it is called by different names in different places."

[2] *Segin* is usually supposed to be Hsi-an Fu, which was in the eighth and ninth centuries the centre of Nestorianism in China. This city in the thirteenth century did not bear the name of Hsi-an Fu, but was called by its older name, Chang-an. However, in popular parlance it may have retained the other name. It is strange, however, that the two

are purely idolaters. The priests of idols of the nations spoken of all wear wide saffron-coloured cowls. There are also among them, as I gathered, some hermits who live in forests and mountains (293) and who are wonderful by their lives and austerity.[1] The Nestorians there know nothing. They say their offices, and have sacred books in Syrian, but they do not know the language, so they chant like those monks among us who do not know grammar,[2] and they are absolutely depraved. In the first place they are usurers and drunkards; some even among them who live with the Tartars have several wives like them. When they enter church, they wash their lower parts like Saracens;[3] they eat meat on Friday, and have their feasts on that day in Saracen fashion. The bishop rarely visits these parts, hardly once in fifty years. When he does, they have all the male children, even those in the cradle, ordained priests, so nearly all the males among them are priests. Then they marry, which is clearly against the statutes of the fathers, and they are bigamists, for when the first wife dies these priests take another.[4] They are all

famous Uigur Nestorians, Mar Jalababa and Rabban Cauma, when on their journey from Koshang in southern Shan-hsi to western Asia in about 1276, while they mention "the city of Tangut," or Ning-hsia on the Yellow River as an important Nestorian centre, do not once refer to Hsi-an Fu or Chang-an. Had Chang-an been at the time the Nestorian episcopal see, one would think that these pilgrims would have visited it, or at least referred to it (Chabot, *Mar Jalababa* 21). *Segin* may represent the Chinese *Hsi Ching* (or *King*) "western capital," a name frequently applied to Hsi-an Fu.

[1] Hermits have always been numerous among the Chinese Buddhists, as well as in the countries where Lamaism is professed.

[2] Badger (ii, 146), speaking of the Nestorian clergy of the present day, says that the clerical Syriac in which their ancient rituals are written is so little understood, that many of the clergy have no certain knowledge of what they read in the churches.

[3] The Manichæans also performed ablutions before each of the four daily prayers (Harnack, *Ency. Brit.*, xv, 484).

[4] This practice arose under the patriarchat of Babaeus, who required that all patriarchs, bishops, presbyters and monks should marry. Later on, the marriage of patriarchs and bishops was forbidden (Assemani, ii, 403, 406, 409, 412; Badger, ii, 178, 180). At the present

simoniacs, for they administer no sacrament gratis. They are solicitous for their wives and children, and are consequently more intent on the increase of their wealth than of the faith. And so those of them who educate some of the sons of the noble Moal, though they teach them the Gospel and the articles of the faith, through their evil lives and their cupidity estrange them from the Christian faith, for the lives that the Moal themselves and the Tuins[1] or idolaters lead are more innocent than theirs.

---

ON the feast of Saint Andrew (30th November) we left this city (of Cailac), and at about three leagues from it we found a village entirely of Nestorians. We entered their church, singing joyfully and at the tops of our voices: "*Salve, regina!*" for it had been a long time since (294) we had seen a church. Proceeding thence three days we came to the head of that province, at the head of the said sea, which seemed to us as tempestuous as the ocean. And we saw a big island in it.[2] My companion approached its shore

---

time, all priests and deacons among the Nestorians may marry a second or third time, being widowers, "as they shall judge the same to serve better to godliness" (Badger, ii, 178).

[1] The word *Tuin* would seem to be an Uigur term. Quatremère (198) says, that in a certain Uigur-Chinese vocabulary of the Paris National Library (title and number not given), this word is explained by the Chinese *shih*, "scholar"; and that in a Persian-Chinese vocabulary it is rendered by *sêng* "a Buddhist priest." The term *Tuin* is used by King Heythum. He says of them that they shaved their heads and beards, wore yellow cloaks, married at twenty, and lived with their wives to the age of fifty. (Klaproth, *Journ. Asiat.*, xii, 289; see also d'Ohsson, ii, 264, Yule, *Cathay*, 241). In using the term, our traveller generally applies it to Buddhists, though here at least it would seem to include Uigur priests also.

[2] The Ala kul is the sea referred to; the traveller took it to be the eastern extremity of Lake Balkash, which is hardly probable, though it is thought that these lakes were connected within the historical period. It may well be, however, that in the thirteenth century the Ala kul and the Sassyk kul to the north of it formed one lake. The island

and moistened a cloth in it, and tasted the water, which was brackish, though drinkable. There opened a valley which came from out high mountains in the south-east, and there amidst the mountains was visible another big sea, and a river came through that valley from that sea into the first one, and there blows nearly continuously such a wind through that valley, that persons cross it with great danger, lest the wind should carry them into the sea. So we crossed this valley, following a northerly direction towards great mountains covered with deep snow, which then covered the ground.[1] On the feast of Saint Nicholas (6th December) we began greatly accelerating our speed, for we already found no one, only those *iams*, that is to say those men who are stationed a day apart to look after ambassa-

---

referred to is the Ala tyube, or "island peak," a small extinct volcano in the Ala kul (Yule, *Cathay*, ccxii ; Bretschneider, *Med. Travel*, 71 ; F. M. Schmidt, 206 ; Spörer, 73, 81). See *supra*, p. 16, Pian de Carpine's account of this part of the route.

[1] This lake to the south-east is the Ebi nor, about ninety-five versts from the Ala kul. A broad straight gorge separates the two lakes, but the stream which flows into the south end of the Ala kul does not come from the Ebi nor, but out of the Ala tau. F. M. Schmidt (207) and Yule (*Ency. Brit.*, xxxi, 47), make out that our traveller went through this gorge (called Dolan kol on the Russian maps), and passed beside the Ebi nor, but the text does not bear out their statement, nor is it all comprehensible why he should have made this *détour*, since, after passing the Ala kul, he says he turned north and passed near Omyl. Yule (*Cathay*, ccxiii) had rightly laid down the route followed; I do not know why he changed his opinion. The violent wind which blows through the Dolan kol is the *ébé* or *yube* of the Kirghiz, the prevailing south-easterly wind of this region from autumn to spring ; it frequently carries such masses of snow and sand with it, that whole camps have been buried in it. This same phenomenon occurs in various other similarly-shaped localities in this region (Spörer, 84). Yuan-chuang noted the violence of the wind of this region (Julien, *Pélerins*, i, 11); while the Chinese traveller, Ch'ang-tê, in 1253, refers to the same locality mentioned by Rubruck, and to the furious wind which comes out of the mountains blowing passers-by into the lake. He also speaks of the island in the Ala kul, which he calls Hai t'uhshan or "the iron hill of the lake" (Bretschneider, *Med. Travel*, 713). The Chinese taoist traveller Ch'ang-ch'un, who passed through this region in 1224, also refers to a "wind hill" somewhere west of Uliassutai (Bretschneider, *op. cit.*, 51).

dors, for in many places in the mountains[1] the road is narrow and the grazing bad, so that from dawn to night we would cover the distance of two *iams*, thus making of two days one, and we travelled more by night than by day. It was extremely cold, so we turned our sheepskins with the wool outside.

On the second Sunday in Advent (13th December) in the evening, while we were passing through a certain place amidst most terrible rocks, our guide sent me word begging me to say (295) some prayers (*bona verba*), by which the devils could be put to flight, for in this gorge devils were wont suddenly to bear men off, and no one could tell what they might do. Sometimes they seized the horse, and left the rider; sometimes they tore out the man's bowels and left the body on the horse, and many such things happened there frequently. So we chanted in a loud voice "*Credo in unum Deum*," when by the mercy of God the whole of our company passed through.[2] From that time they

---

[1] These must be the Tarbagatai mountains. I presume that the traveller followed the river Imil up to its source, and then, crossing the Mus tau in a general easterly direction, came to the southern extremity of the Ulungur nor. From this point, the road he would naturally follow would be up the course of the river Ulungur, as F. M. Schmidt (208 and 210) makes him do. Yule (*Cathay*, ccxiii) supposes that he *crossed* the mountains north of Tarbagatai, then followed the Kara Irtish, and having crossed the Altai to the east of this river, entered the valley of the Jabkan river. I cannot believe that the traveller can have taken such a roundabout and difficult road, especially in winter. While Schmidt makes him follow a too southerly course, between the Ala kul and the upper Ulungur, Yule makes him take one entirely too far to the north. This part of the narrative is rather difficult to follow, for it is not at all clear why the traveller, after leaving the Ala kul, and before reaching the neighbourhood of Kuyuk's *ordu*, which we know to have been on the river Imil, should speak of the gorges of the mountains which he must only have passed later on. The natural explanation is that a paragraph of the narrative has been transposed by an early copyist. If we place after the present phrase the paragraph beginning "After that we entered the plain in which was the *ordu* of Keu chan," the narrative reads much more smoothly and intelligibly.

[2] The Chinese pilgrim, Yuan-chuang, when travelling by the Issy kul, noted the ferocity of the dragons in those parts, and says that travellers must not wear red gowns going through these mountains

began asking me to write cards (*cartas*) for them, to carry on their heads,[1] and I would say to them: "I will teach you a phrase to carry in your hearts, which will save your souls and your bodies for all eternity." But always when I wanted to teach them, my interpreter failed me. I used to write for them, however, the "*Credo in Deum*" and the "*Pater noster*," saying: "What is here written is what one must believe of God, and the prayer by which one asks of God whatever is needful for man; so believe firmly that this writing is so, though you cannot understand it, and pray God to do for you what is written in this prayer, which He taught from His own mouth to His friends, and I hope that He will save you." I could do no more, for it was very dangerous, not to say impossible, to speak on questions of the faith through such an interpreter, for he did not know how.

After that we entered the plain in which was the *ordu* of Keu chan, and which used to be the country of the Naiman,[2] who were the real subjects of that Prester John.

---

(Julien, *Pèlerins*, i, ii). When Ch'ang-ch'un was travelling in the Altai, in 1221, his followers rubbed the heads of their horses with blood to prevent them being charmed by the goblins in the mountains. This traveller mentions a place somewhere north of the Altai which had a very bad fame for goblins. One of his escort told him that a goblin had once pulled him by the hair; and the head of the escort narrated that once the Khan of the Naiman, when passing through this country, was charmed by a goblin (Bretschneider, *Med. Travel*, 27, 29). Friar Odoric tells us that "the Minor Friars (in China) thought it a mere nothing to expel devils from the possessed, no more indeed than to drive a dog out of the house" (Yule, *Cathay*, 155). Grenard (ii, 254) says the people of Chinese Turkestan still believe in a gnome, *Albasty*, who frightens travellers.

[1] Mongols and Tibetans fasten on their guns and spears charms written on bits of paper or cotton, to keep off the devils (see *supra*, p. 147, note 3).

[2] Kuyak Khan lived on the Imil, which flows into the Ala kul. Pian de Carpine (648, 751) speaks of the new city of Omyl which the Emperor Ogodai had rebuilt, and where he was invited to drink. To the south of it was a great desert, in which savages (*sylvestres homines*) lived (d'Ohsson, i, 56, ii, 234; Bretschneider, *Med Geog.*, 221, 305). The country supposed to have been at the time referred to occupied by the Naiman, was to the east of the Imil valley, and

I did not at that time see this *ordu*, but on my way back. I will tell you, however, what befel his family, (296) his son and his wives. When Keu chan died, Baatu wanted Mangu to be chan. As to the death of this Keu I could learn nothing definite. Friar Andrew says that he died from some medicine which was given him, and that it was supposed that Baatu had had this done. I, however, heard another story. He had called upon Baatu to come and do him homage, and Baatu had started in great state. He was in great fear, however, he and his men, so he sent ahead one of his brothers, Stican by name, and when he came to Keu, and had to present him the cup, a quarrel arose, and they killed each other. The widow of this Stican detained us a whole day, to go to her dwelling and bless it, that is, that we might pray for her. So this Keu being dead, Mangu was elected by the will of Baatu, and had already been elected when Friar Andrew was there.[1]

Keu had a brother called Siremon, who on the advice of the wife of Keu and her vassals, went in great state toward Mangu as if to do him homage. In truth, however, he intended to kill him, and to exterminate all his *ordu*. (297) And when he had already got to within a day or two of Mangu, he had to leave on the road one of his carts which broke down; and while the carter was fixing it, there

---

included the Kara Irtish and the Ulungur valleys, though it may have comprised also that of the Imil, but of this I have no positive knowledge.

[1] The quarrel between Kuyuk and Batu has been referred to in a previous note (*supra*, p. 137, note 1). None of the Mohammedan mediæval writers confirm these stories of our traveller. Kuyuk suffered greatly with rheumatism, and his fondness for drink and dissipation seems to have been the primary causes of his premature death at the age of 43 (d'Ohsson, ii, 234). Kutan, a brother of Kuyuk, and Khoja Ogul, Kuyuk's son, are said to have been put to death by poison (d'Ohsson, ii, 232, 234). This Stican, Strican, Stichan, or Stichin—for the MSS. write his name in all these ways—is the *Syban* of Pian de Carpine (667), the *Shiban* of Mohammedan writers (d'Ohsson, ii, 8). The presentation of the cup to the Emperor was a recognized mark of submission. Friar Andrew never saw Mangu, as we learn from Mangu himself.

came along one of Mangu's men who helped him; and he asked so much about their journey that the carter revealed to him what Siremon proposed doing. Then the other, leaving him as if he did not care about it, went to a herd of horses, and taking the strongest horse he could pick in it, rode day and night in great haste till he came to Mangu's *ordu*, and told him what he had heard. Then Mangu promptly called all his men, and caused to be made three circles of men-at-arms around his *ordu*, so that no one could come in. The rest he sent against this Siremon, and they captured him, for he did not suspect that his designs had become known, and led him with all his men to the *ordu*. When Mangu charged him with the crime, he at once confessed. Then he was put to death, he and the elder son of Keu chan, and with them three hundred of the greatest men among the Tartars. And they sent also for their ladies, that they all might be whipped with burning brands to make them confess. And when they had confessed, they were put to death. A young son of Keu, too small to take part in or to know of the plot, was alone left alive, and to him reverted his father's *ordu* with all that belonged (298) thereto in men and animals.[1] And on our way back we passed by it, but

[1] According to d'Ohsson (ii, 187), Shiramun (Pian de Carpine, 667, calls him *Chirenen*) was the eldest son of Guchu, third son of Ogodai, and had been chosen by his grandfather as his successor. Kuyuk was therefore his uncle. D'Ohsson (ii, 255, *et seq.*) tells the story of Siremon's conspiracy from Mohammedan sources in practically the same manner as our traveller. He adds that the man who discovered the plot, and informed Mangu, was a muleteer named Kischk. The Emperor rewarded him with a large sum of money and the title of *tarkhan* (d'Ohsson, ii, 255. 271). This title is an old Turkish one, which insured the holder great privileges. We find it already mentioned by Menander (227), where it is correctly written Ταρχὰν. According to d'Ohss n, however, Siremon was not put to death at this time, but later on Mangu caused him to be drowned. The Empress, Ogul-Gaimish (Rubruck's *Camus*), the widow of Kuyuk, and apparently the instigator of the conspiracy, and also Siremon's mother, were drowned on pretext that they had tried to kill Mangu by witchcraft (see d'Ohsson, ii, 268).

my guides did not dare, either when going or when coming back, to turn off to it, for "the mistress of nations sat in sorrow, and there was no one to console her."

---

AGAIN we ascended mountains, going always in a northerly direction.[1] Finally, on the day of the Blessed Stephen (December 26th) we entered a plain vast as a sea, in which there was seen no hillock, and the following day, on the feast of St. John the Evangelist (December 27th), we arrived at the *ordu* of the great lord. When we were five days from it, an *iam* at whose (station) we were sleeping, wanted to send us by a roundabout road, over which we should have had to plod for more than fifteen days. And this, as I learnt, so that we might pass by Onankerule, which is at it were their original home, and in which is the *ordu* of Chingis chan. Others, however, said that they had wanted to make the journey longer, so as to magnify their importance; and they are in the habit of doing this to persons who come from countries not subject to them. And it was with great difficulty that our guide obtained that we should travel the direct road, after they had detained us over this matter from dawn to the third hour.[2] It was on this part

---

[1] Along some portions of his route while crossing the extremity of the Altai, after leaving the course of the upper Ulungur, the traveller may have followed for a short while a northerly direction, but there can be no doubt that the general direction in this part of the journey was very nearly due east (see F. M. Schmidt, 209).

[2] I have no doubt that the reason given by our author for the attempt to make him follow a roundabout trail is the correct one. The Chinese have often done the same thing to envoys. They used to make them travel overland, from Canton to Peking, for no other purpose. I am reminded in this connection of the remark of Bernardino of Escalanta concerning the missions sent by the kings of Ava, Siam, etc., to Peking: that they always sent four or five

of the journey that that secretary, the one we had waited for at Cailac, told me that in the letters that Baatu was sending to Mangu, it was stated that you asked for troops and aid from Sartach against the Saracens. At this I was (299) much astonished and also annoyed, for I knew the tenor of your letters, and that there was no such request in them, only that you advised him to be the friend of all Christians, to exalt the Cross, and to be the enemy of all the enemies of the Cross. (I feared) that as those who had interpreted (your letters) were Hermenians from Greater Hermenia—great haters of the Saracens—they had perhaps through hatred and for the discomfiture of the Saracens, gratuitously translated as had suited their fancy. I remained silent, saying nothing for or against this, for I feared to contradict Baatu's words lest I should be accused of trickery without reasonable cause. So we came on the day I have mentioned to the said *ordu*. To our guide was assigned a big dwelling, but to us there was given a very small hut in which we could barely store our things, make our beds, and a little fire. Many came to see our guide, and there was brought him rice wine in long narrow-necked flagons, and I could not discern any difference between it and the best Auxerre wine,[1] save that

---

envoys on each mission, because the Chinese used to poison one or two of them in a banquet, "unto whom they make very sumptuous sepulchres, with epitaphs concerning what they were, and the cause of their coming, and by what prince they were sent. And this is for to continue the memory and greatness of the renown of his (the Emperor of China's) realm."—*Account of the Empire of China*, 57 (Osborne's Collection, ii).

[1] *Cervisia de risio*, or, as he calls it in another passage (305), *terracina*, the Mongol *tarassun*, "wine," but here Chinese rice made wine, or *shao hsing chiu*, is meant. Marco Polo (i, 427) says of it: "It is a liquor which they brew of rice with a quantity of excellent spice, in such fashion that it makes a better drink than any other kind of wine; it is not only good, but clear and pleasing to the eye. And being very hot stuff, it makes one drunk sooner than any other wine." Odoric calls it *bigni*, or *bigum* (Yule, *Cathay*, 117; Cordier, *Odoric*, 302, 317). There is another stronger liquor distilled from millet, and called *shao chiu*: in Anglo-Chinese, *samshu*. Mongols

it had not the perfume of wine. We were called and closely questioned as to the business which had brought us. I replied: "We have heard that Sartach was a Christian: we came to him. The King of the French sent him sealed letters by us; he sent us to his father, his father sent us here. He must have written the reason why." They asked if you wanted to make peace with them. I replied: "He sent to Sartach letters as to a Christian, and if he had known that he was not (300) a Christian, he would never have sent him letters. As to making peace, I tell you that he never did you any harm. If he had done something for which you had to make war on him or his people, he would willingly, as a just man, make apology and ask for peace. If you without motive should want to wage war against him, or his people, we trust that God, who is just, would aid them." And they always wondered, repeating: "But why did you come, if you did not come to make peace?" For they are already so puffed up in their pride, that they believe that the whole world must want to make peace with them. Of a truth, if it were allowed me, I would, to the utmost of my power, preach throughout the world war against them. I did not, however, wish to clearly explain the reason of my coming, lest I should say something contrary to what Baatu had stated; and so I gave as the only reason for my coming there that he (Baatu) had sent me.

The next day we were conducted to court, and I thought I could go barefooted, as in our own countries, so I left my shoes. Now, those who come to the court get off their horses about an arrow's flight from the

---

call it *araka*, *arrak*, and *arreki*. Ma Tuan-lin (bk. 327) says that the Moho (the early Nu-chên Tartars) drank rice wine (*mi chiu*), but I fancy that they, like the Mongols, got it from the Chinese.

The dwelling (*domus*) given his conductor, and the little hut (*parvulum tuguriunculum*) assigned him and his party, were in both cases felt yurts.

dwelling of the Chan, and there the horses and the servants keeping the horses remain. So when we had alighted there, and while our guide went to the dwelling of the Chan, there came an Hungarian servant, who recognised us—that is our Order; and as they surrounded us and gazed at us as if we were monsters, especially because we were barefooted, and they asked us if we had no use for our feet, because they supposed that we would at once lose them,[1] this Hungarian (301) gave them the reason, telling them of the rules of our Order. Then came the grand secretary,[2] who was a Nestorian Christian, and whose advice they nearly always follow, to look at us; and he examined us carefully, and called that Hungarian, of whom he made many inquiries. Then we were told to go back to our lodgings; and, as we were going back, I saw before the east end of the *ordu*, the distance of two cross-bow shots from it, a dwelling with a little cross over it. Greatly pleased, and imagining there was something Christian there, I boldly went in, and found an altar right beautifully decked. For there was embroidered[1] on a cloth of gold an image of the Saviour, of the Blessed Virgin, of John the Baptist and of two angels, and the lines of the body and of the garments were marked out with pearls, and there was a great silver cross with gems in the angles and the middle, and many other church ornaments, and an oil lamp having eight lights was burning before the altar; and there was seated there an Hermenian monk, swarthy and lank, and he was dressed in a tunic of the roughest hair-cloth reaching

---

[1] *Quia supponebant quod statim admitteremus eos.* As the text stands in the MSS., I can make nothing out of it. I have read *edmitteremus* (*emitteremus*). Previous translators have either omitted this phrase, or rendered it in the most fanciful manner.

[2] Bulgai by name (see *infra*).

[3] *Brosdate sive bistrate.* These embroidered images took the place among the Armenians and Greeks, of images, the use of which was forbidden them.

halfway down to his shins, and over it he had a stole of black silk lined with vaire, and under his hair-cloth garment he wore an iron girdle. As soon as we entered, and even before saluting the monk, we sang on our knees: "*Ave regina coelorum,*" and he arose and prayed with us. Then, having saluted him, we sat down beside him, and he had a dish with some fire in it before him. We told him the cause of our coming, and he began encouraging us greatly, telling us to speak boldly, for we were the envoys of God, who is greater than any man. (302) After that he told us of his coming there, saying that he had preceded us by a month, and that he had been a hermit in the country of Jerusalem, and that God had appeared to him three times, enjoining on him to go to the Prince of the Tartars. But as he neglected going, God threatened him the third time, striking him down to the ground, and saying that he should die if he did not go; and that he should say to Mangu chan that if he would become a Christian, all the world would come under his rule, and that the Franks and the great Pope would obey him; and then he admonished me to speak in a like way. Then I answered: "Brother, I will willingly advise him to become a Christian; for I have come to preach that to all men. I will promise him also that the French and the Pope will rejoice greatly, and will have him for a brother and a friend. But that they would become his slaves, and pay him tribute as these other nations, that will I never promise, for I should be speaking against my conviction." At this he remained silent. When we went to our lodgings, we found it cold, and we had eaten nothing that day. We cooked a little meat, and a little millet with the broth of the meat to drink. Our guide and his companions had got drunk at the court, and had little care of us. There were then near them (us) envoys of Vastacius, but we did not know it. At dawn (the next day) some men from the court made us get up in all haste. I went with them bare-footed a little way to the dwelling of these envoys, and they asked them if they knew us. Then a Greek knight, recognizing our Order, (303) and also my companion, whom he had seen at the court of Vastacius with Friar Thomas our provincial, he and all the envoys bore great testimony of us. Then they asked if you were at peace or at war with Vastacius. "Neither at peace," I answered, "nor at war," and they enquired how that could be. "Because," I said, "their countries are remote from each other, and they have nothing to do with each other." Then the envoy of Vastacius said that there was peace, and this made me cautious, and I kept silence.

That morning the tips of my toes were frozen, so that I could not thereafter go bare-footed. The cold in these regions is most intense, and from the time it begins freezing it never ceases till May; even in the month of May there was frost every morning, though during the day the sun's rays melted it. But in winter it never thawed, but with every wind it continued to freeze. And if there were wind there in winter as with us, nothing could live; but the atmosphere is always calm till April, then the wind arises. And when we were there, the cold that came on with the wind about Easter killed an infinite number of animals. But little snow fell there during the winter, but about Easter, which was at the end of April, there fell so much that all the streets of Caracarum were full, and they had to carry it off in carts.[1] They brought us from the *ordu* of the first

[1] Pian de Carpine (609) says of the climate of northern Mongolia: "The climate there is most unsettled; in the middle of summer, when in other countries it is usually very hot, there is much thunder and lightning, by which many persons are killed. At the same season there falls there snow in great quantity. They have there also such violent tempests of extremely cold winds, that sometimes men can hardly keep in the saddle . . . . It never rains there in winter, but often in summer; but so little, that ofttimes it barely moistens the dust and the roots of the grass. Hail falls there, often of great

(wife)[1] sheepskin gowns and breeches and shoes, which my companion and the dragoman took; for my part I did not think I was in need of them, for it seemed to me that the fur gown I had brought with me from Baatu's sufficed me.

---

(304)

ON the Octave of the Innocents (3rd January, 1254) we were taken to court; and there came certain Nestorian priests, whom I did not know to be Christians, and they asked me in what direction I prayed. I said "to the east."[2] And they asked that because we had shaved our beards, at the suggestion of our guide, so as to appear before the chan according to the fashion of our country. 'Twas for this that they took us for Tuins, that is idolaters. They also made us explain the Bible. Then they asked us what kind of reverence we wanted to make the chan, according to our fashion, or according to theirs. I replied to them: "We are priests given to the service of God. Noblemen in our country do not, for the glory of God, allow priests to bend the knee before them. Nevertheless, we want to humble ourselves to every man for the love of God. We come from afar: so in the first place then, if it please you, we will sing praises to God who has brought us here in safety from so far, and after that we

---

size . . . . In summer there is suddenly excessive heat, followed immediately by great cold. In winter great quantities of snow fall in some parts, while in others little." Our author's memory served him badly as to the date of Easter in 1254:—it fell on April 12th.

[1] *Attulerunt nobis de curia primo pelliceas arietinas, etc.* It seems to me that *primo* is a clerical error, though all the MSS. give it, for either *principi* or *prime*; the latter would refer to the first wife of Mangu, whom Rubruck calls Cotata Caten (Kutuktai Khatun), and who seems to have greatly favoured the Christians.

[2] The Tuins (see *supra*, p. 159) prayed facing north. The Nestorians faced also the east in praying (Badger, ii, 413).

will do as it shall please your lord, this only excepted, that nothing be required of us contrary to the worship and glory of God." Then they went into the house, and repeated what I had said. It pleased the lord, and so they placed us before the door of the dwelling, holding up the felt which hung before it; and, as it was the Nativity, we began to sing:

> "*A solis ortus cardine*
> *Et usque terre limitem*
> *Christum canamus principem*
> *Natum Maria virgine.*"

When we had sung this hymn, they searched our legs and breasts (305) and arms to see if we had knives upon us. They had the interpreter examined, and made him leave his belt and knife in the custody of a door-keeper. Then we entered, and there was a bench in the entry with *cosmos*, and near by it they made the interpreter stand. They made us, however, sit down on a bench near the ladies.[1] The house was all covered inside with cloth of gold, and there was a fire of briars and wormwood roots—which grow here to great size[2]—and of cattle dung, in a grate in the centre of the dwelling. He (Mangu) was seated on a couch, and was dressed in a skin spotted and glossy, like a seal's skin.[3] He is a little man, of medium height, aged forty-five years, and a young wife sat beside him; and a very ugly, full-grown girl called Cirina, with other children sat on a couch after them. This dwelling had belonged to a certain Christian lady, whom he had much loved, and of whom he had had this girl. Afterwards he had taken

---

[1] That is to say, on the left of Mangu (see *supra*, pp. 24, 58).

[2] Saksaul is meant (conf. Benedict's narrative, *supra*, p. 35).

[3] *Bovis marini*. It was probably otter skin, though a variety of seal was found in lake Baikal, the Caspian, and possibly in other localities then subject to the Mongols. The Bulgars of the Volga carried on a large trade in sea otter skins.

this young wife, but the girl was the mistress of all this *ordu*, which had been her mother's.[1]

He had us asked what we wanted to drink, wine or *terracina*, which is rice wine (*cervisia*), or *caracosmos*, which is clarified mare's milk, (306) or *bal*, which is honey mead.[2] For in winter they make use of these four kinds of drinks. I replied: "My lord, we are not men who seek to satisfy our fancies about drinks; whatever pleases you will suit us." So he had us given of the rice drink, which was clear and flavoured like white wine, and of which I tasted a little out of respect for him, but for our misfortune our interpreter was standing by the butlers, who gave him so much to drink, that he was drunk in a short time. After this the chan had brought some falcons and other birds, which he took on his hand and looked at, and after a long while he bade us speak.[3] Then we had to bend our knees. He had his interpreter, a certain Nestorian, who I did not know was a Christian, and we had our interpreter, such as he was, and already drunk. Then I said: "In the first place we render thanks and praise to God, who has brought us from so far to see Mangu Chan, to whom God has given so much power on earth. And we pray Christ, by whose will we all live and die, to grant him a happy and long life." For it is their desire, that one shall pray for their lives. Then I told him: "My lord, we have heard of Sartach that he was a Christian, and the Christians who heard it rejoiced greatly, and principally my lord the king of the French. So we came to him, and my lord the king sent him letters by us in which were words of peace, and among other

[1] Conf., however, p. 321 of text, which seems to disagree slightly with this statement.

[2] See *supra*, p. 67. *Bal* (or *boal*) may be the Turkish *buzzah*.

[3] This was done to show how unimportant were the envoys and their affairs. When the Chinese Emperor, Yung-lo, received in 1240 the envoys of Shah Rokh at Peking, he kept them standing before him without paying any attention to them, while he tried a number of criminals (Yule, *Cathay*, ccv).

things he bore witness to him as to the kind of men we were, and he begged him to allow (307) us to remain in his country, for it is our office to teach men to live according to the law of God. He sent us, however, to his father Baatu, and Baatu sent us to you. You it is to whom God has given great power in the world. We pray then your mightiness to give us permission to remain in your dominion, to perform the service of God for you, for your wives and your children. We have neither gold, nor silver nor precious stones to present to you, but only ourselves to offer to you to serve God, and to pray to God for you. At all events give us leave to remain here till this cold has passed away, for my companion is so feeble that he cannot with safety to his life stand any more the fatigue of travelling on horse-back."

My companion had told me of his infirm condition, and had adjured me to ask for permission to stay, for we supposed that we would have to go back to Baatu, unless by special grace he gave us permission to stay. Then he began his reply:[1] "As the sun sends its rays everywhere, likewise my sway and that of Baatu reach everywhere, so we do not want your gold or silver." So far I understood my interpreter, but after that I could not understand the whole of any one sentence: 'twas by this that I found out

[1] Pian de Carpine (765) says: "It is the custom of the Emperor of the Tartars never to address directly a foreigner, no matter how great he may be, but to listen and answer through the medium of someone." This custom is still adhered to in audiences granted to foreigners at the Court of China. Rubruck does not refer to it; he only states that he was not at liberty to speak on a subject after the Emperor had once spoken what he had to say about it The bombastic remark of the Emperor is in pure oriental style. Menander states that Turkhan Khan of the Turks told Valentius, the envoy of Tiberius Constantinus, that his realm extended from the rising sun to the farthest point it reached in the west. Theophylactus (*Historia*, 282) says the Khan of the Avars began his letter to the Emperor Maurice by styling himself "Mighty ruler of the seven nations, lord of the seven climes of the world."

he was drunk, and Mangu himself appeared to me tipsy.[1] His speech, it seemed to me, however, showed that he was not pleased that we had come to Sartach in the first place rather than to him. Then I, seeing that I was without interpreter, said nothing, save to beg him not to be displeased with what I had said of gold and silver, for (308) I had not said that he needed or wanted such things, but only that we would gladly honour him with things temporal as well as spiritual. Then he made us arise and sit down again, and after awhile we saluted him and went out, and with us his secretaries and his interpreter, who was bringing up one of his daughters. And they began to question us greatly about the kingdom of France, whether there were many sheep and cattle and horses there, and whether they had not better go there at once and take it all. And I had to use all my strength to conceal my indignation and anger; but I answered: "There are many good things there, which you would see if it befel you to go there."

Then they appointed someone to take care of us, and we went to the monk. And as we were coming out of there to go to our lodgings, the interpreter I have mentioned came to me and said: "Mangu Chan takes compassion on you and allows you to stay here for the space of two months: then the great cold will be over. And he informs you that ten days hence there is a goodly city called Caracarum. If you wish to go there, he will have you given all you may require; if, however, you wish to remain here, you may do so, and you shall have what

[1] Mangu, like Chingis, Ogodai, Kuyuk, Tului, Chagatai, and most of the imperial family, was a hard drinker. The empresses followed in their lead; Rubruck mentions seeing Kutuktai (Cotata) drunk. The Emperor Baber's fondness for *majum* and *arak* is well known. Chingis Khan spoke very strongly against drunkenness in his Ordonnances, but he was not able to live up to his rules of conduct.

you need. It will, however, be fatiguing for you to ride with the court." I answered: "May the Lord keep Mangu Chan and give him a happy and long life! We have found this monk here, whom we believe to be a holy man and come here by the will of God. So we would willingly remain here with him, for we are monks, and we would say our prayers with him for the life of the chan." Then he left us without a word. And we went to a big house, which we found cold and without a supply of fuel, and we were still without (309) food, and it was night. Then he to whom we had been entrusted gave us fuel and a little food.

Our guide being about to return to Baatu, begged of us a carpet or rug which we had left by his order in Baatu's *ordu*. We gave it him, and he left us in the most friendly manner, asking our hand,[1] and saying that it was his fault if he had let us suffer from hunger or thirst on the journey. We pardoned him, and in like manner we asked pardon of him and all his suite if we had shown them an evil example in anything.

---

A CERTAIN woman from Metz in Lorraine, Paquette by name, and who had been made a prisoner in Hungary, found us out, and she gave us the best food she could. She belonged to the *ordu* of the Christian lady of whom I have spoken,[2] and she told me of the unheard-of misery she had endured before coming to the *ordu*.[3] But now she was fairly well off. She had a young

[1] *Postulans dextram nostram.* Hand-shaking is not a Mongol or Chinese custom; the friar's guide had either seen him shake hands, or had noticed the Nestorians do it (see p. 315 of text, where this custom of theirs is noted).

[2] A wife of Mangu, and the mother of the ugly girl Cirina, of whom he has already spoken.

[3] The terrible condition of the captives among the Mongols is thus described by Pian de Carpine (711-713). "In the country of the

Ruthenian husband, of whom she had had three right fine-looking boys, and he knew how to make houses,[1] a very good trade among them. Furthermore, she told us that there was in Caracarum a certain master goldsmith, William by name, a native of Paris: and his family name was Buchier, and the name of his father was Laurent Buchier.[2]

She believed that he had still a brother living on the Grand Pont, called Roger Buchier. She also told me that he supported a young man whom he considered as his son, and who was a most excellent interpreter. But as

---

Saracens, and in those of other nations who live as it were in the midst, the lords take all the best artisans, and use them for all their works; the other artisans pay them of their labour as tribute. They (the captives) store all their crops in the granaries of their lords; they allow them, however, seed corn and enough for their food; to the others they give to each one daily a small weight (of meal), and nothing else but a little portion of meat three times a week. And this they only do for those artisans who live in towns. Whenever it pleases the masters, their wives, or their sons, they take all the young (captives), and make them go after them with all their body servants, who are counted among the Mongols or rather among the captives: for though they are reckoned with them, they are not held in respect as are Tartars, but are looked upon as slaves, and are exposed to all dangers just as other captives; for they are placed in the foremost rank in battles, and if it be necessary to cross a swamp or a dangerous piece of water, they must first try the ford. Furthermore, they must do everything there is to be done. And if they give offence in anything, or if they do not obey orders, they beat them like donkeys. To be brief, they have little to eat, little to drink, and are miserably clad, unless they are able to make some money, as may goldsmiths and other good artisans. But some have such bad masters that they give them nothing, and they have no time to do anything for themselves on account of the amount of work of their masters, unless they take some of the time when they might be resting or sleeping. And this only can they do if they are allowed to have wives or their own tent; but those who are kept in the tent as slaves are full of every kind of misery. I have seen them going about in all weathers with leather breeches, and all the rest of the body bare, under the hottest sun, and enduring the severest cold in winter. I have seen some who have lost their toes and fingers from the great cold, and I heard of others who had died from the intense cold, or had become bereft of the use of all their limbs." See also on foreign captives among the Mongols, d'Ohsson (ii, 133); and Heyd (*op. cit.*, ii, 71).

[1] *Facere domos.* Probably tent-frames are meant, for all the houses at Karakorum were made by the Chinese.

[2] For some details concerning this kind friend of Friar William's see *infra*.

Mangu Chan had given this said master three hundred iascot, that is three thousand marks, and L workmen to do a certain work, she (310) feared he would not be able to send his son to me. She had heard people in the *ordu* saying: "The men who have come from your country are good men, and Mangu Chan would be pleased to speak with them, but their interpreter is worth nothing." 'Twas for this that she was solicitous about an interpreter. So I wrote to this master of my coming, asking him if he could send me his son; and he replied that in that month he could not, but the following he would have finished his task and then he would send him to me.

We were stopping then with the other envoys; for they do differently as regards envoys at the court of Baatu and the court of Mangu. At Baatu's court there is an *Iam* on the west side who receives all those who come from the west; and it is arranged in like fashion for the other quarters of the world. But at the court of Mangu all are under one *Iam*, and may visit and see each other. At the court of Baatu they do not know each other, and one knows not whether another is an envoy, for they know not each other's lodgings, and only see each other at court. And when one is summoned, another perhaps is not: for they only go to court when summoned.

We found there a certain Christian from Damascus, who said he had come for the Soldan of Mont Real and of Crac, who wished to become the tributary and friend of the Tartars. Furthermore, the year before I arrived there, a certain clerk had come there from Acon, who called himself Raymond, but whose name was in truth Theodolus. He had started out from Cyprus with Friar Andrew, and had gone with him as far as Persia, and he brought certain instruments from Ammoric[1] there in Persia, and he re-

---

[1] *Quedam organa ab Ammorico. Organa* in Latin and Greek (ὄργανα) means both drums and wind instruments; but as in another

mained there after Friar Andrew. When Friar Andrew had gone back, he went on (311) with his instruments and came to Mangu Chan, who asked him why he had come; and he said that he was with a certain holy bishop to whom God had sent letters from heaven written in letters of gold, and had ordered to send them to the lord of the Tartars, for he would become the lord of the whole world, and he must persuade men to make peace with him. Then Mangu said to him: "If thou hast brought these letters which have come from heaven and letters of your lord, then thou art welcome." He replied that he had been bringing letters, but that they and his other things being on an unbroken pack-horse, it had run away through forests and over hills, and he had lost everything. Now it is a truth that such accidents frequently do occur, so one must be very careful to hold one's horse when obliged to get off it.

Then Mangu asked the name of the bishop. He said that he was called Oto.[1] And he went on to tell him of Damascus and of master William, who was clerk of the lord legate. Then the Chan asked him in whose kingdom he dwelt. And he answered that he was under a certain king of the Franks, who was called King Moles.[2]

---

passage (362) Friar William says "*sonant timpana et organa*," I take it that he uses it in the sense of horns or wind instruments. Pian de Carpine (662) has "*percutiebant in organis et tympanis et aliis instrumentis.*" *Ab Ammorico* is more embarrassing. Bergeron translates these words by "certains instruments qu'ils appellent d'Amoricus." It is just possible that *Ammorico* is a clerical error for *Hermenia* (Armenia). Joinville (160) speaks of four musicians who came to St. Louis' camp with the Prince of Antioch, "et avoient troiz cors, dont les voiz leur venoient parmi les visages. Quant il encommençoient à corner, vous deissiez que ce sont les voiz des cynes qui se partent de l'estanc; et fesoient les plus douces mélodies et les plus gracieuses, que c'estoit mervieilles de l'oyr."

[1] Odon or Eudes de Chateau-Roux, or Chateau-Raoul, in Berri, Cardinal-Bishop of Tusculum, had preached the crusade in France, and had accompanied St. Louis to the Holy Land as Papal Legate (Michaud, iii, 85).

[2] Or *Meles*, according to some MSS. I am unable to offer any explanation of this word: the whole phrase is obscure, nor do I quite see its

For he had before that heard of what happened at Mensura, and he wanted to say that he was one of your subjects. Furthermore, he said to the chan that the Saracens were between the Franks and him blocking the way: that if the road were open they would send envoys and would gladly make a peace with him. Then Mangu Chan asked if he would (312) take envoys to that king and that bishop. He replied that he would, and also to the Pope. Then Mangu had made a very strong bow that two men could hardly string, and two arrows with silver heads full of holes, which whistled like a pipe when they were shot.[1] And he told the Moal whom he was to send with this Theodolus: "Go to the king of the Franks, to whom this man shall take you, and offer him these from me. And if he will have peace with us, and we conquer the land of the Saracens as far as his country, we will leave him all the rest of the earth to the west. If not, bring back the bow and the arrows to us, and tell him that with such bows we shoot far and hit hard."

Then he made this Theodulus leave his presence, and his interpreter was the son of master William, and he heard (the chan) saying to the Moal: "Go with this man; examine well the roads, the country, the towns, the men and their arms." Then this young man upbraided Theodulus, saying that he did wrong to take envoys of the Tartars with him, who only went to spy. Then he answered that he would put them to sea, so that they

---

connection with the one which follows. Did Theodulus want to invent a name for St. Louis, and so coined the word *Moles* from *Mensura?* On the battle of Mansurah in 1249, and St. Louis' captivity, see Joinville (60 *et seq.*); he writes the name *la Massoure*, and Sarrasin, *la Massore* (see also Michaud, iii, 142, 469).

[1] Already in the sixth century, A.D., the Turks used "sounding arrows" (*ming ti*). *Chou shu*, bk. 50, 3. Such arrow-heads are still used by the Mongols and Manchus, and are called in Chinese *hsiang chien*, "signal arrows." The name sufficiently explains the use to which they are put (see also d'Ohsson, i, 61, *note*).

would not be able to know whence they came nor how they had come back.

Mangu also gave the Moal his bull, which is like a plate of gold a palm broad and a half cubit long, and on it is written his order. He who bears it can command what he pleases, and it shall be done without delay.[1]

So when this Theodulus had come as far as Vastacius, and was wishing to pass on (313) to the Pope, to deceive the Pope as he had deceived Mangu Chan, Vastacius asked him if he had letters of the Pope, since he was an ambassador and had to lead envoys of the Tartars. And when he was unable to show any letters, he seized him and took away from him all that he had got together, and threw him into prison. As to the Moal, he fell ill and died there. Vastacius, however, sent back to Mangu Chan by the attendants of the Moal the bull of gold, and I passed them on the road at Arseron (Erzerum) on the border of Turkuie, and they told me what had befallen this Theodulus. Such adventurers wandering through the world, the Moal put to death when they can lay hands on them.

---

WHEN the feast of the Epiphany (6th January) was nigh, that Hermenian monk called Sergius[2] told me that he would baptize Mangu Chan on that feast. And I begged him to do all in his power that I might

---

[1] Yule (*Marco Polo*, i, 342) has a coloured representation of one of these Mongol *paiza*. The name *paiza*, by which Mohammedan mediæval writers call these tablets, and which was also probably the term used by the Mongols, is Chinese *pai-tzŭ*, "tablet." Devéria (*Journ. Asiat.*, ixe série, viii, 105) describes the various shapes and ornamentation of the Mongol *paiza*. The Kin, in the thirteenth century, used badges of office made of silver. They were rectangular, bore the imperial seal, and an inscription indicative of the duty of the bearer (Chavannes, *Voyageurs chez les Khitan*, 102). The Nü-chên at an earlier date used wooden *pai-tzŭ* tied to each horseman and horse, to distinguish them by (Ma Tuan-lin, bk. 327, 11; see also Palladius, *op. cit.*, 39).

[2] Deguignes (iii, 127) thinks that this Sergius was the Chancellor of

be present, and be an eye-witness to it. And this he promised me. The feast came, but the monk did not call me; however, at the sixth hour I was called to court, and I saw the monk with the priests coming back from the court bearing his cross, and the priests had a censer and the Gospels. Now on that same day Mangu Chan had had a feast, and it is his custom on such days as his diviners tell him are holy, or the Nestorian priests say for some reason are sacred, for him to hold court,[1] and on such days first come the Christian priests with their apparel, and they pray for him and bless his cup. When they have left, the Saracen priests come and do likewise. After them come the priests of idols, doing the same thing (314). The monk told me that (Mangu) believed only in the Christians, but he wanted all to pray for him. But he lied, for he believes in none, as you shall learn hereafter, and they all follow his court as flies do honey, and he gives to all, and they all believe that they are his favourites, and they all prophesy blessings to him.

So we sat for a long time before his *ordu*, and they brought us meat to eat, but I told them that we would not eat there, but that if they wished to provide us with food, they should give it to us in our dwelling. Then they said: "Go then to your dwelling, for you have only been called to eat." So we went back by way of the monk's, who was ashamed of the lie he had told us, and to whom I would not therefore speak of that matter. Some of the Nestorians, however, wanted to assure me that he (Mangu) had been

---

King Heythum of Armenia, who Haithon in his *Hist. Orient.* (39) says baptized Mangu and his family. This is impossible, as King Heythum only arrived at Mangu's court a month after Rubruck had started on his way back to Europe. Furthermore, as our author tells us (323), this Sergius was an impostor, who had never taken holy orders.

[1] The greatest festivals were on the New-year and on the Emperor's birthday.

baptized; I told them that I would never believe it, nor say so to others, for I had not seen it.

We came to our cold and empty dwelling. They had supplied us with couches and bed covering, and brought us fuel, and given to the three of us the flesh of one poor thin sheep for food for six days. Daily they gave us a bowl full of millet and a quart of millet mead,[1] and they borrowed for us a kettle and a tripod to cook our meat; and when it was cooked we boiled the millet in the pot liquor. This was our diet; and it would have been quite sufficient, if they had let us eat in peace. But there were so many suffering from want of food, who as soon as they (315) saw us getting our meal ready, would push in on us, and who had to be given to eat with us. Then I experienced what martyrdom it is to give in charity when in poverty.

---

AT that time the cold began to grow intense, and Mangu Chan sent us three gowns of papion skins, which they wear with the fur outside, and these we received with thankfulness. They inquired also whether we had all the food we required. I told them that a little food sufficed us, but that we had no house in which we could pray for Mangu Chan; for our hut was so small that we could not stand up in it, nor open our books as soon as we lit the fire. So they reported these words to him, and he sent to the monk to know whether he would like our company, and he replied cheerfully that he would. From then on we had a better dwelling, living with the monk before the *ordu*, where no one lodged except ourselves and

[1] *Cervisia de milio.* This must be the common *huang chiu*, or "yellow wine," made in north China with glutinous millet. This is the only passage in the narrative in which Friar William refers to this beverage.

their diviners; but these latter were nearer and in front of the *ordu* of the first lady, while we were on the extreme eastern end, before the *ordu* of the last lady. This was on the day before the octave of the Epiphany (12th January). The next day, that is on the octave of the Epiphany, all the Nestorian priests assembled before dawn in the chapel, beat the board, and solemnly sang matins; then they put on their church vestments, and prepared a censer and incense. And as they thus waited in the court of the church, the first wife, called Cotota Caten (*caten* is the same as "lady," Cotota is a proper name),[1] entered the chapel with several other ladies, and her first-born son called Baltu, and some others of her children; and they prostrated themselves, the forehead to the ground, according to the fashion of the Nestorians, and after that they touched (316) all the images with their right hand, always kissing their hand after touching them;[2] and after this they gave their right hands to all the bystanders in the church. This is the custom of the Nestorians on entering church. Then the priests sang a great deal, putting incense in the lady's hand; and she put it on the fire, and then they incensed her. After that when it was already bright day, she began taking off her head-dress, called *bocca*, and I saw her bare head,[3] and then she told us to leave, and as I was leaving, I saw a silver bowl brought in. Whether they baptized her or not, I know not: but I do know that they do not celebrate mass in

---

[1] Called Kutuktai Khatun by Mohammedan contemporary writers. She was of the Ykiras tribe. She bore Mangu two sons, Baltu and Orenguias. After Mangu's death she espoused the cause of Arik Buga against Kublai (d'Ohsson, ii, 334, 347). The title *Khatún*, in Turkish *Khanum*, is formed from *Khan*, and was given by the Mongols as a title to the wives of emperors or princes (Quatremère, 88).

[2] An old custom among Eastern Christians and Russians; when one cannot kiss a holy image, one kisses the hand which has touched it. The author tells us (320) that Baltu was already married at this time.

[3] Friar William notes this, because married women never appeared in public without the *bogtak* on.

a tent, but in a substantial church. And at Easter (12th April), I saw them baptize and consecrate fonts with great ceremony, which they did not do then.

And as we were going back to our dwelling, Mangu Chan came, and entered the church or oratory, and they brought him a gilded couch, on which he sat beside his lady, facing the altar. Then they summoned us, who did not know of the arrival of Mangu, and the door-keeper searched us, lest we had knives on us. I entered the oratory, with my Bible and breviary in my bosom. First I bowed to the altar, and then to the Chan, and passing to the other side, we stood between the monk and the altar. Then they made us intone a psalm according to our fashion and chant. We chanted this prose: "*Veni, Sancte Spiritus.*"

The Chan had brought him our books, the Bible and the breviary, and made careful inquiry about the pictures, and what they meant. The Nestorians answered as they saw fit, for our interpreter had not come with us. The first time I had been before him, I had also the Bible in my bosom, and he had it handed him, and looked at it a great deal. Then he went away, but the lady remained there and distributed presents to (317) all the Christians who were there. To the monk she gave one *iascot*, and to the archdeacon of the priests another. Before us she had placed a *nasic*, which is a piece of stuff as broad as a cover-lid and about as long,[1] and a buccaran;[2] but as I would

[1] According to Heyd (ii, 698), the *nassit* or *nassith* of Italian mediæval traders in the Levant, which I take to be our author's *nasic*, is a silk gold brocade. The word is derived from the Arabic *necidj*. There was another stuff, differing only from it probably very slightly, called *nacco*, derived from the Arabic *nakh* (see also Yule, *Cathay*, 295, 306; and *Marco Polo*, i, 63, 276, 285; and Bretschneider *Med. Geog.*, 288).

[2] Heyd (ii, 703) says it is very difficult to determine what kind of stuff was sold in the Middle Ages under this name. Victor Gay, he adds, the last writer to have studied the question, is of opinion that it was of fine flaxen cloth. Yule (*Marco Polo*, i, 48) has a very exhaustive

not accept them, they were sent to the interpreter, who took them for himself. The *nasic* he carried all the way to Cyprus, where he sold it for eighty bezants of Cyprus, though it had been greatly damaged on the journey. Then drink was brought, rice mead and red wine, like wine of La Rochelle,[1] and *cosmos*. Then the lady, holding a full cup in her hand, knelt and asked a blessing, and the priests all sang with a loud voice, and she drank it all. Likewise, I and my companion had to sing when she wanted to drink another time. When they were all nearly drunk, food was brought consisting of mutton, which was at once devoured, and after that large fish which are called carp, but without salt or bread; of these I ate. And so they passed the day till evening. And when the lady was already tipsy, she got on her cart, the priests singing and howling, and she went her way. The next Sunday, when we read: "*Nuptie facte sunt in Chana*," came the daughter of the Chan, whose mother was a Christian, and she did likewise, though with not so much ceremony; for she made no presents, but only gave the priests (318) to drink till they were drunk, and also parched millet to eat.

Before Septuagesima Sunday, the Nestorians fast three days, which they call the fast of Jonah, that he preached to the Ninivites; and then also the Hermenians fast for five days, which they call the fast of Saint Serkis, who is one of the greater saints among them, and who the Greeks say was a canon.[2] The Nestorians begin the fast

note on the subject. He thinks it was a quilted material. In a previous passage (290) Friar William uses the expression *stamina rigidata*, where the first word has evidently the meaning of the modern French *étamine*, our buckram.

[1] Red wine was probably brought to the Mongol court from Persia and Turkestan, but it must have been an uncommon drink. Can the drink of which our author speaks have been tea? This beverage was already in general use in Tibet, and probably Mongolia, in his time.

[2] This Nestorian fast is called the fast of the Ninivites or of the Rogation; it is kept on the Monday, Tuesday, and Wednesday

on the third day of the week, and end it on the fifth, so that on the sixth day they eat meat. And at that time I saw that the chancellor, that is the grand secretary of the court, Bulgai by name, gave them a present of meat on the sixth day; and they blessed it with great pomp, as the pascal lamb is blessed. He himself, however, did not eat (meat on Friday), and this is also the principle of master William the Parisian, who is a great friend of his. The monk directed Mangu to fast during the week, and this he did, as I heard say. So on the Sunday of Septuagesima (8th February), which is as it were the Easter of the Hermenians, we went in procession to the dwelling of Mangu, and the monk and we two, after having been searched for knives, entered into his presence with the priests. And as we were entering a servant came out carrying some sheep's shoulder-blades, burnt to coals, and I wondered greatly what he could do with them. When later on I enquired about it, I learnt that he does nothing in the world without first consulting these bones; he does not even allow a person to enter his dwelling without first consulting them. This kind of divination is done as follows: when he wishes to do (319) anything, he has brought him three of these bones not previously charred, and holding one, he thinks of the thing about which he wishes to consult it, whether he shall do it or not; and then he hands it to a servant to burn. And there are two little buildings beside

---

*before* Lent. Their dominical fast, which corresponds with our Lent, lasts seven whole weeks, from our Sunday of Quinquagesima, which they call Entry to the Fast, to Easter, Saturdays and Sundays not excepted (see Chabot, 77, and Badger, ii, 187). The Armenians write the name of Sergius, *Sarkis*. Father Alishan tells me the Armenians still celebrate with great pomp after this fast the feast of Saint Sarkis the General, of his son Sergius, and of the soldiers martyred with them. The feast of this Saint Sergius in the Roman church falls on October 7th (Tournefort, *Voyage*, ii, 164; Chardin, ii, 168). I suppose that our author uses the word *canon* in the Greek sense, Κανονικος, meaning that he was a bishop canonically elected. The text is "*qui est major sanctus inter eos quem Greci dicunt fuisce canon.*"

the dwelling in which he lives, in which they burn these bones, and these bones are looked for diligently every day throughout the whole camp. When they have been charred black, they are brought back to him, and then he examines whether the bones have been split by the heat throughout their length. In that case the way is open for him to act. If, however, the bones have been cracked crosswise, or round bits have been started out of them, then he may not act. For this bone always splits in the fire, or there appear some cracks spreading over it. And if out of the three he finds one satisfactory, he acts.[1]

When then we were going into his presence, we were cautioned not to touch the threshold. The Nestorian priests carried incense to him, and he put it in the censer and they incensed him. They then chanted, blessing his drink; and after them the monk said his benison, and finally we had to say ours.[2] And seeing us carrying Bibles before our

---

[1] This is an extremely accurate description of the method of practising scapulomancy or omoplatoscopy, a form of divination widely spread over Asia and Europe (see Pallas, *Nachrichten*, ii, 350; Quatremère, 272; Klemm, *Culturgeschichte*, iii, 200; Radloff, *Aus Siberien*, i, 474; Gombojew, 654; Rockhill, *Land of the Lamas*, 341; also *Diary*, 198; Vambéry, *Sketches of Central Asia*, 219; Lubbock, *Origin of Civilisation*, 238; Tylor, *Primitive Culture*, i, 124). It was formerly practised in England, where it was known as "reading the speal-bone" (Brand, *Popular Antiquities*, iii, 339). It was also known to the Greeks and Latins. "They sacrificed a sheep or lamb, after having formulated in the mind the question to be answered; then they took a shoulder-blade and roasted it over the fire. According as the middle ridge remained white and intact in the fire, or became cracked, it signified life or death; if the right-side reddened, or if the left-side blackened, it was a sign of war: white signified on either side peace" (Bouché Leclercq, *Divination*, i, 180). In Greece, where this form of divination is still in use among the shepherds, the colour and arrangements of the spots on the bone after being charred are the important signs, while with Asiatics the fissures are chiefly consulted. Rubruck is careful to note the very important fact, that it is necessary, prior to charring the bone, to think of the object of the divination.

[2] Friar Odoric tells of having gone in a procession to meet the Emperor seated in his chariot. The friars carried before them a cross on a high pole, so that it could be seen better, and they sang *Veni, Sancte Spiritus*. "When we came to the chariot by permission of

breasts, he had them handed him to look at, and he examined them very carefully. When he had drunk, and the highest of the priests had served him his cup, they gave the priests to drink. After this we went out, and my companion who had turned his face toward the Chan bowing to him, and following us in this fashion hit the threshold of the dwelling;[1] and as we were proceeding in all haste to the house of Baltu, his son, those who were guarding the threshold (320) laid hands on my companion, stopped him, and would not allow him to follow us; and calling someone, they told him to take him to Bulgai, who is the grand secretary of the court, and who condemns persons to death. But I was in ignorance of all this. When I looked back and did not see him coming, I thought they had detained him to give him lighter clothing, for he was feeble, and so loaded down with furs that he could scarcely walk. Then they called our interpreter, and made him stay with him.

We on our side went to the house of the eldest son of the Chan, who has already two wives, and who lodges on the right side of his father's *ordu*; and as soon as he saw us coming, he got up from the couch on which he was seated, and prostrated himself to the ground, striking the ground with his forehead, and worshipping the cross. Then getting up, he had it placed on high in the most honoured place beside him. He had as a master a certain Nestorian priest, David by name, a great drunkard, who was teaching him. Then he made us sit down, and had given the priests

---

the Lord, for otherwise no one dare approach it, the bishop blessed him, and the Emperor kissed the cross quite devoutly; and as the fashion is that no one shall appear before the Emperor without giving him something, we presented him a silver platter full of apples" (Cordier, *Odoric*, 375, 504).

[1] Friar Bartholomew tried to follow the usage of western courts, and not to turn his back on the sovereign. Like many others since him, he came to grief in this most awkward performance.

to drink. And he also drank, after having been blessed by them.

Then we went to the *ordu* of the second lady, who is called Cota,[1] and who is an idol follower, and we found her lying ill in bed. The monk obliged her to get up from her bed, and made her worship the cross with bended knees and prostrations, the forehead on the ground, he standing with the cross on the west side of the dwelling, and she on the east side. When this was done, they changed places, and the monk went with the cross to the east side, and she to the west; and he commanded her boldly, though she was so feeble she could scarcely stand on her feet, to prostrate herself three times, worshipping the cross facing the east, in Christian fashion: and this she did. And he showed her how to make the sign of the cross before her face. After that, when she had lain down again on her (321) bed, prayers having been said for her, we went to a third house in which the Christian lady used to live. On her death she was succeeded by a young girl[2] who, together with the daughter of the lord (Mangu?), received us joyfully, and all they in this house worshipped the cross most devoutly; and she had it placed in a high place on a silk cloth, and had food brought, to wit, mutton, and it was placed before the master (mistress?), who caused her to distribute it to the priests. I and the monk, however, took neither food nor drink. When the meat had been devoured and a great deal of liquor drunk, we had to go to the apartment of that damsel Cherina, which was behind the big *ordu* which had been her mother's; and when the cross was brought in she prostrated herself to

---

[1] I have not found the names of Mangu's concubines in any contemporary work. D'Ohsson (ii, 334) says he had two sons by his concubines; their names were Shiregui and Assutai.

[2] This is the young girl Cherina (or Cirina) spoken of in the next phrase. Friar William had his first audience of Mangu in this tent (see *supra*, p. 172).

the ground and worshipped it right devoutly, for she had been well instructed in that, and she placed it in a high place on a piece of silk ; and all these pieces of stuff on which the cross was put belonged to the monk.

A certain Hermenian who had come with the monk had brought this said cross from Jerusalem, as he said, and it was of silver, weighing perhaps four marks, and had IIII gems in the angles and one in the centre ; and it did not have the image of the Saviour, for the Hermenians and Nestorians are ashamed to show the Christ fixed to the Cross. And they had presented it to Mangu Chan, and Mangu asked him what he wanted. Then he said he was the son of an Hermenian priest, whose church had been destroyed by the Saracens, and he asked his help to restore this church. (322) Then (Mangu) asked him with how much it could be rebuilt, and he said two hundred *iascot*—that is two thousand marks. And he ordered that he should be given letters to him who receives the tribute in Persia and Greater Hermenia,[1] to pay him this sum of silver. The monk carried this cross with him everywhere, and the priests seeing how he profited thereby began to envy him.

So we were in the dwelling of this damsel, and she gave the priests much to drink. Thence we went to a fourth house, which was the last as to its position and its importance. For he (*i.e.*, Mangu) did not frequent that lady, and her dwelling was old, and she herself little pleasing; but after Easter the Chan made her a new house and new carts. She, like the second, knew little or nothing of Christianity, but followed the diviners and idolaters. However, when we went in she worshipped the Cross, just as the monk and priests had taught her.[2] There

---

[1] Arghun, I take it, is the person referred to. Rubruck states (384) that he resided at Tauris, or Tabriz, in Persia.

[2] The worship of the Cross was reckoned as one of the sacraments n the Nestorian Church (Badger, ii, 132, 414).

again the priests drank; and thence we went back to our oratory, which was near by, the priests singing with great howling in their drunkenness, which in those parts is not reprehensible in man or in woman.

Then my companion was brought in and the monk chided him most harshly, because he had touched the threshold. The next day came Bulgai, who was the judge,[1] and he closely inquired whether anyone had warned us to be careful about touching the threshold, and I answered: "My lord, we had no interpreter with us; how could we have understood?" Then he pardoned him, but never thereafter was he allowed to enter any dwelling of the Chan.

---

IT happened after this that the lady Cota (323), who had fallen ill about the Sunday of Sexagesima (15th February), fell sick even unto death, and the sorcerers of the idolaters could do nothing to drive it out. Then Mangu sent to the monk, asking him what could be done for her, and the monk rashly replied that if she did not get well he could cut off his head. Having made this promise the monk called us, telling us of the affair with tears, and begging us to keep vigils with him that night in the oratory; this we did. And he had a certain root called rhubarb,[2] and he chopped it up till it

[1] Bulgai Aka was not only Chancellor of Mangu, but head of the department of finances and of internal affairs of the empire (d'Ohsson, ii, 260).

[2] Marco Polo (i, 219) says: "Over all the mountains of this province (of Tangut) rhubarb is found in great abundance, and thither merchants come to buy it, and carry it the world over." North-western Kan-su, western Ssŭ-ch'uan, and eastern Tibet, still supply the world with a great deal of this root. The Mongols use it medicinally for animals, as do the Chinese, I believe, but not often for themselves. The Mongols sometimes use it as a dye. See, on the preparation of the root in China, Gemelli Carreri (Churchill's *Collec.*, bk. iii, ch. v, 365). It is said that when Chinghis Khan was pillaging Tangut, the only things

was nearly powder, and put it in water with a little cross which he had, and on which was a raised image of the Saviour, and by which he said he could find out whether a sick person would recover or die. If he was to escape, it stuck on the sick person's breast as if glued there ; if not, it did not stick. And I thought that this rhubarb was something holy which he had brought from Jerusalem in the Holy Land. And he was in the habit of giving this water to drink to all sick persons, and it could not be but their bowels were stirred up by such a bitter draught. But they considered this movement in their bodies something miraculous.

Then I said to him, as he was preparing it, to make the potion with holy water as is done in the Church of Rome, for it has great virtue in expelling devils, for we supposed that she was beset of a devil ; and at his request we made him (324) holy water, and he mixed rhubarb in it, and put the cross to soak in it the whole night. I told him also that if he was a priest, the sacerdotal order had great power in expelling devils. And he said he was ; but he lied, for he had taken no orders, and did not know a single letter, but was a cloth weaver, as I found out in his own country, which I went through on my way back.

The next day then we went to this lady, the monk, I, and two Nestorian priests, and she was in a little (tent) behind her larger dwelling. When we went in, she got up from her couch, worshipped the Cross, put it reverently beside her on a silk cloth, drank some holy water and rhubarb, and washed her breast (with it) ; and the monk requested me to read the Gospel over her. I read the Passion of the Lord according to John. Finally she

---

his minister, Yeh-lü Ch'u-ts'ai, would take as his share of the booty were a few Chinese books and a supply of rhubarb, with which he saved the lives of a great number of Mongols when, a short time after, an epidemic broke out in the army (d'Ohsson, i, 372).

revived and felt better, and she caused to be brought four *iascot* of silver, which she first put at the foot of the Cross, and then gave one to the monk, and she held out one to me, which I would not receive. Then the monk held out his hand and took it. And to either of the priests she gave one ; so she gave that time forty marks. Then she had wine brought, and gave the priests to drink, and I also had to drink three times at her hand in honour of the Trinity. She also began to teach me the language, joking with me because I was silent, not having an interpreter with me.

The next day we again went back to her, and Mangu Chan, hearing that we had passed that way, made us come in unto him, because he had heard that the lady was better ; and we found him with a few of his attendants, and he was drinking what looked like liquid mud, a dish made of paste for (325) the comforting of the head,[1] and charred sheep's shoulder-blades lay before him, and he took the Cross in his hand ; but whether he kissed it or worshipped it I did not notice, but he looked at it, asking I know not what.

Then the monk asked permission to carry the Cross on high on a lance, for he had previously spoken to the monk about this, and Mangu replied : "Carry it as you like best." Then, having saluted him, we went to the said lady, and we found her well and bright, and she drank again of the holy water, and we read the Passion over her. But these miserable priests had never taught her the faith, nor advised her to be baptized. I sat there, however, silent, unable to say a word, so she again taught me some of the language.

---

[1] *Sorbantem liquidam terram, hoc est cibum de pasta, pro comfortatione capitis.* The Chinese in northern China and in Mongolia make a kind of brown gruel, with hot water or tea and parched flour, in which a few very small pieces of fat mutton have been put. It is much used by travellers, and also taken after a drinking bout—such as Mangu had probably been having. The Emperor Baber, on similar occasions, tells us he took a *madjum*.

The priests do not condemn any form of sorcery ; for I saw there four swords half way out of their scabbards, one at the head of the lady's couch, another at the foot, and one of the other two on either side of the entry. I also saw there a silver chalice, of the kind we use, which had perhaps been stolen in some church in Hungary, and it was hung on the wall full of ashes, and on the ashes was a black stone ; and these priests never teach that such things are evil.[1] Even more, they themselves do and teach such things.

We visited her (*i.e.*, Cota) on three days, so that she was completely restored to health. After that the monk made a banner covered with crosses, and got a reed (326) as long as a spear, and we used to carry the Cross on high. I showed him the respect I would to my bishop, because he knew the language. He did, however, many things which did not please me. Thus he had made for himself a folding-chair, such as bishops are wont to have, and gloves and a cap of (with) peacock feathers, and on it a little gold cross, which, so far as the cross went, pleased me well. He had rough claws, which he tried to improve with unguents.[2] He showed himself most presumptuous in his speech. Furthermore these Nestorians used to recite I know not what verses, of a psalm according to them, over two twigs which were joined together while held by two men.[3] The monk stood by during the operation ; and

[1] I cannot explain the purpose of the four swords. The black stone may either have been a rain or thunder-stone, or a *sharir* (*sharira* in Sanskrit, a relic) which Rashideddin says was found in the human body after cremation, and was supposed to bring the fortunate possessor every kind of good luck (Quatremère, 439). Different localities in Asia were famed for the various magic stones found in them (Yule, *Cathay*, clxxxvii).

[2] *Habebat ungulas scabiosas quas laborabat decorare unguentis.* Can our author mean that he used *henneh*, or some such substance to improve the appearance of his nails ?

[3] See the interesting note of Yule (*Marco Polo*, i, 237-238). The mode of divining here referred to is apparently the same as that

other vanities appeared in him which displeased me. Nevertheless, we kept to his company for the honour of the Cross; for we used to carry the cross on high throughout the whole camp, singing "*Vexilla regis prodeunt*," at which the Saracens were greatly astonished.

---

FROM the time when we reached the court of Mangu, he never moved his carts (*bigavit*) but twice toward the south; and then he began going back northward, which was toward Caracarum. One thing I remarked throughout the whole journey, which agreed with what I had been told by Messire Baldwin of Hainaut in Constantinople,[1] who had been there, that the one thing that seemed extraordinary was that he ascended the whole way in going, without ever descending. For all the rivers flowed from east to west, either directly or indirectly—that is to say, deflecting north or south. And I questioned priests, (327) who had come from Cathay, who bore witness to it, that from the place where I had found Mangu Chan to Cathay was XX days journey between south and east; while to Onan Kerule, which is the true country of the Moal, and where is the *ordu* of Chingis, was ten days due east, and that all the way to these eastern parts there was no city. There were, however (they said), people called Su-Moal, which is "Moal of the waters;" for *su* is the same as "water."

---

described by Polo. It must not, however, be confounded with rabdomancy, in which bundles of wands or arrows were used. Ammianus Marcellinus (xxxi, 2, 350) says this mode of divination was practised by the Alans. "They have a singular way of divining: they take straight willow wands and make bundles of them, and on examining them at a certain time, with certain secret incantations, they know what is going to happen."

[1] See *supra*, p. 102, note 2.

They live on fish and by the chase, for they have no flocks, no herds.[1] Likewise to the north there is no city, but a people raising flocks, and called Kerkis.[2] There

---

[1] Pian de Carpine (708) (see also *supra*, p. 112) speaks of the *Su-Mongals.* D'Avezac (532) says that Hammer and Klaproth have found this name, or its Chinese equivalent, in Mohammedan and Chinese works. To judge by their mode of living, this people were probably Tungus, not Mongols. Le Bruyn (*Voyages*, v, 224) speaks of the *Saniongals;* but he is only quoting Pian de Carpine.

[2] Here the Kirghiz are meant. In previous passages (*supra*, pp. 100, 116) the traveller used the name *Kerkis* to designate the Cherkesses, or Circassians. From Chinese sources we learn of the existence of the Kirghiz as a nation as early as the third century, A.D.: they were then known as *Kien-k'un*, *K'ieh-ku* or *K'ü-wu*, and lived where Rubruck placed them, north of northern Mongolia, on the head-waters of the Yenissei, and west of the Baikal. In course of time the Chinese changed the mode of writing this name, first to *Ho-ku* and *Ho-ku-ssŭ*, and in the latter part of the eighth century to *Kieh* (or *Hsia*)-*kia-ssŭ:* meaning in Uigur, we are told, something like "yellow and red face." Down to the time of the adoption of this last name, the earliest form of their name, or *Kien-k'un*, remained in use among the Chinese. The following description of their country and customs, probably in the latter part of the eighth century, is very interesting. I abridge it slightly from Ma Tuan-lin (bk. 348). The Kirghiz country was marshy in summer, and in winter covered with deep snow. The people were tall, and most of them had blonde (literally red, *ch'ih*) hair and green eyes. Those who had black hair were rare, and those who had black eyes were said to be descendants of Li-ling, a famous Chinese general of the Han period, who had taken refuge among them. They raised crops of wheat and barley, and made flour by crushing the grain on querns, and they used also the grain to make wine. They owned great numbers of camels, sheep, cattle and horses. The wild animals in their country comprised wild asses, *ku-tu* (possibly for *ku-no*, a kind of seal), antelope, argali and sables. They had also a variety of fish called *mao*, the smallest of which were seven or eight feet long, without marks on them or any bones, and their mouths were underneath the jaws (sturgeons?). Of birds they had geese, ducks, magpies and hawks. Pine, birch, elm, willow, and a coniferous tree called *p'u-sung* (cypress?), so tall that a man could not shoot an arrow to the top, grew there. Gold, iron and tin were found there. After every rain they found (in the beds of the streams?) a kind of iron called *kia-sha*, which could be made into weapons of extraordinary temper, and which they usually gave to the T'u-küeh (Turks) as tribute. Men were few among them, as compared to women. They wore earrings. The men were brave. They had tattoo-marks on their hands, and the women when they married had them made on the nape of the neck. They lived together promiscuously. Their arms consisted of bows and arrows, and they carried flags and pennons. They made shields of split wood, long enough to cover a horseman to the ground, and had other smaller round ones, reaching to the shoulder, to ward off arrow and sword blows. Their food, besides the flour previously mentioned,

are also the Oengai,[1] who tie polished bones under their feet, and propel themselves over the frozen snow and on the ice, with such speed that they catch birds and beasts. And there is a number of other poor peoples to the north as far as they can extend on account of the cold, and they confine to the west on the land of Pascatir, which is Greater Hungary, of which I have spoken to you previously. The northern end of the angle is unknown,[2] on account of the great cold. For there is eternal snow and ice there.

I asked (these same priests) about the monsters, or human monstrosities, of which Isidorus and Solinus speak.[3]

---

consisted of meat and mare's milk. Their language was very like that of the Uigurs. This people first sent a mission to the court of China in A.D. 648, when they came with a mission of the T'ieh-lê (Oguz Turks). In A.D. 840 the Kirghiz, after more than a century of warfare with the Uigurs, finally overthrew their empire. The name *Kien-K'un* is derived from that of the river Kem, or upper Yenissei. *Kieh-ku* and *Kieh*-(or *Hsia*) *kia-ssŭ* are transcriptions of the word *Hakas*, the early name of the Kirghiz. The name *Ki-li-ki-ssŭ*, or Kirghiz, first appears in Chinese works during the Mongol period (see d'Ohsson, i, 103; Bretschneider, *Anc. Chin. and Arabs*, 13; *ibid.*, *Med. Travel*, 74; and Klaproth, *Tabl. Hist.*, 168).

[1] The *Urianghit bishe*, or "Forest Urianghit" of Rashiddedin. He says they lived in the woods, had no tents, cattle or sheep, only wild cattle and an animal called *hur*, which resembled a mountain sheep. They set up bark shelters wherever they camped. He refers to the wonderful swiftness with which they travelled over the snow, and caught wild animals by means of their snow-shoes, or *chaneh*. During the reign of Chingis, their country was partly occupied by Mongol tribes. Quatremère, in a note to the above passage, remarks that the name *Urianghit* is found in Manchu *orochon*, from *oron*, "reindeer," and that this people is the same as the *Olenni Tongousi*, or "Reindeer Tunguses," of the Russians. Duhalde (*Description*, iv, 44) speaks of the *Orotchon* living near the river Chikiri. The Mongols call these people *Uryangshan* (Ssanang Setzen, 86, 190), and Abulghazi refers to them as *Ur-mankatts* (*Not. et Extr.*, xiii, 274; d'Ohsson, i, 421; F. M. Schmidt, 219). The Chinese annals make frequent mention of these Tungus tribes under a variety of names, and describe their mode of living in very nearly the same terms as Rashiddedin.

[2] *Terminus anguli aquilonaris ignoratur*. I am unable to explain our traveller's notions as to the cartography of northern Asia. He probably refers to the north-east angle.

[3] Solinus (207, 208) (on the authority of Megasthenes) tells of the dog-headed people of India, who were without speech; of the people

They told me they had never seen such, which astonished me greatly, if it be true. All of these said nations, no matter how miserable they may be, must serve (the Moal) in some manner. For it was a commandment of Chingis, that no one man should be free from service, until he be so old that he cannot possibly work any more.

One day a priest from Cathay was seated with me, (328) and he was dressed in a red stuff of the finest hue,[1] and I asked whence came such a colour; and he told me that in the countries east of Cathay there are high rocks, among which dwell creatures who have in all respects human forms, except that their knees do not bend, so that they get along by some kind of jumping motion; and they are not over a cubit in length, and all their little body is covered with hair, and they live in inaccessible caverns. And the hunters (of Cathay) go carrying with them mead, with which they can bring on great drunkenness, and they make cup-like holes in the rocks, and fill them with this mead. (For Cathay has no grape wine, though they have begun planting vines,[2] but they make a drink of rice.) So the hunters hide themselves, and these animals come out of their caverns and taste this liquor, and cry "*Chin, chin,*" so they have been given

---

with one eye; of the people who lived on the odour of wild apples and nothing else. Isidorus (*op. cit.*, xi, 421) says: "We hear of the monstrous faces of people in the remote part of the East; some without noses, their whole face flat and unformed. Others have the upper lip so protruding that they go to sleep shaded by it from the sun's rays. Others, again, are said to be speechless, using signs instead of language." Herodotus (iii, 9, 20) had already spoken of the one-eyed Arimaspians. Pliny (vii, 2, 282) is the authority from which Solinus and Isidorus derived their information. Pliny, in turn, derived his facts from the work of Megasthenes (see also *supra*, p. 12 and p. 36).

[1] This priest must have been a Tibetan lama who had visited China. Chinese priests (whether Buddhist or Taoist) have never worn red gowns, and Friar William has told us that all the *Tuin* among the Mongols dressed in yellow.

[2] Though the Chinese have never made wine from the grape, the vine has been cultivated in China since the second century B.C., when it was brought there from Turkestan by the great traveller, Chang-k'ien.

a name from this cry, and are called Chinchin. Then they come in great numbers, and drink this mead, and get drunk, and fall asleep. Then come the hunters, who bind the sleepers' feet and hands. After that they open a vein in their necks, and take out three or four drops of blood, and let them go free; and this blood, he told me was most precious for colouring purples.[1] They also told me as a fact (which I do not, however, believe), that there is a province beyond Cathay, and at whatever age a man enters it, that age he keeps which he had on entering.[2]

Cathay is on the ocean. And master William told me (329) that he had himself seen the envoys of certain people

---

[1] The story here told is found in a Chinese work, entitled, *Chu ch'uan* or "Record of notes" by Wang-kang of T'ai-yuan, in Chu, but I have been unable to ascertain the date at which it was written. The author says: "Yuan-yen, having been sent on a mission to Feng-chi (in Tongking), learnt from some of the natives that the *hsing-hsing* (a species of gibbon with yellow hair, sharp ears, and human face) love wine. As they have regular paths they travel over in the mountain gorges in bands of hundreds, the country people (set out wine) to catch them with. When they see the wine they know that it is some man's trick to catch them; and as these animals are very clever and know the men's fathers and grandfathers and their names, they revile them, saying: 'You want to kill me, but I don't want (your wine), and I'm off!' Then they go off a little way, but come back, calling each other, and saying, 'Let us all try the wine'; so they drink, and finding the flavour agreeable, they keep on drinking till they are no longer able to escape. Then the people shut them up in a pen to fatten them for food, and when they want a fat one to cook (these *hsing-hsing*) pick it out themselves, and with tears push it out." The other details of Friar William's story are supplied by another Chinese work, entitled *Hua-yang kuo chih*, or "Topographical description of the state of Hua-yang." Hua-yang included part of the present province of Ssŭ-ch'uan. This work says: "The *hsing-hsing* is found in the Shan (*Ai-lao*) country, in the province of Yung-chan. It can speak. A red dye can be made with its blood." The above quotations are taken from Ma Tuan-lin, bk. 329, 8. Yule (*Glossary of References*, 154) says that "the story as told by Rubruck is related with singular closeness of correspondence out 'of the Chinese books of geography' by Francesco Carletti in 1600, in his *Ragionamenti*" (see also *Cathay*, cxxvi).

[2] I have no doubt that this refers to the popular Chinese fables concerning the fabulous Kun-lun mountains, where lives the fairy queen, Hsi-wang mu, and where grows the peach which insures immortality to the fortunate mortal who eats it.

called Caule and Manse, who live on islands the sea around which freezes in winter, so that at that time the Tartars can make raids thither; and they had offered (them) thirty-two thousand *tumen* of *iascot* a year, if they would only leave them in peace. A *tumen* is a number containing ten thousand.[1]

The common money of Cathay is a paper of cotton, in length and breadth a palm, and on it they stamp lines like those on the seal of Mangu.[2] They (*i.e.*, the Cathayans) write with a brush such as painters paint

---

[1] *Caule* is Kao-li, the name of the dynasty which reigned in Korea till the middle of the fifteenth century, when the present dynasty, which styles itself Chao-hsien, came to the throne. The name of the dynasty is applied always to the kingdom. The *Manse* must be the *Manze* of Marco Polo, the empire of the Sung. It is quite out of the question to accept Peschel's view (*Erdkunde*, 169), that the Manse were Manchus. That name was not used in the thirteenth century; the Manchus were then confounded with the Longa and Solanga. It is possible that the person who told William Buchier of this people, and of the islands on which they lived, had in mind the island of Kang-hua off the Korean coast, which was a place of refuge for the Korean kings when pressed by their enemies. In fact, we learn, that when in 1231 Korea revolted against the Mongols, the king took up his residence on this island. In 1241 the King of Korea made his submission to Ogodai, and sent one of his relatives to the Mongol coast (d'Ohsson, ii, 74, 75). This may have been the Korean mission seen by Buchier. The Sung (Rubruck's *Manse*) had allied themselves with the Mongols against the Kin, and probably sent from about 1230 to 1234 numerous missions to the court of Ogodai. As to the extraordinary tribute which our traveller says Buchier told him had been offered by the Caule and Manse, in our money it would be nearly £16,600 millions; this can only be treated as a wild statement made by someone who knew nothing about the subject.

[2] Our traveller says the paper was made of *bombax*, but nearly all other contemporary writers, Oriental as well as Western, say the notes of the Mongols were made of mulberry fibre paper (Yule, *Marco Polo*, i, 409, and *Jordanus*, 46; Cordier, *Odoric*, 380; *Mesalek al-absar*, 223). Palladius (*op. cit.*, 50), says that up to his time (1876) there was kept at Hsi-an Fu a block used for printing the bank notes of the Kin dynasty, from whom the Mongols borrowed the system; and that he had seen a print of these notes. No prints of these bank notes, nor even Mongol ones, are known to me to be now in existence. Those of the Ming dynasty are well known (see Yule, *Marco Polo*, i, 412). As early as B.C. 118, we find the Chinese using "leather money" (*p'i pi*). These were pieces of white deer-skin, a foot square, with a coloured border. Each had a value of 40,000 cash (Ma Tuan-lin, bk 8, 5). See also Vissering, *Chinese Currency*, 38, 160, *et seq.*; and Lacouperie, *Numis. Chron.*, ii, 3rd series, pp. 334-341.

with, and they make in one figure the several letters containing a whole word.[1] The Tebet write as we do, and have characters quite like ours. The Tanguts write from right to left like the Arabs, but they repeat the lines running upwards; the Iugur, as previously said (write) up and down. The ordinary money of the Ruthenians are skins of vaire and minever.[2]

---

WHEN we came (to live) with the monk, he advised us, in all kindliness, to abstain from meat; that our servant would get meat with his servants; and that he would provide us with flour and oil or butter: this we did, though it greatly incommoded my companion on account of his weakness. Consequently, our diet consisted of millet with butter (330), or dough cooked in water with butter, or sour milk and unleavened bread, cooked in a fire of cattle- or horse-dung.

When came Quinquagesima (23rd February), which is the Carnival of all Eastern (Christians),[3] the great lady

---

[1] This is the earliest reference to Chinese writing found in western works. Yule (*Ency. Brit.*, xxxi, 4), justly remarks: "This is a remarkable utterance, showing an approximate apprehension of the nature of Chinese writing."

[2] Already, in the thirteenth century, the Russian princes levied the taxes on their people in honey and in furs. The price of objects was fixed in *kuni*, or "skins." A certain number of *kuni* formed a *grivna*, the equivalent of half a pound of silver. Instead of using the whole skin of the marten or squirrel (Rubruck's "Vaire and Miniver," see *supra*, p. 44, note 1), the head alone was sometimes used: thus we read of *capitata martatorum* (or *kuni mordki* in Russian). Pieces of the skins of martens and squirrels, probably bearing the Government stamp, were also current. In the middle of the thirteenth century, a marten (or sable) skin was worth about ten squirrel skins (Karamsin, i, 308, iii, 371, 372, 376). Ibn Dasta says that the Bulgars of the Volga also used among themselves sable skins for money (Röesler, *Romänische Studien*, 362). The name *polushka* in Russian, given to a small coin worth a quarter of a kopeck, means literally "half a skin."

[3] "*Venit autem quinquagesima, que est carnis primum omnium orientalium.*"

Cotata[1] and her company fasted that week; and she came every day to our oratory, and gave food to the priests and to the other Christians, of whom a great multitude gathered there that first week to hear the services; and she gave me and my companion each of us a tunic and trousers of grey samite,[2] lined with silk wadding, for my companion had complained greatly of the weight of his fur gown. These I received for the sake of my companion, though I excused myself for not wearing such clothes. I gave what belonged to me to my interpreter.

The gate-keepers of the court seeing such a crowd pressing toward the church, which was just beyond the bounds of the court, the warders of the court sent one of their number to the monk, to tell him they would not have such a great multitude congregating there just beyond the court limits. Then the monk replied roughly that he wanted to know if they gave this as the order of Mangu, adding also some threats, as if he would make complaint of them to Mangu. So they forestalled him and accused him to Mangu, saying that he talked too much, and that too great a multitude met together at his talks.

After that, on Quadragesima Sunday (1st March) we were called to court, and when the monk had been so shamefully searched to see whether he had a knife that he of his own accord took off his shoes (331), we entered into the Chan's presence, and he had a charred sheep's shoulder-blade in his hand, and was inspecting it; and then, as if reading on it, he began to reprimand the monk, asking why, since he was a man who ought to pray to

---

[1] Kutuktai Khatun, the first wife of Mangu (see *supra*, p. 184).

[2] *Samico grisio.* Samite was a heavy silk stuff, with gold or silver threads woven in it. It was first manufactured in the islands of Greece, where it was known as *examiton* (ἑξάμιτον), but later on at Acre, Beyrut, Laodicea, Damas and Alexandria (Heyd, ii, 669). I fancy that the samite here referred to was a Chinese brocaded silk.

God, he talked so much to men. I was standing behind with uncovered head, and the Chan said to him: "Why do you not uncover your head, when you come into my presence, as this Frank does?" Then the monk in great confusion took off his hat, against the custom of the Greeks and Hermenians; and when the Chan had said many harsh things to him, we went out. And then the monk handed me the Cross to carry to the oratory, for such was his confusion that he did not want to carry it.

After a few days he made his peace with the Chan, promising that he would go to the Pope, and that he would bring all the nations of the west to owe him obedience. When he came back to the oratory after this conversation with the Chan, he began inquiring about the Pope, whether I believed he would see him, if he came to him on the part of Mangu, and if he would furnish him with horses as far as Saint James.[1] He inquired also concerning you, if I believed that you would send your son to Mangu. Then I warned him to be careful not to make lying promises to Mangu, for he would be making a new mistake more serious than the first, and that God did not want lies from us, or that we should speak deceitfully.

At this time there arose a controversy between the monk and a certain priest called Jonas, a well-read man, whose father had been archdeacon, and whom the other priests looked upon as a teacher and archdeacon. For the monk said that man had been made before paradise, and that the Gospel said so. Then I was called upon to decide this (332) question. I, without knowing that they were arguing on the subject, replied that the paradise had been made the third day, when also all the trees were; and that man had been made on the sixth day. Then the

---

[1] St. James of Compostella, in Galicia in Spain, is meant, I suppose.

monk began to say: "Did not the devil on the first day bring earth from the four parts of the world, and having made mud of it, did he not make the human body, and did not God breathe a soul into it?"[1] Hearing the Manichean heresy, and he thus publicly and impudently proclaiming it, I upbraided him sharply, telling him to put his finger on his mouth, since he did not know the Scriptures, and to be careful not to tell the reason of his fault. But he began to scoff at me, because I did not know the language. So I left him and went to our dwelling.

After that it happened that he and the priests went in procession to the court, without telling me, for the monk was not speaking to me on account of this scolding, and he did not want to take me with him as he used to do. So when they came into the presence of Mangu, and he did not see me among them, he inquired where I was, and why I had not come with them. But the priests were afraid, and excused themselves. When they came back they told me what Mangu had said, and complained of the monk. After that the monk made his peace with me, and I with him, begging him to help me with the language, and that I would help him with the Sacred Scriptures. For "the brother who is aided by the brother is like a strong city."[2]

---

[1] The Manichæans say that Adam was engendered by Satan, in conjunction with sin, cupidity and desire; but the spirit of darkness drove into him all the portions of light he had stolen, in order to be able to dominate them the more surely. Hence, Adam is a discordant being, created in the image of Satan, but carrying within him the stronger spark of light. Eve was given him by Satan as a companion, and Cain and Abel were her sons by Satan (Harnack, *Ency. Brit.*, xv, 483). On this Jonas and his death, see *infra*, p. 216.

[2] *Proverbs*, xviii, 19, in the Vulgate.

AFTER the first week of the fast, the lady ceased to come to the oratory and to give the food and mead we were accustomed to get. The monk did not allow (any food) to be bought, saying that (333) mutton tallow was used in preparing it. He only very rarely gave us oil. Consequently, we had nothing save bread cooked on the ashes, and dough boiled in water, so that we could have soup to drink, as the only water we had was melted snow or ice, and was very bad. Then my companion began to complain greatly; so I told our necessity to that David, who was the teacher of the eldest son of the Chan, and he reported my words to the Chan, who had us given wine and flour and oil. The Nestorians will not eat fish during Lent, neither will the Hermenians;[1] so they gave us a skin of wine. The monk said he only ate on Sunday, when this lady sent him a meal of cooked dough with vinegar to drink.[2] But he had beside him, under the altar, a box with almonds and raisins and prunes, and many other fruits, which he ate all through the day whenever he was alone. We ate once a day, and then in great misery; for it was known that Mangu Chan had given us wine, so they pushed their way in on us like dogs in the most impudent manner, both

---

[1] Tournefort (*Voyages*, ii, 164) says: "The Lent of the Greeks is a high festival compared to that of the Armenians; besides its extraordinary length, it is not allowed them during that time to eat anything but roots; and it is even forbidden them to eat as much of these as will satisfy their appetite. The use of shell-fish, oil, wine, is forbidden, except on Holy Saturday; they take on that day butter, cheese, and eggs. Easter they eat meat, but only such as has been killed that day. . . . Besides the great Fast, they have four others of eight days each during the year. . . . These Fasts are as severe as the great one: there is no question at such times of either eggs, fish, or even oil or butter; some persons there are who take no food whatever for three or four days consecutively."

[2] This dish, called *mien* by the Chinese, is the most common article of diet in northern China and Mongolia. The vinegar, or soy, is used to season the water in which the paste has been cooked, and is drunk as soup.

the Nestorian priests, who were getting drunk all day at court, and the Moal, and the servants of the monk. Even the monk himself, when someone came to him to whom he wished to give drink, would send to us for wine. So it was that that wine brought us (334) more vexation than comfort, for we could not refuse to give of it without causing scandal; if we should give it, we would want it; nor would we dare ask for more from the court, when that was done.

---

TOWARD the middle of Lent, the son of master William arrived bringing a beautiful crucifix, made in French style, with a silver image of the Christ fixed on it. Seeing it, the monks and priests stole it, though he was to have presented it from his master to Bulgai, the grand secretary of the court; when I heard of this I was greatly scandalized.

This young man also informed Mangu Chan that the work he had ordered to be done was finished; and this work I shall here describe to you. Mangu had at Caracarum a great palace, situated next to the city walls, enclosed within a high wall like those which enclose monks' priories among us. Here is a great palace, where he has his drinkings twice a year: once about Easter, when he passes there, and once in summer, when he goes back (westward). And the latter is the greater (feast), for then come to his court all the nobles, even though distant two months journey; and then he makes them largess of robes and presents, and shows his great glory. There are there many buildings as long as barns, in which are stored his provisions and his treasures.[1] In the entry of this great

---

[1] The Mongol palace at Peking was similarly arranged (Marco Polo, i, 356; Bretschneider, *Archæological Researches*, 32; see also on the palace of Karakorum, *infra*).

palace, it being unseemly to bring in there skins of milk and other drinks, master William the Parisian had made for him a great silver tree, and at its roots are four lions of silver, each with a conduit through it, and all belching forth white milk of mares.[1] (335) And four conduits are led inside the tree to its tops, which are bent downward, and on each of these is also a gilded serpent, whose tail twines round the tree. And from one of these pipes flows wine, from another *caracosmos*, or clarified mare's milk, from another *bal*, a drink made with honey, and from another rice mead, which is called *terracina;* and for each liquor there is a special silver bowl at the foot of the tree to receive it. Between these four conduits in the top, he made an angel holding a trumpet, and underneath the tree he made a vault in which a man can be hid. And pipes go up through the heart of the tree to the angel. In the first place he made bellows, but they did not give enough wind. Outside the palace is a cellar in which the liquors are stored, and there are servants all ready to pour them out when they hear the angel trumpeting. And there are branches of silver on the tree, and leaves and fruit. When then drink is wanted, the head butler cries to the angel to blow his trumpet. Then he who is concealed in the vault, hearing this blows with all his might in the pipe leading to the angel, and the angel places the trumpet to (336) his mouth, and blows the trumpet right loudly. Then the servants who are in the cellar, hearing this, pour the different liquors into the proper conduits, and the conduits lead them down into the bowls prepared for that, and then the butlers draw it and carry it to the palace to the men and women.[2]

---

[1] *Lac album jumenti*, by which is meant the dregs left over from the preparation of *caracosmos*, and which, we are told, was given to the slaves as a drink.

[2] Similar works of art and mechanical contrivances were often seen n eastern courts. The earliest I know of is the golden plane tree and

And the palace is like a church, with a middle nave, and two sides beyond two rows of pillars, and with three doors

---

grape vine with bunches of grapes in precious stones, which was given to Darius by Pythius the Lydian, and which shaded the king's couch (Herodotus, iv, 24). The most celebrated, however, and that which may have inspired Mangu with the desire to have something like it at his court, was the famous Throne of Solomon (Σολομώντεος Θρόνος) of the Emperor of Constantinople, Theophilus (A.D. 829-842). Luitprand of Cremona, who was in Constantinople in 946 as ambassador of Berengarius II., describes as follows the audience granted him by Constantine Porphyrogenitus in the Magnaura Palace. "Constantine, as much on account of the Spanish ambassadors who had then recently arrived, as for myself and Luitfred, received us with the following ceremonial. A gilt bronze tree was before the Emperor, and its branches were covered with various kinds of gilt birds, each one of which sang according to its kind. The throne was so artfully contrived that while at one moment it was on the ground, at the next it was off it, and anon it was seen high up in the air. The foot of the throne, which was of great size, and made I know not whether of bronze or wood, had great gilt lions guarding it. I was brought into the presence of the Emperor supporting myself on the shoulders of two eunuchs. As soon as I appeared, the lions roared and the birds sang according to their various kinds. I felt no terror, however, nor was I moved with astonishment, for I had made inquiry concerning all these things of one who knew all about them. Having worshipped (the Emperor) for the third time by a full-length prostration, I raised my head, and whereas I had seen him in the first place seated a little higher up than the floor, I now saw him dressed in other robes, and seated near the ceiling of the room" (Luitprand, *Historia*, vi, 26, in Muratori, *Rerum Italicarum*, ii, 469; see also Constantine Porphyrogenitus, *De Ceremon.*, i, 566-569).

Abulfeda states that in A.D. 917 the envoys of Constantine Porphyrogenitus to the Caliph el Moktader saw in the palace at Bagdad a tree with eighteen branches, some of gold, some of silver, and on them were gold and silver birds, and the leaves of the tree were of gold and silver. By means of machinery, the leaves were made to rustle and the birds to sing.

Mirkhond speaks also of a tree of gold and precious stones in the city of Sultanieh, in the interior of which were conduits through which flowed drinks of different kinds. Clavijo (161) describes a somewhat similar tree at the court of Timur.

Kublai Khan had in his palace at Peking "a large and very beautiful piece of workmanship," from which various liquors were drawn (Marco Polo, i, 369); and Friar Odoric (Yule, *Cathay*, 130) describes a wonderfully richly ornamented jar in the same palace, into which drink was conveyed by conduits from the court of the palace. Bretschneider (*Archæolog. Researches*, 28) describes an organ in the Mongol palace at Peking which was connected in some way with two peacocks seated on a cross-bar, and when the instrument was played, the birds danced.

to the south,[1] and beyond the middle door on the inside stands the tree, and the Chan sits in a high place to the north, so that he can be seen by all; and two rows of steps go up to him: by one he who carries his cup goes up, and by the other he comes down. The space which is in the middle between the tree and these steps by which they go up to him is empty; for here stands his cup-bearer, and also envoys bearing presents; and he himself sits up there like a divinity. On (his) right side, that is to the west, are the men, to the left the women. The palace extends from the north (southward). To the south, beside the pillars on the right side, are rows of seats raised like a platform, on which his son and brothers sit. On the left side it is arranged in like fashion, and there sit his wives and daughters. Only one woman sits up there beside him, though not so high as he.[2]

When then he heard that the work was finished, he ordered the master to put it in place and fix it well, and then toward Passion Sunday (29th March) he started out with his light tents,[3] leaving the big ones behind him. And the monk and we followed him, and he sent us (337) another skin of wine. And on the way we passed between mountains where there was excessive wind and cold and much snow fell. So toward the middle of the night he

---

[1] This palace was evidently built in purely Chinese style, and must have resembled the halls or audience pavilions (*tien* and *t'ing*) of modern Chinese palaces.

[2] Marco Polo (i, 368) says: "The Great Khan sits facing the south, and his chief wife sits beside him on the left. On his right sit his son and his nephews, and other kinsmen of the Blood Imperial, but lower, so that their heads are on a level with the Emperor's feet. And then the other Barons sit at other tables lower still. So also with the women; for all the wives of the Lord's sons and of his nephews and other kinsmen, sit at the lower table to his right; and below them again the ladies of other Barons and Knights, each in the place assigned by the Lord's orders (conf. also Odoric's account, *Cathay*, 141; see also *supra*, p. 24 and p. 38).

[3] *Parvis dominibus*, that is to say, the tents which could be taken down and loaded on camels and horses.

sent to the monk and us, asking us to pray God to temper this cold and wind, for all the animals in the caravan[1] were in danger, particularly as they were then heavy with young and bringing forth. Then the monk sent him incense, telling him that he himself should put it on coals and offer it to God. I know not whether he did this, but the tempest, which had already lasted two days, abated when the third day of it was already beginning.

---

ON Palm Sunday (5th April) we were near Caracarum. At early dawn we blessed some boughs, on which no signs of budding had yet appeared. And toward the ninth hour we entered the city, with raised Cross and banner, and passed through the Saracen quarter, where there is a square and a market, to the church. And the Nestorians came to meet us in a procession. Going into the church, we found them ready to celebrate mass; and when it was celebrated they all communicated and inquired of me whether I wished to communicate. I replied that I had already drunk, and could not receive the sacrament except fasting. When the mass had been said it was already after noon, so master William took us with great rejoicing to his house to dine with him; and he had a wife who was a daughter of Lorraine, but born in Hungary, and she spoke French and Coman well. We found there also another person, Basil by name, the son of an Englishman, and who (338) was born in Hungary, and who also knew these languages. We dined with great

[1] Friar William uses the word *comitatu*. The term "caravan" was, however, known in Europe in his time. Matth. Paris, for example, says: "*omnem illam catervam, quam vulgares karavanam appellant* . . . ."

rejoicing, and then they led us to our hut, which the Tartars had set up in an open space near the church, with the oratory of the monk.[1]

The next day the Chan entered his palace, and the monk and I and the priests went to him, but they did not allow my companion to go because he had trod upon the threshold. I had pondered much within myself what I should do, whether I should go or not; but I feared the scandal if I withdrew from the other Christians, and it pleased the Chan, and I feared it might interfere with the good I hoped to do; so I decided to go, though I saw that their sect was full of sorceries and idolateries. But I did nothing else while there but pray with a loud voice for the whole church, and also for the Chan, that God might guide him in the way of everlasting salvation.

So we entered the court, which is right well arranged; and in summer little streams are led all through it by which it is watered. After that we entered a palace all full of men and women, and we stood in the Chan's presence, with the tree of which I have spoken behind us, and it and the bowls (at its base) took up a large part of the palace. The priests had brought two little loaves of blessed bread, and fruit in a platter, which they presented to him, after saying grace. And a butler took it to him where he was seated on a right high and raised place; and he forthwith began to eat one of the loaves, and the other he sent to his son and to one of his younger brothers, who was being brought up by a certain Nestorian,

[1] The same small tent the travellers had occupied since arriving in Mangu's camp. The oratory of the monk was evidently also a tent. The Mongols when at Karakorum probably lived in tents, just as many of them do at the present day when in Peking. The only houses in Karakorum were, I think, those of the Mohammedan and Chinese quarters; besides these, there were, I suppose, a number of buildings used by Chinese and other foreign officials attached to the Mongol court, and some public offices (see also *infra*, p. 220, and on Basil, *infra*, p. 223).

and he knows the Gospels, and had also sent for my Bible to look at it.

After the priests (339), the monk spoke his oraison, and I mine after the monk. Then he (Mangu) promised that he would come the next day to the church, which is rather large and fine, and the whole ceiling is covered with a silken stuff interwoven with gold. The next day, however, he went his way, telling the priests in excuse that he did not dare come to the church, for he understood that they carried the dead there.[1] We remained, however, with the monk at Caracarum, together with the other priests of the court, to celebrate Easter there.

Holy Thursday and Easter were nigh, and I did not have our vestments, and I was considering the manner of doing of the Nestorians, and was greatly worried about what I should do, whether I should receive the sacrament from them, whether I should say mass in their vestments, with their chalice and on their altar, or whether I should wholly abstain from the sacrament. Then came a great number of Christians, Hungarians, Alans, Ruthenians, Georgians, Hermenians, all of whom had not seen the sacrament since their capture, for the Nestorians would not admit them into their church, so they said, unless they were rebaptized by them. However (the Nestorians) had not told us anything of all this; on the contrary, they confessed that the Roman Church was the head of all churches, and that they should receive their patriarch from the Pope, if the roads were open.[2] And they offered us freely their sacrament, and made us stand in the entry of the choir to

---

[1] This is explained by referring to what the traveller has stated previously (*supra*, p. 80).

[2] When in Rome in 1288, the Nestorian envoy of Arghun, Rabban Sauma, was allowed by Pope Nicolas IV to celebrate mass, and on Palm Sunday the Pope gave him communion. To the Nestorian patriarch Mar Jabalaba III the Pope sent his tiara, his ring, and church vestments of price (Chabot, *op. cit.*, 86, 87, 92).

see their way of doing, and, on Easter eve (11th April), beside the font to see their mode of baptizing. They said that they had some of the ointment with which Mary Magdalen anointed the feet of the Lord, and they always pour in oil to the (340) amount they take out, and they knead it into their bread. For all the Eastern (Christians) put grease into their bread instead of yeast, or else butter or sheep's tail fat or oil.[1] They also say that they have some of the flour with which was made the bread that the Lord consecrated, and they put back in it as much as they take out; and they have a room beside the choir, and an oven where they bake the bread, which they must consecrate with great devotion.

So they make a loaf of bread a palm broad with this oil, and then they divide it first into xii pieces according to the number of the Apostles, and after that they divide these portions according to the number of the people, and a priest gives to each the body of Christ in his hand, and the person takes it from his hand devoutly, and touches the top of his head with his hand.

Then I made them confess through the interpreter as well as I could, stating the x commandments and the vii mortal sins, and the others which one should shun and publicly confess. They excused themselves for theft, saying that without thieving they could not live, for their masters did not provide them with either clothing or victuals. So, considering that they and their belongings

---

[1] Mar Abd Yeshma, the Nestorian Metropolitan of Nisibis at the end of the thirteenth century, in his work entitled "The Jewel," says: "The holy and blessed Apostles Thomas and Bartholomew of the twelve, and Adi and Mari of the seventy, who discipled the East, committed to all the Eastern churches a Holy Leaven, to keep for the perfecting of the administration of the sacrament of the Lord's Body until His coming again" (Badger, ii, 409). On the origin of the custom, see Assemani (ii, 182). The Greeks used leavened bread, but not so the Armenians. The latter make their wafers the day before they are to be consecrated. They are like those used in the Roman Church, but three or four times thicker (Tournefort, ii, 165).

had been carried off without just cause, I said that it was permissible for them to take of their master's things what was necessary for them, and I was ready to say so to (341) Mangu Chan's face. Furthermore, certain among them were soldiers, who excused themselves for being obliged to go to wars, for otherwise they would be put to death. I strongly forbad them to go against Christians, or to injure them; they should rather let themselves be killed, for then they would become martyrs; and I said that if anyone wished to charge me to Mangu Chan with this teaching, I was ready to preach this in his hearing. The Nestorians from the court had approached while I was teaching, and I suspected that they might inform against us.

Then master William had made for us an iron to make wafers, and he had some vestments which he had made for himself; for he had some little scholarship, and conducted himself like a clerk. He had made after the French fashion a sculptured image of the Blessed Virgin, and on the windows surrounding it[1] he had sculptured the Gospel history right beautifully, and he made also a silver box to put the body of Christ in, with relics in little cavities made in the sides of the box. He had also made an oratory on a cart, finely decorated with sacred scenes. I accepted his vestments and blessed them, and we made right fine wafers after our fashion, and the Nestorians gave me the use of their baptistery, in which was an altar. Their patriarch had sent them from Baldach a quadrangular skin for an antimensium,[2] and it had been anointed with chrism;

---

[1] *Fenestris claudentibus.* The image of the Virgin was placed in a recess, with hinged doors (*fenestra*) closing in front of it.

[2] Baldach or Baudas is the usual way employed by western writers of the period to transcribe the name of Bagdad. It is used by the Chinese mediæval writers, in the form *Pao-ta*, though *Pai-ko-ta* is also met with. Consecrated altar-covers, to be used when the altar could not be properly consecrated, were used both in the Latin and the Eastern Church; they were called *antimensium* (from *ante* and *mensa*), in Greek *ἀντιμίσιον*, also written *ἀμτιμίνσιον*. The Greek antimensia

and this they used instead of a consecrated stone. So I celebrated mass on Holy Thursday (9th April) with their silver chalice and patene, and these vases were very large; and likewise on Easter day. And we made the people communicate, with the blessing of God (342), as I hope. As for them they baptized on Easter eve (11th April) more than sixty persons in very good order, and there was great rejoicing generally among all the Christians.

---

THEN it happened that master William fell grievously ill; and, as he was convalescing, the monk, while visiting him, gave him rhubarb to drink, so that he nearly killed him. So when I called on him I found him in this distressing condition, and I asked him what he had eaten or drunk. And he told me how the monk had given him this drink, and how he had drunk two bowls full, thinking it was holy water. Then I went to the monk and said to him: "Either go as an apostle doing real miracles by the grace of the Word and the Holy Ghost, or do as a physician in accordance with medical art. You give to drink to men not in a condition for it, a strong medicinal potion, as if it were something holy; and in so doing you would incur great shame, should it become known among men." From this he began fearing me, and warding himself from me.

It happened also at this time that the priest who was a sort of archdeacon[1] of the others fell ill, and his friends sent for a certain Saracen diviner, who said to them: "A certain lean man, who neither eats, nor drinks, nor sleeps

---

were made of pieces of the altar-cloth which had been used at the consecration of a church, and were sent by the bishops to the various presbyters to use in the absence of a consecrated altar. See Ducange, *s. v. Antimensium*.

[1] See *supra*, p. 205.

in a bed, is angered with him. If he can get his blessing, he may get well." So they understood that this referred to the monk, and toward the middle of the night the wife of the priest and the sister and the son came to the (343) monk, begging him to come and give him his blessing. They aroused us also to ask the monk. And as we asked him he said: "Let him alone, for he and three others who go also in evil ways, have formed the project to go to court, to obtain of Mangu Chan that you and I be driven out of these parts."

Now there had been a dispute among them, for Mangu and his wives had sent on Easter eve four *iascot* and pieces of silk to the monk and the priests to be distributed among them, and the monk had kept one *iascot* as his share, and of the remaining three one was counterfeit, for it was of copper; so it seemed to the priests that the monk had kept too large a share for himself; and it may therefore well have been that they had had some talk among themselves, which had been repeated to the monk.

When it was daylight I went to the priest, who had a very sharp pain in his side and was spitting blood, whence I imagined that it was an abscess. I advised him to recognize the Pope as the father of all Christians, which he at once did, vowing that if God should give him health he would go throw himself at the Pope's feet, and would ask in all good faith that the Pope should send his blessing to Mangu Chan. I advised him also to make restitution, if he had anything belonging to another. He said he had nothing. I spoke to him also of the sacrament of extreme unction. He replied: "We have not that custom, nor do our priests know how to do it;[1] I beg that whatever (344) you do for me, you do it according as you know how to do." I told him also of confession, which they do not

[1] Extreme unction is unknown to the Nestorians; but the Chaldeans have adopted it from the teaching of Rome (Badger, ii, 161).

make. He spoke a few words in the ear of a priest, one of his associates ; after that he began to grow better, and he asked me to go to the monk. I went. At first the monk would not come ; finally, on hearing that he was better, he went with his cross ; and I went carrying the body of Christ in the box of master William, having kept it from Easter day at his request. Then the monk began to stamp upon him with his feet, and the other kissed his feet in all humility. Then I said to him : "It is a custom of the Roman Church that sick persons partake of the body of Christ, as a viatic and protection against all the toils of the enemy. Here is the body of Christ which I have kept from Easter day. You must confess and desire it." Then he said with great faith : "I desire it with all my heart." And as I was about to expose it, he said with great earnestness : "I believe that this is my Creator and Saviour, who gave me life, and will give it me again after death at the general resurrection." And so he received the body of Christ made by me, after the fashion of the Church of Rome.

The monk remained with him after this, and gave him, while I was away, I know not what potion. The next day he began to suffer unto death. So taking some of their oil, which they say is holy, I anointed him according to the fashion of the Church, as he had asked me. I had not any of our oil, for the priests of Sartach had kept everything. And as we were about to repeat the prayers for the dying, and I wanted to be present at his death, the monk sent me word to go away, for if I should be present I could not enter (345) Mangu Chan's house till the year was up. When I mentioned this to his friends, they told me it was true, and they besought me to leave, so as not to interfere with the good I could promote.[1]

---

[1] See *supra*, p. 80.

When he was dead, the monk said to me: "Care not about it; I have killed him with my prayers. He was the only scholar, and was opposed to us. The others know nothing. However, all of them, Mangu Chan included, will come to our feet." Then he told me the above related answer of the diviner, which I did not believe, so I asked priests, friends of the deceased, if it were true. They said that it was; but whether he had been told beforehand, or not, they did not know.

After this I discovered that the monk had called this said Saracen diviner into his chapel with his wife, and had had dust sifted and had them divine for him by it.[1] He had also a Ruthenian deacon with him who divined for him. When I had learned this, I was horrified at his ignorance, and I told him: "Brother, a man who is full of the Holy Ghost, who teaches all things, should not seek answers or advice from diviners; all such things are forbidden, and those who are given to them are excommunicated." Then he began to excuse himself, saying that it was not true that he sought such things. I was not, however, able to leave him, for I had been lodged there by

---

[1] *Cribrari pulverem.* This, apparently, is the well-known method of detecting spirits or devils by strewing ashes around, when their presence is ascertained by the appearance on the ashes of their footprints. Tylor (*Prim. Cult.*, ii, 197) mentions the prevalence of this belief in many countries, among others in England. "On St. Mark's eve, he says (quoting Brand, *Pop. Antiq.*, i, 193), ashes are to be sifted over the hearth, and the footprints will be seen of anyone who is to die within the year." This form of divination is practised among the Koreans to discover the fate of a person who is dying. They place over the bowl in which they keep the brine used with their food a dish on which is strewn fine ashes, and over this they place a sieve. As soon as a person is dead, the sieve is raised and the ashes examined. If traces of small human feet are seen, the deceased has gone to inhabit another human form; if the lines on the ashes are serpentine or only fine lines, he has become a reptile or some crawling or creeping beast, etc. The Greeks had a method of divining by flour, called *ἀλευρομαντεία*, but nothing is known about it (Bouché-Leclercq, *Divination*, i, 182).

order of the Chan, and I could not go elsewhere without his special order.[1]

---

OF the city of Caracarum[2] you must know that, exclusive of the palace of the Chan, it is not as big as the village of Saint Denis, and the monastery of Saint Denis is ten times larger than the palace.

---

[1] While this monk Sergius was an especially ignorant impostor, the Armenian priesthood at that time and in later centuries do not appear to have been much better. Vincent of Beauvaiș (bk. xxx, ch. xcviii, 441a), says of them: "Many of their priests are given to divining, by the inspection of grain, and such-like methods." Chardin (ii, 186, viii, 116) says that the Armenians of his time were taught in their childhood to say *Christus*, to make the sign of the cross, and to fast, and that this was about all their religious education. They were very superstitious, and practised various modes of fortune-telling. Tournefort (ii, 163, 164) speaks also of the deplorable ignorance of the Armenian clergy in his time.

[2] The name of this famous city is Mongol, *Kara*, "black," and *kuren*, "a camp," or properly "pailing." It was founded in 1235 by Ogodai, who called it Ordu Balik, or "the City of the Ordu," otherwise "the Royal City." Mohammedan authors says it took its name of Karakorum from the mountains to the south of it, in which the Orkhon had its source (d'Ohsson, ii, 64). The Chinese mention a range of mountains from which the Orkhon flows, called *Wu-tê kien shan* (*T'ang shu*, bk. 43b). Probably these are the same. Rashideddin speaks of a tribe of Utikien Uigurs living in this country (Bretschneider, *Med. Geog.*, 191; d'Ohsson, i, 437). It would seem more probable that the name of Karakorum, as applied by the Persian mediæval writers to these mountains, was taken from that of the city. The Chinese transcribed the name *Ha-la ho-lin*, which in time was abbreviated to *Ho-lin*, in which form the name is usually written in Chinese works. The determination of the exact site of this city was for many years a much-disputed question, but it appears to have been finally settled in 1889, by the Russian traveller, N. Yadrintzef. The city, according to him, stood on the left bank of the Orkhon river, about thirty miles south of its confluence with the Urtu-Tamir, in 47° 15′ N. lat., and 102° 20′ 15″ E. long. The ruins cover an area of six miles in circumference (*Proc. Roy. Geo. Soc.*, xii, 424). The city within the walls was not, however, large. Juvaini says the wall was half a league long, while Polo says it "was a city of some three miles in compass, surrounded by a strong earthen wall. And beside it was a great citadel, wherein is a fine palace in which the Governor resided" (d'Ohsson, ii, 65; Yule, *Marco Polo*, i, 227, ii, 539). In 1256 Mangu removed the capital of his empire to Shang-tu or Kai-ping Fu, near the present Dolon nor, in S.E. Mongolia, the *Kemenfu* of Marco Polo (i, 26).

As stated in a previous note, the only houses inside the city

There are two quarters in it; one (346) of the Saracens in which are the markets, and where a great many Tartars gather on account of the court, which is always near this (city), and on account of the great number of ambassadors; the other is the quarter of the Cathayans, all of whom are artisans. Besides these quarters there are great palaces, which are for the secretaries of the court. There are there twelve idol temples of different nations, two mahummeries in which is cried the law of Machomet,[1] and one church of Christians in the extreme end of the city. The city is surrounded by a mud wall and has iiii gates. At the eastern is sold millet and other kinds of grain, which, however, is rarely brought there; at the western one, sheep and goats are sold; at the southern, oxen and carts are sold; at the northern, horses are sold.

We arrived there following the court on the Sunday before Ascension (7th May). The next day we, the monk and all his household, were summoned by Bulgai, who is the grand secretary and judge, and all the envoys and foreigners who were in the habit of frequenting the monk's house; and we were separately called into Bulgai's presence, first the monk, and we after him; and they inquired most

were probably those of the Mohammedan and Chinese quarters, and the *yamens*. The four principal markets were, in all likelihood, outside the gates, as is the present custom in all Chinese towns. It was quite natural that grain, oxen and carts should be sold outside the eastern and southern gates, as they were brought from China and the cultivated districts of Manchuria. Horses and sheep were brought from the Kirghiz and Mongol pasture lands to the north and west. Juvaini says there arrived daily at Karakorum, for the use of the court and people, 500 cart-loads of food and drink brought from different parts of the empire (d'Ohsson, ii, 65; see also Cordier, *Sur la position de Ho-lin*; Howorth, *History*, i, pt. i, 182; Palladius, *op. cit.*, 11).

[1] *Due mahummerie in quibus clamatur lex Machometi.* The word *mahummery*, or *mahomerie*, was in common use by writers of the time of the Crusades to designate a mosque. See Joinville (259), where occurs the expression "le maistre mahomerie." In another passage (389) our author speaks of the "synagogues of the Saracens." *Clamatur* refers, of course, to the calling to prayer of the *muezzins*.

minutely whence we were, why we had come, what was our business. And this inquiry was made because it had been reported to Mangu Chan that forty Hacsasins had entered the city under various disguises to kill him. About this time the lady of whom I have spoken[1] had a relapse, and sent for the monk, but he was unwilling to go and said: "She has called back the idolaters around her; let them cure her if they can. I shall go there no more."

On the eve of the Lord's Ascension (20th May) we went into all the houses of Mangu Chan; and I noticed that when he was about to drink, they sprinkled (347) *cosmos* on his felt idols. Then I said to the monk: "What is there in common between Christ and Belial? What share has our Cross with these idols?"

Furthermore, Mangu Chan has eight brothers; three uterine, and five by the father. One of the uterine ones he sent to the country of the Hacsasins, whom they call Mulidet, and he ordered him to put them all to death. Another came toward Persia and has already entered, it is believed, the land of Turkie, and will thence send an army against Baldach and against Vastacius. One of the others he sent into Cathay, against those who do not yet obey him. His youngest uterine brother, Arabuccha by name, he keeps near him, and he holds the *ordu* of their mother, who was a Christian, and William is his slave.[2] For one of his own brothers by the father had captured him in Hungary, in a city called Belgrade, where was also a Norman Bishop from Belevile near Rouen, with the nephew of a bishop,

---

[1] See *supra*, pp. 190, 192; and *infra*, p. 223.

[2] Tului's sons by Siurkukteni (or Siurkukiti-beighi, as the name is also written) were Mangu, Kubilai, Hulagu, and Arik-Boga. By his other wives and concubines he is said to have had six sons (d'Ohsson, ii, 60, and Quatremère, *op. cit.*, 85). Hulagu was sent against the Ismaelians in 1253, Kubilai commanded in China. I do not know who the other brother that was sent to Persia can have been. The MSS. all read *Mulibet* or *Mulihet*. I assume that these are purely clerica errors for *Mulidet*.

whom I saw in Caracarum.[1] And he gave master William to Mangu's mother, for she insisted greatly on having him ; and when she died, master William became the property of this Arabuccha, together with all the other things belonging to the *ordu* of his mother, and through him he became known to Mangu Chan, who after (348) the completion of the work of which I have spoken, gave this master C *iascot*, that is a thousand marks.

The day before Ascension (20th May), Mangu Chan said he wanted to visit his mother's *ordu*, for it was quite near;[2] and the monk said he wanted to go with him and bestow his blessing on the soul of his mother. The Chan gave his approval. In the evening of Ascension day (21st May) the before-mentioned lady (*i.e.*, Cota) grew a great deal worse, so that the chief of the diviners sent to the monk ordering him not to beat his board. The next day, when we left with all the court, the *ordu* of this lady remained behind. When we came to the place for pitching camp, the monk received orders to go farther away from the court than he was wont, which he did. Then Arabuccha came out to meet his brother the Chan, and the monk and we perceiving that he would have to pass beside us, advanced toward him with the cross. He recognized us, for he had been previously to our oratory, and held out his hand and made the sign of the cross at us like a bishop. Then

---

[1] Belgrade on the Danube, the present capital of Servia. The Mongols overran this country during their second expedition to Europe. William Buchier was probably captured about 1242. There is a Belleville-sur-mer in the present department of the Seine Inférieure, of which Rouen is the capital. This nephew of the Norman bishop may be the Englishman called Basil, referred to on p. 212.

[2] There were a number of palaces near Karakorum where the emperors used to pass much of their time, among others Kerchagan, a palace built in Persian style under Ogodai's reign, and distant from it a day's ride. Ormektua (the *Sira Ordu* of Pian de Carpine), where the elections of emperors were held, was also less than a day's ride from the capital and the banks of Lake Keushé, another favourite resort, were only some four days off (d'Ohsson, ii, 84).

the monk got on a horse and followed him, carrying some fruit with him. He (Arabuccha) alighted before the *ordu* of his brother, to wait for him until he should return from the chase. Then the monk got down too, and offered him his fruit, which he accepted. And there were seated beside him two men of high rank at the court of the Chan, and they were Saracens. Arabuccha, who knew of the enmity which exists between the Christians and Saracens, asked the monk if he knew these Saracens. He replied: "I know that they are dogs; why have you got them beside you?" "Why," the latter asked, "do you (349) insult us, when we have said nothing to you?" The monk said to them: "It is true what I say, you and your Machomet are low hounds." Then they began to blaspheme against Christ, but Arabuccha stopped them saying: "You must not speak so, for we know that the Messiah is God." In that very same hour there suddenly arose such a violent wind throughout the whole country, that it seemed as if devils were running through it; and after a little while there came reports that that lady (Cota) was dead.

The next day (22nd May) the Chan went back to his court (at Caracarum) by another way than that by which he had come; for it is one of their superstitions never to come back by the same road by which they go. And furthermore, wherever he sets his camp, after his departure no one may pass through the place where he has been, neither on horseback nor on foot, so long as there are any traces of the fire which has been made there.

That day some Saracens joined the monk on the road, provoking and disputing with him; and they, having the better of him, and he not knowing how else to defend his arguments, wanted to strike them with the whip he had in his hand. He behaved so that his words and actions were reported to the court, and orders were given us to get down (to camp) with the other ambassadors, and not in front of the court as we were in the habit of doing.

---

(350)

I HAD been constantly hoping that the king of Hermenia would come.[1] Moreover, there had arrived about Easter a person from Bolat, where are those Germans, whom I had nearly gone there to see,[2] and he had told me that a German priest was about coming to court; for these reasons I did not make any inquiries of Mangu about our remaining or leaving, though he had only given us permission in the first place to stay there two months, and four months had already gone by, not to say five. For these things took place about the end of May, and we had been there during the whole of January, February, March, April, and May. Not hearing, however, any news of the king (of Hermenia) or of this priest, and fearing lest we be obliged to go back in winter, the severity of which we had experienced, I had inquiry made of Mangu Chan what he wanted to do with us, for we would willingly remain there permanently, if it pleased him; if, however, we must go back, it would be less trying for us to do so in summer than in winter. He at once sent me word not to absent myself, for he wanted to speak to me; he would send for the son of master

---

[1] Heythum I., King of Little Armenia, left his capital, Sis in Cilicia, for the camp of Mangu in 1254. He travelled by way of Sartach's and Batu's camps, thence through the Kara-Khitai and Naiman countries to Mangu's camp, near Karakorum, which he reached on the 13th September, 1254. He started on his return journey on the 1st November of the same year, and arrived in Little Armenia in eight months, *i.e.*, in July, 1255. The Armenian narrative of his journey has been translated by Klaproth (*Journ. Asiat.*, xii., 463 *et seq.*), and by Dulaurier (*Journ. Asiat.*, v^e^ série, xi, 273, *et seq.*). A valuable abstract is also given by Bretschneider (*Med. Geog.*, 297-302).

[2] See *supra*, pp. 136-7.

William, for my dragoman was not competent. He who was speaking with me was a Saracen, and had been an envoy to Vastacius. And he, having been bribed with presents, had advised Vastacius to send ambassadors to Mangu Chan, and that in the meanwhile time would pass; for Vastacius believed that they (*i.e.*, the Mongols) were about to invade his country at once. He sent, and when he had come to know them, he heeded them little, nor did he make a peace with them, nor have they yet entered his country; nor could they do so, so long as he dares defend himself. For they have never conquered any country by force of arms, but only by deceit; and it is because men make peace with them, that they work their ruin under cover of this peace. Then (this Saracen) inquired a great deal (351) about the Pope and the king of the French, and concerning the roads leading to them. The monk, hearing this, cautioned me, unobserved, not to answer him, for he wanted to get himself sent as ambassador; so I was silent, and would answer him nothing. And he spoke to me I know not what injurious terms, for which the Nestorian priests wished to bring a charge against him, and he would have been put to death or soundly beaten; but I would not have it.

The next day, which was Sunday before Pentecost (24th May), they took me to court; and the grand secretaries of the court came to me, and one was the Moal who handed the Chan his cup, and the others were Saracens, and they inquired on the part of the Chan why I had come. Then I repeated what has previously been said; how I had come to Sartach, and from Sartach to Baatu, and how Baatu had sent me thither; then I said to him: "I have nothing to say from the part of any man. (This he must have known from what Baatu had written to him.) I have only to speak the words of God, if he wishes to hear them." They interrupted me, asking what words of God I wished to speak, thinking that I wanted to foretell some piece of good fortune to him, as many others do. I replied to them: "If you want me to speak the words of God to him, procure for me the interpreter." They said: "We have sent for him; but speak (now) through this one as well as you can; we understand you very well." And they urged me greatly that I should speak. So I said: "Of him unto whom much has been given much shall be required. And furthermore, of him to whom much (352) has been given much love is required. By these words of God I teach Mangu, for God hath given him great power, and the riches which he has were not given him by the idols of the Tuins, but by Almighty God, who made heaven and earth, in whose hand are all kingdoms, and who removes it (*i.e.*, power) from one nation to another on account of the sins of men. So if he shall love Him, it shall be well with him; if otherwise, he must know that God will require all things of him to the last farthing." Then one of the Saracens said: "Is there anyone who does not love God?" I replied: "God says: 'If one love me, he keepeth my commandments; and he who loveth me not keepeth not my commandments.'[1] So he who keepeth not the commandments of God loveth not God." Then he said: "Have you been to heaven, that you know the commandments of God?" "No," I replied, "but He has given them from heaven to holy men, and finally He descended from heaven to teach us, and we have them in the Scriptures, and we see by men's works when they keep them or not." Then he said: "Do you wish, then, to say that Mangu Chan does not keep the commandments of God?" I said to him: "Let the dragoman come, as you have said, and I will, in the presence of Mangu, if it pleases him, recite the commandments of God, and he shall judge for

[1] *Gospel according to John*, xiv., 15-24 (Vulgate).

himself whether he keeps them or not." Then they went away, and told him that I had said that he was an idolater, or Tuin, and that he did not keep God's commandments.

The next day (25th May) (the Chan) sent his secretaries to me, who said: "Our lord sends us to you to say that you are here Christians, Saracens and Tuins. And each of you says that his doctrine is the best, and his writings—that is, books—the truest. So he wishes that you shall all meet together, and make a comparison, each one writing down his precepts, so that he himself may be able to know the truth." Then I said: "Blessed be God, (353) who put this in the Chan's heart. But our Scriptures tell us, the servant of God should not dispute, but should show mildness to all; so I am ready, without disputation or contention, to give reason for the faith and hope of the Christians, to the best of my ability." They wrote down my words, and carried them back to him. Then it was told the Nestorians that they should look to themselves, and write down what they wished to say, and likewise to the Saracens, and in the same way to the Tuins.

The next day (26th May) he again sent secretaries, who said: "Mangu Chan wishes to know why you have come to these parts." I replied to them: "He must know it by Baatu's letters." Then they said: "The letters of Baatu have been lost, and he has forgotten what Baatu wrote to him; so he would know from you." Then feeling safer I said: "It is the duty of our faith to preach the Gospel to all men. So when I heard of the fame of the Moal people, I was desirous of coming to them; and while this desire was on me, we heard that Sartach was a Christian. So I turned my footsteps toward him. And the lord king of the French sent him letters containing kindly words, and among other things he bore witness to what kind of men we were, and requested that he would allow us to remain among the men of Moal. Then he (*i.e.*, Sartach) sent us to Baatu, and

Baatu sent us to Mangu Chan; so we have begged him, and do again beg him, to permit us to remain."

They wrote all these things down, and carried it back to him on the morrow.

Then he again sent them to me, saying: "The Chan knows well that you have no mission to him, but that you have come to pray for him, like other righteous priests; but he would know if ever any ambassadors from you have come to us, or any of ours gone to you." Then I told them all about David and Friar Andrew, and they, putting it all down in writing, reported it back to him.

Then he again sent them to me, saying: (354) "You have stayed here a long while; (the Chan) wishes you to go back to your own country, and he has inquired whether you will take an ambassador of his with you." I replied to them: "I would not dare take his envoys outside his own dominions, for there is a hostile country between us and you, and seas and mountains; and I am but a poor monk; so I would not venture to take them under my leadership."[1] And they, having written it all down, went back.

Pentecost eve came (30th May). The Nestorians had written a whole chronicle from the creation of the world to the Passion of Christ; and passing over the Passion, they had touched on the Ascension and the resurrection of the dead and on the coming to judgement, and in it there were some censurable statements, which I pointed out to them. As for us, we simply wrote out the symbol of the mass, "*Credo in unum Deum.*" Then I asked them how they wished to proceed. They said they would discuss in the first place with the Saracens. I showed them that that was not a good plan, for the Saracens agreed with us in saying

---

[1] Conf. *supra*, p. 29, the reasons given by Friar John of Pian de Carpine for not taking Mongol envoys back with him. Rubruck may probably have thought the same, especially in view of what he had been told by William Buchier's adopted son (*supra*, p. 180).

that there is one God: "So you have (in them) a help against the Tuins." They agreed with this. Then I asked them if they knew how idolatry had arisen in the world, and they were in ignorance of it. Then I told them, and they said: "Tell them these things, then let us speak, for it is a difficult matter to talk through an interpreter." I said to them: "Try how you will manage against them; I will take the part of the Tuins, and you will maintain that of the Christians. We will suppose I belong to that sect, because they say that God is not; now prove that God is." For there is a sect there which says that whatever spirit (*anima*) and whatever virtue is in anything, is the God of that thing, and that God exists not (355) otherwise. Then the Nestorians were unable to prove anything, but only to tell what the Scriptures tell. I said: "They do not believe in the Scriptures; you tell me one thing, and they tell another." Then I advised them to let me in the first place meet them, so that, if I should be confounded, they would still have a chance to speak; if they should be confounded, I should not be able to get a hearing after that. They agreed to this.

We were assembled then on Pentecost eve at our oratory, and Mangu Chan sent three secretaries who were to be umpires, one a Christian, one a Saracen, and one a Tuin; and it was published aloud: "This is the order of Mangu, and let no one dare say that the commandment of God differs from it. And he orders that no one shall dare wrangle or insult any other, or make any noise by which this business shall be interfered with, on penalty of his head." Then all were silent. And there was a great concourse of people there; for each side had called thither the most learned of its people, and many others had also assembled.

Then the Christians put me in the middle, telling the Tuins to speak with me. Then they—and there was a great congregation of them—began to murmur against Mangu Chan, for no other Chan had ever attempted to pry into their secrets. Then they opposed to me one who had come from Cathay, and who had his interpreter; and I had the son of master William, who began by (356) saying to me: "Friend, if you think you are going to be hushed up (*conclusus*), look for a more learned one than yourself." I remained silent. Then (the Tuin) inquired by what I wished to begin the discussion, by the subject how the world was made, or what becomes of the soul after death. I replied to him: "Friend, this should not be the beginning of our talk. All things proceed from God; He is the fountain-head of all things; so we must first speak of God, of whom you think differently from us, and Mangu Chan wishes to know who holds the better belief." The umpires decided that this was right.

He wished to begin with these questions, as they consider them to be the weightest; for they all hold this heresy of the Manichaeans, that one half of things is evil, and the other half good, and that there are two (elemental) principles;[1] and, as to souls, they believe that all pass from one body into another. Thus a most learned priest among the Nestorians questioned me (once) concerning the souls of animals, whether they could escape to any place where, after death, they would not be forced to labour. In confir-

---

[1] The whole Manichaean system is one of uncompromising dualism. Mani co-ordinates good with light, evil with darkness—redemption is the physical process of freeing the element light from the darkness. He distinguishes two elemental beings, light (Friar William says "good") and darkness (evil). He did not profess a doctrine of transmigration (Harnack, *Ency. Brit.*, xv, 483, 484). If Friar William's adversary was, as I think he was, an Uigur, this statement of their creed is additionally interesting, as the discussion shows it was an extraordinary jumble of Manichaeism, and of various forms of Buddhism, with perhaps a slight infusion of Chinese philosophical notions. Our author says his adversary came from China, not that he was Chinese. *Infra*, p. 234, he says, however, that the Uigurs (perhaps only some of them) believed in one God.

mation furthermore of this error, as I was told by master William, there had been brought from Cathay a boy who, from the size of his body, was not more than twelve years old, but who was capable of all forms of reasoning, and who said of himself that he had been incarnated three times; he knew how to read and write.[1]

So I said to the Tuin: "We believe firmly in our hearts and we confess with our mouths that God is, and that there is only one God, one in perfect unity. What do you believe?" He said: "Fools say that there is only one God, but the wise say that there are

---

[1] Friar William is the first western traveller to mention incarnate lamas, or, as it is now the custom to call them from the Chinese name (*huo Fo*) "Living Buddhas," a peculiar feature of Buddhist development only found in the religion of Tibet. The system of reincarnation of saints, or Bodhisattwas, founded on a perfectly sound Buddhist theory, assumed its peculiar Tibetan form, not earlier, I am inclined to think, than the eleventh century, with the teaching in Tibet of Atisha, or his disciple Bromton, but it never took any very great extension among the old lamaist school or Nyima sect. It was only after the great lama reformer Tsonghapa had founded in the early part of the fourteenth century the Gelug, or "yellow-capped sect" that Living Buddhas became numerous, the two principal ones being the Talé lama and the Pan-chen lama. The first Talé lama was born in A.D. 1391, the first Pan-chen lama in A.D. 1567. The third great incarnate lama is the Taranata lama, or Jebtsun damba lama of Urga in Mongolia; the first appearance of this incarnation was in the sixteenth century. There are at present about 160 incarnate lamas in Mongolia, Tibet, and China, all of them bearing the Mongol title of *khubilkhan* (pronounced *hubilhan*) (Sarat Chandra Das, *Indian Pandits*, 62, 76; *Sheng-wu-chi*, v, 19; Rockhill, *Jour. Roy. Asiat. Soc.*, 1891, 279, 285, *et seq.*; and *Land of the Lamas*, 290).

When Rubruck was in Mongolia, Tibetan Buddhism had just made its appearance in that country. Saskya Pandita, the first Tibetan lama of any prominence to go thither, visited Kuyuk Khan in 1247; but it was not until the Emperor Kubilai's reign that lamaism was firmly established among the Mongols. Mangu, it is true, appointed (probably in 1247 or 1252) a Tibetan lama named Namo, chief of his religion in the empire, just as he appointed a Chinese hoshang called K'ai-yuan, head of ecclesiastical affairs in China; but it was Kubilai who gave preeminence to the lamas. Our traveller states that the Living Buddha that Master William saw had come from China some years before. It may be that he came with Saskya Pandita; but I am rather inclined to believe that he came from Tangut, the present north-western Kan-su, where lamaism had been firmly established long before by the Tibetans. The remark that he was in his third reincarnation is also very interesting (see Howorth, *History*, I, Pt. I, 188, 504).

many. Are there not great lords in your country, and is not this Mangu Chan a greater lord? So it is of them, for they are different in different regions."

I said to him: "You choose a poor example, in which there is no comparison between man and God; according to that (357) every mighty man can call himself god in his own country." And as I was about to destroy the comparison, he interrupted me, asking: "Of what nature is your God, of whom you say that there is none other?" I replied: "Our God, besides whom there is none other, is omnipotent, and therefore requires the aid of none other, while all of us require His aid. It is not thus with man. No man can do everything, and so there must be several lords in the world, for no one can do all things. So likewise He knows all things, and therefore requires no councillor, for all wisdom comes of Him. Likewise, He is the supreme good, and wants not of our goods. But we live, move, and are in Him. Such is our God, and one must not consider Him otherwise."

"It is not so," he replied. "Though there is one (God) in the sky who is above all others, and of whose origin we are still ignorant,[1] there are ten others under him, and under these latter is another lower one. On the earth they are in infinite number." And as he wanted to spin (*texere*) some other yarns, I asked him of this highest god, whether he believed he was omnipotent, or whether (he believed this) of some other god. Fearing to answer, he asked: "If your God is as you say, why does he make the half of things evil?"[2] "That is not true," I said. "He who makes evil is not God. All things that are, are good." At this all the Tuins were astonished, and they wrote it

[1] *Cujus generationem adhuc ignoramus.* This is a purely Buddhist theory, referring, I take it, to the primordial or Adhibuddha, and the evolved Dhyanibuddhas, Bodhisattwas, etc.

[2] A Manichaean theory, see *supra*, p. 231.

down as false or impossible. Then he asked: "Whence then comes evil?" "You put your question badly," I said. "You should in the first place inquire what is evil, before you ask whence it comes. But let us go back to the first question, whether you believe that any god is omnipotent; after that I will answer all you may wish to ask me."

(358) He sat for a long time without replying, so that it became necessary for the secretaries who were listening on the part of the Chan to tell him to reply. Finally he answered that no god was omnipotent. With that the Saracens burst out into a loud laugh. When silence was restored, I said: "Then no one of your gods can save you you from every peril, for occasions may arise in which he has no power. Furthermore, no one can serve two masters: how can you serve so many gods in heaven and earth?" The audience told him to answer, but he remained speechless. And as I wanted to explain the unity of the divine essence and the Trinity to the whole audience, the Nestorians of the country said to me that it sufficed, for they wanted to talk. I gave in to them, but when they wanted to argue with the Saracens, they answered them: "We concede your religion is true, and that everything is true that is in the Gospel: so we do not want to argue any point with you." And they confessed that in all their prayers they besought God to grant them to die as Christians die.

There was present there an old priest of the Iugurs, who say there is one god, though they make idols; they (*i.e.*, the Nestorians) spoke at great length with him, telling him of all things down to the coming of the Antichrist into the world, and by comparisons demonstrating the Trinity to him and the Saracens. They all listened without making any contradiction, but no one said: "I believe; I want to become a Christian." When this was over (359), the

Nestorians as well as the Saracens sang with a loud voice, while the Tuins kept silence, and after that they all drank deeply.

---

ON Pentecost day (31st May) Mangu Chan called me before him, and also the Tuin with whom I had discussed; but before I went in, the interpreter, master William's son, said to me that we should have to go back to our country, and that I must not raise any objection, for he understood that it was a settled matter. When I came before the Chan, I had to bend the knees, and so did the Tuin beside me, with his interpreter. Then (the Chan) said to me: "Tell me the truth, whether you said the other day, when I sent my secretaries to you, that I was a Tuin." I replied: "My lord, I did not say that; I will tell you what I said, if it pleases you." Then I repeated to him what I had said, and he replied: "I thought full well that you did not say it, for you should not have said it; but your interpreter translated badly." And he held out toward me the staff on which he leaned, saying: "Fear not." And I, smiling, said in an undertone: "If I had been afraid, I should not have come here." He asked the interpreter what I had said, and he repeated it to him. After that he began confiding to me his creed: "We Moal," he said, "believe that there is only one God, by whom we live and by whom we die, and for whom we have an upright heart." Then I said: "May it be so, for without His grace this cannot be." He asked what I had said; the interpreter told him. Then he added: "But as God gives us the different fingers of the hand, so he gives to men divers ways. God gives you the Scriptures, and you Christians keep them not. You do not find (in them, for example) that one should find fault with another, do you?" "No, my lord," I said; "but I told you from the first that I did not want to wrangle (360) with anyone." "I do not intend to say it," he said, "for you. Likewise you do not find that a man should depart from justice for money." "No, my lord," I said. "And truly I came not to these parts to obtain money; on the contrary I have refused what has been offered me." And there was a secretary present, who bore witness that I had refused an *iascot* and silken cloths. "I do not say it," he said, "for you. God gave you therefore the Scriptures, and you do not keep them; He gave us diviners, we do what they tell us, and we live in peace."[1]

---

[1] The *Pien wei lu*, a Chinese Buddhist work, puts in the mouth of Mangu the following opinion of the various religious sects of his time:—"The *Hsien-sheng* (Taoists) say that their teaching is the highest; the *Hsiu-ts'ai* (Literati) say that Confucianism is the first of doctrines; the *Tieh-hsieh* (here meaning Christians), who honour the Messiah, believe in celestial life; and the *Damishmends* (Mollahs) pray to heaven and thank it for its blessings. If all these religions are carefully examined, one will see that no one of them can be compared with Buddhism." Saying this, the Khan held up his hand to make a comparison, and said: "As the five fingers are as regards the palm of the hand from which they project, so are all other religions as compared to Buddhism" (Devéria, *Notes d'épigraphie*, 46).

The Russian archbishop Peter, in 1245, stated to the Council of Lyons regarding the Mongols' religion that "every morning they raised their hands to heaven, adoring the Creator." Matth. Paris (*op. cit.*, iv, 388) and Pian de Carpine (618 *et seq.*) remark: "They believe in one God, who they say is the maker of all things visible and invisible; and they believe that He is the author of all blessings in this world as well as of punishments; but they do not worship Him with prayers or songs of praise or any ceremony whatever." Marco Polo (i, 248) says of them: "They say there is a Most High God of Heaven, whom they worship daily with thurible and incense, but they pray to him only for health of body." Palladius (*op. cit.*, 14), commenting on this passage, says: "The God of Heaven is evidently the *Tengri* of the Mongols, the highest object of their worship. They used to apply to it the epithet of *Dere*, 'Supreme,' and *Munke*, 'Eternal.' The affinity of the Shaman idea of heaven with that of the Chinese is indubitable. It does not appear, however, that Shamanism admits the idea of a personified and intelligent supreme being, similar to that existing in China, where this idea has inspired some thinkers, and raised their minds to high spiritual conceptions." Radloff (*Aus Sibirien*, ii, 3), speaking of the faith of the Shamans, says they teach that "before the earth and heaven were made, all was water; the earth was not, heaven existed not, the sun and moon were not. Then Tengere Kaira Khan, the highest of gods, the beginning of all crea-

He drank four times, I believe, before he finished saying all this. And I was listening attentively for him to say something else of his creed, when he began talking of my return journey, saying: "You have stayed here a long while; I wish you to go back. You have said that you would not dare take my ambassadors with you; will you take my words, or my letters?" And from that time I never found the opportunity nor the time when I could show him the Catholic Faith. For no one can speak in his presence but so much as he wishes, unless he be an ambassador; for an ambassador can say whatever he chooses, and they always ask if he wishes to say something more. As for me, it was not allowed me to speak more; I had only to listen to him, and reply to his questions. So I answered him that he should make me understand his words, and have them put down in writing, for I would willingly take them as best I could. Then he asked me if I wanted gold or silver or costly clothing. I said: "We take no such things; but we have no travelling money, and without your assistance we cannot get out of your country." He (361) said: "I will have you given all you require while in my possessions; do you want anything more?" I replied: "That suffices us." Then he asked: "How far do you wish to be taken?" I said: "Our power extends to the country of the king of Hermenia; if we were (escorted) that far, it would suffice me." He answered: "I will have you taken that far; after that look out for yourself." And he added: "There are two eyes in the head; but though they be two, they have

---

tion, the Father and the Mother of the human race, created in the first place a being resembling himself, and called him *Kishi*, or Man."

As to the early Mongols' conception of a future life, the only writer who has referred to the subject is Pian de Carpine (625). He there says: "As to life eternal and perpetual damnation they know nothing; they believe, however, that after this they will live in another world, and that there they will increase their flocks, eat and drink, and do everything else that is done by living beings in this world."

but one sight, and when one turns its glance there goes the other. You came from Baatu, and so you must go back by way of him." When he had said this, I asked permission of him to speak. "Speak," he said. Then I said: "My lord, we are not men of war. We wish that those should have dominion over the world who rule it most justly, in accordance with the will of God. Our office is to teach men to live after the will of God. For that we have come here, and willingly would we remain here if it pleased you. Since it pleases you that we go back, that must then be. I will go back, and I will carry your letters as well as I can, as you have ordered. I would ask of your majesty that since I shall carry your letters, I may also come back to you with your consent; principally because you have poor slaves at Bolat, who are of our tongue,[1] and who have no priest to teach them and their sons their religion, and willingly would I remain with them." Then he replied: "If your masters should send you back to me (you will be welcome)." I said: "My lord, I know not the will of my masters; but I have their permission to go wherever I wish, where it is needful to preach the word of God; and it seems to me that it is very needful in these parts; so (362) whether he sends back envoys by us or not, if it pleases you I will come back."

Then he remained silent and sat for a long time as if thinking, and the interpreter told me to speak no more. So I waited anxiously for what he would reply. Finally he said: "You have a long way to go, comfort yourself with food, so that you may reach your country in good health." And he had me given to drink, and then I went

[1] *Qui sunt lingue nostre.* It has been supposed from this remark that Rubruck's language was Dutch, Flemish, or German. I fancy he said what he did to Mangu, knowing that he had not a very clear or correct knowledge of the different languages spoken in Western Europe, and wished him only to understand that he was of the same race as these slaves. On Bolat, see *supra*, p. 138.

out from before him, and after that I went not back again. If I had had the power to work by signs and wonders like Moses, perhaps he would have humbled himself.[1]

---

THEIR diviners are, as (Mangu Chan) confessed to me, their priests;[2] and whatever they say must be done is executed without delay. I will tell you of their office, as well as I could learn about it from master William and others who used to speak truthfully to me. They are very numerous, and always have a captain, like a pontiff, who always places his dwelling before the principal house of Mangu Chan, at about a stone's throw from it. Under his custody are, as I have previously said, the carts on which the idols are carried. The others come after the *ordu* in positions assigned to them; and there come to them from various parts of the world people who believe in their art. Some among them

---

[1] Haithon (*Hist. Orient.*, 38, 39) says that Mangu, his whole family, and a number of the great personages of his court, were actually baptised by the Armenian bishop who accompanied Heythum I. to Mangu's court in 1253. The writer's pardonable desire to magnify in the eyes of posterity the influence of this member of his family with the Mongol emperor is probably the only ground for this assertion.

[2] Friar William (259) has given us the native name of these diviners, *cham*, which he wrongly states is the same as that borne by their sovereigns. The word *Kam* has always been used by all peoples of the Turki and Tartar races to designate their doctors, quacks and magicians, the "medicine-men" of the American Indians. It occurs in this sense in the *Kudatku Bilik*, the earliest monument of Turkish literature, dating from A.D. 1069. The Beltire Tartars still have their *Kamen*, those of Kachinzi their *Kamnoe*, the Kirghiz their *Kamtscha*, and the Manchus their *Shamas*, whence we derive our word *Shaman* (Pallas, *Voyages*, i 620, iii, 433, iv, 509, 579; Radloff, *Aus Siberien*, ii, 67; Hyacinthe, *Chamanisme*, 289, *et seq.*). Armenian chronicles of the thirteenth century attribute to the Mongol women great powers as witches. "Their women, they say, bewitched everything. It is only after the decision of their sorcerers and magicians, and after they have made their oracles, that they start on their marches" (Dulaurier, *op. cit.*, 250). The knowledge of astronomy which our traveller says the Shamans at the Mongol court possessed, was unusual; it was probably gained from the Chinese.

know something of astronomy, particularly the chief, and they predict to them the eclipses of the sun and moon; and when one is about to take place all the people lay in their food, for they must not go out of the door of their dwelling. And while the eclipse is taking place, they sound drums and instruments, and make a great noise and clamour. After the eclipse is over, they give themselves to drinking and feasting, and make great jollity. They predict lucky and unlucky days for the undertaking of all affairs; and so it is that they never assemble an army nor begin a war without their assent (363), and long since (the Moal) would have gone back to Hungary, but the diviners will not allow it.[1]

All things which are sent to the court they take between fires, and for this they retain a certain portion of them. They also cleanse all the bedding of deceased persons by taking them between fires. For when anyone dies, they put aside all that belongs to him, and they are not allowed to the other people of the *ordu* until they have been purified by fires. This I saw in connection with the *ordu* of that lady who died while we were there. On account of this (custom) there was a double reason why Friar Andrew and his companion should have gone between fires; they bore presents, and they were destined for one who was already dead, Keu Chan. Nothing of the sort was required of me, because I brought nothing. If any animal or any other thing falls to the ground while passing between the fires, it is theirs.[2]

---

[1] The belief that eclipses are brought about by a dragon or some other monster attempting to swallow the sun or moon, is general over most of Asia, and in many other parts of the world. The Mongols, Chinese, and Tibetans of the present day, believe that the dragon can be driven away, and the calamity averted, by making a great noise.

[2] The earliest mention of this method of purifying among Asiatics is found in Menander's account of Zemarchus' mission to the Turks in A.D. 569 (see Menander, 227, and Yule, *Cathay*, clxiii). In the

On the ninth day of the month of May, they get together all the white horses of the herds, and consecrate them.[1]

seventh century we hear of its prevalence in Japan, where it was customary for a newly-married woman to straddle over (*k'ua*) fire before entering her husband's house (Ma Tuan-lin, bk. 324, 15). Pian de Carpine (627) says of the Mongols: "They believe that everything is purified by fire; so when there come to them ambassadors, or princes or other persons, they and the presents they bear must pass between fires, so that they shall be purified, lest otherwise they should do some bewitching or bring some poison or some evil. Likewise, if fire falls from heaven on the flocks or men, which happens frequently, or if something of the kind befalls them which they deem unlucky, they must in like way dispel it by incantations. In fact, nearly all their hope is in such things." He describes (632) the method of purifying by fire as follows: "They make two fires, and place two spears beside the fires, and a cord across the top of the spears, and on this cord they tie bits of buckeram; and underneath the cord and the rags, and between the two fires, men, beasts, and tents must pass. And there are two women, one on one side, the other on the other, who sprinkle water and sing charms; and if any cart breaks down while passing through here, or anything falls to the ground, the sorcerers take it" (see also V. M. Mikhailov, *Journ. Anthrop. Inst.*, xxiv, 89; E. B. Tylor, *Primitive Culture*, i, 85; Gombojew, *op. cit.*, 661, and *supra*, pp. 9 and 35).

Of the other superstitions of the early Mongols, Pian de Carpine (624) says: "Though as to justice and wrong doings they have no law, nevertheless they have certain traditions handed down to them from their forefathers, which establish certain things as wrong doings. One is, to put a knife in the fire, or to touch the fire in any way with a knife; or to take meat out of the kettle with a knife. Another is to chop wood with an axe near the fire, for they think the head of the fire would be taken off by so doing (*quod sic auferri debeat caput igni*). Likewise, to lean on a whip used to strike a horse (for they use not spurs). So likewise to touch arrows with a whip; to catch or kill young birds; to strike a horse with a bridle; to break a bone on another; to spill on the ground milk or any other drink or food; to urinate in a tent; and if this done voluntarily, the person is put to death, but if otherwise he must pay the diviner a large sum of money for purifying them, and making the tent and all of them pass between two fires. And before the tent has thus been purified, no one dares enter it or take anything out of it. Likewise, if one takes a piece in his mouth and cannot chew it and spits it out, they make a hole underneath the tent, take him out by it and at once put him to death" (see Gombojew, 653, and conf. Vambery, *Sketches of Central Asia*, 292; and E. B. Tylor, *Early History*, 277).

[1] Marco Polo (i, 291) refers to this feast, which in his time was celebrated on the 28th of August. See also Yule's remarks in *Marco Polo* (i, 300). Pallas (*Voyages*, iv, 579) says: "The most solemn feast of the Tartars of Kachinzi and other idolatrous Tartars is the *Jun* or spring feast, in the month of June, which they call on that account *Ulu-shilker-ai*. . . . After the first (partial and private) feasts, several Ulus meet together for a public sacrifice. . . . In the public.

And the Christian priests are obliged to come to this with their censer. Then they sprinkle new *cosmos* on the ground and hold a great feast on that day, for they consider that they then first drink new *cosmos*, just as in some places among us is done with wine (364) at the feast of Bartholomew or Syxtus, and with fruit at the feast of James and Christopher.

They (*i.e.*, the *Kam*) are also called in when a child is born, to tell its fortune;[1] and when anyone sickens they are called, and they repeat their incantations, and tell whether it is a natural malady or one resulting from witchcraft. And in this connexion that woman of Metz, of whom I have spoken, told me a most remarkable thing.

Once some valuable furs were presented, which were to be deposited in the *ordu* of her mistress, who was a Christian, as I have previously said; and the diviners carried them between fires, and took of them more than they should have done. A certain servant-woman who had charge of the treasure of this lady, accused them of this to her mistress; so the lady reproved them. Now it happened

---

sacrifices they have present one of their *Kams*, or magicians. It is he who blesses the horse which is to be used as a holocaust. They call this horse *Isik*. They choose for this purpose an isabel or iron-grey one. It is, however, the magician who makes the choice of colour; but they may not take a stallion. This ceremony only takes place when the Kam orders it, and thinks it necessary for the well-being of the herds. As soon as a horse has become *isik*, they renew with him each spring the same ceremony with the feast of the *Jun*. They wash him with milk or a decoction of absinth, and perfume him with this plant. They plait strips of red and white stuff into his mane and tail, and leave him in complete liberty. His master may only mount him after snow has fallen, then he must use him." Radloff (*Aus Siberien*, i, 378) describes this feast in about the same terms; he only differs in his statement that the *isik* is always a stallion or a mare. Pian de Carpine (620) seems to refer to the *isik* when he says that the Tartars "offered horses to their deceased emperors, which no one dared mount as long as they lived."

[1] The custom of having a child's horoscope cast is nearly everywhere observed in Asia, and is so well known that no confirmation of our author's statement is necessary: see, however, Ploss, *Das Kind*, i, 83-89.

after this that this lady fell ill, and had shooting pains through her limbs. The diviners were called, and they, while seated at a distance, ordered one of the maids to put her hand on the painful spot, and to pull out whatever she should find. So she arose and did this, and she found in her hand a piece of felt, or some other thing. Then they told her to put it on the ground; when it was put there it began to wriggle like some live animal.[1] Then it was put into water, and it became like a leech, and they said: "Lady, some sorceress has done you this harm with her sorceries." And they accused her who had accused them about the furs. And she was taken outside the camp into the fields, and for vii days she was beaten and tried with other torments, so that she should confess. And in the meanwhile the lady died. When she heard of this she said (365) to them: "I know that my mistress is dead; kill me, that I may go after her, for I never did her wrong." And as she would confess nothing, Mangu commanded that she be allowed to live; and then those diviners accused the nurse of the daughter of the lady of whom I have spoken;[2] and she was a Christian, and her husband was most respected among all the Nestorian priests. And she was taken to the place of execution with one of her maids, to make her confess; and the maid confessed that her mistress had sent her to speak to a horse, to get an answer from it.[3]

---

[1] The extraction of diseases in the shape of stones, splinters, worms, bits of rag, has been practised by Shamans and medicine-men in many parts of the world. The Chinese, Mongols, Tibetans, and other peoples of Eastern and Northern Asia still attribute many diseases to the presence of worms or some material object in the body (see on the subject in general, Bartels, *Medecin der Naturvölker*, 183, *et seq.*, and E. B. Tylor, *Primitive Culture*, ii, 146, *et seq.*)

[2] This daughter is Chirina, frequently mentioned in preceding pages.

[3] *Loqui cum quodam equo, ut quereret ab eo responsa.* The Armenian chronicles of the thirteenth century speak of the Tartar magicians "who cause horses, camels, and felt idols to speak" (Dulaurier, *op. cit.*, 50). I have no doubt some Shamanistic ceremony similar to those still performed in the Altai is referred to. Radloff

The woman (*i.e.*, the nurse) also confessed that she had done something to make herself liked by her master (*i.e.*, Mangu ?), so that he should show her favour, but she had never done anything which could have injured him. She was asked whether her husband knew what she had done. She made excuse for him, having burnt characters and letters she had made herself.[1] So she was put to death; and Mangu sent her husband, this priest, to the bishop who was in Cathay, to try him, though he had not been found guilty.

In the meanwhile it happened that the first wife of Mangu Chan bore a son; and the diviners were called in to tell the child's fortune, and they all foretold it good luck, saying that it would live long and become a great lord. But after a few days it happened that the child died. Then the mother in a rage called the diviners, saying: "You told me that my son would live, and here he is dead." Then they replied: "Lady, here we see the witchcraft of the nurse of Chirina, who the other day (366) was put to death. She killed your son, and now we see her carrying him off." There still lived a grown-up son and daughter of this woman in the camp, and the lady in a fury sent for them, and caused a man to kill the youth, and a woman the daughter,

---

(*op. cit.*, ii, 20, *et seq.*) describes in great detail a Shaman sacrifice in which a horse is the offering. Its soul is supposed to ascend to Bai Ülgön, an emanation of Tengere Kaira Khan, the highest of gods. It is accompanied on this journey by the soul of a person who takes part in the ceremony, and who is called a *Bash-tutkan*. These two bring back from heaven various information interesting the person who has paid for the ceremony.

[1] I presume she had caused Mangu to drink certain charms which, having been written on paper, had afterwards been burnt and the ashes mixed with the Chan's drink. This woman was a Nestorian, and Badger (i, 238-240) says their priests still supply the people with charms. He gives translations of a number of them; among them one "to excite love in a man toward a woman." D'Ohsson (iv. 54) states that Tutshak, wife of Arghun, when tried for the death of that Ilkhan, confessed that she had tried to gain his affection by the use of certain writing as a charm, and which I presume she also caused him to swallow in his drink.

in revenge for her son, who the diviners had said had been killed by their mother. After this the Chan dreamed of these children, and on the morrow he asked what had been done with them. His servants were afraid to tell him; but he inquired the more solicitously where they were, for they had appeared to him in a vision of the night. Then they told him; and he forthwith sent to his wife, and asked her where she had found out that a wife could pass a death sentence, leaving her husband in ignorance (of what she had done); and he had her shut up for vii days, with orders that no food be given her. As to the man who had killed the youth, he had him decapitated, and had his head hung around the neck of the woman who had killed the young girl, and he caused her to be beaten with burning brands through the camp, and then put to death. And he would have put his own wife to death had it not been for the children he had had of her; but he left her *ordu*, and did not go back there for a month.

These same diviners disturb the atmosphere with their incantations;[1] and when it is so cold from natural causes that they can bring no relief, they pick out some persons in the camps whom they accuse of having brought about the cold, and they are put to death at once.

A short time before I left there, there was one of the concubines (367) who was ill, and she had languished for a long time; so they said incantations over a certain German female slave of hers, who went to sleep for three

---

[1] Rashideddin states that when the Urianghit wanted to bring a storm to an end, they said injuries to the sky, the lightning and thunder. (I have seen this done myself by Mongol storm-dispellers. See *Diary*, 201, 203.) "The other Mongol people," he adds, "do the contrary. When the storm rumbles, they remain shut up in their huts, full of fear." The subject of storm-making, and the use of stones for that purpose, is fully discussed by Quatremère, *Histoire*, 428-440 (see also *infra*, p. 254, and Yule, *Marco Polo*, i, 292, 300). Grenard (ii, 257) says the sorcerers called *djaduger*, in Chinese Turkestan, use a jade stone to make rain or fine weather.

days. And when she came back to herself they asked her what she had seen; (and she said) she had seen a great many persons, all of whom they declared would soon die; but she had not seen her mistress among them, so they declared that she would not die of her complaint. I saw the girl, who had still a good deal of pain in her head from her sleep.[1]

Some among them evoke devils, and assemble at night in their dwelling those who want to have answers from the devil, and they place cooked meat in the centre of the dwelling; and the *cham* who does the invocation begins repeating his incantations, and strikes violently the ground with a drum he holds. Finally he enters into a fury, and causes himself to be bound. Then comes the devil in the dark, and gives him the meat to eat, and he gives answers.[2]

Once, as I was told by master William, a certain Hungarian hid himself among them; and the devil who was on top of the dwelling cried that he could not come in, for

---

[1] This mode of divining or fortune-telling by hypnotic sleep is so commonly used by savage and barbarous tribes the world over, that no confirmation of Friar William's statement seems necessary.

[2] This is a very accurate description of these well-known shaman ceremonies. The placing of the sacrificial meat in the centre of the hut is common to most of these rites. The devil usually comes in through the hole in the top of the tent, in America as well as in Asia and Africa (see Pallas, *Voyages*, i, 569; Radloff, *Aus Sibirien*, ii, 20; and on the subject of shaman drums, Bartels, *Medecin der Naturvölker*, 174).

Pian de Carpine (626) says: "They pay great attention to divinations, auguries, soothsayings, sorceries and incantations. And when the devils answer them they believe that a god has spoken to them; and they call that god *Itoga*, but the Comans name it *Kam*. And they fear and reverence it wonderfully, and offer it many oblations, and the first-fruits of their food and drink; and according to its reply they do everything. At the new moon or at the full moon they begin whatever they have to do, so they call it (*i.e.*, the moon) the Great Emperor, and bow the knee to it and pray to it. They say that the sun is the mother of the moon, for it receives its light from the sun." Some writers are disposed to see in this word *itoga* the Mongol *etugen*, "earth," Marco Polo's *Natigai* (see Palladius, 15; Yule, *Marco Polo*, i, 249, ii, 479; and on the subject of divination, Vambery, *Sketches*, 292; Schuyler, *Turkestan*, ii, 31; Castren, *Reisen im Norden*, 221 *et seq.*; and Grenard, ii, 254-257).

there was a Christian among them. Hearing this, he fled in all haste, for they set about looking for him. This and many other things they do, which it would take too long to tell of.

---

WITH the feast of Pentecost (31st May) they began preparing the letters which he (the Chan) was to send you. In the meanwhile he came back to Caracarum, and held his great ceremony on the octave of Pentecost (7th June), and he wanted all the ambassadors to be present the last day of it. He sent also for me; but I had gone (368) to the church to baptize three children of a poor German I had found there. Master William was the chief butler at this feast, for he it was who had made the drink-flowing tree; and everyone poor and rich was singing and dancing and clapping hands before the Chan. Then he spoke to them, saying: "I have sent my brothers away, and have exposed them to danger among foreign nations. Now, let it be seen what you will do, when I shall want to send you to increase our realm." Each day during these four days, they changed their raiment, which was given them each day all of one colour from their boots to their turbans (*tyaram*).[1] At this time I saw there the envoy of the Caliph of Baldach, who used to be brought to court in a litter between two mules, and some said of him that he would make a peace with them, in view of which he was to give him X thousand horse soldiers for his army.

[1] Pian de Carpine (755 and *supra*, p. 19), Marco Polo (i, 374), and Odoric (Yule, *Cathay*, 141) all speak of this custom of wearing different robes on each day of a feast. Odoric, however, says that the colours differed according to the rank. The custom of presenting *khilats* is still observed in Central Asia and Persia. I cannot learn from any other authority that the Mongols ever wore turbans. Odoric, *loc. sup. cit.*, says the Mongols at the imperial feasts wore "coronets" (*in capite coronati*).

Others said that Mangu had said that he would not make a peace unless they destroyed all their fortresses, and that the envoy had replied: "When you bring all the hoofs of your horses, we will destroy all our fortresses." I saw also the envoy of a certain Soldan of India, who had brought VIII leopards and ten greyhounds taught to sit on horses' backs, as leopards sit.[1] When I asked them concerning India, in what direction it was from that place, they pointed to the west. And these envoys went back with me for nearly three weeks, always going westward. I saw there also envoys of the Soldan of Turkia, who had brought him rich presents;[2] and he (*i.e.*, Mangu) had answered them, as I heard, that (369) he did not want gold or silver, but men; so he wanted to be given troops. On the feast of saint John he held a great drinking bout, and I counted an hundred and five carts and ninety horses loaded with mare's milk; and on the feast of the apostles Peter and Paul likewise.

Finally, the letters he sends you being finished, they called me and interpreted them to me. I wrote down their tenor, as well as I could understand through an interpreter, and it is as follows:

"The commandment of the eternal God is, in Heaven

---

[1] Marco Polo (i, 290) says the Great Khan frequently carried a hunting leopard (*cheeta*) behind him on his horse's croup. I have not seen mention made of greyhounds being carried about in this fashion.

[2] This sultan was Azzeddin, son of Ghaisheddin Keikhosrew II. The Turks made a treaty in 1245 with the Mongols, by which they bound themselves to pay them an annual tribute of 1,250,000 *iperpera* (about £625,000), 14 camels and 1,000,000 sheep, all of which they had to deliver in the plain of Mongan (at the mouth of the river Kur, near the Caspian). Simon of St. Quentin, from whom I derive this information, adds that, exclusive of this regular tribute, the Turks had to pay vast amounts to the Mongols as presents to officers travelling officially, for their horses, victuals, etc., etc. The Notary of the Sultan of Turkey had calculated these expenses incurred for Tartar missions to Iconium for two years, and found that, exclusive of bread and wine, they had amounted to 600,000 *iperpera* (about £300,000) (Vincent of Beauvais, bk. XXX, ch. XXVIII, 451*b*).

there is only one eternal God, and on Earth there is only one lord, Chingis Chan, the Son of God, Demugin, (or) Chingis 'sound of iron.'" (For they call him Chingis, "sound of iron," because he was a blacksmith ;[1] and puffed up in their pride they even say that he is the son of God). "This is what is told you. Wherever there be a Moal, or a Naiman, or a Merkit or a Musteleman, wherever ears can hear, wherever horses can travel, there let it be heard and known; those who shall have heard my commandments and understood them, and who shall not believe and shall make war against us,[2] shall hear and see that they have eyes and see not; aud when they shall want to hold anything they shall be without hands, and when they shall want to walk they shall be without feet: this is the eternal command of God.

"This, through the virtue of the eternal God, through the great world of the Moal, is the word of Mangu (370) Chan to the lord of the French, King Louis, and to all the other lords and priests and to all the great realm of the French, that they may understand our words. For the word of the eternal God to Chingis Chan has not reached unto you, either through Chingis Chan or others who have come after him.

"A certain man by the name of David came to you as the ambassador of the Moal, but he was an impostor; and you sent back with him your envoys to Keu Chan. After the death of Keu Chan your ambassadors reached this

---

1 The belief that Chingis Khan was a blacksmith at times is still universal in Mongolia. I have seen several hills which derive their names from legends placing Chingis's smithy on their summits. The mistake arises from confounding Chingis's name of *Temuchin*, which means "best iron," with *Temurji*, in Turkish "a blacksmith." As to the name Chingis, it means "mighty." The title "Son of God" is but the old Chinese imperial title of *T'ien-tzŭ*, "Son of Heaven" (see d'Ohsson, i, 36, 99, and Pian de Carpine, 715).

2 The text is certainly incorrect here; it reads: *et voluerunt credere, et noluerunt facere exercitum contra nos.*

court. And Camus his wife sent you *nasic* stuffs and letters. But as to affairs of war and of peace and the welfare and happiness of a great realm, what could this woman, who was viler than a dog, know about them?" (For Mangu told me with his own lips that Camus was the worst kind of a witch, and that she had destroyed her whole family by her witchcraft.)[1]

"These two monks, who have come from you to Sartach, Sartach sent to Baatu; but Baatu sent them to us, for Mangu Chan is the greatest lord of the Moal realm. Now then, to the end that the whole world and the priests and monks may be in peace and rejoice, and that the word of God be heard among you, we wanted to (371) appoint Moal envoys (to go back) with these your priests. But they replied that between us and you there is a hostile country, and many wicked people, and bad roads; so they were afraid that they could not take our envoys in safety to you; but that if we would give them our letters containing our commandments, they would carry them to King Louis himself. So we do not send our envoys with them; but we send you in writing the commandments of the eternal God by these your priests: the commandments of the eternal God are what we impart to you. And when you shall have heard and believed, if you will obey us, send your ambassadors to us; and so we shall have proof whether you want peace or war with us. When, by the virtue of the eternal God, from the rising of the Sun to the setting, all the world shall be in universal joy and peace, then shall be manifested what we are to be. But if you hear the commandment of the eternal God, and understand it, and shall not give heed to it, nor believe it, saying to yourselves: 'Our country is far off, our mountains are strong, our sea is wide,' and in this belief you make war

---

[1] On Ogul Gaimish and her death, see *supra*, p. 164.

against us, you shall find out what we can do. He who makes easy what is difficult, and brings close what is far off, the eternal God He knows."

They had in the first place called us in the letters your ambassadors. So I told them: "Call us not ambassadors, for I explained thoroughly to the Chan that we were not the ambassadors of King Louis." They then went to him and told him. But they came back to me and said that (though) he had used it as a great (372) compliment, he had directed that they should write as I should tell them. I told them, nevertheless, to strike out the word 'ambassador,' and to call us monks or priests. While this was being done, my companion, hearing that we would have to go back to Baatu by way of the desert, and that a Moal would guide us, ran, without my knowing it, to Bulgai, the grand secretary, and intimated to him by signs that he would die if he went that way; and so when the day arrived on which we were to take our leave, to wit, a fortnight after the feast of saint John,[1] when we were called to court, the secretaries said to my companion: "Now Mangu Chan wants your companion to go back by way of Baatu, and you say that you are ill, as is evident you are. So Mangu says, if you want to go with your companion, go. But it rests with you; for perhaps you may be left in some *Iam*, and you will not be looked after, and you will be a burden on your companion. If you choose to stay here, he will provide you with everything necessary, till some other ambassadors come with whom you can go back leisurely and along a road on which towns are found." The friar replied: "God bless the Chan. I will stay." But I said to the friar: "Brother, see to it what you do. I will not leave you." "You," he said, "will not be leaving me; but

[1] The feast of the Nativity of St. John the Baptist falls on the 24th June. Rubruck's visit to court was therefore on or about the 8th July 1254, a day or two before he started on his journey back to Syria.

I leave you; for should I go with you, I can see danger of death to my soul and body; for it cannot bear such terrible hardships."

Now they were holding in their hands three gowns or tunics, and they said to us: "You will not accept gold or silver, and you have stayed here a long time praying for the Chan. He begs that each of you will accept at least a plain gown, so that you go not away empty-handed." So we had to accept them through respect for him, for they hold it (373) very bad that one should scorn their gifts. At first he used to make inquiries as to what we wanted, and we always replied in the same way, so that the Christians used to abuse the Idolaters for wanting nothing else than gifts. And these made answer that we were foolish, for if he (*i.e.*, the Chan) wanted to give them his whole *ordu*, they would take it with pleasure and do wisely. Having taken the gowns, they asked us to say an oraison for the Chan, and this we did; and having been granted leave, we went back to Caracarum.[1]

It happened, however, on a day (before that) when we were with the monk and the other ambassadors some distance from the court, that the monk beat the board so loudly that Mangu Chan heard it, and asked what it was. And they told him. Then he asked why he was so far from the court. They told him that it was troublesome to send him daily horses and oxen (to come) to court, and they added that it would be better if he remained in Caracarum beside the church and there did his praying. So the Chan sent to him to say that if he would go to Caracarum and remain there by the church, he would give him all he required. The monk, however, replied: "I came here from Jerusalem, in the Holy Land, by the command

[1] Mangu was probably camped somewhere in the vicinity of the city.

of God, and I left a city in which there were a thousand churches better than that in Caracarum. If he wants me to remain here and pray for him, as God commanded me, I will stay; otherwise I will go back whence I came." That very same evening oxen harnessed to carts were brought him, and the next morning he went back to the place he had been in the habit of occupying in front of the *ordu*.

A little while before we left there, a certain Nestorian monk arrived, and he seemed to be a wise man. Bulgai, the grand secretary, established him in front of the *ordu*; and the Chan sent him his books to bless.

---

WE returned then to (374) Caracarum; and while we were in the house of master William, my guide came, bringing x *iascot*, five of which he placed in the hand of master William, telling him to spend them on the part of the Chan for the wants of the friar;[1] the other v he put in the hands of Homo Dei, my interpreter, with directions to spend them on the journey for my wants. Master William had told them to do this, without our knowing it. I at once caused one (*iascot*) to be sold, and distributed the change among the poor Christians who were there, all of them having their eyes fixed upon us; another we spent in buying what was necessary for us in clothing and in other things; with the third, Homo Dei bought a few things on which he could make a small profit, which he did. The balance we also expended, for from the time we entered Persia they never gave us enough of what we needed, nor did they ever even among the Tartars; but there we rarely found anything to buy.

---

[1] Bartholomew of Cremona, who had decided to remain in Mongolia.

Master William, once your subject, sends you a girdle ornamented with a precious stone, such as they wear against lightning and thunder ;[1] and he sends you endless salutations, praying always for you ; and I cannot sufficiently express to God or to you the thanks I owe him. In all I baptized VI persons there.

So we separated with tears, my companion remaining with master William, and I alone with my interpreter going back with my guide (375) and one servant, who had an order by which we were to receive every four days one sheep for the IIII of us.[2]

---

IN two months and ten days we came to Baatu, and (on the way there) we never saw a town, nor the trace of any building save tombs, with the exception of one little village,[3] in which we did not eat bread ; neither did we ever take a rest in those two months and

---

[1] I do not know of any stone worn as a charm to avert lightning. The Mongols used a stone, called *yedu* or *yada*, to bring on storms, to draw rain. Rashideddin says the ceremony to bring on a storm by this means was called *yeda mishi*. "Certain stones," he remarks, "when they have been soaked in water and dried, have the property of attracting, even in summer, storms accompanied by flurries of snow and excessive cold, or torrents of rain" (d'Ohsson, ii, 614) ; Bergmann (iii, 183) says the Kalmuks use for this purpose bezoar stones (see also Baber, *Mémoires*, i, 86 ; E. B. Tylor, *Prim. Cult.*, ii, 263, and *Early History*, 223, 226). The Chinese call "thunderstone" (*lei ta shih*) any meteoric stone or stone implement of unknown origin dug out of the earth.

[2] His party travelled, however, in company of the mission of a Sultan of India for the first three weeks (see *supra*, p. 248).

[3] This little village must have been Imil, where Kuyuk Khan had his *ordu*. Friar William states (*supra*, p. 163) that he passed by this *ordu* on his way back. F. M. Schmidt (231, 232) agrees with this view (conf. Pian de Carpine, *supra*, p. 15). This identification agrees with the additional fact related by the traveller (281), that in going west he travelled by the north side of Lake Balkash. It must be noted that our traveller only states that he saw this village ; he did not break bread there. He has, in fact, remarked in a previous passage (p. 165) that his guide did not dare enter the place.

x days, except for one day only, when we could not get horses. We came back for the most part of the way through the same peoples, though generally through different districts; for we went in winter and came back in summer by parts farther to the north, fifteen days excepted, when both in going and in coming back we had to keep along a river between mountains, where there is no grass except close to the river.[1] We had to go for two days—sometimes for three days—without taking any other nourishment than *cosmos*. Sometimes we were in great danger, not being able to find any people, at moments when we were short of food, and with worn-out horses.

When I had ridden XX days I got news of the King of Hermenia; he had passed there at the end of August, going to meet Sartach, who was on his way to Mangu Chan with his flocks and herds,[2] his wives and children;

---

[1] For reasons previously stated, I take this river to be the Ulungur, though in the lower part of its course it does not flow between mountains, but in a tolerably broad valley, with ranges of low hills on either side (see F. M. Schmidt, 230). Fifteen days is rather a long time to take to descend the valley of the Ulungur river, which, from the point where it takes a westerly course till it empties into the Ulungur lake, is not much more than 375 versts (259 miles) long; still the scarcity of grass along this part of the road may have obliged them to go slowly; and I am inclined to think the reference in the next phrase to worn-out horses and the total absence of inhabitants, may apply to this part of the journey in particular. This would explain the time consumed; the average distance made daily would be about 16½ miles.

[2] This seems to be at variance with the Armenian chronicles and the statements of Mohammedan contemporary writers. King Heythum was received in audience by Mangu, at or near Karakorum, on the 13th September, 1254. On his way thither, he had visited both Sartach's and Batu's *ordus*, which were on either side of the Volga. This was in the early part of 1254, so this visit cannot be the one here referred to. The king left Mangu's camp to return to Armenia on November 1st, 1254; and when at Barchin, on the Syr daria, he turned north to go and again visit Sartach, who was then on his way to the Great Khan's court. Heythum, we are told, took eight months on his return journey to Cilicia; he cannot, therefore, have met Sartach the second time before the early spring of 1255. Mohammedan writers disagree as to the date of Sartach's journey to Mangu's court; some say he started in 1256, before Batu's death; while others state that it was after his death (d'Ohsson, ii, 334, 336,

though his big dwellings had been left behind between the Etilia and the Tanais.

I paid my respects (to Sartach) and told him that I would right willingly stay in his country, but that Mangu Chan wished me to go back and carry his letters. He replied that one must do the bidding of Mangu Chan. Then I asked Coiac about our servants. He replied that they were in Baatu's *ordu*, carefully looked after. I reminded (376) him also of our vestments and books: he replied: "Did you not bring them to Sartach?" I said: "I brought them to Sartach, but I did not give them to him, as you know;" and I repeated to him what I had replied when he had asked whether I would give them to Sartach. Then he answered: "You speak the truth, and no one can resist the truth. I left your things at my father's, who stays near Sarai, the new town that Baatu is making on the Etilia; but our priests have some of your vestments here with them." "As to the vestments," I said, "keep what you want of them, so long as my books are given back to me." Then he said that he would tell Sartach what I said. "I must have," I said, "a letter for your father, so that he will give me back all my things." As they were then just on the point of starting, he said: "One of the *ordu* of the ladies is following us closely; stop

---

and Dulaurier, 401). We will assume, however, that the Armenian chronicles are correct, and that in 1255 he was on his way to the court of the Great Khan. The distance between Batu's camp on the Volga and Karakorum by the route followed by Friar William, and probably by King Heythum on his journey east, is roughly about 2,600 miles. Friar William made the distance in 70 days; this supposes an average speed of 37 miles a day; the king, on his side, took 123 days, or an average of 21 miles daily. At the end of August, 1254, Heythum must therefore have been about 320 miles from Karakorum. I suppose the twenty days should be counted from the time our traveller left Karakorum; he had probably covered about 400 miles of the journey by that time. This passage has puzzled previous editors of Friar William's narrative. F. M. Schmidt, (231) suggests the reading of LX instead of XX. Friar William, in a subsequent passage (377) refers to the first visit of the king to Sartach, and to his kindly interest in his man Gosset.

there, and I will send you by this man here the answer of Sartach." I was anxious that he should not deceive me; but I could not wrangle with him. The man he had pointed out to me came in the evening, bringing with him two tunics, which I took for a whole piece of uncut silk stuff, and he said to me: "Here are two tunics: Sartach sends you one, and the other, if you see fit, you may present (377) to the King from him." I replied: "I do not make use of such clothes; I will present both to the King for the honour of your lord." "No," he said, "do as you choose with them." Now it pleases me to send them both to you, and I do so by the bearer of these presents. He gave me also letters to the father of Coiac, to return to me all that belonged to me, for he wanted nothing of mine.

We reached the *ordu* of Baatu the same day we had left it a year previously, the second day after the Elevation of the holy Cross (16th September), and I found with pleasure our servants in safety, but suffering from great poverty, as Gosset told me; and had it not been for the King of Hermenia, who had comforted them greatly and recommended them to Sartach, they would have been lost, for they thought that I was dead; and the Tartars were already inquiring of them if they knew how to herd cattle or milk horses. For had I not come back, they would have been made their slaves.

After that, Baatu caused me to come into his presence, and had interpreted to me the letters Mangu Chan sends you. For Mangu had written to him that if he wished to add, strike out, or alter anything in them, he was to do so. Then he said to me: "Take these letters and make them understood." He asked me also which road I wanted to take, by sea[1] or by (378) land. I told him the sea route was closed, for it was winter, so I would have to go by

[1] I suppose he means from the mouth of the Volga, or Sarai, by boat down the Caspian to Derbend.

land. I still thought at that time that you were in Syria, and I took the road toward Persia. If I had imagined that you had crossed over into France, I should have gone to Hungary and should have come sooner to France; and by that road I should have travelled with less trouble than in Syria.

We drove about for a month with him (*i.e.*, Baatu) before we could get a guide. Finally they appointed an Iugur, who, understanding that I would not give him anything, though I told him that I wanted to go straight to Hermenia, had letters given him to take me to the Soldan of Turkie, hoping to receive a present from the Soldan and make more along that road.[1]

---

SO we started XV days before the feast of All Saints (*i.e.*, 16th October) in the direction of Sarai, going due south, and descending along the Etilia, which divides below there into three great branches, each of which is nearly twice as large as the river of Damietta. The rest (of the river) forms four minor branches, so that we crossed that river in VII places by boat. On the middle branch is a town called Summerkeur, which is without walls; but when the river is in flood it is surrounded by water. For VIII years the Tartars were around it before they got it. And there were Alans in it, and Saracens.[2] We found there a German with his wife, and

---

[1] The guide's method of making money is explained in two other passages (389, 391).

[2] Yule (*Cathay*, 287) thinks the name *Summerkeur* (or *Summerkent* as some of the MSS. give it) is a clerical error for Sittarkent, Pegolotti's *Gintarchan* or *Gittarchan*, that is, old Astrakan. Purchas had already made the same identification. The position assigned by the early Mahommedan geographers to the town of Itil, or Atel, the capital of the Khazars, and the description they have left us of it, agree so well with our traveller's statement, that I am disposed to think the

he was a right worthy man, with whom Gosset (379) had stopped ;[1] for Sartach had sent him there to rid his *ordu* of him. Round about these parts Baatu is on one side of the river and Sartach on the other about Christmas time ; and they go not down any farther. And it happens that the whole river freezes over, and then they pass across. About here there is very great plenty of pasturage, and (the Tartars) live among the reeds till the ice begins to thaw.

When the father of Coiac received the letters of Sartach, he gave me back my vestments, excepting three albs, an amice embroidered in silk, a stole, a girdle, a gold-fringed altar cloth[2] and a surplice ; he gave me back also the silver vases, excepting a censer and a little vase in which was holy oil, all of which latter things the priests who were with Sartach had kept. He gave me back the books, with the exception of the psalter of my lady the queen, which he kept with my consent ; I could not refuse

two places are identical. The name *Summerkeur* may also be a corrupt form of the name *Sacassin*, which the Mahommedan geographer of Baku, Abdelrashid, applies to the city of Atel, and which he says was in his time submerged (d'Ohsson, i, 346 ; see also Ishtakri, 103 ; Ibn Haukal, 185, 186 ; and F. M. Schmidt, 241-243). Ishtakri (*loc. cit.*) says that Atel was inhabited by Mahommedans and Christians, a detail which our traveller confirms. Friar William seems to have visited the town on his way to Sarai, so this makes Yule's identification of it with Old Astrakan quite unacceptable. It must, however, have been quite near Sarai, for Ibn Haukal (185) only counts 14 days' travel from Derbend to the town of Atel, while Ishtakri (106), counts 12 ; but perhaps part of the journey—or the whole—was made by boat on the Caspian and the Volga. I have been no more fortunate than previous commentators of Rubruck in finding any mention of the capture of this city by the Mongols. The text seems only to imply that they occupied it eight years after their arrival in the country.

[1] One MS. reads *hyemaverat*, "had passed the winter" (of 1253-54, I suppose).

[2] *Tualiam ornatam aurifrigio. Tualia* may be a barbarous form of the French *toile*, though in another passage our traveller uses the word *telle de cotone*, "a cotton cloth." There is an Italian word, *tavalia*, which means an altar-cloth. Purchas translates this by "a Tualia adorned with golden embroyderie."

it him, for he said it would please Sartach greatly. He also asked me, in case I should come back that way, to bring a man knowing how to make parchment. He was making, by order of Sartach, a big church and a new village on the west bank of the river, and (380) wanted, he said, to make books for Sartach's use. I know, however, that Sartach cares not for such things.

Sarai and the palace of Baatu are on the eastern shore, and the valley through which flow these branches of the river is more than VII leagues wide, and there is a great quantity of fish there.[1] The versified Bible and a book in Arabic, worth thirty bezants, and several other things, I did not get back.

---

LEAVING it (*i.e.*, Sarai) then on the feast of All Saints (1st November), and going constantly south, we reached by the feast of saint Martin (15th December) the mountains of the Alans. Between Baatu and Sarai, for XV days we found no one save one of his (*i.e.*, Baatu's) sons preceding him (south) with his hawks and hawkers, who were very numerous. From the feast of All Saints for XV days we found no one, and there were two days on which we nearly died of thirst: for a whole day and a night, and a day following to the third hour, we did not find any water.

---

[1] *Mesalek-al-absar* (285, 287) says Sarai, meaning "the Palace," was founded by Bereké, brother of Batu. It stood in a salty plain and was without walls, though the palace had walls flanked by towers. The town was large, had markets, *madrasas* and baths. It is usually identified with Selitrennoyé Gorodok, about 70 miles above Astrakan (see Ibn Batuta, i, 79, ii, 446; Yule, *Marco Polo*, i, 5, ii, 495, 537, and *Cathay*, 231, 233, 287; and Heyd, ii, 227). Pallas (*Voyages*, v, 162) says he crossed the Volga near Selitrennoyé in June, 1773, when the waters were high. The main stream and its branches were about 30 versts (20 miles) broad.

The Alans in these mountains still hold out against (the Tartars), so Sartach has had to send two out of every ten men to hold the mouths of the defiles, lest they come out and lift their cattle in the plains between them, the Alans and the Iron Gate, which is two days thence, and where begins the plain of Arcacc.[1] Between the sea and the mountains are Saracens called (381) Lesgi, (who live) in the mountains and who also withstand (the Tartars); so the Tartars at the foot of the mountains of the Alans had to give us twenty men to escort us beyond the Iron Gate. And this pleased me much, for I hoped to see them under arms; for I had never been able to see their arms, though most anxious to. When we came to a dangerous passage, out of the XX (only) two had haubergeons. I asked them how they came by them, and they said they had got them from the Alans, who are good makers of such things,[2] and excellent artisans. So it seems to me that they have few arms except arrows and bows and fur gowns. I saw given to them iron plates and iron caps from Persia, and I also saw two who had come to present themselves before Mangu, armed with jackets of convex pieces of hard leather, which were most unfit and unwieldy.[3]

---

[1] *Planicies Arcacci.* As F. M. Schmidt (246) remarks, the name *Arcacc* is absolutely unknown. Our traveller appears to use it to designate the extreme south-eastern extremity of the plain held by the Alans.

[2] The *Zafer nameh* refers to this country of the Alans as "the country of the cuirass-makers" (Quatremère, *op. cit.*, 71).

[3] All contemporary western writers speak of the leather armour used by the Mongols (Matth. Paris, *op. cit.*, iv, 77, 115, 388). Vincent of Beauvais, on the authority, of course, of Simon of St. Quentin (bk. xxix, ch. lxxix, 420) says: "When the archers let fly their arrows, they withdraw entirely their right arm from out their armour, and put it back when the shaft has left the bow. But only the barons and the military chiefs, the standard-bearers and the constables wear this armour, so it is believed that not a tenth part of them have it or wear it. . . . They do not use shields, and very few of them have lances. . . ." Pian de Carpine (684-689) describes at great length the arrows and armour of the Mongols. "All of them," he says, "must have at least the following arms: two or three bows, at least one good one, three

Before we reached the Iron Gate, we came to a walled hamlet (*castellum*) of the Alans, which was Mangu Chan's, he having conquered that (part of the) country. Here we found grape-vines for the first time and drank wine. The next day we came to the Iron Gate, which Alexander the Macedonian made; and it is a town whose eastern end is on the sea-shore, and there is a small-sized plain between the sea and the mountains across which this town stretches to the top of the mountain adjoining it on the west; so it is that there is no road higher up, on account of the steepness of the (382) mountain, nor any lower down by the sea, but only straight through the town where is the iron gate from which the town takes its name.

The town is more than a mile long, and on the top of the mountain is a strong fort; its width, however, is but a stone's throw. It has very strong walls without moats, and towers of great dressed (*politis*) stones; but the Tartars have destroyed the tops of the towers and the parapets of the walls, making the towers even with the walls. Below this town the country used to be a real paradise.[1]

---

big quivers full of arrows, an axe and ropes (*funes*) to pull machines. . . . Their helmets are of iron or steel on top, but that portion which goes round the neck and throat is of leather. . . . Some of them have spears, and at the lower end of the heads is a hook to pull people out of the saddle. Their arrows are two feet one palm and two fingers long. . . . The heads of their arrows are very sharp, and they always carry files to sharpen them. . . . They have shields made of wickerwork, but I do not think they carry any except in camp, and when on guard over the emperor and the princes, and then only at night" (see also Marco Polo, i, 252; ii, 458). The arrows which Strabo (vii, 3, 254) says the Scythians carried were practically the same. He states that they used raw oxhide helmets and cuirasses, wicker shields, spears, bows and swords.

[1] Derbend is called *Demir kapi*, or "the Iron Gate," by the Turks. It is the *Carpiae pilae* of classical authors, "the *Gate of Zur*" of Procopius (iv, 3), the *Djora* of the Armenian chronicles (Klaproth, *Jour. Asiat.*, xii, 277) the *Bab-el Abwab*, or "Gate of Gates" of the early Mohammedan geographers. Ishtakri (86) says the wall and the gates were built by Kosroes Anushirwan; and Ibn Haukal (158) refers to the two walls of Derbend, the one of stone, the other of earth, besides the walls of stone bound with lead projecting into the sea to

Two days thence we found another town called Samaron,[1] in which were many Jews; and when passing through it we noticed walls coming down from the mountains to the sea. Leaving the road by the sea at these walls, for at that point it turned eastward, we went uphill toward the south.

The next day we crossed a valley, where we saw the foundations of walls running from one mountain to another, and along the tops of the mountains there was no road. These were once the barriers of Alexander,[2] shutting out the wild tribes, that is the desert nomads, so that they could not get in on the cultivated lands and the towns.

---

form the port (see also Ibn Kordadbeh, 490-496, and Masudi, ii, 2, 7, 72). Barbaro (86) speaks of it as *Derbenth*, and says that the town from one gate to another is half a mile broad, and that the walls are of great stones, after the Roman style of building. On the Alexander legend concerning the building of the wall and Iron Gate, see Peschel (*Erdkunde*, 93) and Yule (*Marco Polo*, i, 55 ; ii, 537). Barbaro (90) speaks of the country around Derbend as follows : "Of Derbenth I shall tell yo one marvailous matter. Going from the one gate towardes this place, even till ye come under the walles, ye shall finde grapes and fruictes of all sortes, specially almons. On the other parte there are neither fruictes nor any trees, except it be certein qwynces ; and so it endureth x, xv, or xx myles of that side."

[1] Samaron is unquestionably, as pointed out by F. M. Schmidt (246), Edrisi's *Semmur*, but it is not easy to locate it accurately. It must have been a little to the north of Beshbarmak on the Caspian. There is a little bay, some 15 miles south of Derbend, called Samur, but our traveller's Samaron was probably some 60 to 70 miles from that town. Pian de Carpine (748) speaks of a people called *Brutachi*, "who are said to be Jews and who shave their heads," as living somewhere in this region (see d'Avezac, 496, and *supra*, p. 12). Benjamin of Tudela (36) refers to the great number of Jews living in his time (latter part of twelfth century) among the Alans in the Caucasus. On the Jews in Transcaucasia, see Haxthausen, *Transcaucasia*, 136 *et seq.*, and conf. Maundevile, 265.

[2] *Claustra Alexandri*, the *Sedd-Iskender* of Persian writers. Vincent of Beauvais (bk. xxix, ch. lxxxix, 422*b*), says (quoting Friar Simon, of course) "As our scholastic histories say that Alexander the Great, King of the Macedonians, besought God to shut up the Jews within the Caspian mountains, our Friars of the Holy Order of Preachers, who have for the last seven years been in Triphilis (Tiflis), in Georgia, near the Caspian mountains, have diligently inquired of Georgians, Persians, as well as of Jews, concerning this shutting up, and they have all said, even the Jews, that they knew nothing certain of it, except what they have found in their histories."

There are other barriers within which are Jews, but I could learn nothing precise concerning them ; however, there are many Jews in all the towns of Persia.[1]

The next day we came to a big city called Samag ;[2] and the day after that we entered a vast plain called (383) Moan,[3] through which flows the Cur, from which the Curges, whom we call Georgians, take their name.[4] It flows through the middle of Tefilis, which is the capital city of the Curges, coming straight from the west and flowing eastward into that sea, and it has most excellent salmon. In that plain we again found Tartars. The Araxes also flows through this plain, coming out of Greater Hermenia from due south-west, out of what is called the Ararat country, which is Hermenia ; thus it is that in the book of Kings it is said of the sons of Senacherib, that their father having been killed they fled into the country of the Hermenians ; while in Isaiah it is said that they fled into the country of Ararat.[5]

To the west of this beautiful plain is Curgia, and the

---

[1] Benjamin of Tudela (48) estimated the number of Jews in Persia when he was there at over 70,000.

[2] The town of Shamakhi or Shamaka. Barbaro (86) says it had between four and five thousand houses in his time, and that it manufactured silks, fustians and other things. It was at one time the capital of Shirwan. Anthony Jenkinson (98, 131) speaks of "Shamakye in Media."

[3] Jordanus correctly transcribes the name Mogan, which is still the name of the plain between the Aras and the Kura. The Armenian chroniclers sometimes refer to it under the name of *Taran* or *Tahin*.

[4] Conf. *supra*, p. 39, where Friar Benedict gives another explanation of the name Georgian. The MSS. of Rubruck write the name *Gurgi* and *Curgi*. In view of the etymology stated by the author, I have written *Curgi* throughout. The kingdom of Georgia was first attacked by the Mongols in 1221. Pian de Carpine (709) speaks of the *Obesi sive Georgiani*, thus identifying them, as d'Avezac (479) notes, with the Abazes on the coast of the Black Sea. As used by Friar William, however, the name has a much wider application. Persian writers called Georgia *Gurgestan*. Clavijo (80) calls the Kura *Corras*, and Jenkinson (98) speaks of the *Cyrus* and the *Arash*.

[5] 4 (2) Kings, xix, 37 ; Isaiah, xxxvii, 38. Chardin, *Voyages*, ii, 158, makes the same remark as our author.

Crosminians[1] used to be in this plain; and there at the base of the mountains is a great city called Ganges,[2] which used to be their capital, and which prevented the Curges from coming down into the plain.

So we came to a bridge of boats held by great iron chains stretched across the river, there where the Cur and the Araxes fall into each other.[3] Here the Araxes loses its name. From this point we ascended continually along the Araxes, of which it is said—

. . . . . . . . . . . . *pontem dedignatur Araxes*,[4]

(384) leaving Persia on our left to the south, and the Caspian mountains and Greater Curgia on our right to the north, and going toward Africa to the south-west.

We passed through the camp of Baachu, who is the chief of the army there on the Araxes, and who has conquered the Curges, the Turks and the Persians. There is another (chief) at Tauris in Persia, who superintends the tribute, and whose name is Argun; and Mangu has recalled both of them to give their places to his brother who is coming to these countries.[5] This country I am describing to you is

---

[1] The Khorazmians conquered Georgia in 1225. The name occurs in Arrian, *Expeditio*, vii, 185, in the form Χωράσμιοι. In western mediæval works it is usually written *Corasmini*, *Chorosmini*, *Coremins* or *Corvins*.

[2] F. M. Schmidt (248) has identified Rubruck's *Ganges* with Gaush or Gendje, the present Elisabethpol.

[3] The point of junction of the Araxes with the Kura seems to have shifted considerably. Ibn Haukal (162) says it was on the border of the plain of Mugan, near Mahmudabad. Le Bruyn (*Voyage*, iv, 4) says it was about half a league from the village of Sgavad. Modern maps make the confluence near the town of Kalakoiny.

[4] Virgil, *Æneid*, viii, 728.

[5] Friar Simon of St. Quentin calls this Mongol General *Bajothnoy*. *noy* representing the Mongol word *noin* or *noian*, "lord," a title first given to chiefs of a *tuman*, and later to all persons of distinction. Guillaume of Nangis (364) calls him *Bachou*, while Mahommedan writers transcribe his name *Baiju*, and Armenian chronicles call him *Bachu Ghurchi*. This general was placed at the head of the Mongol army in Georgia and Armenia in 1242, to succeed Charmaghan (or

not Persia proper, but that which used to be called Hircania.[1]

I was in the house of Baachu, and he gave me wine to drink; he himself drank *cosmos*, which I should have preferred to drink if he had given it to me. Though the wine was new and good, *cosmos* satisfies better a famished man.

So we ascended along the Araxes from the feast of saint Clement (23rd November) to the second Sunday of Quadragesima (15th February) till we reached the head of the river. And beyond the mountain in which it rises is a goodly city called Aarserum,[2] which is the Soldan of Turkie's, and near these to the north, at the foot of the mountains of the Curges, rises the Eufrates. I would have

---

Djurmagun); who had commanded it since 1232 (Klaproth, *Jour. Asiat.*, xii, 205, d'Ohsson, ii, 221, 229). He it was who in 1247 received Friar Ascelin and Simon of St. Quentin. Arghun aka, according to Mahommedan historians, set out from Persia for the court of Mangu in 1256, leaving his son as his substitute during his absence with Hulagu, the brother of Mangu referred to in the text, who arrived in Samarkand in September, 1255. In 1258, Arghun took up again his post in Persia (d'Ohsson, ii, 141, 267). According to Armenian writers, Arghun made a census of the western portion of the Mongol empire in 1255. He is described by these writers as a very harsh, cruel man (Klaproth, *op. cit.*, 208, 213; and Dulaurier, 460).

[1] Isidorus (*op. cit.*, xiv, 501), our author's usual geographical authority, limits Hircania on the east by the Caspian, on the south by Armenia, on the north by Albania, and on the west by Iberia. This was practically identical with the Hircania of Pomponius Mela (603, 650). Ptolemy (vi, 7) applies the name to a much larger area.

[2] Erzerum. Guillaume of Nangis (341) writes the name *Arseron* (or *Arsaron*). He says it was the land of Hus where Saint Job lived and reigned. Vincent of Beauvais (bk. xxx, ch. cxlvii) repeats the same story, and adds that the town was captured by the Tartars in 1243, after a siege of twenty days. Pascalis of Victoria, who was martyred in Almalik in 1341, says that *Urganth* was Us, and that the body of Job was there (*Analecta Francis.*, iii, 533). In Urganth we have no difficulty in recognizing *Urfah*, which is believed by Mahommedans to be the Ur of the Chaldees (Badger, i, 331). Marco Polo (i, 47) writes the name of Erzerum, *Arziron*, a form which Tournefort also uses, though he remarks (ii, 111) that *Arzerum* is the correct form. Clavijo (78) uses the form *Aseron*, and Maundevile (147) *Artyroun*. The Armenians called it *Garin*, and the Greeks *Theodosiopolis*.

gone to its source, but there was so much snow that no one could go outside the beaten path. On the other side, to the south of the mountains of the Caucasus, the Tigris takes its rise.

---

WHEN we left Baachu, my guide went to Tauris[1] to speak with Argun, taking my interpreter with him. But Baachu had me taken to a certain city called Naxua,[2] which used to be (385) the capital of a great kingdom, and was a large and beautiful city; but the Tartars have reduced it to nearly a desert. And there used to be in it eighty Hermenian churches; but there are only two small ones now, for the Saracens have destroyed them. In one of these I kept the Christmas feast as well as I could, with our clerk. The next day the priest of the church died, and a bishop and XII monks from the mountains came to his funeral. All the bishops of the Hermenians are monks, as are those of the Greeks for the most part.[3] This bishop told me that near there was the

---

[1] *Taurinum.* According to Persian historians, the town of Tauris, or Tabriz, was founded A.D. 792 (see Chardin, *Voyages*, ii, 320 *et seq.*). Maundevile (149) refers to the "Cytie of Thauriso or Taxis."

[2] Or Nadjivan. The name is also written *Nakhdjevan*, *Neshewy*, and *Neksh-djehan.* Clavijo (80) writes the name *Naujua.* It is said to be Armenian *nakhid-shevan*, "the first landing-place," and was thus called because Noah got out of the ark near where it stands. Armenians say it is the oldest town in the world. Persian writers state that it once had 40,000 houses, and was one of the largest and finest cities of Armenia (Chardin, ii, 297 *et seq.*). A resident of Erzerum writes to me that one is shown in the monastery of Nadjivan the tomb of Noah and his wife. Chardin, however, states (ii, 318) that these are at a place called Maraut. See James Bryce, *Transcaucasia*, 222.

[3] This is quite correct. Chardin (ii, 185) states that the *Vertabied* or Armenian bishops were usually taken from among the monks, though sometimes a secular priest was appointed, "for it must be noted that this dignity is only obtained with money." Among the Greeks the prelates are taken from among the monks or Καλογεροι. The *Papas* or secular priests can only attain the dignity of *Protopapa.*

church in which blessed Bartholomew and also blessed Judas Thadeus were martyred;[1] but the road was impassable on account of the snow.

He told me also that they have two prophets: the first is Methodius the martyr,[2] who was of their race, and he prophesied concerning the Ysmaelites, which prophecy has been fulfilled in the Saracens. The other prophet is called Acatron, who on his death-bed prophesied concerning the race of Archers to come from the north,[3] saying that they would acquire possession of all the countries of the Orient, and that (God) would spare the Eastern kingdom so as to deliver unto them the kingdom of the West; but our brethren, like the Catholic Franks, would not believe in them, and they (*i.e.*, the Archers) would occupy the earth from the north even unto the south, and would come to Constantinople, and would occupy (386) the port of Constantinople; and one of them, who would be called a sage, would enter the city, and seeing the churches and the ceremonies

---

[1] Friar Jordanus (4), describing Armenia the Greater, states that three of the apostles suffered martyrdom there—Bartholomew, Simon, and Judas. "I saw a prison in which the two latter apostles were kept; and likewise springs of water which they produced from the living rock, smiting it with a rod, . . . and hard by there was a church built, beauteous and of wonderful bigness." St. Judas Thadeus was martyred, it is believed, at a place called Maku, on Persian territory west of Nadjivan. There is a monastery of St. Thadeus about twenty miles from Maku (see also *Acta Sanctorum*, 27 October, 440). As to the place of the martyrdom of the apostle Bartholomew, great uncertainty reigns. Some writers have placed it in India, others in Persia; the weight of testimony seems to favour the town of Albana or Albanopolis in Albania, on the shore of the Caspian (*Acta Sanctorum*, 27 August, 30). Some writers, among others de Morgan (*op. cit.*, i, 13), identify Albana with Derbend. No work I have been able to consult places the scene of the martyrdom of the two saints in or even near the same place.

[2] The works of Saint Methodius are well known to Armenian scholars. A complete edition of them is now being published by the Fathers of St. Lazarus at Venice.

[3] The prophecy here attributed to Acatron (or one of identical tenor) is stated by some Armenian historians to be due to the patriarch Narses, who was Catholicos of the Aghuanks from A.D. 1236 to 1263 (Dulaurier, 210). The Armenian historians of the thirteenth century habitually refer to the Mongols as "the Archers."

of the Franks would be baptised, and he would tell the Franks how to kill the lord of the Tartars, and how to confound them. On learning this the Franks of the centre of the world, that is Jerusalem, would fall upon the Tartars in their borders, and with the help of our people, that is the Hermenians, would pursue them, so that the King of the Franks would place his royal throne in Tauris in Persia, and then all the Orientals and all the infidels would be converted to the faith of Christ, and there would be such peace on earth that the living would say to the dead: "Woe is you, unfortunate ones, why lived ye not to these times?"

I had read this prophecy in Constantinople, brought there by the Hermenians who live there, but had paid no particular attention to it; when I had had this conversation, however, with the bishop, it came back vividly to my memory; and throughout Hermenia they hold this prophecy as sure as the Gospel. They used also to say to me: "As the souls in limbo expect the coming of Christ for their liberation, so we look to your coming to deliver us from this bondage in which we have so long been."

Near this city are mountains in which they say that
(387) Noah's ark rests; and there are two mountains, the one greater than the other; and the Araxes flows at their base; and there is a town there called Cemanum, which interpreted means "eight," and they say that it was thus called from the eight persons who came out of the ark, and who built it on the greater mountain.[1] Many have

[1] Vincent of Beauvais (bk. xxx, ch. xcvii, 440*b*) says that near the city of Ain (Ani) is Mount Arach. "Here rests Noah's ark, and at the foot of this mountain is the first (of all) cities, which Noah built there, and he called the city *Laudumie*, and around it flows the river *Arathosi* (Araxes), which flows through (the plain of) Mongan, where the Tartars winter, and into the *Mare Servanicum* (Caspian Sea)." Maundevile (148) speaks of "the cytee of Dayne, that Noe founded." Dayne may be the Laudumie of Vincent. Clavijo (80) says the city of Calmarin (Etchmiadzin?) was the first built in the world, "and it

tried to climb it, but none has been able. This bishop told me that there had been a monk who was most desirous (of climbing it), but that an angel appeared to him bearing a piece of the wood of the ark, and told him to try no more. They had this piece of wood in his church, they told me. This mountain did not seem to me so very high, that men could not ascend it. An old man gave me quite a good reason why one ought not to try to climb it. They call the mountain Massis, and it is of the feminine gender in their language. "No one," he said, "ought to climb up Massis; it is the mother of the world."[1]

---

was built by the lineage of Noah." In another passage (82) he describes the ruins he saw at the foot of Ararat, and which were a league in length, and were the remains of a city founded by Noah and his sons. The MSS. write this name in different ways—*Cemanium*, *Cemaurum*, and *Cemanum*. I have adopted the last form, as it approximates more closely the Arabic *Temanin*, the name given by early Mohammedan writers to the town built here by Noah. Ibn Haukal (60) says that at the foot of the mountain on which Noah's ark rested is a village called *Themabim*, "and they say that the companions of Noah descended here from the ark and built this village." Masudi (i, 75) has it that Noah and his family, in all eighty persons, on coming out of the ark built a town which they called *Temanin* (eighty), a name which it retained to Masudi's time.

Jordanus (4) describing Ararat, speaks of a dwelling on it which Noah is said to have built on leaving the ark; and "there, too, is said to be that original vine which Noah planted, and whereby he got drunk." Yule identifies it with the village of Arguri, the only one on Ararat, which name means "He planted the vine" (*argh urri*). Chardin (*Voyages*, ii, 193) says that at the foot of Ararat, in a Christian village, is a monastery called *Arokilvane*, or "the Monastery of the Apostles," which the Armenians revere especially, believing that Noah made there his first residence and his first sacrifices after the deluge. (See also Chabot, *op. cit.*, 52, note.)

[1] Isidorus (*op. cit.*, xiv, 521) says that pieces of the timbers of the ark are still seen on Mount *Ararath*. Vincent of Beauvais (bk. xxx, ch. xcvii, 440*b*) tells this legend differently. He says Arach has never been scaled but once by a certain monk, who had previously tried many times. An angel of the Lord appeared to him and told him to try again. He did so, reached the summit, and brought back with him a piece of the ark. He then built a monastery at the foot of the mountain, in which the piece of wood was placed and worshipped like a holy relic. Chardin (*op. cit.*, ii, 191) tells the legend exactly as our traveller does. He adds that the monk was called James, that he was from the great monastery of Etchmiadzin, near Erivan, and

In that city (of Naxua) Friar Bernard of Catalognà, of the Order of Preaching Friars, found me; he had remained in Georgia with a certain prior of the Holy Sepulchre, who had large holdings in land there; and he had learned a little Tartar, and had been with a certain friar from Hungary to Argun at Tauris, to ask leave to go through to Sartach. When they came there they were refused entry, and the Hungarian friar went back by way of Tefilis with a servant; but Friar Bernard had remained at Tauris with a German lay brother, whose language he did not understand.

(388) We only left this city (of Naxua) on the Octave of the Epiphany (13th January), for we were kept there a long while on account of the snow. In IIII days we came to the country of Sahensa, once the most powerful Curgian prince, but now tributary to the Tartars, who have destroyed all its fortified places. His father, Zacharias by name, had got this country of the Hermenians, for delivering them from the hands of the Saracens.[1] And there are very fine villages there, all of Christians and

that he became Bishop of Nizibe, and was canonised. I am told that a piece of the ark is still shown in the monastery of Nadjivan. Bryce (*op. cit.*, 321) says it is in the treasury of Etchmiadzin.

*Massis* is the Armenian name of Ararat, and the monks on the mountains still tell travellers that the mountain cannot be scaled because it is the cradle of the human race, so a man can no more reach its top than re-enter his mother's womb. Maundevile (148) speaks of "Ararathe which the Jewes clepen Tanuz." Rubruck was misinformed about the gender of this word, as inanimate objects have no gender in Armenian (see also Chardin, *op. cit.*, ii, 189; and Klaproth, *Jour. Asiat.*, ii, 301-304; conf. also Marco Polo, i, 47). The first recorded ascent of Ararat was made in 1829 by Prof. Parrot; he gives its altitude as 17,325 ft., while Chodzko made it 16,916 (Bryce, *op. cit.*, 225).

[1] Sahensa is the Shahenshah prince of Ani of Georgian and Armenian chroniclers. He was son of Zacharias (or Zakharê) and nephew of John (or Ivané), Constable of Georgia. The family was of Armenian (Orpelian) descent. He was a favourite of the Queen of Georgia, Rusudan. After the capture and destruction of Ani in 1239, he had to serve with the Mongol troops. He and the other Georgian princes were present at the siege and capture of Erzerum in 1242 or 1243 (Klaproth, *op. cit.*, 196, 202; and Dulaurier, 216, 231, 241, *et seq.*).

having churches, just like the French; and every Hermenian has in his home, in the most honoured spot, a hand of wood holding a cross, and he places a burning lamp before it; and what we do with holy water to drive away the evil spirit, they do with incense. For every evening they burn incense, carrying it to every corner of the house to drive out every kind of evil.[1]

I took a meal with this Sahensa; and he showed me great politeness, as did his wife and his son called Zacharias, a very fine and prudent young man, who asked me, whether if he should come to you, you would keep him with you; for so heavily does he bear the domination of the Tartars, that though he has abundance of all things, he would prefer to wander in foreign lands to bearing their domination.[2] Moreover, they told me that they were sons of the Roman Church; and if the lord Pope would send them (389) some assistance, they would themselves subject all the neighbouring countries to the Church.

In fifteen days from that city (of Naxua?) we entered the country of the Soldan of Turkie on the (second) Sunday of

---

[1] Armenian scholars whom I have consulted have not been able to give me any information concerning the hand holding the cross mentioned by our author. Father Alishan thinks Friar William was misinformed. As to the custom of burning incense throughout the house, it is still observed by Armenians on Saturday nights, to drive away evil spirits. The same custom obtains in Greece. The Armenians, on Saturday night also, keep a lamp burning in a holy place. Perhaps the cross seen by our traveller was some kind of *ickôn*, before which the Greeks keep a lamp burning.

[2] The Armenian chronicles speak at length of this young Zakharé, son of Shahenshah. They say that in 1249 or 1250, when Avak Sarkis, son of Ivané (uncle of Shahenshah) died, his principality was given to Zakharé, but after a little while the Tartars took it away from him to give it to Vartoish-Kontsa, widow of Avak. Zakharé served at the head of the Georgian contingent in the Tartar army. He was present in 1258 at the capture of Bagdad, and rose high in Hulagu's favour on account of his courage. Somewhere about 1260 he was, however, accused of conspiring against the Mongols, and Hulagu had him quartered and his body thrown to the dogs. His father died of grief shortly after. (Klaproth, *op. cit.*, 211; Dulaurier, 456, 488, 502.)

Quadragesima (15th February), and the first town we found was called Marsengen.[1] All the people in the burg were Christians: Hermenians, Curges and Greeks. The Saracens had only the lordship. The castellan said that he had received orders not to give provisions to any Frank, or to ambassadors of the king of Hermenia or of Vastacius; so from this place, which we reached on the (second) Sunday of Quadragesima, all the way to Cyprus, which I entered eight days before the feast of saint John the Baptist (16th June) we had to buy our provisions. He who was guiding me procured us horses; he received also money for our provisions, but he put it in his purse. When we came to some field and saw a flock, he would carry off a sheep by force, and give it to his followers to eat, and was greatly astonished because I would not eat of his theft.

---

ON the (feast of the) Purification (2nd February) I was in a town called Aini, belonging to Sahensa, the position of which is very strong; and there are in it a thousand churches of Hermenians and two synagogues of Saracens.[2] The Tartars have

---

[1] The traveller says he left Naxua on the 13th of January, 1255, and that he was in Sahensa's country (*i.e.*, Ani) after four days, or on the 16th of January. Here he remained until after February 2nd, leaving there on the 3rd or 4th of February. In eleven days (*i.e.*, fifteen days in all from Naxua) he reached Marsengen, on the second Sunday of Quadragesima (15th of February). F. M. Schmidt (251) says he arrived in Marsengen on March 7th; this, I suppose, is simply a slip of the pen. Marsengen is the modern Medshingert, between Kars and Erzerum.

[2] Ani was situated in the ancient Armenian canton of Shirag. a little above the confluence of the Akhurean or Arpachai, and the Rhah or Magazbert, an affluent of the Araxes. The town already existed in the fifth century, A.D. From A.D. 961 to 1045 it was the capital of Armenia. In 1064 it was captured by the Seldjuk Turks, who lost it in 1124. It was entirely destroyed by an earthquake in 1319 (Klaproth, *op. cit.*, 194). Vincent of Beauvais (bk. xxx, ch. xcvii, 440*b*) says: "In Armenia there is a noble city called Ain (Ani), where there are a thousand churches, and an hundred thousand families

placed a bailiff[1] in it. Five preaching friars found me there. Four of them had come from the Province of France, and the fifth had joined them (390) in Syria; and they had only one infirm servant, who knew Turkish and a little French; and they had letters from the lord Pope to Sartach,[2] to Mangu Chan and to Buri, like those you gave me, requesting that they be allowed to stay in his country, and to preach the word of God, etc. When I had told them what I had seen, and how they had received me, they took the road to Tefilis, where are some of their friars, to hold council with them as to what they should do. I told them that, thanks to those letters, they could get through if they chose, but that they must provide themselves well with patience and with reasons for their coming, for having no other mission than preaching, they would show them scant courtesy, especially as they had no interpreter. What they did after this, I know not.

---

dwell therein, and the Tartars took it after a twelve days' siege." It was captured by the Mongols in 1239 (Dulaurier, 237). The Armenian princes had built so many churches and chapels in it that it became the custom to swear by the thousand and one churches of Ani (Dulaurier, 237). Clavijo (79) speaks of "the strong city called Auniqui."

[1] *Ballivum.* Probably a *daruga*, as the Mongols called such officers. They were under the orders of a *Mingatan* or commander of a thousand (Hammer, *Gold. Horde*, 238, and Devéria, *Journ. Asiat.*, ixe série, viii, 104).

[2] We learn from Raynaldus (*Annales*, ii, 492-494), that on the 14th March, 1254, Pope Innocent IV wrote letters to the Sultan of Turkey by certain Dominican friars, exhorting him to become a Christian, and that on the 4th September of the same year he wrote to Sartach, whom he called *Sattachi illustri Regi Tartarorum*, congratulating him on his conversion to Christianity, of which he had learnt from "our beloved son John, a presbyter, and your chaplain, whom you sent to us bearing presents" (see also Rémusat, *Mémoire*, 61). It is just possible that the Dominicans whom our traveller met at Ani were the bearers of these letters. I have found no record of any letters of the Pope to Mangu and to Buri. Buri, by the way, had been put to death by Batu in 1252 (*supra*, p. 137); possibly we should read Batu instead. In 1253 Innocent IV had founded additional missions among the Comans, Iberians, Alans, the Ungarians of greater Hungary, etc. (Raynaldus, *op. cit.*, ii, 489). The Dominicans had been established at Tiflis since 1240, when the Pope sent eight members of the order thither (Raynaldus, ii, 246, 248)

So on the second Sunday after Quadragesima (15th February) we came to the head of the Araxes, and after crossing a mountain, we came to the Eufrates, along which we descended for eight days, going always westward till we came to a certain fort called Camath.[1] Here the Eufrates turns southward toward Halapia.[2] We crossed the river, continuing westward through very high mountains and deep snow. That same year there was such an earthquake there that in one city called Arsengen[3] X thousand persons known by name were lost (391), exclusive of the poor, of whom there was no record. During three days' ride we saw a rent in the ground as if split in the commotion, and masses of earth which had slid down from the mountains and filled the valleys: had the earth been shaken a little more, what Isaiah said would have been fulfilled to the letter: "Every valley shall be filled up, and every mountain and hill shall be made low."[4]

We crossed the valley in which the Soldan of Turkie had been defeated by the Tartars. It would take too long to write how he had been defeated, but a servant of my guide, who had been with the Tartars (in the battle), said that there were not over X thousand Tartars in all; and a Curgian slave of the Soldan's said that there were with the Soldan two hundred thousand, all on horses. In that

---

1 The Κάμαχα of Constantine Porphyrogenitus (*De Adminis.*, 226), the *Kamkh* of Edrisi, the *Camag* of Clavijo (73), the *Kemakh* or *Gemash* of modern maps (F. M. Schmidt, 251). Schiltberger (43) spells the name *Kamach*. He says it was situated on a high mountain, at the base of which flowed the Euphrates. This is the Kara Su, or western branch of the Euphrates.

2 The *Haleb* of Mohammedan writers, our Aleppo. Some MSS. read *Alapia*, but *Halapia* is the usual form found in western mediæval works.

3 The *Arsinga* of Clavijo (67). The modern Erzinghian, about thirty miles east of Gemash (Camath), on the Kara Su.

4 Isaiah, xl, 4. Here again our traveller does not quote the text correctly. He has "*Omnis vallis implebitur.*" The Vulgate has, however, "*Omnis vallis exaltabitur.*"

plain in which that fight and that rout occurred, a large lake burst out in the earthquake; and I said to myself that that whole country had opened its mouth to drink in the blood of the Saracens.[1]

We were in Sebaste in Lesser Hermenia in the Greater Week,[2] and we visited there the sepulchre of the Forty Martyrs. There is at that place a church of saint Blaise, but I could not go there, for it was up in the citadel. On the Octave of Easter (4th April) we came to Cesarea of Capadocia, where there is a church of saint Basil the Great. After that in XV days (*i.e.*, 19th April), we came to Yconium,[3] travelling by short stages and resting in many places, for we could not get horses very quickly. And my guide used to do this trick: he would sell (392) in every

---

[1] Vincent of Beauvais (bk. xxx, ch. cl, 447*b*) says this battle was fought in the plains of Achsar, and that the Sultan had 50,000 men with him. Armenian historians say it was fought near a village called Acetshman-Gadug (Vincent's Achsar), in the plain between Erzerum and Erzinghian (Dulaurier, 429). The Sultan here referred to is Ghaiatheddin Keikosrew II. The battle was fought in 1243 or 1244. Baidju (Rubruck's Baachu) commanded the Mongol forces. Rashi-deddin calls the place of this celebrated battle, which put an end to the independence of the Kingdom of Rum, *Kuseh-dag*, evidently the same as *Consedrack*, the name given it by the historian Haithon (Quatremère, 225; and Haithon, *Hist. Orient.*, 33). This latter writer says that Baidju had a force of 30,000 men (see also d'Ohsson, iii, 80).

[2] In 1255 Palm Sunday fell on March 21st, and Easter on the 28th. Sebaste is the modern Sivas. Guillaume of Nangis (342) writes the name *Savastre*. In 1281 Friar Marcus of Montefeltro built a house at Sivas for the Franciscans "remaining among the Tartars" (*Analecta Francis.*, ii, 96). Sivas was pillaged in 1244 by the Mongols, after the defeat of Ghaiatheddin. The Forty Martyrs of Sebaste suffered death in A.D. 320, in a pond outside the city. Their bodies were burnt and the ashes thrown in the river. I cannot find a record of any of these martyrs having been buried. The pool where they were martyred is still visited by pilgrims, and the Forty Martyrs are adored alike in the Greek, Armenian and Latin Churches (*Acta Sanct.*, 10 March, 12-29; and Bedjan, *Acta Marty. et Sanct.*, ii, 325). St. Blaise was beheaded at Sivas, in A.D. 315. His feast is celebrated on February 3rd (*Acta Sanct.*, 3 February, 342; see also *Marco Polo*, i, 46).

[3] Guillaume of Nangis (343) writes the name *Ycoine*, Joinville *Coyne*, which is the more usual form in works of the period. It is the modern Konieh.

town his requisition on it for three days.[1] I was much worried over this; but I dared not speak, for he could have sold or killed me or our servants; there would have been no one to say him nay. I found several Franks in Yconium, and a Genoese trader from Acon, Nicholas by name, from Santo-Siro, who with his partner, a Venetian called Benefatius de Molendino, had monopolised all the alum in Turkie, so that the Soldan could sell none of it to any save these two; and they resold it so dear that what used to be sold for XV besants is sold for L.[2]

My guide presented me to the Soldan. The Soldan said he would be pleased to have me taken to the sea of Hermenia or of Silicia.[3] But this trader (Nicholas) knowing that the Saracens would take little care of me, and that I was wearied beyond measure with my guide's company, who pestered me daily for presents, had me taken to Curta, a port of the king of Hermenia.[4] Here I arrived the day

---

[1] *Sumendo in qualibet villa procurationem suam tribus diebus.* He probably had an order from Baidju to supply Friar William with horses, food and lodgings. Chinese officials of the present day, travelling in Mongolia, are supplied with like orders, called *ula piao*; they frequently get paid in money, instead of taking the horses and supplies due to them (conf. *supra*, p. 258, 273). Purchas (51) translates this phrase: "And my guide did this of purpose; taking upon him to sollicite his owne business three days, in every Towne."

[2] Heyd (*op. cit.*, i, 302) says of this Molendino that he probably belonged to the Venetian family of Molino, and this Bonifacius de Molendino must be the same as the "Bonifacius de Molinis de Venetiis," Condottiere in the service of the Sultan of Iconium at the time of the invasion of Asia Minor by the Tartars in 1242-43, of whom Sanuto speaks. Joinville (44) says that in his time, "le soudanc du Coyne estoit le plus riche roy de toute la paennime." Jordanus (5) describes in detail the process of making alum as he saw it done in a camp on the coast of Turkey, held by a noble Genoese called Andreolo Cathani.

[3] One MS. reads *Ecilie*, which Vivien de St. Martin (*Asie Mineure*, i, 494) thinks is the better reading, as it reproduces the name *Itch-ili*, by which the Turks called Cilicia. Writing to St. Louis it seems hardly probable, however, that our traveller would have used the Turkish form.

[4] Curta is the *Corycus* of classical writers, and was situated a little to the north of the Gök Su, on the coast of Cilicia. Writers of the

before the Ascension (5th May), and remained to the day after Pentecost (17th May). Then I heard that messengers had come from the king (of Hermenia) to his father,[1] so I put our things in a ship to be carried to Acon, and I myself went at once to the king's father, to learn whether he had received any news from his son. I found him at Assis[2] with all (393) his sons, save one called Barunusin,[3] who was having a castle built; and he had received messengers from his son (saying) he was coming back, and that Mangu Chan had greatly reduced the tribute for him, and that he had granted him the privilege that no ambassadors should enter his country;[4] on account of this the old man with all his sons and all his people were holding a great feast. He had me taken to the sea, to a port called Auax;[5] and from there I passed over into Cyprus,[6] and at Nicosia I found your Provincial,[7] who the same day took me with him to

---

time of the Crusades called this place *Curca*. Barbaro calls it *Curco*. He visited it about the middle of the fifteenth century, and says (44): "It is a castell both stronge and faire and well wrought, though at this present it be greatly decaied."

[1] When Heythum left in 1254 for Mangu's court, he committed the regency of Little Armenia to his father Constantine, and to his two sons, Levan (Lewis) and Thoros (Theodore) (Klaproth, *op. cit.*, 214).

[2] Sis in Cilicia, the capital of Little Armenia.

[3] Baron Oschin was the son of Heythum, according to most writers (Dulaurier, 433). Father Alishan tells me, however, that he was his brother.

[4] This was a valuable concession (see *supra*, p. 248, note 2). We may note that no mention is made of the king having induced Mangu and his family to be baptised: a story which Haithon gives in his *Hist. Orient.*, 37, 39 (see *supra*, p. 239; also d'Ohsson, ii, 313). Maundevile (229), quoting possibly Haithon, says of Mangu that he "was a gode Christene man, and baptized."

[5] The Polos, when coming back from their first journey to the court of Kubilai, came to this port on the Gulf of Alexandretta. Marco Polo calls it Layas, and says that "whatsoever person would travel to the interior (of the East), merchants or others, they take their way by this city of Layas." Ayas is now an insignificant village (Yule, *Marco Polo*, i, 16, 43, 45).

[6] He reached Cyprus on the 16th June (*supra*, p. 273).

[7] *Ministrum vestrum.* Franciscans in Cyprus and those parts of Palestine which had been held by St. Louis, belonged probably to the Province of France.

Antioch, which is in a most dilapidated condition. We were there for the feast of the Apostles Peter and Paul (29th June). Thence we came to Tripoli, where we held our chapter on the Assumption of the Blessed Virgin (15th August); and the Provincial ordered me to remain at Acon, not allowing me to come to you, directing me to write you whatever I had to say by the bearer of these presents. Not daring to disregard my vow of obedience, I did as best I could and have written; and I beg grace from your great kindness for what is said either too much or too little, or injudiciously or foolishly, as it comes from a man with little ability, and not accustomed to compose[1] such long stories.

May the peace of God, which passeth all understanding, keep your heart and mind.

I would gladly see you and those particular friends[2] I have in your kingdom; so if it displeases not Your (394) Majesty, I would beg you to write to the Provincial that he allow me to come to you, to return after a little while to the Holy Land.

---

[1] *Dictare.* Though in mediæval Latin *dictare* rarely or never means "to dictate," it may be that Friar William used it in that sense. The work as we have it shows that it was hastily written and badly revised. The frequent error of *eum* for *meum* seems to point to the report having been dictated. F. M. Schmidt (166) is of opinion that it was. Yule (*Marco Polo*, i, 87) calls attention to the fact that many of the most notable narratives of the Middle Ages have been dictated instead of being written by their authors, and that in cases where it is impossible to ascribe this to ignorance of writing. He cites Joinville, Marco Polo, Odoric, Nicolo Conti, Ibn Batuta, and the monk Haithon. Perhaps to this number we must add William of Rubruck.

[2] *Amicos speciales.* Some of the MSS. read *spirituales.* Purchas (51) has "spirituall friends."

YOU must know of the Turks that not one man out of ten (among them) is a Saracen; nearly all are Hermenians and Greeks, and (the country) is governed by children. For the Soldan who was defeated by the Tartars (as I have related) had as a legitimate wife an Iberian woman, by whom he had one son, a weakling, who he ordered should be Soldan (after him).[1] By a Greek concubine, whom he gave (later on) to a certain powerful emir, he had another; and he had yet another by a Turk; and a lot of Turks and Turkemans conspired with this one to kill the sons of the Christian (women). They arranged, as I was told, that when they had gained the victory they would destroy all the churches, and put to death all those who would not become Saracens. He was, however, defeated, and many of his followers were

---

[1] Ghaiatheddin's favourite wife was his second; her name was Thamar; she was daughter of Rusudan, Queen of Georgia, and, if we are to believe the statements of Armenian historians about Rusudan, it is quite impossible to say who was Thamar's father (Dulaurier, 216, 427). Vincent of Beauvais (bk. xxxi, ch. xxvi, 451*a*) says that in October, 1245, Gaiasadin, Soldan of Turquie, died; and his son, whose name was Raconadius (Rokneddin), succeeded him. This child was the son of the daughter of a Greek priest. He left another son called Azadin (Azzeddin Kaikawus), born, it is said, of the daughter of a certain burgher or captain of Iconium; and a third called Aladin (Alaeddin Kaikobad), by the daughter of the Queen of Georgia, who had been his wife. Raconadius was (at the time of his father's death) eleven years old, Azadin seven. Vincent then goes on to tell, at considerable length, of the rise to power of a certain Persian called Losyr (probably the Perwané of Mohammedan historians), who had been the deceased sultan's chancellor, and who, on Ghaiatheddin's death took as his wife the dead sultan's wife, the mother of Rokneddin, whom he placed on the throne, though Azadin (Aladin?) had been designated by his father as his successor, and all the emirs had sworn him allegiance. This narrative agrees clearly with that of our traveller, the Losyr of Vincent being "the powerful emir" of whom friar William speaks. Rubruck's Pacaster is Rokneddin.

Deguignes (*Histoire*, ii, pt. II, 67, *et seq.*) gives another account, and Hammer (*Histoire*, i, 44) still another. I will not attempt to unravel the discrepancies in all these narratives. It suffices that Alaeddin dying in 1254 while on his way to Mangu's court, Azzeddin drove his brother Rokneddin out of the part of the kingdom which had been assigned him by the Mongol emperor, and for a while reigned alone in Turkey.

killed. A second time he got together an army, and that time he was made prisoner, and is still kept in chains. Pacaster, the son of the Greek woman, has arranged with his half-brother[1] that he shall be Soldan, for the latter is delicate, and they have sent him to the Tartars; and this has angered his relatives on the side of his mother, the Iberian or Georgian woman. So it is that a child governs in Turkie without a treasure, with few soldiers and many enemies. The son of Vastacius (395) is delicate, and is at war with the son of Assan, who likewise is a youth, and under the yoke of the Tartars;[2] so if the army of the Church were to come to the Holy Land, it would be very easy to conquer or to pass through all these countries. The King of Hungary has not at most XXX thousand soldiers. From Cologne to Constantinople is not over XL days in a cart. From Constantinople it is not so far as that to the country of the King of Hermenia. In times past valiant men passed through these countries, and succeeded, though they had most powerful adversaries, whom God has since removed from the earth.[3] Nor should we (if we followed this road) be exposed to the dangers

---

[1] *Pacaster, filius Grece, procuravit de filiastro suo quod soldanus sit.* Purchas (52) renders this "Pacaster the Sonne of the Greeke Concubine procured of Filiaster, that he might be Soldan."

[2] Theodore Lascaris II could hardly be called a youth in 1255, for he was then thirty-four. He succeeded his father, John Vataces, in 1254. He was a man of considerable ability and of a cultivated mind, but his health was ruined and his intellect affected by repeated attacks of epilepsy. He died in 1258 or 1259 (Finlay, *History*, iii, 303, 321; Gibbon, vii, 360). Michel, the reigning sovereign of Bulgaria, ascended the throne in 1245 or 1246, when an infant. There was war between John Vataces and Bulgaria from 1245; it terminated in 1255 by the utter defeat of the Bulgarians (Finlay, iii, 309, *et seq.*).

[3] He refers to the march of Peter the Hermit and the Crusaders through Germany, Hungary, Bulgaria and Turkey in 1096. The "powerful adversaries" may either be the Bulgarians who, provoked by the massacres of their people by the Crusaders, defeated them at Nissa (Nisch); or the Turks who, in 1097, under Kilidjarslan, Sultan of Nicea, opposed so vigorously the advance of Godfrey of Bouillon and his army.

of the sea or to the mercies of the sailor men, and the price which would have to be given for a fleet would be enough for the expenses of the (whole) land journey.[1] I state it with confidence, that if your peasants—I speak not of the princes and noblemen—would but travel like the Tartar princes, and be content with like provisions, they would conquer the whole world.

It seems to me inexpedient to send another friar to the Tartars, as I went, or as the preaching friars go; but if the Lord Pope, who is the head of all Christians, wishes to send with proper state a bishop, and reply to the foolishness they have already written three times to the Franks (once to Pope Innocent the Fourth of blessed memory,[2] and twice to you: once by David, who (396) deceived you, and now by me), he would be able to tell them whatever he pleased, and also make them reply in writing. They listen to whatever an ambassador has to say, and always ask if he has more to say; but he must have a good interpreter—nay, several interpreters—abundant travelling funds, etc.

---

[1] Rubruck probably had in mind the contract made by the Council of the fourth Crusade in 1201 with the Doge of Venice, to carry the army to the Holy Land. The sum agreed upon was about £180,000 (Pears, *Fall of Constantinople*, 234).

[2] This is the letter of Kuyuk Khan, brought to Lyons by Friar John of Pian de Carpine, the text of which is in d'Avezac, *op. cit.*, 594.

# INDEX.

THE

# HAKLUYT SOCIETY.

1900.

---


**President.**

SIR CLEMENTS MARKHAM, K.C.B., F.R.S., Pres. R.G.S.

**Vice-Presidents.**

THE RIGHT HON. THE LORD STANLEY OF ALDERLEY.

REAR-ADMIRAL SIR WILLIAM WHARTON, K.C.B., F.R.S.

**Council.**

C. RAYMOND BEAZLEY, M.A.
COLONEL G. EARL CHURCH.
SIR W. MARTIN CONWAY.
ALBERT GRAY.
F. H. H. GUILLEMARD, M.A., M.D.
EDWARD HEAWOOD, M.A.
DUDLEY F. A. HERVEY, C.M.G.
ADMIRAL SIR A. H. HOSKINS, G.C.B.
J. SCOTT KELTIE, LL.D.
F. W. LUCAS.
A. P. MAUDSLAY.
MAJOR M. NATHAN, C.M.G., R.E.
E. J. PAYNE, M.A.
E. G. RAVENSTEIN.
HOWARD SAUNDERS.
H. W. TRINDER.
CHARLES WELCH, F.S.A.

**Hon. Secretary and *(pro tem.)* Treasurer.**

WILLIAM FOSTER, B.A., BORDEAN, HOLLY ROAD, WANSTEAD, N.E.

**Bankers in London.**

MESSRS. BARCLAY & Co., 1, PALL MALL EAST, S.W.

**Bankers in New York.**

THE MORTON TRUST CO., CORNER OF CEDAR AND NASSAU STREETS.

**Agent for distribution, &c., of Volumes.**

MR. B. QUARITCH, 15, PICCADILLY, W.


---

**Annual Subscription.—One Guinea (in America five dollars.)**

---

THE HAKLUYT SOCIETY, established in 1846, has for its object the printing of rare or unpublished Voyages and Travels. Books of this class are of the highest interest and value to students of history, geography, navigation, and ethnology; and many of them, especially the original narratives and translations of the Elizabethan and Stuart periods, are admirable examples of English prose at the stage of its most robust development.

The Society has not confined its selection to the books of English travellers, to a particular age, or to particular regions. Where the original is foreign, the work is given in English, fresh translations being made, except where it is possible to utilise the spirited renderings of the sixteenth or seventeenth century.

More than a hundred volumes have now been issued by the Society. The majority of these illustrate the history of the great age of discovery which forms the foundation of modern history. The discovery of AMERICA, and of particular portions of the two great western continents, is represented by the writings of COLUMBUS, AMERIGO VESPUCCI, CORTES and CHAMPLAIN, and by several of the early narratives from HAKLUYT'S collection. The works relating to the conquest of PERU, and to the condition of that country under the Incas, are numerous and of the highest value; similar interest attaches to STRACHEY'S *Virginia Britannia*, DE SOTO'S *Discovery of Florida*, and SIR ROBERT SCHOMBURGK'S edition of RALEIGH'S *Discoverie of Guiana*. The works relating to AFRICA already published comprise BARBOSA'S *Coasts of East Africa*, the *Portuguese Embassy to Abyssinia* of ALVAREZ, and *The Travels of Leo the Moor*. Notices of AUSTRALIA, INDIA, PERSIA, CHINA, JAPAN, etc., as they appeared in early times to European eyes, both before and after the discovery of the Cape route, are also included in the series, a well-known example being the work on *Cathay and the Way Thither*, contributed by a former President, SIR HENRY YULE. The search for the North-west and North-east Passages is recorded in the narratives of JENKINSON, DE VEER, FROBISHER, DAVIS, HUDSON, BAFFIN, etc.; whilst more extensive voyages are signalised by the great names of MAGELLAN, DRAKE, and HAWKINS.

The works selected by the Council for reproduction are printed (with rare exceptions) at full length. Each volume is placed in the charge of an editor especially competent—in many cases from personal acquaintance with the countries described—to give the reader such assistance as he needs for the elucidation of the text. Whenever possible, the interest of the volumes is increased by the addition of reproductions of contemporary portraits, maps, and other illustrations.

As these editorial services are rendered gratuitously, *the whole of the amount received from subscribers is expended in the preparation of the Society's publications*.

The subscription should be paid to the Society's Bankers on the 1st January in each year. This entitles the subscriber to receive, free of charge, the current publications of the Society. Usually two volumes are issued each year; but it is hoped to add from time to time a third volume, whenever the state of the funds will permit. Members have the sole privilege of purchasing sets of the previous publications; and the more recent of the Society's volumes are also reserved exclusively for its subscribers. In addition, they are allowed a special discount of 15 per cent. on the volumes permitted to be sold to the public. It may be mentioned that the publications of the Society tend to rise in value, and those which are out of print are now only to be obtained at high prices.

The present scale of charges for back volumes is as follows :—

TO MEMBERS.—*Sets of the* FIRST SERIES, omitting Nos. 1-10, 12, 19, 25, 36, 37, to be sold for . . . . . . . . . . . *net* **£30.**

N.B.—*Most of the out-of-print volumes have been, or are being, reprinted as later volumes of the series.*

Nos. 82-87, 90-100, at . . . . . . . *net* **10s.**

Nos. 88, 89, at . . . . . . . . . *net* **15s.**

---

TO THE PUBLIC GENERALLY.—*A limited number of single copies* as follows :—

Nos. 23, 26, 29, 31, 34, 40, 47, 50, at . . . . . **8s. 6d.**

Nos. 21, 24, 28, 30, 35, 46, 48, 51, 53, 55, 56, 58, 60 to 81, at . . . . **10s.**

Nos. 20, 27, 33, 38, 41 to 45, 49, 52, 57, at . . . . . . **15s.**

Nos. 54 and 59, at . . . . . . . . . **20s.**

*** Subject in case of Members to a discount of 15%.

*The volumes of the* SECOND SERIES *can only be obtained by paying the arrears of subscription.*

A list of works in preparation is given at page 11. The Secretary will be happy to furnish any further information that may be desired.

Gentlemen desiring to be enrolled as members should send their names to the Secretary. Applications for back volumes should be addressed to MR. QUARITCH.

# WORKS ALREADY ISSUED.

## FIRST SERIES.

**1—The Observations of Sir Richard Hawkins, Knt.,**

In his Voyage into the South Sea in 1593. Reprinted from the edition of 1622, and edited by Capt. C. R. D. BETHUNE, R.N., C.B.

*(First Edition out of print. See No. 57.) Issued for* 1848.

**2—Select Letters of Columbus,**

With Original Documents relating to the Discovery of the New World. Translated and Edited by R. H. MAJOR.

*(First Edition out of print. See No. 43.) Issued for* 1849.

**3—The Discoverie of the Empire of Guiana.**

By Sir Walter Raleigh, Knt. Edited by SIR ROBERT H. SCHOMBURGK, Ph.D.

*(First Edition out of print. Second Edition in preparation.) Issued for* 1850.

**4—Sir Francis Drake his Voyage, 1595,**

By Thomas Maynarde, together with the Spanish Account of Drake's attack on Puerto Rico. Edited by W. D. COOLEY.

*(Out of print.) Issued for* 1850.

**5—Narratives of Early Voyages to the North-West.**
Edited by THOMAS RUNDALL.
*(Out of print.)* *Issued for* 1851.

**6—The Historie of Travaile into Virginia Britannia,**
Expressing the Cosmographie and Commodities of the Country, together with the manners and customs of the people, collected by William Strachey, Gent., the first Secretary of the Colony. Edited by R. H. MAJOR.
*(Out of print.)* *Issued for* 1851.

**7 - Divers Voyages touching the Discovery of America**
And the Islands adjacent, collected and published by Richard Hakluyt, Prebendary of Bristol, in the year 1582. Edited by JOHN WINTER JONES.
*(Out of print.)* *Issued for* 1852.

**8- A Collection of Documents on Japan.**
With a Commentary by THOMAS RUNDALL.
*(Out of print.)* *Issued for* 1852.

**9 The Discovery and Conquest of Florida,**
By Don Ferdinando de Soto. Translated out of Portuguese by Richard Hakluyt; and Edited by W. B. RYE.
*(Out of print.)* *Issued for* 1853.

**10 Notes upon Russia,**
Being a Translation from the Earliest Account of that Country, entitled Rerum Muscoviticarum Commentarii, by the Baron Sigismund von Herberstein, Ambassador from the Court of Germany to the Grand Prince Vasiley Ivanovich, in the years 1517 and 1526. Two Volumes. Translated and Edited by R. H. MAJOR. Vol. 1.
*(Out of print.)* *Issued for* 1853.

**11—The Geography of Hudson's Bay,**
Being the Remarks of Captain W. Coats, in many Voyages to that locality, between the years 1727 and 1751. With Extracts from the Log of Captain Middleton on his Voyage for the Discovery of the North-west Passage, in H.M.S. "Furnace," in 1741-2. Edited by JOHN BARROW, F.R.S., F.S.A.
*Issued for* 1854.

**12—Notes upon Russia.**
Vol. 2. *(Out of print.)* *Issued for* 1854.

**13—Three Voyages by the North-East,**
Towards Cathay and China, undertaken by the Dutch in the years 1594, 1595 and 1596, with their Discovery of Spitzbergen, their residence of ten months in Novaya Zemlya, and their safe return in two open boats. By Gerrit de Veer. Edited by C. T. BEKE, Ph.D., F.S.A.
*(See also No. 54.)* *Issued for* 1855.

**14-15—The History of the Great and Mighty Kingdom of China and the Situation Thereof.**
Compiled by the Padre Juan Gonzalez de Mendoza. Reprinted from the Early Translation of R. Parke, and Edited by SIR GEORGE T. STAUNTON, Bart. With an Introduction by R. H. MAJOR. 2 vols.
*Issued for* 1855.

**16—The World Encompassed by Sir Francis Drake.**
Being his next Voyage to that to Nombre de Dios. Collated with an unpublished Manuscript of Francis Fletcher, Chaplain to the Expedition. Edited by W. S. W. VAUX, M.A. *Issued for* 1856.

**17—The History of the Tartar Conquerors who subdued China.**

From the French of the Père D'Orleans, 1688. Translated and Edited by the EARL OF ELLESMERE. With an Introduction by R. H. MAJOR.
*Issued for* 1856.

**18—A Collection of Early Documents on Spitzbergen and Greenland.**

Edited by ADAM WHITE. *Issued for* 1857.

**19—The Voyage of Sir Henry Middleton to Bantam and the Maluco Islands**

From the rare Edition of 1606. Edited by BOLTON CORNEY.
(*Out of print*). *Issued for* 1857.

**20—Russia at the Close of the Sixteenth Century.**

Comprising "The Russe Commonwealth" by Dr. Giles Fletcher, and Sir Jerome Horsey's Travels. Edited by E. A. BOND.
*Issued for* 1858.

**21—The Travels of Girolamo Benzoni in America, in 1542-56.**

Translated and Edited by ADMIRAL W. H. SMYTH, F.R.S., F.S.A.
*Issued for* 1858.

**22—India in the Fifteenth Century.**

Being a Collection of Narratives of Voyages to India in the century preceding the Portuguese discovery of the Cape of Good Hope; from Latin, Persian, Russian, and Italian Sources. Edited by R. H. MAJOR.
*Issued for* 1859.

**23—Narrative of a Voyage to the West Indies and Mexico,**

In the years 1599-1602, with Maps and Illustrations. By Samuel Champlain. Translated from the original and unpublished Manuscript, with a Biographical Notice and Notes by ALICE WILMERE. *Issued for* 1859.

**24—Expeditions into the Valley of the Amazons**

During the Sixteenth and Seventeenth Centuries: containing the Journey of Gonzalo Pizarro, from the Royal Commentaries of Garcilasso Inca de la Vega; the Voyage of Francisco de Orellana, from the General History of Herrera; and the Voyage of Cristoval de Acuna. Translated and Edited by CLEMENTS R. MARKHAM. *Issued for* 1860.

**25—Early Indications of Australia.**

A Collection of Documents shewing the Early Discoveries of Australia to the time of Captain Cook. Edited by R. H. MAJOR.
(*Out of print.*) *Issued for* 1860.

**26—The Embassy of Ruy Gonzalez de Clavijo to the Court of Timour, 1403-6.**

Translated and Edited by CLEMENTS R. MARKHAM.
*Issued for* 1861.

**27—Henry Hudson the Navigator.**

The Original Documents in which his career is recorded. Edited by GEORGE ASHER, LL.D. *Issued for* 1861.

**28—The Expedition of Ursua and Aguirre,**

In search of El Dorado and Omagua, A.D. 1560-61. Translated from the "Sexta Noticia Historiale" of Fray Pedro Simon, by W. BOLLAERT, with an Introduction by CLEMENTS R. MARKHAM.
*Issued for* 1862.

**29—The Life and Acts of Don Alonzo Enriquez de Guzman.**

Translated and Edited by CLEMENTS R. MARKHAM.
*Issued for* 1862.

**30—Discoveries of the World**

From their first original unto the year of our Lord 1555. By Antonio Galvano. Reprinted, with the original Portuguese text, and edited by VICE-ADMIRAL BETHUNE, C.B. *Issued for* 1863.

**31—Marvels described by Friar Jordanus,**

From a parchment manuscript of the Fourteenth Century, in Latin. Edited by COLONEL H. YULE, C.B. *Issued for* 1863.

**32—The Travels of Ludovico di Varthema**

In Syria, Arabia, Persia, India, etc., during the Sixteenth Century. Translated by J. WINTER JONES, F.S.A., and Edited by the REV. GEORGE PERCY BADGER. *Issued for* 1864.

**33—The Travels of Cieza de Leon in 1532-50**

From the Gulf of Darien to the City of La Plata, contained in the first part of his Chronicle of Peru (Antwerp, 1554). Translated and Edited by CLEMENTS R. MARKHAM. *Issued for* 1864.

**34—The Narrative of Pascual de Andagoya.**

Containing the earliest notice of Peru. Translated and Edited by CLEMENTS R. MARKHAM. *Issued for* 1865.

**35—The Coasts of East Africa and Malabar**

In the beginning of the Sixteenth Century, by Duarte Barbosa. Translated from an early Spanish manuscript by the HON. HENRY STANLEY. *Issued for* 1865.

**36-37—Cathay and the Way Thither.**

A Collection of all minor notices of China, previous to the Sixteenth Century. Translated and Edited by COLONEL H. YULE, C.B. Two Vols. (*Out of print.*) *Issued for* 1866.

**38—The Three Voyages of Sir Martin Frobisher.**

With a Selection from Letters now in the State Paper Office. Edited by REAR-ADMIRAL COLLINSON, C.B. *Issued for* 1867.

**39—The Philippine Islands,**

Moluccas, Siam, Cambodia, Japan, and China, at the close of the 16th Century. By Antonia de Morga. Translated from the Spanish, with Notes, by the LORD STANLEY of Alderley. *Issued for* 1868.

**40—The Fifth Letter of Hernan Cortes**

To the Emperor Charles V., containing an Account of his Expedition to Honduras in 1525-26. Translated from the Spanish by DON PASCUAL DE GAYANGOS. *Issued for* 1868.

**41—The Royal Commentaries of the Yncas.**

By the Ynca Garcillasso de la Vega. Translated and Edited by CLEMENTS R. MARKHAM. Vol. 1. *Issued for* 1869.

**42—The Three Voyages of Vasco da Gama,**

And his Viceroyalty, from the Lendas da India of Gaspar Correa; accompanied by original documents. Translated and Edited by the LORD STANLEY of Alderley. *Issued for* 1869.

**43—Select Letters of Christopher Columbus,**

With other Original Documents relating to his Four Voyages to the New World. Translated and Edited by R. H. MAJOR. 2nd Edition (see No. 2). *Issued for* 1870.

**44—History of the Imâms and Seyyids of 'Omân,**

By Salîl-Ibn-Razîk, from A.D. 661-1856. Translated from the original Arabic, and Edited, with a continuation of the History down to 1870, by the REV. GEORGE PERCY BADGER. *Issued for* 1870.

**45—The Royal Commentaries of the Yncas.**

Vol. 2. *Issued for* 1871.

**46—The Canarian,**

Or Book of the Conquest and Conversion of the Canarians in the year 1402, by Messire Jean de Bethencourt, Kt. Composed by Pierre Bontier and Jean le Verrier. Translated and Edited by R. H. MAJOR.

*Issued for* 1871.

**47—Reports on the Discovery of Peru.**

Translated and Edited by CLEMENTS R. MARKHAM, C.B.

*Issued for* 1872.

**48—Narratives of the Rites and Laws of the Yncas.**

Translated and Edited by CLEMENTS R. MARKHAM, C.B., F.R.S.

*Issued for* 1872.

**49—Travels to Tana and Persia,**

By Josafa Barbaro and Ambrogio Contarini; Edited by LORD STANLEY of Alderley. With Narratives of other Italian Travels in Persia. Translated and Edited by CHARLES GREY. *Issued for* 1873.

**50—Voyages of the Zeni**

To the Northern Seas in the Fourteenth Century. Translated and Edited by R. H. MAJOR. *Issued for* 1873.

**51—The Captivity of Hans Stade of Hesse in 1547-55,**

Among the Wild Tribes of Eastern Brazil. Translated by ALBERT TOOTAL, Esq., and annotated by SIR RICHARD F. BURTON.

*Issued for* 1874.

**52—The First Voyage Round the World by Magellan.**

Translated from the Accounts of Pigafetta and other contemporary writers. Edited by LORD STANLEY of Alderley.

*Issued for* 1874.

**53—The Commentaries of the Great Afonso Dalboquerque,**

Second Viceroy of India. Translated from the Portuguese Edition of 1774, and Edited by WALTER DE GRAY BIRCH, F.R.S.L. Vol. 1.

*Issued for* 1875.

**54—Three Voyages to the North-East.**

Second Edition of Gerrit de Veer's Three Voyages to the North-East by Barents. Edited by Lieut. KOOLEMANS BEYNEN, of the Royal Dutch Navy.

*Issued for* 1876.

**55—The Commentaries of the Great Afonso Dalboquerque.**

Vol. 2. *Issued for* 1875.

**56—The Voyages of Sir James Lancaster.**

With Abstracts of Journals of Voyages preserved in the India Office, and the Voyage of Captain John Knight to seek the N.W. Passage. Edited by CLEMENTS R. MARKHAM, C.B., F.R.S.

*Issued for* 1877.

**57—The Observations of Sir Richard Hawkins, Knt.,**

In his Voyage into the South Sea in 1593, with the Voyages of his grandfather William, his father Sir John, and his cousin William Hawkins. Second Edition (see No. 1). Edited by CLEMENTS R. MARKHAM, C.B., F.R.S. *Issued for* 1877.

**58—The Bondage and Travels of Johann Schiltberger,**

From his capture at the battle of Nicopolis in 1396 to his escape and return to Europe in 1427. Translated by Commander J. BUCHAN TELFER, R.N.; with Notes by Professor B. BRUUN. *Issued for* 1878.

**59—The Voyages and Works of John Davis the Navigator.**

Edited by Captain ALBERT H. MARKHAM, R.N. *Issued for* 1878.

**The Map of the World, A.D. 1600.**

Called by Shakspere "The New Map, with the Augmentation of the Indies." To illustrate the Voyages of John Davis. *Issued for* 1878.

**60-61.—The Natural and Moral History of the Indies.**

By Father Joseph de Acosta. Reprinted from the English Translated Edition of Edward Grimston, 1604; and Edited by CLEMENTS R. MARKHAM, C.B., F.R.S. Two Vols. *Issued for* 1879.

**Map of Peru.**

To Illustrate Nos. 33, 41, 45, 60, and 61. *Issued for* 1879.

**62 The Commentaries of the Great Afonso Dalboquerque.**

Vol. 3. *Issued for* 1880.

**63—The Voyages of William Baffin, 1612-1622.**

Edited by CLEMENTS R. MARKHAM, C.B., F.R.S. *Issued for* 1880.

**64—Narrative of the Portuguese Embassy to Abyssinia**

During the years 1520-1527. By Father Francisco Alvarez. Translated and Edited by LORD STANLEY of Alderley. *Issued for* 1881.

**65—The History of the Bermudas or Somer Islands.**

Attributed to Captain Nathaniel Butler. Edited by General Sir J. HENRY LEFROY, R.A., K.C.M.G. *Issued for* 1881.

**66-67—The Diary of Richard Cocks,**

Cape-Merchant in the English Factory in Japan, 1615-1622. Edited by EDWARD MAUNDE THOMPSON. Two Vols. *Issued for* 1882.

**68—The Second Part of the Chronicle of Peru.**

By Pedro de Cieza de Leon. Translated and Edited by CLEMENTS R. MARKHAM, C.B., F.R.S. *Issued for* 1883.

**69—The Commentaries of the Great Afonso Dalboquerque.**

Vol. 4. *Issued for* 1883.

**70-71—The Voyage of John Huyghen van Linschoten to the East Indies.**

From the Old English Translation of 1598. The First Book, containing his Description of the East. Edited by A. C. BURNELL, Ph.D., C.I.E., and P. A. TIELE, of Utrecht. *Issued for* 1884.

**72-73—Early Voyages and Travels to Russia and Persia,**

By Anthony Jenkinson and other Englishmen, with some account of the first Intercourse of the English with Russia and Central Asia by way of the Caspian Sea. Edited by E. DELMAR MORGAN, and C. H. COOTE. *Issued for* 1885.

**74—The Diary of William Hedges, Esq.,**

Afterwards Sir William Hedges, during his Agency in Bengal; as well as on his Voyage out and Return Overland (1681-1687). Transcribed for the Press, with Introductory Notes, etc., by R. BARLOW, and Illustrated by copious Extracts from Unpublished Records, etc., by Col. Sir H. YULE, K.C.S.I., R.E., C.B., LL.D. Vol. 1, The Diary. *Issued for* 1886.

**75—The Diary of William Hedges, Esq.**
Vol. 2. Sir H. Yule's Extracts from Unpublished Records, etc.
*Issued for* 1886.

**76-77—The Voyage of François Pyrard to the East Indies,**
The Maldives, the Moluccas and Brazil. Translated into English from the Third French Edition of 1619, and Edited by ALBERT GRAY, assisted by H. C. P. BELL. Vol. 1. Vol. 2, Part I.
*Issued for* 1887.

**78—The Diary of William Hedges, Esq.**
Vol. 3. Sir H. Yule's Extracts from Unpublished Records, etc.
*Issued for* 1888.

**79—Tractatus de Globis, et eorum usu.**
A Treatise descriptive of the Globes constructed by Emery Molyneux, and Published in 1592. By Robert Hues. Edited by CLEMENTS R. MARKHAM, C.B., F.R.S. To which is appended,

**Sailing Directions for the Circumnavigation of England,**
And for a Voyage to the Straits of Gibraltar. From a Fifteenth Century MS. Edited by JAMES GAIRDNER; with a Glossary by E. DELMAR MORGAN. *Issued for* 1888.

**80—The Voyage of François Pyrard to the East Indies, etc.**
Vol. 2, Part II. *Issued for* 1889.

**81—The Conquest of La Plata, 1535-1555.**
I.—Voyage of Ulrich Schmidt to the Rivers La Plata and Paraguai. II.—The Commentaries of Alvar Nunez Cabeza de Vaca. Edited by DON LUIS L. DOMINGUEZ. *Issued for* 1889.

**82-83—The Voyage of François Leguat**
To Rodriguez, Mauritius, Java, and the Cape of Good Hope. Edited by Captain PASFIELD OLIVER. Two Vols.
*Issued for* 1890.

**84-85—The Travels of Pietro della Valle to India.**
From the Old English Translation of 1664, by G. Havers. Edited by EDWARD GREY. Two Vols. *Issued for* 1891.

**86—The Journal of Christopher Columbus**
During his First Voyage (1492-93), and Documents relating to the Voyages of John Cabot and Gaspar Corte Real. Translated and Edited by CLEMENTS R. MARKHAM, C.B., F.R.S. *Issued for* 1892.

**87—Early Voyages and Travels in the Levant.**
I.—The Diary of Master Thomas Dallam, 1599-1600. II.—Extracts from the Diaries of Dr. John Covel, 1670-1679. With some Account of the Levant Company of Turkey Merchants. Edited by J. THEODORE BENT, F.S.A., F.R.G.S. *Issued for* 1892.

**88-89—The Voyages of Captain Luke Foxe and Captain Thomas James**
In Search of a N.-W. Passage, 1631-32; with Narratives of Earlier N.-W. Voyages. Edited by MILLER CHRISTY, F.L.S. Two Vols.
*Issued for* 1893.

**90—The Letters of Amerigo Vespucci**
And other Documents relating to his Career. Translated and Edited by CLEMENTS R. MARKHAM, C.B., F.R.S. *Issued for* 1894.

**91—The Voyage of Pedro Sarmiento to the Strait of Magellan, 1579-80.**
Translated and Edited, with Illustrative Documents and Introduction, by CLEMENTS R. MARKHAM, C.B., F.R.S.
*Issued for* 1894.

**92-93-94—The History and Description of Africa,**
And of the Notable Things Therein Contained. The Travels of Leo Africanus the Moor, from the English translation of John Pory (1600). Edited by ROBERT BROWN, M.A., Ph.D. Three Vols.
*Issued for* 1895.

**95—The Discovery and Conquest of Guinea.**
Written by Gomes Eannes de Azurara. Translated and Edited by C. RAYMOND BEAZLEY, M.A., and EDGAR PRESTAGE, B.A. Vol. I.
*Issued for* 1896.

**96-97—Danish Arctic Expeditions.**
Book 1. The Danish Expeditions to Greenland, 1605-07; with James Hall's Voyage in 1612. Edited by C. C. A. GOSCH. *Issued for* 1896.
Book 2. Jens Munk's Voyage to Hudson's Bay in 1619-20. Edited by C. C. A. GOSCH. *Issued for* 1897.

**98—The Topographia Christiana of Cosmas Indicopleustes.**
Translated and Edited by J. W. MCCRINDLE, M.A., M.R.A.S.
*Issued for* 1897.

**99—The First Voyage of Vasco da Gama.**
Translated from the Portuguese, with an Introduction and Notes, by E. G. RAVENSTEIN. *Issued for* 1898.

**100—The Discovery and Conquest of Guinea.**
Written by Gomes Eannes de Azurara. Translated and Edited by C. RAYMOND BEAZLEY, M.A., and EDGAR PRESTAGE, B.A. Vol. 2.
*Issued for* 1898.

---

## SECOND SERIES.

**1-2—The Embassy of Sir Thomas Roe to the Court of the Great Mogul, 1615-19.**
Edited from Contemporary Records by WILLIAM FOSTER, B.A.
*Issued for* 1899.

**3—The Voyage of Sir Robert Dudley to the West Indies and Guiana in 1594.**
Edited by GEO. F. WARNER, M.A., F.S.A., Assistant Keeper of Manuscripts, British Museum. *Issued for* 1899.

**4—The Journeys of William of Rubruck and John of Pian de Carpine**
To Tartary in the 13th century. Translated and Edited by the Hon. W. W. ROCKHILL. *Issued for* 1900.

## OTHER WORKS UNDERTAKEN BY EDITORS.

Raleigh's Empire of Guiana. Second Edition (see No. 3). Edited, with Notes, etc., by EVERARD F. IM THURN, C.B., C.M.G.

The Strange Adventures of Andrew Battell of Leigh in Essex. Edited by E. G. RAVENSTEIN.

Histoire de la Grande Isle Madagascar, par le Sieur De Flacourt, 1661. Translated and Edited by Captain S. PASFIELD OLIVER.

The Voyages of Cadamosto, the Venetian, along the West Coast of Africa, in the years 1455 and 1456. Translated from the earliest Italian text of 1507, and Edited by H. YULE OLDHAM, M.A., F.R.G.S.

The Voyages of the Earl of Cumberland, from the Records prepared by order of the Countess of Pembroke. Edited by W. DE GRAY BIRCH, LL.D., F.S.A.

The Voyage of Alvaro de Mendaña to the Solomon Islands in 1568. Edited by the LORD AMHERST OF HACKNEY and BASIL H. THOMSON.

De Laët's Commentarius de Imperio Magni Mogolis (1631). Translated and Edited by Sir ROPER LETHBRIDGE, K.C.I.E., M.A.

The Voyages of Willoughby and Chancellor to the White Sea, with some account of the earliest intercourse between England and Russia. Reprinted from Hakluyt's Voyages, with Notes and Introduction by E. DELMAR MORGAN.

Dr. John Fryer's New Account of East India and Persia (1698). Edited by ARTHUR T. PRINGLE.

The Expedition of Hernan Cortes to Honduras in 1525-26. Second Edition (see No. 40), with added matter. Translated and Edited by A. P. MAUDSLAY.

The Letters of Pietro Della Valle from Persia, &c. Translated and Edited by MAJOR M. NATHAN, C.M.G., R.E.

The Journey of Pedro Teixeira from India to Italy by land, 1604-05; with his Chronicle of the Kings of Ormus. Translated and Edited by W. F. SINCLAIR, late I.C.S.

The First English Voyage to Japan, 1611-14. Edited by H. E. SIR ERNEST M. SATOW, K.C.M.G.

# LAWS OF THE HAKLUYT SOCIETY.

I. The object of this Society shall be to print, for distribution among its members, rare and valuable Voyages, Travels, Naval Expeditions, and other geographical records, from an early period to the beginning of the eighteenth century.

II. The Annual Subscription shall be One Guinea (for America, five dollars, U.S. currency), payable in advance on the 1st January.

III. Each member of the Society, having paid his Subscription, shall be entitled to a copy of every work produced by the Society, and to vote at the general meetings within the period subscribed for; and if he do not signify, before the close of the year, his wish to resign, he shall be considered as a member for the succeeding year.

IV. The management of the Society's affairs shall be vested in a Council consisting of twenty-two members, viz., a President, two Vice-Presidents, a Treasurer, a Secretary, and seventeen ordinary members, to be elected annually; but vacancies occurring between the general meetings shall be filled up by the Council.

V. A General Meeting of the Subscribers shall be held annually. The Secretary's Report on the condition and proceedings of the Society shall be then read, and the meeting shall proceed to elect the Council for the ensuing year.

VI. At each Annual Election, three of the old Council shall retire.

VII. The Council shall meet when necessary for the dispatch of business, three forming a quorum, including the Secretary; the Chairman having a casting vote.

VIII. Gentlemen preparing and editing works for the Society, shall receive twenty-five copies of such works respectively.

# LIST OF MEMBERS.

1900.

Aberdare, The Right Hon. Lord, Longwood, Winchester.
Adelaide Public Library, per Messrs. Kegan Paul, Trench, Trübner & Co.
Admiralty, The (2 *copies*), per Messrs. Eyre and Spottiswoode.
Advocates' Library, Edinburgh, per Mr. Eccles, 96, Great Russell-street.
Alexander, W. L., Esq., Pinkieburn, Musselburgh, N.B.
All Souls College, Oxford.
American Geographical Society, 11, West 29th-street, New York City, U.S.A.
Amherst, of Hackney, The Right Hon. Lord, Didlington Hall, Brandon, Norfolk.
Antiga Casa Bertrand, José Bastos, 73, Rua Garrett, Lisbon.
Antiquaries, the Society of, Burlington House, Piccadilly, W.
Army and Navy Club, 36, Pall-mall.
Athenæum Club, Pall Mall.

Baer, Joseph & Co., Messrs., per Messrs. Epstein, 47, Holborn Viaduct, E.C.
Bain, Mr., 1, Haymarket, S.W.
Ball, John B., Esq., Ashburton Cottage, Putney Heath, S.W.
Barclay, Hugh G., Esq., Colney Hall, Norwich.
Barlow, R. Fred., Esq., 71, Marine Parade, Worthing, Sussex.
Basano, Marquis de, per Messrs. Hatchard, Piccadilly W.
Basset, M. René, Correspondant de l'Institut de France, Directeur de l'Ecole supérieure des lettres d'Alger, L'Agha 77, rue Michelet, Alger-Mustapha.
Baxter, James Phinney, Esq., 61, Deering-street, Portland, Maine, U.S.A.
Beaumont, Rear-Admiral L. A., 3, Sloane-gardens, S.W.
Beazley, C. Raymond, Esq., 13, The Paragon, Blackheath, S.E.
Belhaven and Stenton, Col. the Lord, R.E., 41, Lennox-gardens, S.W.
Berlin Geographical Society, per Messrs. Sampson Low.
Berlin, the Royal Library of, per Messrs. Asher and Co.
Berlin University, Geographical Institute of (Baron von Richthofen), 6, Schinkelplatz, Berlin, W., per Messrs. Sampson Low.
Birch, Dr. W. de G., British Museum.
Birmingham Central Free Library, Ratcliff-place, Birmingham.
Birmingham Old Library (The), Birmingham.
Bodleian Library, Oxford *(copies presented)*.
Bonaparte, H. H. Prince Roland, 10, Avenue d'Jéna, Paris.
Boston Athenæum Library, U.S.A., per Messrs. Kegan Paul.
Boston Public Library, per Messrs. Kegan Paul.
Bowdoin College, Brunswick, Maine, U.S.A., per Messrs. Kegan Paul.
Bower, Major Hamilton, per Messrs. Grindlay & Co., 54, Parliament Street.
Bowring, Thos. B., Esq., 7, Palace Gate, Kensington, W.
Brewster, Charles O., Esq., University Club, New York City, U.S.A.
Brighton Public Library.
Brine, Vice-Admiral Lindesay.
British Guiana Royal Agricultural and Commercial Society, Georgetown, [Demerara.
British Museum *(copies presented)*.
Brock, Robert C. H., Esq., 1612, Walnut-street, Philadelphia.
Brodrick, Hon. G., Merton College, Oxford.
Brooke, Thos., Esq., Armitage Bridge, Huddersfield.
Brookline Public Library, Mass., U.S.A.
Brooklyn Mercantile Library, per Mr. E. G. Allen.
Brown, Arthur W. W., Esq., 37, Evelyn Mansions, Carlisle-place, Victoria-street, S.W.
Brown, General J. Marshall, 218, Middle-street, Portland, Maine, U.S.A.

Brown, H. T., Esq., Roodeye House, Chester.
Brown, J. Allen, Esq., J.P., 7, Kent-gardens, Ealing.
Brown, J. Nicholas, Esq., per Messrs. Ellis & Elvey, 29, New Bond-st., W.
Brown University, Providence, Rhode Island (H. L. Koopman, Librarian).
Buda-Pesth, the Geographical Institute of the University of.
Bunting, W. L. Esq., The Steps, Bromsgrove.
Burgess, Jas., Esq., C.I.E., LL.D., 22, Seton-place, Edinburgh.
Burns, J. W., Esq., Kilmahew, Dumbartonshire.
Buxton, E. North, Esq., Knighton, Buckhurst-hill.

Cambridge University Library, per Mr. Eccles.
Canada, The Parliament Library, per Mr. E. G. Allen.
Cardiff Public Library, Cardiff (J. Ballinger, Esq., Librarian).
Carles, W. R. Esq., British Consulate, Tientsin, China.
Carlton Club, Pall-mall.
Carlisle, The Rt. Hon. the Earl of, Naworth Castle, Bampton, Cumberland.
Carnegie Library, Pittsburgh, U.S.A., per Mr. Stechert.
Cawston, Geo., Esq., Warnford Court, Throgmorton-street, E.C.
Chamberlain, Right Hon. Joseph, M.P., 40, Princes-gardens. S.W.
Chetham's Library, Hunt's Bank, Manchester.
Chicago Public Library, per Messrs. Stevens and Brown.
Christ Church, Oxford
Christiania University Library, c/o Messrs. T. Bennett and Sons, Christiania, per Messrs. Cassell and Co., Ludgate Hill.
Church, Col. G. Earl, 216, Cromwell-road, S.W.
Cincinnati Public Library, Ohio, U.S.A.
Clark, J. W., Esq., Scroope House, Trumpington-street, Cambridge.
Colgan, Nathaniel, Esq., 1, Belgrave-road, Rathmines, Dublin.
Colonial Office (The), Downing-street, S.W.
Constable, Archibald, Esq., India.
Conway, Sir W. Martin, The Red House, Hornton-street, W.
Cooper, Lieut.-Col. E. H., 42, Portman-square, W.
Copenhagen Royal Library, c/o Messrs. Lehman and Stage, Copenhagen, per Messrs. Sampson Low.
Cora, Professor Guido, M.A., Via Goito, 2, Rome.
Cornell University, per Mr. E. G. Allen.
Corning, C. R., Esq. } Vesaleanum, Bâle, Switzerland.
Corning, H. K., Esq. }
Cortissoz, Royal, Esq., Editorial Room, *New York Tribune*, New York, U.S.A.
Cow, J., Esq., Elfinsward, Hayward's Heath.
Cruising Club, The, 40, Chancery Lane, W.C.
Cunningham, Lieut.-Col. G., Junior U.S. Club, Charles-street, S.W.
Curzon of Kedleston, Right Hon. Lord, Carlton-gardens, S.W.

Dalton, Rev. Canon J. N., M.A., C.M.G., The Cloisters, Windsor.
Danish Royal Naval Library, per Messrs. Sampson Low (Foreign Dept.).
Davis, Hon. N. Darnell, C.M.G., Georgetown, Demerara, British Guiana.
De Bertodano, B., Esq., 22, Chester-terrace, Regent's-park, N.W.
Derby, The Earl of, c/o the Rev. J. Richardson, Knowsley, Prescot.
Detroit Public Library, Michigan, U.S.A.
Dijon University Library, Rue Monge, Dijon.
Dorpat University, per Herr Koehler, 21, Täubchenweg, Leipzig.
Doubleday, H. Arthur, Esq., 2, Whitehall-gardens, S.W.
Dresden Geographical Society, per Herr P. E Richter, Kleine Brüdergasse, 11, Dresden.
Droutskoy Lubetsky, S.A.S. le Prince, Kovensky per. 2, St. Petersburg.
Ducie, The Right Hon. Earl, F.R.S., Tortworth Court, Falfield.

Eames, Wilberforce, Esq., Lenox Library, 890, Fifth avenue, New York, U.S.A., per Mr. B. F. Stevens.
Edinburgh Public Library.
Edwards, Francis, Esq., 83, High-street, Marylebone, W.
Ellsworth, James W., Esq., 2, West 16th Street, New York, U.S.A.
Elton, Charles I., Esq., Q.C., F.S.A., 10, Cranley-place, Onslow-square, S.W.

Faber, Reginald S., Esq., 90, Regent's Park-road, N.W.
Fanshawe, Admiral Sir Edw., G.C.B., 74, Cromwell-road, S.W.
Fellows Athenæum, per Messrs. Kegan Paul, Trench, Trübner, & Co.
Ferguson, D. W., Esq., 5, Bedford-place, Croydon.
Field, W. Hildreth, Esq., 923, Madison-avenue, New York City, U.S.A.
Fisher, Arthur, Esq., St. Aubyn's, Tiverton, Devon.
Fitzgerald, Edward A., Esq., per Mr. Jas. Bain, 1, Haymarket, S.W.
Foreign Office (The), per Messrs. Eyre and Spottiswoode.
Foreign Office of Germany, Berlin, per Messrs. Asher and Co.
Forrest, G. W., Esq., C.I.E., Savile Club, 107, Piccadilly, W.
Foster, William, Esq., India Office, S.W.
Fothergill, M. B., Esq., c/o Imperial Bank of Persia, 25, Abchurch-lane, E.C.
French, H. B., Esq., 429, Arch Street, Philadelphia, U.S.A.

Georg, Mons. H., Lyons, per Messrs. Sampson Low.
George, C. W., Esq., 51, Hampton-road, Bristol.
Gladstone Library, National Liberal Club, Whitehall-place, S.W.
Glasgow University Library, per Mr. Billings, 59, Old Bailey, E C.
Godman, F. Ducane, Esq., D.C.L., F.R.S., 10, Chandos-street, Cavendish-square, W.
Gosch, C. A., Esq., 21, Stanhope-gardens. S.W.
Gosset, General M. W. E., C.B., Island Bridge House, Dublin.
Göttingen University Library, per Messrs. Asher and Co.
Grant-Duff, Rt. Hon. Sir M. E., G.C.S.I., 11, Chelsea Embankment, S.W.
Gray, Albert, Esq., Catherine Lodge, Trafalgar Square, Chelsea, S.W.
Gray, M. H., Esq., India-rubber Company, Silvertown, Essex.
Greever, C. O., Esq., 1345, East Ninth-street, Des Moines, Iowa.
Grosvenor Library, Buffalo, U.S.A.
Guildhall Library, E.C.
Guillemard, Arthur G., Esq., Eltham, Kent.
Guillemard, F. Henry H., Esq., M.A., M.D., The Old Mill House, Trumpington, Cambridge.

Haig, Maj.-General Malcolm R., Rossweide, Davos Platz, Switzerland.
Hamburg Commerz-Bibliothek, c/o Herrn Friederichsen and Co., Hamburg, per Messrs. Drolenvaux and Bremner, 36, Gt. Tower-street, E.C.
Hannen, The Hon. H., Holne Cott, Ashburton, South Devon.
Harmsworth, A. C., Esq., Elmwood, St. Peter's, Kent.
Harrison, Edwin, Esq., Church Gates, Cheshunt.
Harvard College, Cambridge, Massachusetts, per Messrs. Kegan Paul.
Harvie-Brown, J. A., Esq., Dunipace, Larbert, Stirlingshire, N B.
Haswell, Geo. H., Esq., Ashleigh, Hamstead Road, Handsworth, Birmingham.
Hawkesbury, The Rt. Hon. Lord, 2, Carlton House-terrace, S.W.
Heap, Ralph, Esq., 1, Brick-court, Temple, E.C.
Heawood, Edward, Esq., M.A., F.R.G.S., 3, Underhill-road, Lordship-lane, S.E.
Hervey, Dudley F. A., Esq., C.M.G., The Elms, Aldeburgh.
Hiersemann, Herr Karl W., 3, Königsstrasse, Leipzig, per Mr. Young T. Pentland, 38, West Smithfield, E.C.
Hill, Professor G. W., West Nyack, New York.
Hippisley, A. E., Esq., c/o J. D. Campbell, Esq., C.M.G., 26, Old Queen-st., S.W.
Hobhouse, C. E. H., Esq., The Ridge, Corsham, Wilts.
Horner, J. F. Fortescue, Esq., Mells Park, Frome, Somersetshire, per Mr. J. Bain.

Hoskins, Admiral Sir Anthony H., G.C.B., 17, Montagu-square, W.
Hoyt Public Library, per Messrs Sotheran and Co., 140, Strand.
Hubbard, Hon. Gardiner G., 1328, Connecticut-avenue, Washington, D.C.
Hudson, John E., Esq., 125, Milk-street, Boston, Mass., U.S.A.
Hull Public Library (W. F. Lawton, Esq., Librarian).
Hull Subscription Library, per Messrs. Foster, Fore-street.

Im Thurn, E. F., Esq., C.B., C.M.G., 23, Edwardes-square, Kensington, W.
India Office (21 *copies*).
Inner Temple, Hon. Society of the (J. E. L. Pickering, Esq., Librarian).

Jackson, Major H.M., R.E., 3, Ravelston Place, Edinburgh.
James, Arthur C., Esq., 92, Park-avenue, New York, U.S.A.
James, Walter B., Esq., M.D., 268, Madison-avenue, New York.
Johns Hopkins University, Baltimore, U.S.A., per Mr. E. G. Allen.
Johnson, General Sir Allen B., 60, Lexham-gardens, Cromwell-road, S.W.
Johnson, Rev. S. J., F.R.A.S., Melplash Vicarage, Bridport.
Jones and Evans, Messrs., 77, Queen-street, Cheapside, E.C.

Kearton, G. J. Malcolm, Esq., F.R.G.S., 28, Fenchurch Street, E.C.
Keltie, J. Scott, Esq., LL.D., 1, Savile-row, W.
Kelvin, The Rt. Hon. Lord, F.R.S., LL.D., Netherhall, Largs, Ayrshire.
Key, John J., Esq., Colorado Springs, Colorado, U.S.A.
Kinder, C. W., Esq., M.I.C.E., Tongshan, North China.
King's Inns Library, Henrietta-street, Dublin.
Kimberley Public Library, per Messrs. Sotheran and Co., Strand.
Kitching, J., Esq., Oaklands, Kingston Hill, S.W.
Kleinseich, M., per Mr. Wohlleben, 45, Gt. Russell-street, W.C. (3 *copies*).

Larchmont Yacht Club, Larchmont, N.Y., U.S.A. (F. D. Shaw, Esq., Chairman of Library Committee).
Leechman, C. B., Esq., 10, Earl's-court-gardens, S.W.
Leeds Library, Commercial-street, Leeds.
Lehigh University, U.S.A.
Leipzig, Library of the University of, per Herr O. Harrassowitz, Leipzig.
Lewis, Walter H., Esq., 11, East 35th-street, New York City, U.S.A.
Levy, Judah, Esq., 17, Greville-place, N.W.
Liverpool Free Public Library.
Liverpool Geographical Society (Capt. D. Phillips, R.N., Secretary), 14, Hargreaves-buildings, Chapel-street, Liverpool.
Loch, Right Hon. Lord, G.C.B., G.C.M.G., 23, Lowndes-square, S.W.
Loescher, Messrs. J., & Co., Via del Corso, 307, Rome, per Messrs. Sampson Low.
Logan, Daniel, Esq., Solicitor-General, Penang, Straits Settlements.
Logan, William, Esq., per Messrs. Grindlay & Co., 54, Parliament-street.
London Institution, Finsbury-circus.
London Library, 12, St. James's-square.
Long Island Historical Society, Brooklyn, U.S.A.
Lowrey, Joseph, Esq., The Hermitage, Loughton.
Lucas, C. P., Esq., Colonial Office, S.W.
Lucas, F. W., Esq., 21, Surrey-street, Victoria Embankment, W.C.
Luyster, S. B., Esq., c/o Messrs. Denham & Co., 27, Bloomsbury-square, W.C.
Lydenberg, H. M., Esq., Lenox Library, Fifth Avenue, New York.
Lyttelton-Annesley, Lieut.-Gen. A., Templemere, Weybridge.

Macmillan & Bowes, Messrs., Cambridge, per Messrs. Foster, Fore-street.
Macrae, C. C., Esq., 93, Onslow-gardens, S.W.
Manchester Public Free Libraries.
Manierre, George, Esq., 184, La Salle-street, Chicago, Ill., U.S.A.

Margesson, Lieut. W. H. D., R.N., Findon Place, Worthing.
Markham, Vice-Admiral Albert H., F.R.G.S., 65, Linden-gardens, W.
Markham, Sir Clements, K.C.B., F.R.S., 21, Eccleston-square, S.W.
Marquand, Henry, Esq., 160, Broadway, New York, U.S.A.
Martelli, E. W., Esq., 4, New Square, Lincoln's Inn, W.C.
Massachusetts Historical Society, 30, Tremont-street, Boston, Mass., U.S.A., per Messrs. Kegan Paul.
Massie, Capt. R. H., R.A.
Mathers, E. P., Esq., Glenalmond, Foxgrove-road, Beckenham.
Maudslay, A. P., Esq., 32, Montpelier-square, Knightsbridge, S.W.
McClymont, Jas. R., Esq., 201, Macquarie-street, Hobart Town, Tasmania.
Mecredy, Jas., Esq., M.A., B.L., F.R.G.S., Wynberg, Stradbrook, Blackrock, Dublin Co.
Melbourne, Public Library of, per Messrs. Melville, Mullen & Slade, 12, Ludgate-square, E.C.
Meyjes, A. C., Esq., 42, Cannon-street, E.C.
Michigan, University of, per Messrs. H. Sotheran & Co., 140, Strand, W.C.
Milwaukee Public Library, Wisconsin, per Mr. G. E. Stechert.
Minneapolis Athenæum, U.S.A., per Mr. G. E. Stechert, 2, Star-yard, W.C.
Mitchell Library, 21, Miller-street, Glasgow.
Mitchell, Alfred, Esq., per Messrs. Tiffany, 221, Regent-street, W.
Mitchell, Wm., Esq., 14, Forbesfield-road, Aberdeen.
Monson, The Rt. Hon. Lord, C.V.O., Clarence House, St. James's, S.W.
Morgan, E. Delmar, Esq., 15, Roland-gardens, South Kensington, S.W.
Morris, H. C. L., Esq., M.D., Gothic Cottage, Bognor, Sussex.
Morris, Mowbray, Esq., 59A, Brook street, Grosvenor square, W.
Moxon, A. E., Esq., c/o Mrs. Gough, The Lodge, Sculdern, near Banbury.
Mukhopadhyay, The Hon. Dr. Asutosh, M.A., LL.D., etc., etc., 77, Russa-road North, Bhowanipore, Calcutta.
Munich Royal Library, per Messrs. Asher & Co.

Nathan, Major, C.M.G., R.E., 11, Pembridge-square, W.
Natural History Museum, Cromwell-road, per Messrs. Dulau & Co., Soho-sq.
Naval and Military Club, 94, Piccadilly, W.
Netherlands, Geographical Society of the, per Mr. Nutt, 57, Long Acre.
Nettleship, E., Esq., c/o R. S. Whiteway, Esq., Brownscombe, Shottermill, Surrey.
Newberry Library, The, Chicago, U.S.A., per Messrs. Stevens & Brown.
Newcastle-upon-Tyne Literary and Scientific Institute.
Newcastle-upon-Tyne Public Library.
New London Public Library, Conn., U.S.A.
New York Athletic Club, Central Park, South, New York (John C. Gulick, Esq., chairman of Library Committee).
New York Public Library, per Messrs. Stevens & Brown.
New York State Library, per Mr. G. E. Stechert, 2, Star-yard, Carey-st., W.C.
New York Yacht Club (Library Committee), 67, Madison-avenue, New York City, U.S.A.
New Zealand, Agent-General for, per Messrs. Sotheran & Co.
Nicholson, Sir Charles, Bart., D.C.L., The Grange, Totteridge, Herts.
Nijhoff, M., per Mr. D. Nutt, 57, Long Acre, W.C.
Nordenskiold, Baron, 11, Tradgardsgatan, Stockholm.
North Adams Public Library, Massachusetts, U.S.A.
Northbrook, The Right Hon. the Earl of, G.C.S.I., Stratton, Micheldever [Station.
North, Hon. F. H., C 3, The Albany, W.
Northumberland, His Grace the Duke of, per Mr. Cross, 230, Caledonian-road, N.

O'Byrne, P. Justin, Esq., "British-Indian Commerce," 21, St. Helen's-place, E.C.
Oliver, Captain S. P., Findon, near Worthing.
Oliver, Commander T. W., R.N., 16, De Parys-avenue, Bedford.

Omaha Public Library, Nebraska, U.S.A.
Ommanney, Admiral Sir Erasmus, C.B., F.R.S., 29, Connaught-sq., Hyde Park.
Oriental Club, Hanover-square, W.

Parmly, Duncan D., Esq., 160, Broadway, New York.
Payne, E. J., Esq., 2, Stone Buildings, Lincoln's Inn, W.C.
Peabody Institute, Baltimore, U.S., per Mr. E. G. Allen.
Peckover, Alexander, Esq., Bank House, Wisbech.
Peech, W. H., Esq., St. Stephen's Club, Westminster.
Peek, Sir Cuthbert E., Bart., 22, Belgrave-square, S.W.
Peixoto, Dr. J. Rodrigues, 8, Rue Almte. Comandaré, Rio de Janeiro.
Pequot Library, Southport, Conn., U.S.A.
Petherick, E. A., Esq., 85, Hopton-road, Streatham, S.W.
Philadelphia Free Library, U.S.A., per Mr. G. E. Stechert, 2, Star-yard, W.C.
Philadelphia, Library Company of, U.S.A., per Mr. E. G. Allen.
Poor, F. B., Esq., 160, Broadway, New York, U.S.A.
Poor, Henry W., Esq., per Messrs. Denham & Co., 27, Bloomsbury-square.
Pope, Alexander, Esq., Methven House, King's-road, Kingston-on-Thames.
Portico Library, Manchester.
Pringle, Arthur T., Esq., c/o Messrs. G. W. Wheatley & Co., 10, Queen-st., E.C.

Quaritch, Mr. B., 15, Piccadilly, W. (*12 copies*).

Rabbits, W. Thos., Esq., 6, Cadogan Gardens, S.W.
Raffles Library, Singapore, per Messrs. Jones & Evans, Queen-street, E.C.
Ravenstein, E. G., Esq., 2, York Mansions, Battersea Park, S.W.
Reform Club, Pall-mall.
Reggio, André C., Esq., c/o Messrs. Baring Bros. & Co., 8, Bishopsgate-street Within, E.C.
Rhodes, Josiah, Esq., The Elms, Lytham, Lancashire.
Richards, Admiral Sir F. W., G.C.B., 34, Queen Anne's Gate, S.W.
Riggs, E. F., Esq., 1311, Mass. Avenue, Washington, U.S.
Ringwalt, John S., Jun., Esq., Mt. Vernon, Knox County, Ohio, U.S.A.
Rittenhouse Club, 1811, Walnut-street, Philadelphia, U.S.A.
Rockhill, The Hon. W. W., Department of State, Washington.
Rodd, Sir Rennell, C.B., K.C.M.G., c/o Foreign Office, Downing-street, S.W.
Röhrscheid and Ebbecke, Herrn, Strauss'sche Buchhandlung, Bonn.
Rose, C. D., Esq., 10, Austin Friars, E.C.
Royal Artillery Institute, Woolwich.
Royal Colonial Institute, Northumberland Avenue, W.C.
Royal Engineers' Institute, Chatham.
Royal Geographical Society, 1, Savile-row, W. (*copies presented*).
Royal Scottish Geographical Society, Edinburgh (Jas. Burgess, Esq., LL.D., C.I.E., Librarian).
Royal Societies Club, St. James's-street, S.W.
Royal United Service Institution, Whitehall, S.W.
Russell, Lady A., 2, Audley-square, W.
Rutherford, Rev. W. Gunion, D.D., Westminster School, S.W.
Ryley, J. Horton, Esq., } Melrose, Woodwarde-road, Dulwich, S.E.
Ryley, Mrs. Florence, LL.A., }

San Francisco Public Library, per Mr. G. E. Stechert.
Satow, H. E. Sir E., K.C.M.G., 104, The Common, Upper Clapton, E.
Saunders, Howard, Esq., 7, Radnor-place, Gloucester-square, W.
Saxe-Coburg and Gotha, H.R.H. the Reigning Duke of (Duke of Edinburgh) K.G., K.T., etc., c/o Col. the Hon. Sir W. J. Colville, K.C.V.O., Clarence House, St. James's.
Schwartz, J. L., Esq., P.O. Box 594, Pittsburg, Pa.

Science and Art Department, South Kensington.
Seawanhaka Corinthian Yacht Club, 7, East 32nd-street, New York, U.S.A.
Seymour, Vice-Admiral Sir E. H., K.C.B., 9, Ovington-square, S.W.
Sheffield Free Public Libraries (Samuel Smith, Esq., Librarian).
Shields, Cuthbert, Esq., Corpus Christi College, Oxford.
Signet Library, Edinburgh (Thos. G. Law, Esq., Librarian), per Mr. D. Nutt.
Silver, S. W., Esq., 3, York-gate, Regent's Park, N.W.
Sinclair, W. F., Esq., c/o Messrs. H. S. King & Co., Pall Mall, S.W.
Smith, F. A., Esq., Thorncliff, Shoot-up-Hill, N.
Smithers, F.O., Esq., F.R.G.S., Dashwood House, 9, New Broad-street, E.C.
Sneddon, Geo. T., Esq., 8, Merry-street, Motherwell.
Societá Geografica Italiana, Rome.
Société de Géographie, Paris, per Mr. J. Arnould, Royal Mint Refinery, Royal Mint-street, E.C.
South African Public Library, per Messrs H. S. King & Co., 65, Cornhill, E.C.
Southam, S. Clement, Esq., F.S.A., F.R.G.S., F.R.Hist.S., F.R.S.L., Elmhurst, Shrewsbury.
Springfield City Library Association, Mass., U.S.A.
Stairs, James W., Esq., c/o Messrs. Stairs, Son and Morrow, Halifax, Nova Scotia.
Stanley, Right Hon. Lord, of Alderley, 15, Grosvenor-gardens, S.W.
St. Andrew's University.
St. John's, N. B., Canada, Free Public Library (J. R. Ruel, Esq., Chairman).
St. Louis Mercantile Library, per Mr. G. E. Stechert, 2, Star-yard, W.C.
St. Martin's-in-the-Fields Free Public Library, 115, St. Martin's-lane, W.C.
St. Petersburg University Library, per Messrs. Kegan Paul.
St. Wladimir University, Kief, per Messrs. Sotheran & Co., 140, Strand.
Stephens, Henry C., Esq., M.P., Avenue House, Finchley, N.
Stevens, J. Tyler, Esq., Park-street, Lowell, Mass., U.S.A.
Stevens, Son, & Stiles, Messrs., 39, Great Russell-street, W.C.
Stockholm, Royal Library of, per Messrs Sampson Low.
Stockton Public Library, per Messrs. Sotheran & Co., 140, Strand.
Strachey, Lady, 69, Lancaster-gate, Hyde-park, W.
Stride, Mrs. Arthur L., Bush Hall, Hatfield, Herts.
Stringer, G. A., Esq., 248, Georgia-street, Buffalo, N.Y., U.S.A.
Stubbs, Captain Edward, R.N., 13, Greenfield-road, Stoneycroft, Liverpool.
Sydney Free Library, per Mr. Young J. Pentland, 38, West Smithfield, E.C.
Sykes, Major P. Molesworth, H.M.'s Consul at Kerman, Persia, *viâ* Tehran.

Tate, G. P., Esq., c/o Messrs. W. Watson & Co., Karachi, India.
Taylor, Captain William R., 1, Daysbrook-road, Streatham Hill, S.W.
Temple, Lieut.-Col. R. C., C.I.E., per Messrs. Kegan Paul.
Thin, Mr. Jas., 54, 55, South Bridge, Edinburgh, per Mr. Billings, 59, Old Bailey, E.C.
Thomson, B. H., Esq., Governor's House, H.M.'s Prison, Northampton.
Tighe, W. S., Coalmoney, Stratford-on-Slaney, Co. Wicklow.
Toronto Public Library. } per Messrs. Cazenove & Son.
Toronto University. }
Transvaal State Library, Pretoria, Transvaal, South Africa, per Messrs. Mudie.
Travellers' Club, 106, Pall-mall, S.W.
Trinder, H. W., Esq., Northbrook House, Bishops Waltham, Hants.
Trinder, Oliver Jones, Esq., Mount Vernon, Caterham, Surrey.
Trinity College, Cambridge, care of Messrs. Deighton, Bell & Co., per Messrs. Simpkin, Marshall & Co. (Enclo. Dept.).
Trinity House, The Hon. Corporation of, Tower-hill, E.C.
Troop, W. H., Esq., c/o Messrs. Black Bros. & Co., Halifax, Nova Scotia.
Trotter, Coutts, Esq., Athenæum Club, S.W.
Trübner, Herr Karl, Strasburg, per Messrs Kegan Paul.
Turnbull, Alex. H., Esq., 7, St. Helen's-place, Bishopsgate-street, E.C.

Union League House, Broad-street, Philadelphia, U.S.A.
Union Society, Oxford. per Messrs. Cawthorn & Hutt, 24, Cockspur-street.
United States Congress, Library of, per Mr. E. G. Allen.
United States National Museum (Library of), per Messrs. W. Wesley & Son, 28, Essex-street, W.C.
United States Naval Academy, per Messrs. Stevens & Brown.
University of London, per Messrs. Sotheran & Co., 37, Piccadilly, W.
Upsala University Library, per C. J. Lundstrom, Upsala.

Van Raalte, Charles, Esq., Aldenham Abbey, Watford, Herts.
Vienna Imperial Library, per Messrs. Asher & Co.
Vignaud, Henry, Esq., Ambassade des Etats Unis, 18, Avenue Kleber, Paris.

Wahab, Mrs., Knowle, Godalming.
Ward, Admiral Hon. W. J., 79, Davies-street, Berkeley-square, W.
Warren, W. R., Esq., 81, Fulton-street, New York City, U.S.A.
Washington, Department of State, per Messrs. Stevens & Brown.
Washington, Library of Navy Department, per Messrs. Stevens & Brown.
Watkinson Library, Hartford, Connecticut, U.S.A.
Watson, Commander, R.N.R., Ravella, Crosby, near Liverpool.
Webster, Sir Augustus, Bart., Guards' Club, 70, Pall-mall.
Weld, Geo. F., Esq., Quincy-street, Cambridge, Mass., U.S.A.
Westminster School (Rev. G. H. Nall, M.A., Librarian).
Wharton, Rear-Admiral Sir W. J. L., K.C.B., Florys, Princes-road, Wimbledon Park, S.W.
Wildy, A.G., Esq., 14, Buckingham-street, W.C.
Williams, O. W., Esq., Fort Stockton, Texas, U.S.A.
Wilson, Edward S., Esq., Melton Grange, Brough, East Yorkshire.
Wisconsin State Historical Society, per Messrs. Sotheran & Co., 140, Strand.
Worcester, Massachusetts, Free Library, per Messrs. Kegan Paul.
Wright, John, Esq., 2, Challoner Terrace West, South Shields.
Wyndham, Geo., Esq., M.P., 35, Park Lane, W.

Yale College, U.S.A., per Mr. E. G. Allen.
Young, Alfales, Esq., Salt Lake City, Utah, U.S.A.
Young, Sir Allen, C.B., 18, Grafton-street, W.
Young & Sons, Messrs. H., 12, South Castle Street, Liverpool.

Zürich, Bibliothèque de la Ville, care of Messrs. Orell, Turli & Co., Zürich, per Mr. D. Nutt.